ISRAEL AFTER BEGIN

SUNY Series in Israeli Studies
Russell Stone, Editor

ISRAEL AFTER BEGIN

EDITED
BY
GREGORY S. MAHLER

STATE UNIVERSITY OF NEW YORK PRESS

Published by
State University of New York Press, Albany

©1990 State University of New York

For information, address State University of New York
Press, State University Plaza, Albany, N.Y., 12246

Library of Congress Cataloging-in-Publication Data

Israel after Begin / edited by Gregory S. Mahler.
    p.   cm. -- (SUNY series in Israeli studies)
    Includes bibliographical references.
    ISBN 0-7914-0367-X. -- ISBN 0-7914-0368-8 (pbk.)
    1. Israel--Politics and government--Congresses. 2. Israel-
-Foreign relations--Congresses. 3. Political Parties--Israel-
-Congresses. 4. Begin, Menachem, 1913-   --Congresses. I. Mahler,
Gregory S., 1950-   . II. Series.
JQ1825.P3A176   1990
956.9405'4--dc20   89-28079
                                                             CIP

10 9 8 7 6 5 4 3 2 1

Contents

CHAPTER ONE

Israel After Begin

Gregory S. Mahler

Fully a month after the elections for Israel's Twelfth Knesset (parliament) in November 1988, Israel's two major political parties, Likud and Labor, were still engaged in a battle over which was more capable of forming a coalition government. Likud had received the first post-election "mandate" from the president to attempt to create a coalition, but by the end of three weeks was still unable to put together a parliamentary majority without the assistance of Labor. At the same time, both Likud and Labor were loudly and firmly articulating their intentions of avoiding another "national unity" government of the type in which they had both served during the preceding four years. Eventually, despite their protestations to the contrary, Likud and Labor created precisely the kind of national unity coalition that they had promised their followers in the election campaign that they would never form again.

That this could have been the case at all would have shocked someone who had not observed the politics of the preceding political decade. Prior to 1977, the idea that Likud could be even a *part of* a government coalition was — with the exception of a brief National Unity Government in the Seventh Knesset — almost unbelievable. The Mapai/Alignment/Labor block had so thoroughly dominated Israeli politics for Israel's first thirty years that many perceived the Likud as an "unrealistic" party, capable of serving in the Opposition, or perhaps as part of a broad National Unity Government, but clearly *not* capable of creating a coalition government on its own.

The 1977 election of the Ninth Knesset changed the political landscape, however. The final words of a 1981 national study of political behavior in the Knesset included the observation that

1

Israeli Borders Today

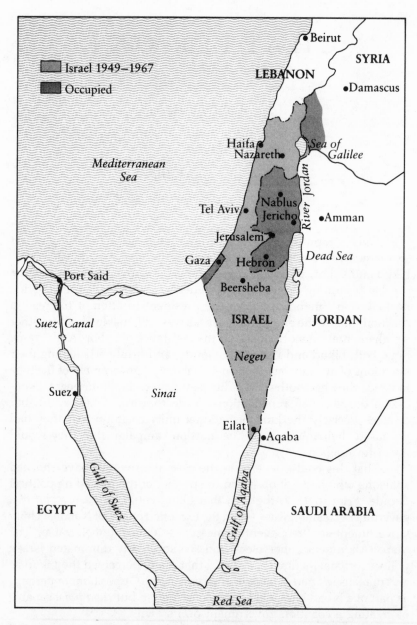

Regardless of how or why Likud came into power [in 1977], it seems clear that forming the Government has given the Likud a certain respectability that many Israelis felt it lacked prior to 1977, feeling that the Likud was only an opposition party.

Whether a Likud or a Labor alignment ends up winning a plurality in the 1981 election, it seems clear that another thirty-year period of Labor rule is extremely unlikely . . . Many in Israel, who in the past would never have supported the Likud because it was perceived as an extremist party, perpetually in the opposition, have now decided that the Likud is a reasonable alternative to the Labor alignment, and having proven its ability to govern — regardless of policy outcomes — the Likud has become a much more viable alternative to Labor hegemony than it was before it had a chance to demonstrate its ability.[1]

Time has proven this prediction to be an accurate one. Since the 1977 election, Likud has either served as the sole "major partner," or shared the role as major partner, in all Israeli coalition governments, and Labor has served as the secondary, sometimes "almost equal" party, but has proven unable to regain its position as the dominant party in the political system, which it enjoyed for virtually all of Israel's early years.

The man credited for changing the relationship between the political parties in Israel was Menachem Begin. Historians suggest that he was more than just a Resistance fighter and a party leader; he was the agent of some fundamental changes in the nature of the Israeli polity. Among the many facets of Israeli politics affected by Begin might be included the nature and degree of competition offered by the Likud in elections, the role of Sephardic Jews in the polity, the pattern of Israeli settlements on the West Bank, Israel's relations with her Arab neighbors, a peace treaty with Egypt, and other structures equally significant in the Israeli political landscape. Begin's influence can be seen in sociocultural variables, in party structures, in electoral competition, in foreign policy, and in economics. Many of these changes are described in the essays in this volume.

In fact, scholars in recent years have begun to refer to a "Begin era" in Israeli political history. In this framework, Menachem Begin is seen as a "watershed" in Israeli politics, and it is possible to speak of a "pre-Begin era," a Begin era, and a "post-Begin era" when we seek to study both Israeli domestic policy and Israeli foreign policy. Scholars contributing to this volume focus on a relatively new theme in the study of Israeli politics: "What is the nature of Israel in this post-Begin era?"

The Contributions in this Volume

Almost all of the papers included in this volume were presented at the Israel Studies Association Conference held at the University of Vermont in June 1987. The title of the Conference was "Israel in the Post-Begin Era," and papers were sought that would cover a wide variety of perspectives of Israeli politics and society. The papers were revised in 1988 for their inclusion in this volume, but readers should keep in mind — as is the case with so much of the scholarship dealing with this region of the world — that political events outpace the printed word, and the words on these pages were set down long before this volume was printed. To this end, a brief editor's note has been added at the end of several of these chapters to indicate events relevant to the discussion in the chapter that took place after the authors' revisions.

Ilan Peleg's essay, "The Legacy of Begin and Beginism for the Israeli Political System," introduces many of the themes found throughout the rest of the volume. He suggests that "with the exception of David Ben-Gurion, Menachem Begin was the single most important personality in the political history of the State of Israel." Although the personal contributions of Begin are somewhat problematic, Peleg suggests, it *is* safe to claim that Begin was the primary *agent* of many significant changes.

As an agent of change in the system of Israeli political parties, Begin was crucial in the development of a true second party in Israel. His leadership brought Herut from the position of being perceived as an "unrealistic" and "irresponsible" Right Wing party "beyond the limits of the Israeli national consensus," to a point at which it gained legitimacy in the eyes of the Israeli middle class: "Herut blurred its own controversial image without actually giving up its long-held ideological positions." Peleg shows that the "seeds of the 1977 revolution which brought Begin to power were sown a decade earlier, in the summer of 1967," and in the National Unity Government (1967–1970) in which he served. He was able to use an age factor, a socioeconomic factor, and an ethnic factor to develop a "Second Israel," converting what had been a "political underclass" into a dominant class. Peleg suggests, though, that this increase in the strength of the Right helped to create a "potentially destructive social division within Israel," because it reinforced "deep disagreement regarding the central political question on the Israeli national agenda, the future of the occupied territories."

As an ideological innovator, Begin developed and "radicalized the Revisionist belief system," including increased territorial claims, a negation or mistrust of the outside world, an increase in the "tendency to use mystical justifications in support of its territorial and other claims," its "Holocaust fixation," and an increasingly hostile attitude toward the Arabs.

As a foreign policy innovator, Begin supported the traditional Herut values of (1) territorial expansion, (2) the use of force, (3) a pro-Western foreign policy, and (4) increased nationalism. Peleg points out two distinct eras of Begin foreign policy: the first (1977–1980) moderated by the influence of Moshe Dayan and Ezer Weizmann, and the second (1980–1983) radicalized with Begin, Ariel Sharon, and Yitzak Shamir. Peleg suggests that the Lebanese War was characteristic of this second, "radicalized," era, and was "truly reflective of Herut's traditional foreign policy goals, style of operation, and even fundamental values," specifically (a) to annex the West Bank and Gaza, and (b) to destroy the Palestine Liberation Organization. Begin saw Israel, Peleg tells us, as a "regional superpower" and wanted to act accordingly.

Ilan Peleg is head of the Department of Government and Law at Lafayette College, and has published widely in the area of Israeli politics. Among his most recent publications are works dealing with Israeli foreign policy and Israeli political culture.

Ehud Sprinzak develops a second theme dealing with the Begin era in his article "Illegalism in Israeli Political Culture," focusing on the "illegalistic orientation" of Israel's top political leaders. He defines these "illegalistic orientations" as the leaders' "conviction that security considerations, party interests, and their own political survival stand above the law." Sprinzak uses the "Pollard Affair," the case of an American Jew caught spying for Israel, and the "Shin Beth Affair," the case involving the "mysterious" killings of two Arab terrorists who were alive when taken into custody, to demonstrate the increase in what he calls "Israeli illegalism." The three components of this "illegalism" are: (a) there is in the Israeli political culture a greater-than-normal behavioral disrespect for the legal norms in a democracy; (b) beyond the "behavioral illegalism" lies a significant "cultural layer of illegalism"; and (c) this "illegalistic syndrome" is not a new development in Israeli politics, but has been developing since the beginning of the century "side by side with the Zionist policy." Israel's illegalism, Sprinzak tells us, is "illegalism from the top," developed and nourished by Israel's political leaders.

Sprinzak shows the evolution of this "illegalistic" culture and the various components that have contributed to its makeup today. Illegalism was a *necessary* (and perceived as both legitimate and just) response to British rules and British political behavior under the

Mandate, for example violating the British Mandatory laws to encourage illegal Jewish immigration; the pattern simply continued that there could be — and was — a "higher law" than the legal system of the day, whether it was Zionism, or "security interests of the state," and the pattern suggests that one's obligation to follow the rules of the state ("legalism") could be limited by these "higher laws," resulting in a pattern of ignoring the rules of the state ("illegalism").

Sprinzak discusses the four historical stages of this illegalism in Israel: (a) the "functional illegalism" of the Yishuv era, which helped Zionism develop in Palestine; (b) subsequent "latent illegalism", a version of pragmatism that could not be constrained by rigid regulations in the early years of the Israeli State under the Ben-Gurion government; (c) the "manifest illegalism" of Eshkol and Sapir in the post-Ben-Gurion years; and (d) the "rediscovered illegalism" of the Likud and National Unity Government years. Sprinzak concludes that Acton's observation about power corrupting and absolute power corrupting absolutely is as true in Israel as it has been true in other settings over time.

Ehud Sprinzak is a member of the Political Science Department at the Hebrew University of Jerusalem. His recent research has focused upon terrorism and democracy and the Radical Right in Israel.

Aaron Rosenbaum's essay on "Tehiya as a Permanent Nationalist Phenomenon" is especially interesting in light of the remarkable increase in the support for the Religious Right in recent elections. Rosenbaum describes Tehiya as a "confluence" of several components involving orthodoxy and Zionism, and describes the political principles of the movement. These are illustrated through a description of each of the Tehiya MKs in the Tenth Knesset, showing their common beliefs, bonds, and backgrounds. He states that "as a social movement Tehiya shares with Islamic fundamentalism the same atavism, the same reaction to the modern world, and the same feeling of powerlessness in the face of misguided change." Rosenbaum further suggests that it is possible that Tehiya, as a political party organization, might "break up or metamorphose, . . . but Tehiya's worldview and agenda are now irreversibly established in Israel's political dialectic." He then describes the main component of what he refers to as the "Tehiya agenda," and analyzes the Tehiya party structure and its political strength. Much of what we see in Rosenbaum's essay is corroborated by the November 1988 electoral results, in which the parties of the Religious Right increased their representation in the Knesset by almost 50 percent.

Aaron Rosenbaum is president of Aaron Rosenbaum and Associates, a consulting firm in Washington, D.C., specializing in international politics and defense.

The second section of this book focuses upon national security and foreign policy. The essay by Avner Yaniv, "Israeli National Security: The Crisis of Overload," provides an overall analysis of the foreign policy setting. Yaniv begins with a general discussion of two broad types of national security policy. The first, which lasted from the time of independence through 1960, "was distinguished by striking coherence and sense of purpose." The second period, the post-Ben-Gurion period, displayed less leadership, and saw a more institutionalized style of policymaking. Levi Eshkol, Golda Meir, and Moshe Dayan all lacked Ben-Gurion's vision, Yaniv tells us, and the Rabin-Peres (1974–1977) era illustrated the "Peter Principle" of individuals being promoted to their levels of declining competence. Begin, Yaniv adds, restored some of the Ben-Gurion style, but was not able to live up to many people's expectations. Indeed, Yaniv suggests that Begin, without the assistance of Dayan and Weizmann, was "an ignoramus in matters of national security," leading to a "recipe for a disaster" in the national security field.

Yaniv discusses the "overloaded" agenda of the Begin and post-Begin era in the national security and foreign policy arena, including (a) the development of doctrine, (b) the question of Israel's nuclear development and capability, (c) Israel's management of its alliances, primarily with the United States, (d) its orientation to regional issues, (e) its policy regarding the need for self-sufficiency in weapons supply, (f) its role as an arms exporter (especially regarding South Africa and Latin America), (g) its policy in regard to the Occupied Territories, and (h) its strategy in South Lebanon.

Yaniv concludes that the eight "clusters" of issues "constitute a formidable hurdle that no Israeli government in the foreseeable future — be it Labor-based, Likud-based, or a power-sharing coalition — will be able to resolve satisfactorily." What lies ahead for Israeli policy, Yaniv tells us, is a period of "muddling through" in foreign policy, and an increased likelihood of "mishaps, blunders, 'rogue operations', setbacks, *mechdalim* [acts of oversight or omission], and quite likely, tragedies."

Avner Yaniv was a visiting professor at Georgetown University, on leave from the University of Haifa, when he authored this article. His research interests include security issues and military policy.

In a detailed study of Soviet policy toward Israel, Robert Freedman analyzes "Changes in Soviet Policy Toward Israel and Soviet

Jewry in the First Two Years of the Gorbachev Era." Freedman reviews
Soviet policy toward the Middle East as a whole, and traces the Soviet
efforts to "weaken and ultimately eliminate Western influence from
the Middle East, and particularly the Arab world, while promoting
Soviet leadership." He then describes and analyzes new Soviet signals
to Israel, including the July 1985 (secret) ambassador-level meeting in
France, a public consular-level meeting in Helsinki in August 1986, a
meeting between Mr. Peres and Soviet Foreign Minister Shevardnadze
at the United Nations in September 1986, and several meetings between
Soviets and Israelis in 1987.

Freedman suggests that there are two major reasons that explain
recent Gorbachev initiatives: issues related to Middle East relations,
and issues related to Soviet-American relations. The apparent progress
of the Middle East peace process motivated Gorbachev to make some
gestures to Israel to gain entrance to the peace process, and to enhance
the Soviet regional and international standing as contributing to the
peace process. Peres saw the Soviet initiatives as offering a real opportunity, and pursued the initiatives, to the extent of trying to use the
opening as an excuse to bring down the National Unity Government
in which he was involved with Shamir.

Freedman also demonstrates the importance of the issue of Soviet
Jewry in the realm of Soviet-Israeli relations. The Israelis have regarded
the issue of emigration as the litmus test by which normalization can
be measured; the Soviets, in turn, have focused their attention upon
the degree to which Israel demonstrates flexibility in negotiations
dealing with the peace process in the Middle East.

The innovations of the new Gorbachev regime have promised
a great deal in the realm of Soviet-Israeli relations, but Freedman argues
that the establishment of formal diplomatic relations "would appear
to be a long way off unless an international peace conference is unexpectedly convened." Thus, Freedman concludes, we see appearances
of change in Soviet-Israeli relations, but whether these appearances
will produce real change is yet to be determined.

Robert Freedman is dean of the Graduate School of Baltimore
Hebrew University. He has published widely in the area of Soviet-
Israeli relations.

In the turbulent setting of the Middle East there have been two
moderate actors in recent years, Egypt, which signed a peace treaty
with Israel in 1979, and Morocco, which has served as a communication
facilitator over the last two decades. This volume includes three
chapters on Israel's political relations in the Middle East political
system: a broadly constructed chapter on Israel in the Middle East sets

the scene with discussion of the context within which bilateral relations exist; an essay on Israeli-Moroccan relations examines the role and motivations of King Hassan in Morocco's participation in the quest for peace; and an essay on Israeli-Egyptian relations discusses the effects and current status of the peace treaty on bilateral relations between these two nations.

Laurie Mylroie's essay, "Israel in the Middle East," focuses on two general themes. First, she focuses on a quiet but general pattern of increasing normalization between Israel and many of her neighbors. Mylroie traces the history of bilateral relations between Israel and Egypt, Israel and Morocco, Israel and Lebanon, Israel and Jordan, and Israel and Iraq, as an illustration of marked erosion of Arab hostility toward Israel.

Mylroie subsequently examines several regimes as examples of what she refers to as cases of "persistent intractability," illustrations of states maintaining hostile attitudes toward Israel. These case studies include substantial discussion of Syria, Iran, and the Palestine Liberation Organization (although Mylroie recognizes that the PLO is not a state and there is not, strictly speaking, a "comparable case" in this context).

What distinguishes the "moderate" states from the "intractable" states? According to Mylroie, the single most highly rated factor that was associated with the hostility of a neighboring state "was whether that state deemed itself a radical regime or not. Governments that professed a harsh, uncompromising anti-Zionism generally consider themselves revoluntionary states. Their anti-Zionism can be understood ultimately as a function of their domestic politics."

Laurie Mylroie is assistant professor of government at the Center for Middle Eastern Studies of Harvard University, and is now a Bradley Fellow there.

One of the most stable and moderate actors in the Middle East arena in recent years has been Morocco. Mark Tessler describes the Moroccan role in the Middle East in his essay "Israel and Morocco: The Political Calculus of a 'Moderate' Arab State." The central thesis of the essay is that King Hassan's moderation has been based upon several factors, including (a) a belief that he could play a constructive role in encouraging a dialogue toward peace in the Middle East, and (b) the desire of Morocco to stay in the "good graces" of the United States to maximize the amount of financial assistance that the regime receives from the United States.

Tessler reviews Moroccan-Israeli contacts going all the way back to 1965, including indirect communication through France in the mid-1960s, direct secret contacts in the mid-1970s that led to the Camp David accords in 1978, secret meetings between (then) Prime Minister Peres and King Hassan in 1981, up to the public meeting between (now Foreign Minister) Peres and King Hassan in 1986. Tessler then explains the agenda of the 1986 Peres-Hassan summit, Hassan's desire to focus on the (1982) Fez Plan related to the Palestinians and a Palestinian state, and Peres's negative responses to Hassan's Fez-based discussion. He also discusses at some length the significance of the 1986 Peres-Hassan summit in the context of the broader Arab-Israeli conflict, focusing upon the openness of the summit, Hassan's unusual step of having consulted with other Arab actors, the general restraint with which other Arab leaders reacted to the summit, and the significance of the formal communiqué at the end of the summit — even though no agreement was reached — emphasizing the public nature of the meeting.

The other major theme developed at length by Tessler is the causal relation between U.S. assistance and Moroccan moderation. Although it has been suggested that King Hassan genuinely "regards himself as a bridge between Arabs and Jews," that he "is motivated by a desire to demonstrate the strategic value of a Moroccan connection to the United States and other Western powers and, in so doing, to acquire tangible benefits in return," and that he is pursuing a strategy "which he sincerely believes to be in the interest of the Arabs in general and the Palestinians in particular," the "U.S. contribution" theme is developed by Tessler in some detail, using several case studies in his explanation. Morocco receives a great deal of United States support in a variety of forms, and this assistance — and a desire for more assistance — has provided King Hassan with a motive for being perceived as a "moderate."

Morocco's Jewish community, the historic tradition of Hassan's concern — and the concerns of Hassan's father Mohammed V — for Morocco's Jews, and Hassan's views of himself "as a leader capable of transcending local quarrels and of working for Arab-Jewish accommodation on the international level," are also reasons offered for Morocco's moderate position in this area. Tessler concludes by noting that although, so far at least, Hassan's efforts have not produced any tangible results, his moderation "has sought to help the Palestinians as well as himself and that his invitiation to Shimon Peres was not an entirely cynical and manipulative act." In the final analysis, he has worked hard to keep the parties involved talking, not fighting, and that must be regarded as a step in the right direction.

Mark Tessler is professor of political science at the University of Wisconsin, Milwaukee. His recent research activity has included work on the Israeli-Palestinian conflict.

Ann Lesch contributes an analysis of the bilateral relationship between Egypt and Israel, examining how it can be that "the promise and hope offered by Camp David have not been realized, and yet the accord has not been annulled." She traces the three distinct phases of Egyptian-Israeli relations, 1977 through the Israeli invasion of Lebanon in 1982, 1982 through September 1986, when Israel and Egypt reached an agreement on the procedure for resolving the Taba conflict, and 1986 to the present time.

Lesch shows that from the time of the signing of a peace treaty between Israel and Egypt, their attitudes on a wide range of issues have varied widely, and their goals have varied, as well, with Israelis "pressing for friendship" and Egyptians "reacting warily." She traces progress, and lack of progress, in a number of different areas of bilateral cooperation, including tourism, trade, cultural relations, and scientific exchanges, and shows how each of these areas has been affected by both domestic and international factors, as well as the "Palestine issue." She concludes that

> In the current environment, few positive signs can be discerned. Without a fundamental change in the official Israeli approach to the Palestine issue and serious efforts to achieve a comprehensive peace, the bilateral relationship will remain circumscribed. Normalization will remain abnormal.

Several other points of tension are examined in this study as well, including the protection of Israeli diplomats in Egypt, an attack on Israeli tourists in 1985, and the treatment of an Israeli caught smuggling drugs in Egypt in 1985. In each case Lesch describes the setting, shows the positions of the two governments, and illustrates the effects, temporary or lasting, that the action had on the bilateral relationship. The issue of Taba, and the conflict between Israel and Egypt over a "250-acre triangle of land southwest of Eilat," has been another focus of tension between the two nations, and the development of Taba as a point of contention, and the progress toward a peaceful resolution of the dispute between 1981 and the present time, are discussed here in some detail.

Lesch concludes with a broader assessment of the bilateral relationship, stating that "the promise inherent in the peace between Egypt and Israel has not been realized." She indicates that although there are differences in positions on issues and approaches to those issues between the two nations, the basic problem is "that the bilateral relationship cannot be separated from the broad regional context."

Pressure from Arab states, and the recent Palestinian *intifadah* have resulted in an uneasy peace between the two nations.

Ann Lesch is a professor of political science at Villanova University. She has published widely on Arab politics and issues related to the Palestinians.

The Israeli-American Jewish relationship is also highly significant in the Israeli foreign policy process. George Gruen describes the association in his essay "The Not-So-Silent Partnership: Emerging Trends in American Jewish-Israeli relations." American Jews, according to Gruen, "have started to reexamine the traditional boundaries between legitimate involvement and improper interference by one community in the affairs of the other." The questions Gruen studies here involve the American Jewish lobby in United States policy, and the duty — and the right — of American Jews to try to influence Israeli foreign policy.

Gruen examines the basic principles underlying this relationship, tracing the evolution of the "American citizen and a Jew" role over time. In the light of the Pollard Affair, Gruen discusses the fundamental principles governing the relations between American Jews, the United States Government, and the Government of Israel. This relationship is not always clear:

> During the 1988 Israeli election campaign both major Israeli parties . . . actively solicited contributions from American Jews. Estimates of the total were as high as $10 million. It is ironic that some of those who regard public criticism of Israeli policies by American Jews as unwarranted interference are nevertheless eager to receive foreign money to strengthen their own party and its political positions.

Gruen discusses the issues of "participation" and "interference" in several different areas, including issues of Aliyah and immigration, the role of Diaspora Jewry in the management of worldwide Jewish and Zionist organizations, and efforts to reform and modify Zionist organization bureaucracies.

The issue of the degree to which Diaspora Jews are obligated to "toe the party line" is also discussed by Gruen; as a case in point he discusses American Jews' public statements in 1987 and 1988 supporting an international peace conference under United Nations auspices, opposed by Prime Minister Shamir, and how "appropriate" it was deemed to be for American Jews to advise the Israeli government on issues of this kind. Shamir's position was that "Jews abroad have a moral duty . . . to support Israeli government, never a foreign government against Israel. It is absolutely un-Jewish and very dangerous to join an anti-Israel front with non-Jews.'' Not all American Jewish leaders agreed, and Gruen discusses this difference of opinion.

Gruen also discusses the reasons why Diaspora Jews have increased the level of their discussion and dissent in recent years. Part of the reason is attributed to Israel's Lebanon campaign, and part is attributed to the continuing troubles in the Occupied Territories. Gruen concludes by noting that ''disagreement doesn't mean divorce,'' and notes that despite increasing feeling on the part of American Jews that they have a right to express their own views on issues of importance, they continue to strongly support Israel's right to exist.

George Gruen is director of Israel and Middle Eastern affairs for the American Jewish Committee. He has published widely in the area of American-Israeli relations.

The final section of this volume focuses upon the domestic political environment, and includes chapters on the Herut party, the Labor party, the religious parties, and a chapter on recent issues in Israeli economic policy. These chapters focus upon changes in these political structures in recent years, in the post-Begin era.

The chapter by Zuckerman, Herzog, and Shamir, entitled ''The Party's Just Begun: Herut Activities in Power and After Begin,'' is an empirical analysis of survey data gathered in 1986 from delegates to the Labor and Herut party conventions. The authors examine ethnic makeup of the parties, social identifications and friendship networks of the delegates, and describe the types of factors drawing Herut supporters into the Herut ''family.''

Following an analysis of the growth of Herut and the expansion of its political base, they describe the emergence of conflict within Herut, primarily as a function of the entry of new members and activists to Herut, the control of patronage positions, and Begin's retirement. The power struggle within Herut, between David Levy, Ariel Sharon, and Yitzhak Shamir, is described and analyzed, and the sociocultural correlates of the conflict are examined.

The authors conclude with the assertion that the changes in Herut and the followers of Herut ''illustrate the transformation of Herut from a movement to a party,'' with a greater number of party professionals (as distinct from volunteers), and more competition among party factions for leadership positions and patronage. ''Herut politics,'' they say, ''is faction politics.''

Alan Zuckerman is professor of political science at Brown University. Hannah Herzog and Michal Shamir are both members of the Political Science Department at Tel-Aviv University.

The chapter by Myron Aronoff, "Better Late Than Never: Democratization in the Labor Party" is an analysis of the changes made in the nominations process for the selection of Labor candidates for the Knesset, something that is "key to evaluating the extent to which Labor is undergoing internal democratization."

Aronoff describes the background of the Labor nominating process, and how the unreformed system of nomination contributed to the party's loss of power in 1977 and again in 1981. The election of Uzi Baram to the position of party Secretary General in October 1984 was a crucial point in the reform process — Baram saw reform as mandatory if the party was to regain power. The party convention held in April 1986 is described in some detail in this essay; this convention adopted new party nomination rules.

Aronoff illustrates in great detail the May 1988 election of party candidates at the party convention in Tel Aviv, the "carnival atmosphere" that existed there, and the results of the new process, something that *Ma'ariv* called a "revolutionary" level of "internal democratization." He explains the ways in which the new selection process for the electoral list is more representative than earlier methods of selection, and concludes that "the result of this more open and competitive process was a more attractive and representative list of Knesset candidates than Labor has ever fielded." The fact that the party list did not do better than it did in the November election was a function of external events, not internal democratization.

Myron Aronoff is professor of political science at Rutgers University. His recent research activity includes work on Israeli ideology.

The contribution by Gary Schiff, "Beyond the Begin Revolution: Recent Developments in Israel's Religious Parties," is an especially timely essay in light of the results of the November 1, 1988 election in which the religious parties increased their representation in the Knesset by 50 percent. Here, Schiff describes the "core" religious parties and explains why he feels they are fundamentally very different from one another.

Schiff describes the origins of the religious parties, and the many factors which serve to distinguish between and among them, arguing that they have "clearly distinguishable political and social characteristics, as well as often divergent roles in the Israeli political system." Both the National Religious party (NRP) and Agudat Israel are examined in detail, in terms of their origins, developments, structures, and ideology. Schiff then describes the "winds of change" for both the NRP and the Agudat Israel organizations, explaining the importance of the increasing Religious Right, ethnic (Ashkenazic versus

Sephardic) factors, and "nonreligious" factors (such as defense, foreign policy, the Occupied Territories, and the economy) in contributing to the changes in the parties.

Schiff concludes that "in many ways the problem of the religious parties mirror those — albeit on a much smaller scale — of the highly divisive and fragmented political system as a whole." The dominant issues of the Begin era have affected the religious parties as they have affected the secular parties.

Gary Schiff is president and professor of Middle East studies at Gratz College in Philadelphia. He is the author of numerous works on Israeli politics and society.

The volume's final essay, by Yakir Plessner, is titled "Israel's Economy in the Post-Begin Era," and focuses on an aspect of the Israeli polity not covered in the other essays here. Plessner briefly describes the economic situation that existed when Begin came into office in 1977, and undertakes a more detailed analysis of the economic policies of the first Shamir government from 1983 to 1984. One of the major problems faced in both the Begin and (first) Shamir governments was that the prime ministers were not interested in economics, and economic policy was left to cabinet ministers who were unable, or unwilling, to take the "big picture" into consideration.

Plessner then describes the initial period of the National Unity Government, and the types of economic policies it initiated to resolve the economic crisis posed by an annual rate of inflation of almost 1,000 percent. We see how the coalition government was able to make substantial progress in the face of this economic disaster, and Plessner shows why, for both political and economic reasons, the initial success of the coalition could not be sustained. Plessner then shows how "the utter failure of the various attempts to combat inflation convinced the policymakers that an altogether different approach was needed," and how the ideologically antagonistic coalition partners were forced to reach some crucial economic compromises in the areas of devaluation, subsidization, freezing of prices and wages, increased taxation, bank deposit policy, and cuts in government expenditures. These policies appeared to work, and the plan achieved its objective.

Plessner concludes with the observation that the economic crisis faced in the early Shamir years was not the fault of Menachem Begin: "decades of economic mismanagement by all of Israel's governments, including Begin, produced the grapes of wrath that the Begin government was too weak and unwilling to uproot. It all exploded in the face of the first post-Begin government . . ." However, after tracing the causes of the crisis, and explaining those policies that helped to resolve the crisis, Plessner tells us that the "jury is still out" as far as an overall verdict is concerned. The economic problems might have been resolved, but maybe not.

Yakir Plessner is a professor at the Levi Eshkol School of Agriculture of the Hebrew University of Jerusalem. He wrote this essay while he was a visiting professor at Dartmouth College.

Israel After Begin

The chapters that follow each contribute one piece to the jigsaw puzzle that is the Israeli political world in post-Begin times. Although no single essay provides a global view of the nature of Israeli politics and society in recent times, when taken as a collectivity they provide with a remarkable degree of insight and clarity a perspective on recent Israeli politics that instructs the reader as to the issues, values, and behaviors that are characteristic of the contemporary Israeli political system.

PART ONE

Beginism, the Rule of Law, and
the Radical Right in Israel

CHAPTER TWO

The Legacy of Begin and Beginism for the Israeli Political System*

Ilan Peleg

> We Fight, Therefore We Are!
> Menachem Begin, *The Revolt*

At this historical juncture, Israel's fortieth anniversary, it could be argued that with the exception of David Ben-Gurion, Menachem Begin was the single most important personality in the political history of the State of Israel. His impact was significant in a number of areas: (a) Begin was instrumental in the development of a bipartisan system in a country that traditionally had one dominant party; (b) Begin contributed to the development of a new ideology in Israel by introducing a large number of people (and eventually the entire population) to a new psycho-ideological framework (here called Neo-Revisionism); and (c) Begin changed some of the most fundamental assumptions of Israel's foreign and defense policy and was directly responsible for some innovations in the thinking about Israel's fundamental problems (e.g. in the area of solution to the status of the Palestinians, nuclear deterrence, the type of Arab-Israeli peace that Israel should aspire for, the nature of Israel's relations with Western powers, etc.). Begin also initiated processes (particularly on the West Bank, the Gaza Strip, and

*The author wishes to thank Myron Aronoff and Ian Lustick for comprehensive comments made on a previous version of the paper. The analysis in the paper is still the author's, unless specifically mentioned otherwise.

the Golan Heights) that are likely to have long-term effects on the Israeli political system.

One cautionary remark ought to be made in the outset. Methodologically, the assessment of the exact *personal* contribution of Menachem Begin in any of these areas is extremely difficult. Governmental decisions are usually made by scores of individuals and implemented by thousands. The task of the historian, generations after the event, is to assess the precise impact of a particular individual on a specific decision, policy or development. Begin left office only five years ago and much of the material regarding his activities (especially as premier) is still unavailable to scholars; therefore, it would be presumptuous to claim precise knowledge as to his involvement in any defined area. This paper, therefore, will offer only a general analysis of the legacy that Begin left behind him. Because most of Begin's activities in the years 1977–1983 were public, the reconstruction of his record is possible. Although definitive interpretation is problematical, it is necessary and important.

Begin as an Agent of Bipartisanship*

The establishment of the State of Israel in 1948 found the Israeli Right in shambles. Two important Right Wing parties made an appearance in the elections for the First Knesset, and both failed even to mount a serious challenge to Mapai, the dominant labor party. The General Zionists, a party representing the middle and upper-middle class and supportive of a laissez-faire economy, received only seven seats in the newly established Knesset; it quickly became a partner in the government of David Ben-Gurion. Herut, the other Right Wing party, received fourteen seats in 1949 and dropped to only eight seats in 1951, a performance that led its leader, Menachem Begin, seriously to contemplate withdrawal from political life altogether.[1]

The birth of Herut in 1948 signaled the victory of the military branch within the Revisionist movement, represented by the Irgun Zvai Leumi (IZL) under Begin, over the more moderate, "civilian" branch. Many of the veteran Revisionists were removed from power and denied influence in favor of the young Irgunists.[2] In fact, immediately upon its inception, Herut published a ten–page programmatic booklet,

---

*Much of this section is based on an article of mine in a book on the Middle East since 1967 edited by Yehuda Lukacs, *The Arab-Israeli Conflict: Twenty Years After the Six Day War*, Westview, 1988.

entitled *The Herut Movement (established by the Irgun Zvai Leum): Its Foundation and Principles.*

Herut's close association with the IZL led to its defeat in the first election and in many more elections to come: the IZL was generally unpopular among the great majority of the Jews of Palestine and, later, among the Israelis. The lack of support for the IZL was based not only on widespread opposition to its tactics in fighting against the British government but on even wider rejection of the ideological stance of the organization. Because Herut, under Begin, fully adopted the IZL demand for Jewish control of *both* the East and the West Banks of the Jordan River, it practically placed itself beyond the limits of the Israeli national consensus regarding the important question of the State's boundaries.

Even after the armistice agreements with the Arabs were signed, Herut refused to join in the general acceptance of the agreed upon lines of demarcation (including the Green Line, the armistic border between Israel and Jordan). In April 1949 Begin, now a member of the Knesset, called for a no-confidence vote in the Ben-Gurion government for having signed an agreement with (and thereby bestowing recognition on) the Hashemite Kingdom of Jordan. The motion was easily defeated, signifying Herut's isolation, and even irrelevance, in regard to the territorial question and foreign policy in general.

The ultranationalist position of Herut enabled Ben-Gurion and the Mapai leadership to paint the party as utterly irresponsible, its leader (Begin) as a warmonger, and its possible rise to power as a recipe for a national disaster. In forming all his governments, Ben-Gurion started with the assumption that these governments might include all parties "with the exception of Herut and Maki [the Communists]." Similarly, Ben-Gurion even refused to call Begin by his name, preferring derogatory terms such as "the spectacled religious pretender," the "court jester," and "the man who usually sits next to Knesset Member Bader." Until Ben-Gurion's departure from political life in 1963, Herut suffered from total denial of legitimacy, at least insofar as the majority of Israeli voters were concerned. Between 1949 and 1961 it decisively lost five consecutive elections.

In many ways, Herut reinforced its negative image in the collective mind of the public by its behavior. In 1952 it led an unruly attack on the government and a physical assault on the Knesset building itself in order to prevent Israeli-German negotiations on monetary reparations. A few years later, Herut tried (and succeeded) to exploit the Kastner trial for political purposes (doubling in the process its Knesset delegation from eight to fifteen). Throughout the 1950s the party had a superhawkish stance on all foreign policy matters: it continued to adhere to the old dream of Jewish control over the East Bank; it supported the extension of Israel's military reprisals and condemned any restraint; when Israel attacked Egypt in 1956, Herut supported the campaign enthusiastically but demanded an attack on Jordan as well; when Ben-Gurion ordered the Israeli army to withdraw from the Sinai, Begin criticized him and demanded a new election. The ultranationalist stance created a severe image problem for the party, a problem that continued well into the 1960s.

Ben-Gurion's resignation as Israel's prime minister (1963) gave Herut an opportunity for political recovery for three reasons. First, Ben-Gurion had been involved in a long-term, often personal battle with the Revisionists since the 1920s. He sharply condemned IZL terror and personally opposed Begin on bitter issues such as the Altalena affair and the crisis over the German reparations. By far the most dominant leader of Mapai, Ben-Gurion was committed to the denial of even minimal legitimacy to Herut.

Second, the relatively long peace along Israel's borders prior to the Six-Day War enabled Herut to gain a measure of respectability in the eyes of the public. In the years prior to the war very few, if any, disagreements over major foreign policy issues emerged within Israel. Although Herut remained verbally militant throughout this period, the long period of political calm enabled the party to erase the memory of its belligerent past.

Third, and most important, Ben-Gurion's departure led to a political realignment in Israel, a process through which Herut gained legitimacy in the eyes of the moderate middle class and even among some segments within the labor camp (ironically, mainly those associated with Ben-Gurion). *Begin's role in this important process was decisive:* his most long-lasting impact on the Israeli political process was possibly his willingness and ability to build bridges to other political forces.

Though at the time it was not widely known, Ben-Gurion's unexpected resignation in 1963 was the result of an internal feud within Mapai, Israel's leading party. The leadership around Ben-Gurion opposed the old man not only because of his domineering attitude but also his inclination to quickly promote some of the younger leaders to positions of power. Leaders such as Levi Eshkol, Pinchas Sapir, and Zalman Aranne looked worryingly at the political emergence of younger men such as General Moshe Dayan and Shimon Peres. Superimposed on these personal rivalries, there was also an ideological disagreement: Mapai's young guard under Dayan and Peres, was, on the whole, more hawkish on foreign policy questions and domestically less committed to socialism than were the members of the old guard.

Following his departure from the premiership, Ben-Gurion, along with his younger disciples, adopted a strong position against Mapai's old guard, led by the new prime minister, Levi Eshkol. In order to strengthen its position, the new leadership opened negotiations on political unification with a smaller labor party, *Ahdut Ha'avoda*. These negotiations proved successful, and a new labor party known as *Hama'arach* (the Alignment) came into being in May 1965. Ben-Gurion and six other Knesset members representing Mapai (including Dayan and Peres) decided not to join, establishing instead their own party, *Rafi* (Israel Workers' List).

The realignment process on the left was accompanied by a realignment process on the right. Early in 1965, prior even to the conclusion of the Alignment agreement, Herut and the Liberals announced the creation of *Gahal*, the Herut-Liberal Bloc. The establishment of Gahal was, politically, a highly significant act. One of the important components of the Liberal party was the General Zionists, a group that for many years had refused to join Herut in a large, middle-class political organ, particularly because its members strongly disagreed with Herut's annexationist zest. Now, however, with Herut's image considerably improved, the movement toward unity on the left, and the hope that Herut had finally deserted its vision of conquest and grandeur, the General Zionists in the Liberal party (but still not all Liberals) decided to establish Gahal together with Herut (April 1965).

The establishment of Gahal represented a great political victory for Begin. The respectable middle class signaled that it was ready to cooperate with the ultranationalists, assuming (mistakenly, as it was learned shortly thereafter) that the latter's annexationist zest had dissipated. In order to maintain a measure of autonomy, the two components of Gahal agreed that they would continue to maintain independent political organizations. Yet, it was clearly understood that the leadership of the new bloc would be in the hands of Menachem Begin.

The elections for Israel's Sixth Knesset (November 1965) provided an opportunity to test the relative power of the newly established political blocs, the Alignment and Gahal. The Alignment won handily, indicating general approval for the practical, moderate policies of Eshkol and his team. Gahal failed badly at the polls, receiving only twenty-six seats in the new Knesset, and the hawkish Rafi also lost its credibility.

Nonetheless, the establishment of Gahal was a strike in favor of Begin and his political ideas, and it signaled a long-term change in the political system as a whole. By starting to build bridges to other parties, *Herut blurred its own controversial image without actually giving up its long-held ideological positions.* An examination of the Agreement for Establishment of a Herut-Liberal Bloc indicates that in respect to foreign policy Herut clung to its fundamental nationalistic stance. Article 2 of the preface to that agreement read: ''The Herut Movement will continue to bear aloft in the midst of the nation the principle of the integrity of the homeland, the right of the Jewish people to Eretz Israel in its historic completeness as an eternal right which accepts no denial.''

Although for the first time since 1948 there was no specific reference to Transjordan, Herut still supported a revision of the armistice lines and continued to hope for territorial expansion, a position regarded in Israel prior to the Six-Day War as extremely radical. With its ideological position intact, the future of the Israeli Radical Right represented by Herut was, by and large, unpromising. It continued to adhere to an ideological position almost universally unacceptable to the majority of the Israeli public. Although Herut was successful in receiving a measure of legitimacy by the creation of Gahal, the elections of 1965 revealed that in political terms this was far from enough: while Mapai and Adhut Ha'avoda received forty-five mandates, Gahal got only twenty-six (as against thirty-four received by Herut and the Liberals running separately in 1961).

The dramatic events of May and June 1967, however, reinforced the legitimation of Herut, a process that had started with the establishment of Gahal in 1965. In retrospect, it gave the legitimation process enough momentum and *a critical mass sufficient to change the complexion of the Israeli political system.* The acute crisis helped Begin to achieve wide-based acceptance not only among Israel's Right Wing voters and the middle class but, for the first time, the nation.

When the 1967 crisis erupted, as the Egyptians moved their armed forces into the Sinai, Begin worked diligently and publicly for the establishment of a National Unity Government, a position that enhanced his popularity across the spectrum of Israeli public opinion. Furthermore, at one stage of the political crisis in Israel, with growing demands for the resignation of Levi Eshkol as prime minister, Begin proposed that Eshkol transfer the premiership to David Ben-Gurion, Begin's longtime political and personal rival. This act of magnanimity earned Begin almost universal applause. When Gahal was finally invited to join a National Unity Government, Begin insisted that the defense minister in such a government should be Moshe Dayan, Ben-

Gurion's protegé. The 1967 crisis had an interesting side effect, an unplanned but enormously important result: it enhanced Menachem Begin's status in wide circles of the Israeli body politic, and it erased his image as an ambitious, unrestrained and irresponsible politician. *The seeds of the 1977 revolution that brought Begin to power were sown a decade earlier, in the summer of 1967.*

While the 1967 crisis initially appeared to be a great victory for the political leadership of the Alignment (Mapai and Ahdut Ha'avoda), and for the foreign and security policies of this elite, in fact it was a victory for the Right. First, the hawkish elements within the historical Mapai elite, now represented by Dayan, returned to power, with the active assistance of the Herut leadership under Begin. Thus, a strong hawkish bloc was created within the government immediately following the 1967 war, a Trojan horse of sorts. Second, and more importantly, the circumstances under which the war erupted gave credence to the attitude that one cannot rely on or expect Arab moderation and that Arab radicalism requires more than an occasional Israeli reprisal. The crisis also proved that total war could have some quick, handsome rewards. By undermining the long-term stability of the region, the Six-Day War gave much needed credibility to Herut's hawkish position on foreign policy matters; moreover, Hussein's decision to join Nasser in the war against Israel gave Herut's claim on the West Bank at least a measure of credibility for the first time since 1949. The appearance of the Palestinian Liberation Organization (PLO) prior to the Six-Day War was also a God-sent gift to Herut because it signified the radicalization of the Arab position toward Israel.

Begin made the most of his brief service (1967–1970) in the National Unity Government. As a minister without portfolio he was not burdened with the management of a ministry, and could devote all his time and energy to issues of real importance for him, foreign policy and especially the future of the Occupied Territories. As a gentleman from the Old World, he treated Prime Minister Eshkol and his successor Golda Meir with respect and deference, an exception to the informal, blunt Israeli style, which many voters welcomed. The deferential manners led to the further erasing of Begin's traditional image. At the same time, while he outwardly appeared deferential and conciliatory, Begin stuck to his old maximalist positions. Although according to the Rabin memoirs Begin agreed (along with all other ministers) on June 19, 1967, that in return for a peace treaty Israel would withdraw to its international borders with Egypt and Syria and that the future of the West Bank would be dealt with separately,[3] Begin's position grew more and more hawkish, and he adopted Herut's traditional stance. Thus, when Israeli officials met with Ambassador Gunnar Jarring, the United Nations-designated mediator, Begin protested, as he did when Israel accepted Resolution 242 (on May 1, 1968)[4] and when plans to hold Rhodes-style negotiations were discussed.[5]

Furthermore, while still a member of the National Unity Government, Begin argued in the Knesset for setting up Jewish quarters in the Arab cities of the West Bank in order to create, as he put it, "an atmosphere of mutual trust" between the native Arabs and their Jewish neighbors.[6] Within the government Begin routinely sided with the hawks, especially General Dayan; some referred to him as "Abba Eban's watchdog."[7] Finally, when the government decided in August 1970 to accept an American diplomatic initiative calling for Israeli-Arab discussions through Ambassador Jarring, Gahal withdrew from participation in the government at Begin's insistence.

Begin's resignation from the Meir government in August 1970 allowed him, and Herut, to further radicalize their political positions. The withdrawal from the government gave Herut and Begin personally much greater freedom of action in the political arena. They quickly became pillars of the annexationist movement in Israel, a movement that included, in addition a few small political factions, Gush Emunim and the Greater Israel Movement.

Despite the growing strength of the movement, it was clear to Begin, a seasoned politician, that unless all the nationalist forces were politically united, they would not be able to control the fate of the territories occupied by Israel in 1967. This was the rationale for the establishment of the Likud, the political coalition on which Begin finally rode to power. The Likud was created as a result of the efforts of General Ariel (Arik) Sharon, an ultranationalist paratrooper with a long history of radical involvement in the Arab-Israeli conflict, much of it accompanied by severe criticism from fellow Israelis. The original Likud ("Unity") included Gahal (Herut and the Liberals), the State List (La'am) composed of individuals close to Ben-Gurion and Dayan, the Free Center of Shmuel Tamir,[8] and the Greater Israel Movement.

From the very beginning it became clear that the Likud would be dominated by Herut. The political program of the new body was a carbon copy of Herut's traditional ideological perspective. The Likud platform for the 1973 election declared that the Jewish people had an inalienable right to all of biblical Palestine and that the Likud would not accept any Israeli withdrawal from the West Bank. The party leaders also stated that formal peace treaties between Israel and its Arab neighbors must recognize Israel's right to control areas that the Arabs had used as a springboard for attacks on Israel prior to the 1967 war, namely, the West Bank, the Gaza Strip, the Golan Heights, and possibly the Sinai as well. The territorial message of the Likud was simple: "not an inch!"[9]

The 1973 platform also called for intensifying the settlement campaign, particularly in Judea and Samaria, as a step toward annexation. As a way of dealing with the local inhabitants, the Likud proposed allowing them to choose between Israeli citizenship or the citizenship of another country. The platform contained no hint of the possibility of recognizing the right of the "inhabitants" as a distinct national group.

While the Likud failed to defeat the Labor parties in the 1973 elections, the establishment, for the first time in Israel's history, of an ultranationalist coalition of forces indicated the movement of the entire political system to the right. Begin was now not only the head of the "fighting family," as the IZL veterans called themselves, but the recognized leader of a large bloc of political parties unified around the concept of "Greater Israel." He was ready to fight for the biggest political prize, Israel's premiership, a prize that would enable him to change history.

Begin was not only instrumental in creating a bipartisan system in Israel, but also important in facilitating the political appearance of a more active, distinct, and possibly dominant group of younger voters of lower socioeconomic background and of non-European origin. A few factors could be identified as explaining Begin's electoral success in 1977 and 1981 and Likud's performance in 1984:

> *The Age Factor.* Since the late 1970s the Likud had clearly led the Alignment among voters under 30 (while it tied the Alignment among the middle-aged and trailed among older voters). Likud's superiority was particularly evident in the army, where it led the Alignment by a margin of roughly two to one. The 1967 generation was certainly more pro-Likud than any previous generation in Israel.
>
> *Socioeconomic Status (Occupation, Education, and Income).* While low-income, blue-collar people voted mostly for the Likud, the more prosperous, educated, and the white-collared tended to prefer the Alignment. The superhawkish message of Menachem Begin, rich in emotionality, symbolism and mystique, was always attractive to the less educated Israelis.
>
> *Ethnic Origin.* While Jews from European (or American) descent voted mostly for the Alignment, the non-Europeans (known as Sephardim or Orientals) voted in overwhelming numbers for the Likud. In the Development Towns, where the population is mostly from the Arab

countries, Likud led Labor in 1977 by roughly a two-to-one margin, and often more. In 1984 the preference ratio for the two parties among Israel's ethnic groups was about three to one, with the Sephardim prefering the Likud and the Ashkenazim the Alignment.[10] While about two-thirds of the Alignment's voters were Ashkenazim, two-thirds of the Likud's were Sephardim.

The rise of Begin marked the emergence of what was known in the country as *Israel Hashnia*—the Second Israel: Jews from non-European contries, relatively poor, mostly employed as blue-collar workers, individuals who had immigrated to the country after the establishment of the state in 1948 (or their descendants). While most of these people had hardly ever heard of Jabotinsky, they felt much closer to Begin than to the Alignment leadership. The Alignment represented for them the First Israel: the wealthy and the educated, the secular, and the Ashkenazic (European). Begin, forever the man in the opposition, represented the Second Israel, even though he was not one of them in terms of demographic characteristics.

From a broad historical perspective, Begin had an important role in a rather dramatic development: the growing bipartisanship of the Israeli political system. While in the first three decades of Israel's existence (1948–1977), practically all power was concentrated in one party (Mapai) or a bloc of parties (Alignment), the situation changed in 1977. Within Mapai there was an ongoing political competition[11] and on occasions that competition focused even on major foreign policy issues,[12] but still the way to power was traditionally through a single dominant organization. The rise of Begin to power in 1977 changed the structure by creating a bipolar system with two large blocs alongside a few smaller parties.

In changing Israel's fundamental political structure, Begin succeeded in bringing into power what was, traditionally, *a political underclass*. This underclass had a rather strange composition, and it included a variety of elements: (a) the ultranationalist leadership of Herut and the underground organizations (IZL and Lechi); (b) the bourgeois of the Liberals; (c) the urban *lumpen-proletariat*,[13] blue-collar, underpaid workers of Sephardi descent, concentrated in the crowded quarters of some of Israel's major cities or in the Development Towns. These groups had little in common beside being politically "out" (seemingly in a permanent way) and perceiving Menachem Begin as the leader who could bring them "in." With the exception of the bourgeois, all the out elements tended to be highly nationalistic, hawkish in foreign policy, and suspicious of the outside world, an attitudinal syndrome that their would-be savior, Menachem Begin, personified.

In order to be considered a potential national leader, Begin had to overcome Mapai's traditional ostracism, an attitude on the part of the establishment that, ironically, strengthened his image as the permanent underdog. Begin had to pass the threshold of legitimacy and acceptability in order to be considered by the public at large as a viable alternative to the old Mapai guard. He did so with tremendous speed during the crisis preceeding the 1967 war.

Begin's 1977 revolution had, potentially, far-reaching significance, over and above the creation of a bipartisan, competitive political structure. Political scientists have traditionally assumed that the success of a stable, working democracy depends on the overlapping of social groups within political organizations, rather than the reinforcement of social cleavages. In this sense, the Begin revolution amounted to the evolution of *potentially destructive social division within Israel.* Multifaceted polarization grew with Likud voters concentrated among the religiously more traditional, Sephardim, less educated, lower status workers, while Alignment voters dominated among the secular, Ashkenazi, upper class voters. This "demographic" differentiation, of which the public itself was acutely aware, was further *reinforced by deep disagreement regarding the central political question on the Israeli national agenda,* the future of the Occupied Territories.

It could be argued that Begin contributed to the development of this pattern of political polarization through his extremist rhetoric: during the electoral campaign of 1981, for example, he openly accused his opposition of disloyalty to the State; in 1984, Begin's successors similarly referred to themselves as the "National Camp" (ha'machaneh ha'leumi), indicating that those who opposed them were unpatriotic. Begin's rise coincided with the increase in political intolerance and violence in Israel and decrease in communication and understanding among different social groups, and the prime minister was not entirely free from responsibility. Wrote one commentator upon Begin's resignation in 1983:

> We are facing a testing time for our democracy once more because of the palpable presence of the anti-democratic forces, never far below the Herut surface, that have been allowed to emerge during Likud rule. Menachem Begin, the stickler for due process and democratic procedure, in his passion for the entire Land of Israel has let loose menaces to the democratic system such as the forces backing Ariel Sharon and the Gush Emunim zealots in Kiryat Arba and elsewhere.[14]

One could argue that the most significant "menace to the democratic system" in Israel, or at least to the long-term stability of that system, that Menachem Begin left behind was his ideological legacy. I now turn to this legacy.

The Ideological Legacy of Menachem Begin

For about a quarter of a century before he became Israel's premier, especially since he assumed control of the IZL, Menachem Begin had been the chief spokesman of the Zionist Right. When he resigned Israel's premiership he left behind a well-defined, explicit, highly developed ideology, a belief system that is likely to continue to influence those who see themselves as his disciples and many others. Therefore, it is important to identify some of the main components of Begin's thinking and to analyze their implications for the future.

Begin was strongly influenced by the great Zionist leader Vladimir Jabotinsky (1880–1940), to whom he customarily referred as "our teacher, master, and father," describing him as the greatest man of his era. Nevertheless, there is no straight line leading from Jabotinsky to Begin: the two often disagreed bitterly on important issues[15] and, in fact, while Begin adopted some of Jabotinsky's fundamental ideas about the nature of the world and the appropriate Jewish response to it, *he systematically emotionalized and radicalized the Revisionist belief system*, so much so, that the ideology of Begin is justifiably called Neo-Revisionism.[16] Begin, representing the generation of persecuted East European Jews of the period between the two World Wars, the same generation which lost most of its sons and daughters in the Holocaust, developed a much more combative ideology than classical Revisionism ever was. The Israeli premier was, as one of his admirers stated, "a product of the militant Hebrew nationalism that was rising out of the depth of the *galut* despair."[17]

What are the main elements of Neo-Revisionism, the radicalized version of Jabotinsky's ideology, the belief system that may be justifiably called "Beginism" in view of Menachem Begin's contribution to its development and eventual political triumph? *First,* Neo-Revisionism, as Revisionism before it, is based on a set of territorial assumptions, namely that Jews have a valid claim to Eretz Israel in its entirety, that no other national group has such valid claim, and that within the land Jews alone should rule. The territorial imperative of Neo-Revisionism (and of Revisionism in the past) is fundamental and nonnegotiable. Begin's refusal to negotiate the return of the West Bank and Gaza was based on the Neo-Revisionist territorial imperative, an attitude that he left as a sacred legacy to the Israeli Right.

Those who were unaware of the territorial imperative to which Begin was wedded, naively believed that at Camp David he signalled his willingness to compromise on the West Bank and Gaza. In fact, at Camp David Begin was trying to obtain the tacit agreement of the United States and Egypt to the eventual annexation of Judea, Samaria, and Gaza to Israel, while promising the Palestinians merely personal autonomy. His position rested on principles formulated by Jabotinsky in the 1920s.

Although it is more difficult to identify the fundamental values on which Begin's ideology rests, it seems that these values are the supremacy of the nation and the belief in an inevitable conflict between nations. The outlook is, in other words, ultranationalistic and Social Darwinist.[18]

A *second* distinctive feature of Neo-Revisionism is found in its fundamental position toward the outside world, a position that is a somewhat surprising deviation from Jabotinsky's attitude. Neo-Revisionism often reflects a *fundamental negation of the outside world*, a world which is perceived as anti-Semitic in its essence. While others view anti-Semitism as fundamentally social, political, and economic, that is, explainable in behavioral or historical terms, the Neo-Revisionist sees the rejection of the Jew in ahistorical terms. While most Neo-Revisionists feel uneasy describing anti-Semitism in theological terms, as Gush Emunim adherents do, they nevertheless often describe it as a permanent condition that can never change, somewhat of a metaphysical reality.

For the Neo-Revisionists, headed by Begin, the current criticism of Israeli policies (particularly their own) reflects merely the traditional rejection of the Jew as a Jew. The continuous Arab-Israeli dispute thus *reinforces the powerful sense of mistrust toward the world*. As the chief Neo-Revisionist ideologue and spokesman, Begin very often levied the accusation of anti-Semitism at his opponents. When Begin was asked to explain his government's role in the massacre in the Sabra and Shatila camps, he immediately identified the inquiry itself as a "blood libel," a return to vicious anti-Semitism. The very same attitude has characterized the Neo-Revisionist response to more general policy issues. In a personal statement he issued on June 11, 1979, Begin attacked those who dared argue that Israeli settlements on the West Bank were provocative. Alluding to the anti-Semitism of his opponents, he said: "One recalls times when it was asserted that the very presence of Jews was in and of itself a provocation."[19] The image of a hostile, murderous world is central to the Neo-Revisionist belief system, affecting issues of specific and general nature alike.

A *third* characteristic of Begin's Neo-Revisionist ideology is a pronounced tendency to use mystical justifications in support of its territorial and other claims. Thus, the Neo-Revisionist claim to the West Bank is often couched in biblical terms, emphasizing historical rights and ignoring political realities. Menachem Begin in particular was an effective promoter of national myths.[20]

A *fourth* element within the Neo-Revisionist ideology is its attitude toward the possibility or even the desirability of a normal Jewish existence in the world; for Begin and his associates "normalcy" was unachievable in the first place, and hardly desirable in any event. Their negation of the world and their position toward Jewish integration within it were highly consistent. The negation of normalcy is a serious deviation on the part of contemporary Neo-Revisionism from the basic principles of Zionism to which even Jabotinsky adhered. The emphasis on Jewish uniqueness, separation and even secession from the rest of the world is one of Neo-Revisionism's most far-reaching attitudes.

A *fifth* element of the Neo-Revisionist belief system is different than the other elements in that it describes a *positive image of national salvation*. Approaching the world with a fundamentally negative image, the Neo-Revisionist sees it as an extremely hostile and dangerous place, a profoundly anti-Semitic environment to which the Holocaust was an organic, almost inevitable result. Yet, within that belief system there is also a positive, compensatory image: the Jew, who in the negative image is perceived as an eternal victim, is now perceived as a powerful, almost superior being; the Holocaust, the most horrible disaster for a living nation, is transformed now by the reemergence of the Jewish people in a powerful, dominant, universally fulfilling role. Begin, a man who suffered from a severe case of Holocaust-fixation, was also an enthusiastic supporter of Israeli military might, extensively applied to the country's environment.

The Revisionist and later the Neo-Revisionist gospels differed from the ones offered by Herzl and the Labor camp in Palestine. For Herzl the overwhelming Zionist goal was, simply put, Jewish survival, and he believed that it should be achieved in a modern, Western, liberal society in Palestine or elsewhere. For Labor the Zionist dream was that of a model society based on principles of equality and sharing. The Revisionists argued for national grandeur, military might, conquest and expansion, not merely survival. They demanded a move from total insecurity to total security, from being dominated by others to the domination of others, from statelessness to powerful statehood. Under Neo-Revisionism, in the post-Holocaust era, the dream of grandeur and power grew to enormous, abnormal proportions. Neo-Revisionism, more than any other brand of Zionism with the possible exception of Gush Emunim's messianism, reflected "a rapid transition from inferiority to overcompensation," a phenomenon known also among individuals.[21]

A *sixth* element in the Neo-Revisionist ideology that ought to be emphasized is that of Holocaust-fixation. Direct experience of the Holocaust distinguishes Begin's Neo-Revisionism from Jabotinsky's Revisionism, and this difference explains why the former is significantly more radical than the latter. The Holocaust is Neo-Revisionism's center of gravity, it dominates its worldview. For the Neo-Revisionists, as represented by Begin, the lines of cause and effect between the Holocaust and the tenets of Israeli foreign policy have been clearer, stronger, and more direct than for most Israeli political groups. As in the case of Jewish presence in ancient Eretz Israel, the Neo-Revisionists view the Holocaust experience as not merely affecting present situations but as *controlling* them. The Jewish presence in ancient Eretz Israel determined for Begin and his associates the boundaries of modern Israel; the Holocaust meant that Israel had to be completely independent of the rest of the world and in total control over its international environment.

In fact, the absorption of the Holocaust among the Neo-Revisionists has been so profound that a tendency has developed to see any conflict between Jews and others in apocalyptic terms. All opponents, as such, were considered Hitleric, bent on destroying the Jewish people. Throughout the period of Neo-Revisionist control over the government of Israel (1977–84), security and foreign policy decisions and positions were Holocaust-centered. Not only did Prime Minister Begin refer to the Holocaust in virtually all of his numerous speeches, but his policies were heavily influenced by the memories of the horrible past. In deciding whether to bomb Iraq's nuclear reactor, for example, Begin said that he had thought about a new Holocaust. Even during the Lebanese War, a war in which the IDF enjoyed overwhelming superiority, Begin constantly referred to the Holocaust as a relevant historical experience.

For Begin the Holocaust functioned not only as a powerful symbol, but as a measure of all things, an analytical device. In this context, the pre-1967 borders became "Auschwitz borders," the Palestinian national covenant was *Mein Kampf*, Arafat was called Hitler, and the PLO became the "Arab S.S." Commenting on the Venice initiative of the European countries, which his government rejected out of hand, Begin openly accused all European countries ("with the exception of the Danes") of collaboration with the Nazis.[22]

A *seventh* characteristic of Neo-Revisionism is an attitude toward the Arabs that is an extension of the attitude toward the rest of the non-Jewish world. The Arab problem is perceived as an integral part of the fundamental problem of Jewish existence, that of anti-Semitism. The theory of Arab anti-Semitism is extremely widespread among Neo-Revisionists, although it could be found among others as well. The Arab is often perceived as the reincarnation of the eternally present anti-Semite seeking the annihilation of the Jew. While classical Revisionism as reflected in the writing of its founder, Jabotinsky, viewed the Arab-Jewish dispute as a genuine interethnic conflict, modern Neo-Revisionism developed a more mythical outlook denying in some cases even the existence of an Arab national entity within the borders of Eretz Israel. The demonology of the Arabs reached new heights under Begin.

Begin as a Foreign Policy Innovator*

During his tenure as prime minister (1977–1983), Menachem Begin had a historical opportunity to implement some of the ideas of the Revisionism movement and his own Neo-Revisionist concepts. His policies as prime minister must be understood on the background of the foreign policy adopted by his party, Herut, in the first 30 years of Israel's existence, a policy that had a few major characteristics:

Territorial Expansion

Herut's line on the question of Israel's final boundaries was essentially a continuation of the line taken by the Revisionist movement and the Irgun.[23] When Ben-Gurion declared the establishment of a Jewish state, acting on the basis of the United Nations partition resolution of November 1947, Begin, as IZL commander, issued a declaration reflecting a different position:

> The State of Israel was established. But we shall remember that the homeland has not yet been liberated. . . . We shall carry the vision of full liberation and full redemption. Five-sixths of our national territory are at stake. . . . Our plows will yet plow the fields of the Gilad.[24]

Herut consistently criticized Mapai, the ruling party, and Ben-Gurion himself, for having missed a "golden opportunity" (in 1948)

---

*Parts of this section are based on an article in a book on Israeli politics, edited by Bernard Reich and Gershon Kieval (*Israeli National Security Policy*, Greenwood Press, 1989).

to conquer the West Bank.[25] Begin maintained that Mapai's territorial position, which favored partition, was a crime that made Chamberlain's sin of appeasement in Munich pale in comparison. In its first public document Herut stated that "the main objective of the Hebrew foreign policy will be to ensure the unification of the torn homeland."

With the termination of active hostilities, in 1949, a national consensus of accepting the armistice lines emerged in Israel. Herut alone among Israel's political parties remained outside of this consensus. When the Sinai/Suez campaign erupted, in 1956, Begin bitterly criticized the Ben-Gurion government for not initiating an attack on Jordan; Herut consistently was waiting for an opportunity for territorial expansion. Its position on the territories following the 1967 war was merely a continuation of its historical, ideologically grounded line.

Use of Force

Throughout Israel's first thirty years, Herut's foreign policy was activist, supportive of frequent and extensive use of force as an instrument for dealing with Israel's political and military problems. While within Mapai, the ruling party, two opposing approaches, a dovish and a hawkish, emerged,[26] Herut's policy remained monolithically what Harkabi called "hawkish-hawkish."[27] When Israel's reprisals policy was initiated in the early 1950s, it found in Herut a consistent supporter. In fact, Herut demanded even more extensive reprisals than Ben-Gurion, Dayan, and Peres were willing to approve. Furthermore, while the reprisal policy of Mapai's hawks was designed to keep the political and territorial status quo, Herut's support for reprisals was designed to initiate a total war that would give Israel an opportunity to "liberate" the occupied homeland. Herut's position was entirely consistent with its ideological stance.

Relationships with External Powers

It is often assumed that Herut, by its very nature, was inherently pro-Western and anti-Soviet. After all, communism and Zionism, let alone communism and Revisionism, were always incompatible, and Herut's leader, Menachem Begin, served a term in a Soviet labor camp for Zionist activity, as did many other activists in Jabotinsky's movement.

In fact, however, the pro-Western, anti-Soviet position of Herut was not a fundamental position but a stance taken on the basis of cold calculation based on Herut's ideological inclinations. Dr. Yochanan Bader wrote in his memoirs and told me in a personal interview (July

1985) that Herut, at the begining, had a position of neutrality and non-alignment, but that Begin unilaterally changed it following his visit to the United States in 1951. At this time, following the outbreak of the Korean War, Herut's leader understood that the cold war would remain a fundamental feature of the international scene for many years and concluded that Israel would benefit from close relationships with the United States, a position that Ben-Gurion's government had also adopted. Herut maintained and intensified the pro-American, pro-Western line of the early 1950s.

Herut leaders had fundamental attachment to one idea alone: *shlemut hamoledet* (greater Israel). This vision took as a given a long-term, violent conflict with the Arabs. Herut thought that in this conflict Israel would need powerful allies, preferably the United States. The pro-American line, in other words, was the function of the fundamental ideological line.

In some of his writing, Begin expressed his views on the appropriate relationships between Israel and the West openly and clearly. Thus, in a piece in *Hauma*, 1966, written to the party loyalists, Begin talked not only about territorial expansion, but actually defended Israel's "right" to remain a foreign entity in the Middle East: "We better call Israel not a Middle Eastern state but a *Mediterranean state.*"[28] He then proceeed to reject ideas for an association between Israel and the Arab world, and promoted an open alliance with Western countries. Hinting to his Strategic Understanding with the United States more than fifteen years later, Begin stated in this remarkable article: "Being a *Mediterranean* state, we can *serve as a link beyond our own limited area,* where we are surrounded by enemies. We have an opportunity to establish alliances in different directions."[29] Herut was one of the most enthusiastic supporters of the Israeli-French link in the 1950s and 1960s.

Nationalism

In a general way, beyond all specific issues, Herut's position always reflected a strong sense of nationalism, sometimes even beyond rational calculations of self-interest. The issue of the reparations from Germany (1952) is a case in point. Despite the fact that Israel had strong economic reasons to be interested in receiving the reparations, as well as significant political reasons, Herut vocally opposed the efforts of the government to obtain them. Begin called the negotiations with the Germans *chilul hashem* (the defamation of God's name), "the ultimate abomination, the likes of which we have not known since we became a nation."[30]

Herut's foreign policy was of limited importance as long as the party was in opposition (until 1967) or served as a relatively small partner within a larger coalition led by Labor. This policy became very important once Menachem Begin assumed the position of Israel's prime minister (1977). His policies in the region and beyond reflected not only the traditional Herut ideology, but they were backed by the considerable force of the Israeli State and armed forces. Likud's policies, in totality, created a new regional order in the Middle East.

The cornerstone of Likud's foreign policy throughout its reign was the effort to maintain Israel's control over the West Bank, the Gaza Strip and the Golan Heights, although the international pressures, internal dissent, and the demographic reality prevented the government from a *de jure* annexation of the Occupied Territories. Some even argued that having recognized his inability to annex the territories, Begin decided to focus instead on the southern (Egypt) and northern (Lebanon) fronts in order to facilitate such annexation in the future.[31] Both operations, the peace with Egypt and the war in Lebanon, were intimately linked with the central goal of annexation.

On the whole, there were two distinct periods during the Likud's rule, periods that do not exactly match the first and the second Begin governments. In the first period, that of *moderation* (1977–79), Foreign Minister Dayan and Defense Minister Weizman implemented what was generally perceived in the West as Begin's peace policy. The highlights of this period were the Sadat visit to Jerusalem, the Camp David Accords, and the Egyptian-Israeli peace treaty, and it came to an end with the resignation (in frustration) of both Dayan and Weizman and the stalemate in the negotiations over West Bank autonomy. In the second period, that of *radicalization* (1980–83) a new policy was implemented by Begin himself, Defense Minister (since 1981) Ariel Sharon, Foreign Minister Yitzhak Shamir, chief of Staff Eitan, and the Ambassador to Washington Moshe Arens. A new political elite, substantially more radical than the previous one, had emerged, and it carried a series of actions, which, in their totality, constituted *a departure from the tough but restrained policy of the past:* extensive and public settlement effort, annexation of the Golan Heights, the attack on the Iraqi nuclear reactor (Osiraq), the Lebanon war, etc.

The first Likud government was dominated by Camp David. Because it was there that Begin recognized the "legitimate rights of the Palestinians," many believed that at Camp David Begin really deviated from the Revisionist orthodox dogma. In fact, however, Begin's Camp David actions were (for him, although not to many of his supporters) merely a tactical, momentary deviation, taken under conditions of extreme personal duress (American *and* Israeli, the pressure on the Israeli side put mainly by Dayan and Weizman).[32] On the whole, Begin went to Camp David in order to guarantee his vision of Greater Israel, to neutralize Egypt as an active confrontation state and to buy some time in the face of unprecedented American pressure. When he finally freed himself from his "prison" at Camp David, Begin immediately returned to his annexationist stance, approved an accelerated settlement effort, and refused to allow any but the most limited autonomy to the local inhabitants. The failure of the autonomy talks meant a Begin victory.[33]

What could be called Begin's "diplomacy of annexation," was accompanied on the ground by a series of policies designed to guarantee eventual incorporation of the territories to Israel: (a) a large-scale settlement effort, which put the number of settlers at the end of Begin's rule at 28,400 (it was merely 3,200 at the end of Labor's rule in 1977) and which was designed to make the eventual separation of the West Bank from Israel impossible by encouraging Jewish presence in Central Samaria; (b) a dramatic increase in land seizure on the West Bank (from 35,000 *dunams* under Labor to more than 400,000 *dunams* under the Likud, and a claim for over forty percent of the total area of the West Bank as "state land"),[34] as well as the opening of the territories for private buyers; (c) an open and enthusiastic governmental support for Gush Emunim as a settling *avant garde* on the West Bank, a force of armed zealots; (d) the establishment of a civilian administration (Nov. 8, 1981; Military Order no. 947) in the territories as a step toward eventual annexation and a more effective control of the population.

All the above actions, and more, were part of a large-scale effort designed to guarantee an Israeli control and eventually annexation of the Occupied Territories. The autonomy plan devised by Begin was to serve as a legal framework within which real annexation could be effected. When it met with the opposition on the international level (United States, Egypt), domestic level (in Israel itself, including Begin's own government) and, as expected, in the territories themselves, the efforts to establish autonomy were replaced by efforts to cultivate a new, collaborationist leadership on the West Bank (the Village Leagues). When this attempt also failed, mainly due to internal opposition in the territories, the Lebanon war was launched (June 1982) as a means for destroying the *political power* of the PLO and eliminating its influence on the West Bank. Begin and Sharon thought that this would lead to the pacification of the territories and to the quiet imposition of the autonomy plan.

The Lebanon war marked a new strategic concept in the thinking of any Israeli government — it was *truly reflective of Herut's traditional foreign policy goals, style of operations, and even fundamental values:* in sharp contrast with the recent past, Begin's second government conducted unlimited, unrestrained Lebanese policy. An examination of Labor's policy in Lebanon indicates that the Rabin government recognized the limits of its ability to influence internal Lebanese affairs,[35] instructed the IDF to conduct military operations against PLO targets exclusively, limited these operations in size and duration, and reached an overall (albeit unwritten) understanding with Syria on areas of influence in Lebanon.

Begin's ascendence and the formation of the Likud government led to important changes in Israel's Lebanese policy. The new prime minister falsely defined the Lebanese situation as "genocide" against the Christians, a situation that Israel could not and would not allow (thereby committing Israel to a long-term, unlimited involvement in Lebanon). In March 1978 the government authorized the Litani Operation, signaling a new level of Israeli involvement.

Ezer Weizman, Begin's first defense minister, attempted to halt the chain of events and to limit Israel's Lebanese involvement. The Litani Operation, even though unprecedented, was carried out (under Weizman) in a moderate fashion. Weizman rejected the repeated requests of the Maronites for an IDF intervention on their behalf, including an advance toward Beirut during the Litani Operation itself.[36] He and foreign minister Dayan were afraid that an adventurist policy in Lebanon would hurt Israel's chances of making peace with other Middle Eastern countries.

These signs of moderation completely disappeared with the installment of the second Begin government. The new defense minister, Sharon, wanted to eject the Syrians completely from Lebanon, to force his ally Bashir Gemayel on the country (as president), to destroy the PLO base militarily *and* politically, possibly to lead to mass Palestinian evacuation of Lebanon, and, in general, to establish Israel as a controlling political force in the country. The June 1982 invasion was designed to achieve these goals.

The main and most immediate goal of the Lebanon war was to achieve Herut's long-held ideological goal: the annexation of the West Bank and Gaza. By destroying the PLO in Lebanon, Likud leaders hoped to force the inhabitants of the West Bank to accept the autonomy plan offered by Begin. Chief of Staff Eitan said candidly that the war in Lebanon was a continuation of "the battle that, he thought, had lasted already 100 years."[37] Eitan openly unveiled the *real* reason for the invasion, a reason carefully concealed by Begin when he called the operation "Peace for the Galilee."

A secondary, yet important, cause for the Lebanon invasion was the desire of Begin to free Israel from what he considered past national traumas that could negatively affect the national resolve in the future. Related to that goal was Begin's effort of reunification of the Israeli Right around himself. The prime minister spoke often of the trauma of the 1973 war,[38] and he believed that a clear-cut victory in Lebanon would once and for all erase that trauma. A second and much more personal trauma that Begin had to erase was the one caused by his signature on the Camp David Accords and the Israeli concessions to which they led, including the painful evacuation of the Israeli-built town in the Sinai, Yamit. Camp David led to bitter criticism of Menachem Begin's otherwise impeccable credentials as a nationalist, the recognized spokesman of the nationalist right in Israel. The assault on Lebanon (as the annexation of the Golan Heights before) was, at least partially, motivated by Begin's decision to reestablish his status as Jabotinsky's heir.

Lebanon can be seen as a "case study" of Likud's foreign policy in the region. Other interesting cases, such as the attack on Osiraq or the Golan annexation, do not necessitate a detailed analysis here, but some general comments regarding Likud's regional foreign policy are in order.

In regional terms, Israel's goal prior to 1977 was that of maintaining the balance of power between herself and the neighboring Arab countries as a means of maintaining the status quo in the region. While many leaders of Labor and other parties even spoke about an eventual return of most of the West Bank to Arab hands, about a territorial change in favor of the Arabs, all were committed to the maintenance of the military balance of forces established as a result of the Six-Day War.

The Likud government under Begin pursued a radically different policy, which was unrecognized by most political observers prior to the departure of Dayan and Weizman from the government. Begin, acting on a basis of a neo-Revisionist set of assumptions,[39] did not believe that peaceful coexistence between Jews and Arabs — in Israel, on the West Bank or in the region in general — was possible. He was determined to establish Israeli hegemony in the area, a new balance of power in which Israel would be completely dominant.[40] The war in Lebanon, the annexation of the Golan Heights, and similar actions were logical extensions of this new set of goals.

The traditional Israeli position vis-a-vis the Arab states tended to be defensive in nature. This posture has a few general characteristics:

limited objectives in case of war;[41] restrained military operations even under conditions of total superiority;[42] and a position of deterrence of Arab attack as a fundamental objective of the IDF. The Likud quickly deserted the traditional Israeli defensive posture, of which Begin was highly critical in the first three decades of Israel when Herut was in opposition. The government adopted an offensive posture character- ized by declared expansionist goals,[43] extensive and frequent use of Israel's military machine, and a political compeller rather than military deterrence as a controlling factor.[44] The final objective of the leading figures in Begin's second government was to create a new, Israeli- dominated order in the Middle East, an order that would have as one of its elements nominal autonomy for the West Bank Palestinians. For the purpose of shaping the new order, the Likud was willing to shift from a position of deterrence and prevention, which characterized Labor's defense policy, to a position of compeller and control. The position became Clausewitzian, the use of warfare for purely political goals.[45]

Although some leaders of the Labor governments (1967–77) were accused of stubbornness and reluctance to explore all alternatives for a regional peace,[46] Labor carefully avoided the unilateral introduction of long-term changes in the regional status quo. With the exception of Jerusalem, on which there was a national consensus (almost unanimity), no legal action was taken to annex Arab territories. The Likud, on the other hand, did everything in its power to impose unilateral revisions in the legal status of Jerusalem, the West Bank and Gaza, Lebanon and the Golan Heights. It often did so by using crude force, as in launching the attack on Lebanon. Power politics came to replace diplomacy, and Israel's foreign policy became growingly militaristic until Begin's resignation. This change in the character of Israel's foreign policy was enthusiastically supported by Right Wing writers, opinion makers who, in fact, helped to bring it about. Wrote Zvi Shiloah, a former Laborite turned annexationist:

> Just as France emerged from its hundred-year war with England strong, fortified, united and large, so would Israel come out of her hundred-year war strong, fortified, united and large. Then there will be peace....The real peace between Israel and the Arabs will be signed in Baghdad.[47]

For Shiloah and his associates, but also for Begin and his lieutenants, war had become an acceptable tool for the achievements of their nationalistic, ideologically determined goals. While in the past Israel had fought in response to massive Arab attacks (1948, 1969–70,

1973) or within the contexts of preventive (1956) or preemptive (1967) war,[48] the Begin government, especially the second one, initiated a major war for the purpose of attaining purely political objectives.[49] While prior Israeli governments saw war as a means of last resort, Begin's second government perceived war as an instrument of political objectives over which there was deep disagreement within the Israeli public. General (Ret.) Benny Peled of the Israeli Air Force often expressed publicly the view that "Israel must determine her political objectives according to her military capabilities, define her desired borders and attain them through her army."[50] Begin shared Peled's prescription: he defined the desired borders and then used the IDF to attain them.

Because the concepts of Greater Israel and regional peace proved incompatible, the Begin government found it necessary to use Israel's military might beyond the boundaries of Western Palestine. A new concept of Israel and its role in its immediate region had emerged and actually been acted upon, Israel as a *regional superpower*. Begin, and particularly his defense minister, Sharon, perceived Israel as having not only immediate defensive needs, but far-reaching territorial and political objectives. They both worked to establish a large regional sphere of influence that would enable Israel to maintain political control over the internal affairs of its neighbors. This policy rested not only on an attempt to maintain an overwhelming conventional superiority but also monopoly over nuclear weapons.[51]

The new policy relied on the sharp increase in the size of Israel's standing army. In 1973 the IDF's regular force numbered merely 70,000 troops; by 1982 it had increased to 170,000 troops,[52] enabling the government to order the invasion of Lebanon without the immediate use of the reserve force. The use of the IDF beyond deterrence and prevention was much easier under these circumstances, and in 1982, with a new political elite in control, the willingness to use the IDF beyond deterrence and prevention became a dominant factor in determining the country's regional policy.[53]

As a seasoned politician, Menachem Begin was reluctant to reveal the full scope of his new regional policy. Yet others on the Right wrote and spoke about it more candidly. Ariel Sharon, who was in charge of implementing the new regional policy, serving as Begin's second defense minister (1981–83), prepared in December 1981 a lecture for a symposium sponsored by the Jaffe Institute for Strategic Studies at Tel-Aviv University. In his lecture he presented his strategic thinking, which reflected, at least partially, that of the prime minister. Sharon argued[54] that Israel has strategic interest in three circles: (a) the confrontation states (toward which the defense minister had clear-cut plans: an attack on Lebanon, designed to create a new political order there; an assault on the Syrian forces in Lebanon; the overthrow of the monarchy in Jordan, etc.); (b) the outer Arab states; (c) other outer states that by their political status and orientation could dangerously influence Israel's national security. Sharon's geostrategic scope was quite broad:

> We must broaden the domain of our strategic and security interests *beyond that of the Middle Eastern states and the Red Sea*, so that in the 1980s this domain will include such states as Turkey, Iran and Pakistan, and regions such as *the Persian Gulf and Africa, particularly northern and central Africa*.[55]

Sharon's ideas reflected the thinking of a growing number of Right Wing Israeli writers. Oded Yinon, a journalist and a former employee of Israel's Foreign Ministry, wrote in 1982 that Israel ought to encourage the dissolution of Egypt, Lebanon, Syria, Jordan, Iraq, Saudi Arabia, and the states of the Persian Gulf area.[56] The primary goal of Israel's policy should be the creation of many weak, ethnic mini-states in the Middle East: four in Syria, three in Iraq, at least two in Egypt, etc. The Yinon article was an authentic mirror of the thinking mode of the Israeli Right at the height of Begin's rule; it reflected a sense of unlimited and unrestrained power. Yinon recommended the reconquest of the Sinai, the toppling of the Jordanian monarchy, and similar actions.

There can be no question that the hard-core Neo-Revisionist camp as a whole subscribed, at least until the Lebanese fiasco, to ideas similar to those of Yinon. Dan von Wiesel, for example, proposed immediately following the 1967 war that Israel's foreign policy should be extended far beyond the state's immediate borders.[57] Hanan Porat, one of Gush Emunim's most sophisticated leaders, explained to a *Jerusalem Post* journalist (March 27, 1983) his views on Israel's long-term policy in the region:

> For the time being, Judea and Samaria are all we can handle; but we believe that one day the Jews will have the entire land [that is, also the east bank of the Jordan River], just as the temple will be rebuilt. If we create a real Jewish state worthy of the name, the Arabs will be glad to join us.

On the whole, Likud's regional policy rested on a few sources. First, geostrategic analysis emphasized raw force as a tool for reshaping

the map of the Middle East; this kind of thinking was reflected in
Sharon's and Yinon's articles. Second, the messianic zest of Gush
Emunin and its associates, as reflected in Porat's ideas. Third, growing
hatred in Right Wing circles towards Arabs in general, an irrational
force of great importance, enabled prime minister Begin to take anti-
Arab action with virtual impunity. This irrational, overwhelming hatred
was expressed, for example, by General Dr. Aharon Davidi:

> The Arabs deserve the hatred of the entire world and the united action
> of the entire civilized world against them — a vigorous and extreme
> action. . . . The Arabs want only to enrich themselves, so that they can
> control the entire world. They, the Arabs, do not contribute a thing
> to the world. They are unproductive people, the least productive
> people in the entire world. They sell petroleum in which they did
> not invest even one cent. They choke the world. . . they merely steal
> from the world economy.[58]

*Begin's political genius was that he knew how to crystallize the
geostrategic ideas, the messianic zest and the irrational hatred into a coherent
whole, a purposeful regional policy.* This policy finally collapsed under
its own weight — being unrealistic it could not have succeeded, and
being inhumane it led to powerful opposition in the IDF and in the
nation —but for a few years the prime minister rode on the forces identified here.

The regional policy of Menachem Begin should be primarily
assessed by examining his actions, not his words. Nevertheless, while
in office Begin often discussed his foreign policy publicly, allowing the
analyst a rare look into his thinking. Such insight into Begin's overall
position can be gained by studying one of his last public speeches, a
speech given during the Lebanese War at Israel's national Security College.[59] In this speech, Begin dealt with the conditions under which a
nation should go to war:

> On the basis of international relations and our own national experi-
> ence, it is clear that a state does not have to go to war only when
> there is no other choice. . . . On the contrary, a free, soverign, war-
> hating, peace-loving, security-oriented nation must create the condi-
> tions under which a war, if required, will not be without a choice.

An examination of what Begin said indicates that the prime
miinster saw war as a legitimate act to be taken for purely political
reasons, not only in self-defense. When there is ''no other choice,''
the conditions justify self-defense; Begin, however, argued for

additional reasons for the use of violence, and was willing to use military might rather extensively to achieve a large number of political goals.

Summary

On the whole, then, Menachem Begin's legacy is extremely important for the future of the Israeli polity. First, he facilitated the development of a bipartisan system in Israel, enabling voters to make more meaningful choices between alternative policies. More important-ly, Begin developed a full-fledged ideology, which is likely to serve as the intellectual foundation of the Israeli Right for years to come. Third, he left behind a model for a foreign policy that Israel may pur-sue in the future, particularly under a Right Wing government. This model is, of course, not uncomplicated, but its content, its main features are clear: insistence on eventual annexation of the West Bank and Gaza to Israel, domination of the region through military means, and reliance on extremely close relations with the United States. In a way, at Camp David Begin presented a model for an Arab-Jewish reconciliation based on Arab recognition of exclusive Jewish control over Eretz Israel and limited personal autonomy for the Palestinians. Since Camp David (September 1978) it has become abundantly clear that such a model cannot lead to a comprehensive peace in the region. On the other hand, Begin demonstrated, following Camp David, that strong political leadership is capable of convincing the Israeli public to agree to far-reaching concessions.

The cornerstone of Begin's policy, and eventually the most important element in his legacy, was his policy on the West Bank. Begin apparently realized that he did not have enough power to annex the territory with impunity: the likely international pressure and internal dissent and the demographic situation on the West Bank made annex-ation extremely unattractive. Yet, Begin tried to make Israel's future disengagement from the territories much less likely if not virtually im-possible. Lustick believes that:

> Any Israeli government now contemplating policies leading toward disengagement knows that in addition to risking its coalition majority, it is putting at risk the legal-parliamentary order itself.[60]

Put in other words, by encouraging extensive settlement in all parts of the West Bank and by giving the policy of eventual annexa-tion legitimacy, Begin increased the stakes of withdrawal. Many now believe that a decision to withdraw, even if approved overwhelmingly by the Knesset, could led to widespread violence, initiated by Right Wing elements, which subscribed to Begin's ideological legacy or versions thereof.[61]

In a more general way, Begin was instrumental in tilting Israel's foreign policy in the direction of a much harder line, growing militarism, and enhanced national egotism. Since 1948 there was in Israel a delicate balance between a dovish and a hawkish approach to Israel's foreign and security policies. The dovish approach emphasized diplomatic means; the hawkish approach often preferred military means, but used them with caution and restraint and in close cooperation with at least some Western powers. Begin and Herut were outside of both camps: they called for an offensive posture, promoting opportunities for territorial expansion. This approach received legitimation as a result of the 1967 war and became a controlling attitude in 1977.

The Begin regime (1977–1983) not only increased signficantly the power of the Israeli Right but, possibly, made it into Israel's largest political bloc. Begin left behind a legacy in which the gap between the Revisionist Right and the Labor camp decreased, and in which the traditional rivals found themselves in a situation of actual cooperation with each other (albeit *forced* cooperation). This cooperation pushed the Israeli left, the determined antiannexationists, to a position of seemingly permanent opposition. Since 1984 the left had assumed the role that was Herut's prior to the Six-Day War, the role of an almost irrelevant ideological camp.

One of the most interesting questions regarding Begin is whether he was a true revolutionary: did his policy amount to qualitative change or a merely quantitative one (e.g. more settlements, somewhat more reliance on military force than his predecessors, etc.). On the whole, *the totality of Begin's legacy seems to indicate the revolutionary nature of his regime.* He intitiated a foreign policy carried out in big strikes, deviating systematically from the incremental pattern characterizing that policy traditionally. Begin's vigorous approach reideologized the Israeli political system, with the future of the Occupied Territories as a main focal topic.

As a writer, Begin did not leave behind a comprehensive essay explaining his ideological position in a consistent manner. In fact, I would accept Aronoff's judgment that

> Begin's genius was less as an original ideological thinker than as a politician who could creatively pull together the strands of different political ideas and capitalize on them in the mobilization of political

support. Begin's talents in the manipulation of symbol, myth, and ritual were greater than his intellectual prowess as an ideologue.[62]

Nevertheless, if one looks at Begin's legacy in its totality, it seems that it amounts to not only a behavioral message to Israel of the future but an ideological message as well. On the whole it seems that the Beginist understanding of Israel's predicament and solution to it has been adopted by most factions of what might be termed the Israeli Right and, furthermore, in some cases Begin's attitudinal prism has been further radicalized.

First, all factions on the Right remain expansionist: the territorial imperative is, for them, a given assumption, not a political option. Furthermore, some people on the Right have radicalized Begin's territorial stance, which at the end of his political life amounted to a demand for an Israeli control over the West Bank while ignoring the traditional Revisionist claim for the East Bank. Thus, during the early parts of the Lebanese invasion, some nationalist elements hinted at the "historical rights" of Israel in Lebanon; appropriate maps, depicting Beirut as Beerot, were quickly printed.

The more abstract elements of Begin's ideological package have also been adopted by the entire Right; they are functional and indeed necessary in maintaining the combative stance of the Right. The negation of the World, the rejection of normalcy as an objective, the use of mystical justifications as a basis for national policy are all part and parcel of the nationalist camp's baggage.

The process of attitude radicalization on the Right is quite systematic, as could be shown for example on the issue of relationships with the Arabs. On the whole, Menachem Begin was a fair-minded man, a supporter of civil rights and due process in general. Although on some occasions he was carried away by his own nationalistic fervor, as when he called the Palestinians "two-legged animals," he always subscribed to Jabotinsky's idea that Arabs, like all citizens in the Jewish state, ought to be given all fundamental civil rights. It was even reported that he specifically ordered the Shin Beth (Security Service) to refrain from torturing Arabs suspected of terrorist acts.

Begin's ideological successors are much less pedantic in maintaining civil rights of "minorities." Furthermore, and much more importantly, significant radicalization had occurred on the ideological, symbolic level. Thus, a growing number of opinion-makers on the Right refer now to the Arabs, in Israel proper and in the Occupied Territories, as Amalek, the biblical nation whom God commanded the Israelites to annihilate. Others talk openly about "transfer," the expulsion of the Arabs. This radicalization is not unrelated to the political atmosphere that Begin left behind him, as well as to his policies. Leon Wieseltier was apparently right when he wrote that "the phenomenon of Kahanism must be understood in the context of a seismic shift in the political culture of Israel occasioned by the rise to power of Menachem Begin and Ariel Sharon."[63]

Begin left behind him an ideology that can be and has been used by like-minded men in promotion of their own agendas. This ideology is the glue that holds together all factions of the Israeli Right. Begin's genius was in his ability to convincingly transfer the Jewish experience in Europe, especially anti-Semitism and the Holocaust, and apply it to the current Middle East situation.

The danger in Begin's legacy is that the process of ideological radicalization he started, demonstrated dramatically by the election of Kahana to the Knesset and the electoral success of Tehiya (both in 1984), will continue. In fact, the lack of solution to the conflict guarantees *accelerated* radicalization of the ideology left behind by Begin.

[Editor's Note: Ilan Peleg's comments about the growth of the Radical Right and the increased militarization of their positions were demonstrated in the campaign for the Twelfth Knesset and the reaction of many Israelis to the *intifadah*, the uprising that began in the West Bank in 1987. The Right has become more intense in its demands for settlements and stronger anti-Palestinian policy. Even though the Kach Party of Rabbi Kahane was disqualified from competing in the 1988 elections because of its advocacy of "racist" and anti-Palestinian doctrine, the Radical Right has convinced more of the Israeli electorate that moderation is not the way to respond to the *intifadah*.

In the final year of the Eleventh Knesset the Shamir government increased the number of settlements in the West Bank and took an increasingly hard-line stand against Palestinian resistance to occupation. Although substantial portions of the electorate supported the moderation advocated by Shimon Peres in the campaign, and the campaign was labeled as "too close to call" up to the very end, a terrorist explosion on the morning of the election was credited by many with swinging several seats in the Twelfth Knesset to the Likud Party, giving it a 40-to-39 edge over Labor. The new National Unity government led by Prime Minister Shamir — with Peres playing a clearly secondary role (as distinct from the power-sharing model of the previous National Unity government, which involved Peres and Shamir exchanging the position of prime minister halfway through the term of the Knesset) — has continued to take a hard anti-Palestinian position in regard to the *intifadah,* and, many have said, has offered conditions for negotiations with the Palestinians that are so extreme that they cannot be met, thus effectively freezing any progress on the issue of the West Bank and the Palestinians.]

CHAPTER THREE

Illegalism in Israeli Political Culture: Theoretical and Historical Footnotes to the Pollard Affair and the Shin Beth Cover Up

Ehud Sprinzak

Several recent scandals that took place in Israel, most noteworthy the Pollard Affair and the obstruction of justice by the Shin Beth (Israel's Secret Service), have called attention to the *illegalistic orientation* of Israel's top political leaders: the conviction that security considerations, party interests and their own political survival stand above the law.

The Jonathan Pollard issue involved an American Jew who spied for Israel in one of the most sensitive intelligence agencies in the United States. Yet the case became "an affair" not because of the shameful act of spying on one's best friend, but as a result of a series of incredible denials, lies and deceptions. The Israeli government, whose operators were caught red-handed, simply did not understand why it had to admit guilt and trade a full disclosure of the facts for a full and friendly pardon. The leaders continued to lie and pretend nothing of significance happened. They even promoted the officers involved. They left no choice for the American Justice Department but to disclose in court the full story.

The Shin Beth Affair displayed a similar attitude on behalf of Israel's ruling masters. The leading ministers in the Israeli Cabinet were so determined to save the methods and reputation of their secret service that they were ready to disregard the most flagrant obstruction of justice ever committed by the directors of any defense agency. The head of Shin Beth and his chief lieutenants conspired to lie to a governmental investigation committee, which studied the mysterious killing of two

Arab terrorists caught alive. A top Shin Beth man, who was made an official member of the committee, would meet every night, for months, with his chieftains to coordinate the next day's false presentations and testimonies. The conspiracy, which was plotted to conceal Shin Beth's responsibility for the killing, was highly successful. The blame was shifted to the military, and one of Israel's most illustrious generals, innocent by all standards, almost lost his job and reputation. When the whole story was disclosed by several unhappy Shin Beth officers, the leading Cabinet Ministers remained unmoved. The only officials to leave the organization were the informers. Only an immense public outrage and the resignation of the state's attorney general forced the government to fire the guilty Intelligence heads, but they were not fired before a special pardon, worked out by the government and Israel's president, made sure they could not be prosecuted. Responding to public pressure during the Shin Beth Affair, Israel's Prime Minister Itzhak Shamir compared the law to the bread we all eat:

> The Law is not an end in itself. Like bread, which is eaten not for itself but in order to keep the body alive, the law ought to serve the state and not vice versa. It is possible to imagine situations of a dictatorship of law as of *Yikov Hadin Et Hahar* (the law can penetrate the mountain), but something like that is unacceptable. The law was only destined to make orderly life possible.[1]

When viewed against the background of the successive affairs that brought down the Labor hegemony in the 1970s and characterized the second Likud administration (1981–1984), these scandals appear indicative of more than a series of unfortunate accidents. They show that there exists in Israel's political culture a salient dimension of illegalism, an instrumental orientation towards the law and the idea of the rule of law.

The issue of Israeli illegalism has attracted, in the last decade a great deal of public attention. It came up in countless press editorials and articles, reports of investigation committees and public statements. For some strange reason it did not draw the theoretical attention of the people who were supposed to identify it first, political scientists and sociologists. None of the writers on Israel's political culture has, thus far, noticed that the instrumental orientation towards the law was a *key feature* of the Israeli political culture and of the behavior of Israel's politicians. Israeli politologists have in a sense, displayed the same attitude to the issue as Israel's politicians: they did not know about it. The purpose of this chapter is to fill in this theoretical gap. Its main thesis, which is explored in depth in a book, *A Law Unto Itself: Illegalism in Israeli Society*,[2] that was just published in Israel, is that:

(a) Israel is formally established on the principle of the rule of law, but it is possible and necessary to identify in its political culture a salient dimension of behavioral illegalism, which far exceeds the normal and expected sphere of disrespect for the legal norms in a democracy.

(b) Beyond the salient behavioral illegalism, there exists in Israel's political society a deep cultural layer of illegalism. The characteristic features of this layer are an instrumental orientation towards the legal order and a conviction that democracy can work without a strict adherence to the law.

(c) The illegalistic syndrome, which is behavioral just as it is cultural, did not emerge in the last decade when it appeared in a rather sensational way, but had developed since the beginning of the century side by side with the Zionist policy in Palestine.

The proposition that this chapter argues is that legalism in the Western sense of the term never was an integral part of the democratic system established in Israel by the Zionist parties and their leaders. Israel's illegalism has consequently been an illegalism from the top. Instead of curtailing grass roots illegalistic orientations brought in by immigrants from nondemocratic societies, it has nourished them from above and continues to do so.

Four historical stages of Israeli illegalism are examined:

(1) *The functional illegalism*—the illegalism of the Yishuv era, which was necessary for the establishment of a Zionist polity in Palestine, but which produced all the presently prevailing patterns of Israel's illegalism.

(2) *The latent illegalism*—the hidden illegalism that had developed after the establishment of the state, under Ben-Gurion's "universalistic" Mamlachtiut (Statism).

(3) *The manifest illegalism*—the manifest illegalism of the post-Ben-Gurion era that flourished under Levy Eshkol and Pinchas Sapir.

(4) *The rediscovered illegalism*—the illegalism that reemerged under the Likud government and has been sustained by the Unity government.

Illegalism as a Feature of Political Culture

While the concept of illegalism is rarely explored in the dictionaries and encyclopedias, it can easily be understood as the opposite
of legalism, a well-defined term. The *Compact Edition of Oxford Dictionary
of the English Language* defines legalism as "a disposition to exalt the
importance of law or formulated rule in any department of action."
Random House Dictionary defines legalism as "a strict adherence, or the
principle of strict adherence, to law or prescription." The idea implied
in these definitions, which is followed by most other dictionaries, is
that legalism is not just a form of behavioral obedience to the law but
also a prescriptive norm. A respect for the law and for the idea of the
rule of law is not, according to this prescription, mandatory because
of the material gains involved but because of the intrinsic value of the
legal order. "A society with law," writes H.L.A. Hart, "contains those
who look upon its rules from the internal point of view as accepted
standards of behavior and not merely as reliable predictions of what
will befall them at the hands of officials if they disobey."[3]

The precise meaning of the rule of law is today a subject of an
intense academic debate.[4] Nevertheless, it appears that the study of
political culture may benefit a great deal from the legalism-illegalism
distinction. If we agree with the students of political culture that it
basically amounts to the orientations of the citizens and the key political
actors towards the conduct of public affairs[5], then, it is quite possible
to place political societies on a continuum that spreads from an orientation of strict obedience to the law to an orientation that implies a total
disregard for it. A useful way of conducting research seems to follow
Max Weber and test the empirical reality against two opposing ideal
types:

Legalism as an ideal type of a political culture—a comprehensive
conception of the rule of law, which is expressed in influential writings
of legal authorities, major juridical documents, ruling of the courts,
legislation and regulation of the regime in question; a genuine identification of the leading ideologues, politicians and civil servants of the
regime with this conception and its elevation to a normative behavior;
a negative attitude of all these authorities towards illegal excesses; a
general citizens' respect for the law. In order to have the legalistic ideal
type approximate reality, its characterization should leave room for
certain struggles and cases of civil disobedience that do not presuppose
a general instrumental attitude towards the law, for clear cases of
personal disrespect for the law as a result of faults in the law itself,
and for general criminality and a reasonable universal lawbreaking
expressed in traffic violations, drinking problems, etc.

Illegalism as an ideal type of political culture—does not require a negation of a general commitment to the rule of law by all the authorities concerned. It represents, however, the existence of a *deep gap* between the legal conception espoused by juridical authorities, the courts, and the reality. This ideal type should, therefore, be characterized by the existence of a prestigious and influential ideology, which either degrades the rule of law or assigns it a low priority; a salient disregard for the idea of the rule of law, by top politicians and civil servants, in the name of an ulterior state norm, ideology or party interests; an enactment of laws that cannot be enforced; outstanding cases of political and politically related corruption and administrative white collar crime, clientelism, patronage; low-level corruption and a comprehensive citizens' disregard for the law and for what it means.

Functional Illegalism: The Yishuv Period

Even a cursory examination of the Zionist literature, including the debates on the political nature of the movement, may show that the founding fathers of Israeli Zionism were never aware of the rule of law as a principle of good government. It is not difficult to see why. All of them came from Eastern Europe, from countries with no democratic culture and no tradition of civil and individual rights. Critical of the oppressive regimes in those countries, they entertained several conceptions of democracy (people's, class, Jewish), but none of these included the idea of the rule of law and its elevation to a public norm. For Jews who never even experienced the rudimentary elements of democracy — free elections, free press and majority rule — the niceties of the rule of law and civil rights were totally irrelevant. This unawareness and its byproducts were strengthened by three pre-Yishuv influential cultural orientations, which played an important role in shaping the political mentality of the growing community in Palestine: the Ghetto culture, the Bakshish culture, and the culture of Naive Socialism.[6]

The Ghetto culture was the system of orientations that had developed for hundreds of years in the Jewish Shtetle (small town), or the Jewish Ghetto, in Eastern Europe. Almost everything in the Ghetto was informal. Everyone knew everybody else, and there was no need for official code or written law. The only formal law was the Torah and its Halacha interpretation, as understood by the local rabbi. This law, which had no features of positive, state law, was a basis for communal behavior along with many other informal modes of behavior like *shmor li ve'eshmor lecha* (You help me and I'll help you.), etc. The attitude towards the formal law of the land was full of suspicion because no Jew of the Shtetle could trust the law of the Gentiles. The state's law was seen as another part of the Gentile society. One had to survive, not respect, it. The art of Jewish living within the Ghetto included an elaborate system of using the law, avoiding the law, or sidestepping it.[7]

The Bakshish culture was an essential part of the organizational culture of the Orient, the Middle East and North Africa, which the Jews, most of whom also lived in Ghettos, shared. Bakshish, a Turkish synonym for an instant bribe one gives to an official who can help or do a favor, was not a Jewish invention. It was a permanent feature of the Ottoman Empire, which instituted an organizational polinor-mativity.[8] Side by side with the formal, legal, norms of the colonial bureaucracy, which the citizen (in many cases a conquered minority) was expected to respect, there existed an informal, illegal, system of bribery and favoritism. If one could not get along through the formal, legal, channels, it was always possible to make it through Bakshish. Jews, like many other minorities, learned to live with Bakshish and to use it for their needs.

The culture of Naive Socialism did not have deep historical roots but was highly influential among the idealist pioneers who came from Eastern Europe. Its main feature was an ideological animosity towards formal and legal bureaucracy, which, it was assumed, was an essential part of capitalism.[9] Strongly believing in the good nature of man, certainly of the socialist Zionist, the Naive Socialists were sure that good intentions and hard work were a solution for every problem. Bureaucracy, legality and formality implied false consciousness and bourgeoise mentality.

Having a strong psychopolitical background of illegalism, Israel's founding fathers were unlikely to discover the virtues of the rule of law in the first place. The circumstances they encountered in Palestine made such tentative learning all the more difficult. The declining Ottoman colonial administration that ruled Palestine before World War I was extremely hostile to the Zionist endeavor. Even Bakshish rarely worked. The British, whose legal system could indeed help shape a new Zionist legal culture, were seen as early as the 1920s as renouncing the Balfour Declaration. By the late 1930s and as result of their notorious White Paper, which barred immigration almost totally, the British assumed the status of "foreign rulers." Their system of justice may have been *legal*, but according to the yishuv leaders and ideologists it was *illegitimate*. So strong was the anti-British sentiment that a whole nomenclature of *prestigious illegalism* evolved: *Aliya Bilti-legalit, Hagana*

Bilti-legalit, Hityashvut Bilti-legalit (illegal immigration, illegal defense, illegal settlement).[10] A whole generation of young Zionists, some of whom were to take part in the scandals of the 1980s as key actors, was socialized into public life by the spirit of a typical speech of Berl Katzenelson, the chief ideologist of Mapal:

> There is an immigration which is named 'illegal' . . . Everything in this legal world is legal — legal regimes, legal conquests, legal documents, even a legal breaking of commitments. Jewish immigration only, based on the old charter of Exodus is illegal . . . if this immigration is illegal, what immigration is legitimate and legal? It is not the blame of the refugees, our blame, that we have become law breakers. He who broke the fundamental constitution of the land, made us criminals.[11]

The evolution of the Yishuv's defiant illegalism vis-à-vis the British did not help the internal Zionist structures, which were to a great extent autonomous, to adopt legal manners, but this was not the sole reason. Of much greater importance was the lack of interest of the individuals and movements who established these institutions. Yonathan Shapira, who studied Achdut Haavoda and its relation to the emerging Histadrut, has shown that since their inception, the *raison d'etre* of these organizations, and the sole measure of their success, was *the interest of the movement*.[12] Considerations of efficiency, good management, accountability, and profit were never allowed to interfere. Politicians and ideological activitists were made paid directors of Histadrut economic corporations and were judged by the dedication to the party and the cause. This was the atmosphere in which *Protektzia*[13] for *Anshei Shlomenu* (our people) flourished and public money, which was very scarce, had started to become cheap.

In contrast to the common belief that Labor scandals only started in the 1970s, the Histadrut (the General Federation of Labor) and other Labor organizations have faced scandals since time immemorial. A Histadrut investigation committee, which studied one of the earliest collapses of Sollel Boneh (its subsidiary construction corporation) found out in 1928 that its directors were overpaid in many forms and had constantly defied the egalitarian ideology of this socialist organization, which required that all workers, rank notwithstanding, be paid the same[14]. Answering the call for the resignation of the responsible directors, David Ben-Gurion, at the time the secretary general of Histadrut, said:

> We were never trained in business administration. Had we only been a business, we should have all had resigned. But we represent

a social movement and we have to learn from our mistakes . . . Had
we been deterred by our inexperience and incompetence, we would
have never created Degania, Ein Harod and Nahallal . . . Had we
concluded that they should have resigned it would have been
immoral, apolitical and unreasonable . . . I believe in the hegemony
of Labor in Zionism. But this hegemony will never be based on the
fact that we are more able or honest but rather on the fact that we
are more Zionist than the others.[15]

In this classical defense of the Labor Movement's wrong-doers,
Ben-Gurion made it clear that the movement, which established
Degania, Ein Harod and Nahallal, could not go wrong. Zionism, not
honesty or ability, was the name of the game, and no one was (could
ever be?) more Zionist than the Labor movement and its leading party,
Mapai.

As "illegal" and damaging as the illegalism of the Yishuv was,
most of it was *functional*. Facing the immense animosity of the Ottoman
regime and later the growing British hostility, the founding fathers of
the Yishuv had little choice. Had they become fully legal, sticking to
the spirit and the letter of the law, they might have ended up with
high grades on civics, but might never have established a state. There
was a sense and purpose in the Yishuv illegalism. It was necessary
to save Jewish refugees escaping Nazi Germany with or without British
consent. It was just as necessary and right to establish a strong Jewish
polity in Palestine before the Arabs launched their attack, Great
Britain's formal law notwithstanding. The problem of the functional
illegalism of that period was that it created and formatted strong
patterns of illegal behavior that far outlived their functionality. These
prestigious patterns were not forsaken when the Zionists got rid of
the foreigners and established their own state.

Latent Illegalism—The Case of Ben-Gurion's Mamlachtiut

A common anecdote in the early 1950s was the joke about the
Zionist volunteers, who served in the British army during World War
II, stole from the British (for the Jewish underground in Palestine), but
forgot to stop when the state of Israel was established. While simple
and unidimensional, the anecdote, nevertheless, tells a sad story: the
inability of the new state to change direction and embark upon a full
legalistic course.

To say that Israel simply continued to be run in the pre-state
fashion would be erroneous. The early achievements of the Jewish

polity were, in fact, very impressive. In the midst of Israel's most devastating war, the Jewish leaders formed an effective executive and a viable parliament. A comprehensive court system was established and a decent Civil Service started to shape up. It was all orchestrated by David Ben-Gurion, a self-educated man, who carved a unique philosophy of government, out of an immense, but highly unsystematic, body of reading. Ben-Gurion's new philosophy, Mamlachtiut (Statism), had many universalistic elements. The new system was a great improvement upon the old "Bolshevik" approach of Mapai, which maintained that everything that was good for Mapai, was good for the Yishuv[16]. The key Mamlachtiut theme was "from a class to a nation." The theme expressed Ben-Gurion's recognition that the old sectarian socialist philosophy of Mapai was irrelevant for nation-building. A regime that intended to triple its population in five years and to bring together persecuted refugees from all corners of the earth could not afford the old thinking. Mamlachtiut's greatest accomplishments were undoubtedly, the creation of Zahal, Israel's apolitical people's army and Hinuch Mamlachti, the state's unitary educational system. The two had the fingerprints of Ben-Gurion, and both made a great contribution to the socialization of the Israeli youth to a modern political society.

However, Ben-Gurion's Mamlachtiut had three fundamental flaws. First, it was hardly shared by most of his colleagues in Mapai. Second, the prime minister himself applied it only selectively. Third, and most important of all, it lacked a built-in legal theory.

Most of Ben-Gurion's colleagues, the powerful Mapai veterans, did not fully identify with their leader's new vision. While symbolically endorsing it, they were very reluctant to adopt its conclusions. Their Mapai, a very innovative and powerful machine they built from scratch, was too precious to sacrifice on the altar of Mamlachtiut.[17] They were especially hostile to Ben-Gurion's efforts to operationalize Mamlachtiut by bringing in new blood, ambitious and successful young wolves like Moshe Dayan and Shimon Peres, who "did not dry up swamps in Hadera," and were not party veterans. These old party hands, individuals like Golda Meir, Zalman Aran, Levy Eshkol and Mordechai Namir, were not as powerful as David Ben-Gurion, but were strong enough to slow Mamlachtiut down. Holding key executive positions, they kept the old Mapai machine in good shape and made sure that many official jobs remained in the hands of party loyalists[18] and that new immigrants were absorbed to the "party" well before they were absorbed by the state.[19] No Mamlachtiut was allowed to touch the powerful Histadrut and its subsidiary economic corporations or the very influential Jewish Agency. A whole echelon of Israeli executives heard of Mamlachtiut only over the radio.

While his junior colleagues were diluting Mamlachtiut a great deal, Ben-Gurion himself was selective in its application. No general criteria of qualification for Mamlachtiut were set, and its determination was exclusively the "Old Man's." The Arab citizens of Israel, for example, were never considered legitimate subjects for this policy of equalization. They were a "security risk."[20] Former members of the Irgun and Lehi were also not equal partners, for they were "Fascists" or "putchists." Many of them could not get decent jobs in any public agency and for years paid for their pre-state sins.[21] "Ben-Gurion's youngsters" had an interpretation of their own for the new ideology. According to Shimon Peres and Moshe Dayan, Mamlachtiut meant efficiency, smooth operation that gets results. Rules, regulations and orderly procedures were invented, from the perspective of the young guards, in order to be ignored or sidestepped. Thus, under the direct command of the prime minister, Shimon Peres, the director general of the Ministry of Defense, sidestepped Golda Meir, Israel's minister of foreign affairs, and ran his own European secret diplomacy.[22] Moshe Dayan, Israel's soldier no. 1, who believed he was above all rules and regulations, in fighting, driving, womanizing, and archeology collecting, became a role model for a whole Sabra generation.[23]

The major flaw in Mamlachtiut was its total ignorance of any legal theory. Nowhere in his writings and public speeches of the 1950s had Ben-Gurion assigned any significance to the role of law or to the rule of law. There is no doubt that the man was not anarchist and that discipline, law and order were very much on his mind. But he never recognized that he himself, the great David Ben-Gurion, or the party (under his guidance), could go wrong. The idea that the best way to introduce Mamlachtiut is to place the entire political system, including the government, under a strict legal umbrella was not part of his vision. Ben-Gurion, a stranger to the liberal and constitutional traditions that were always suspicious of power, truly believed that good intentions and correct political education could produce a decent republic, and it was, of course, very convenient politically not to have one's own hands tied up by unnecessary legal procedures.

David Ben-Gurion, the father of Mamlachtiut, was responsible for the single greatest constitutional blunder in Israel's history: *the failure to introduce a constitution.* No doubt, in 1948, the new state was committed to a written constitution, which was first set as an essential condition in the 1947 U.N. Partition Resolution that sanctified the establishment of a Jewish state in Palestine.[24] It was restated in Israel's own Declaration of Independence of May 15, 1948. The document, which was solemnly signed by the entire gallery of the nation's leaders, secular and religious alike, stated unequivocally that Israel's first elected constituent assembly was to make a constitution, but declarations aside, the commitment for a constitution was very superficial. The religious partners of the coalition government were strongly opposed to the whole notion. They already had a constitution, the Torah, the book of books. The idea of a man-made sacred document was anathema for them. Mapai, Ben-Gurion's party which was nearly twenty years in control, did not like the idea either. A constitution threatened to put its political domination under strange legal arrangements such as a bill of rights, and checks and balances.

Hesitant to break their public obligation and spit in the face of the United Nations and the entire world, the representatives of the Israeli political majority crafted a brilliant ploy. The relegated the draft constitution to a committee. Two years later, when everybody was already tired and unexpecting, the Knesset quietly passed a resolution that postponed the issue indefinitely.[25] Neither a bill of rights nor a system of effective controls of the government were ever introduced to the Jewish state. Only partially has Israel's Supreme Court been successful in defending civil rights. The Knesset, on the contrary, has never been able to control the government or balance its excessive power. It was, and remains, a feeble legislature dominated by Israel's coalition government. None of its committees was given subpoena powers, and it has always been short on resources and resolve to conduct a serious investigation of its own.

At the critical historical moment of Israel's initiation, the authority of the Old Man could make a difference. Had Ben-Gurion really had a legal philosophy, he must have known that there was no better way to introduce the entire system into Mamlachtiut than through an elevated constitutional document that would guarantee civil rights to all, introduce systemic checks and balances into the government, and serve as a permanent legal model for the nation. Prevailing upon the religious parties might not have been easy, but if there ever was a man to do it, it was David Ben-Gurion. None of the religious leaders refused to sign Israel's declaration of independence because it categorically committed the new state to a future constitution. None was in a position, in 1949–1950, to challenge him on an issue that was agreed upon since 1947. But neither the understanding nor the will were there. In the debate that finally ended up with an indefinite postponement, the people of Israel were told by their prime minister:

The circumstances that necessitated and justified a supreme and ennobled constitution in America and even France, do not obtain in our country. On the contrary, if we wish to educate the people to respect the law we have to educate them to respect every law, not just "an ennobled" law which is called "constitution". The dynamism of the land cannot stand a rigid framework and artificial chains. The laws of Israel should follow this dynamic development.[26]

Unclear is the issue of whether Ben-Gurion's stand was a product of instrumental considerations of a leader who wanted to avoid constitutional checks on his government or really believed in his words. Nearly forty years after the event, however, it is clear that he was wrong in both of his propositions. No sign that the people of Israel were educated to respect the law exists, and there certainly are no indications that the "educators" themselves were ever in a position to educate.

Manifest Illegalism—the Post-Ben-Gurion Era

The illegalism of the 1950s may be called "the latent illegalism," which existed, as we say, but was concealed under the heavy cover of the universalistic Mamlachtiut. An event of historical significance took place in the beginning of the 1960s, the Lavon Affair, which changed the entire orientation of Mapai. The Lavon Affair did many things to many people, but its major effect was the near demise of the Ben-Gurion mystique and authority.[27] The old lion and his new party, Rafi, did not give up on Mamlachtiut. To their great dismay they discovered, on the contrary, that because of the lack of legal procedures they lost the Labor hegemony. The leadership of the country passed to the hands of the old Mapai guard, Levy Eshkol, Pinchas Sapir and Golda Meir, for whom the entire Mamlachtiut symbology was anathema.[28] They did not like it, did not want to hear about it, and had no intention of practicing it. Unfortunately they had no alternative universalistic ideology. What they were best at was the art of pragmatic politics, a method full of innovative compromises, half-baked solutions, brilliant maneuvers and, necessarily, intense illegalism. Levy Eshkol's orientation to public life was already demonstrated in the early 1950s, when he was the treasurer of the Jewish Agency. When severely criticized by the institute's comptroller for allowing two officials to use the Agency's foreign currency for their own private purposes, he responded:

the purchase was made in frozen Lirot (pounds), not in foreign currency. But even had it been conducted in foreign currency, I would not have seen any wrongdoing in it. We would have followed *Mikra Meforash* (the original Torah Text): *'Lo Tachsom Shor Bedisho'* ('Do not muzzle the ox while he threshes the corn').[29]

Eshkol's rule: "do not muzzle the ox while he threshes the corn," was, certainly, not an action-oriented prescription, and he and Pinchas Sapir, the grand master of Israel's economy, were good Zionists and decent individuals. The two sincerely believed that they could run the country in a personal way through some trustworthy lieutenants, therefore, threshing the corn became their *modus operandi*. Pinchas Sapir, Israel's minister of finance, a financial genius, was the mastermind of the whole system. He had a personal knowledge, and control, of everything that was happening in the public and private sectors of Israel's economy. Very few Israelis could be nominated to influential positions in the economy without his personal approval. Using the immense sources under his command, and especially the less controllable money that came from foreign resources, the German reparations, the United Jewish Appeal, the Israel Bonds loans and the United States government grants, he could, and did, make and break. Genuinely eager to build and strengthen Israel's economy, Sapir did not care about procedures and rules. He was the rules.[30] Everything was written and memorized in his own small black notebook, the most notorious notebook in Israel's history. All that was expected from an obscure and unknown entrepreneur who wanted to start a government supported industry in Israel, was to come to Shapir with a brilliant idea. Sapir belonged to the old school, which believed that everything that was good for Mapai was good for the country; therefore, all the new debtors were expected to line up with many Histadrut corporations and contribute financially to the ruling party.[31] Not all of this was formally illegal, for Israel's laws of parties' finance were, in the 1960s, very primitive. The Sapir system uplifted the old Mapai clientelism and favoritism to unprecedented heights. Never before was so much easy money moved so easily into politics without an external review or control.[32]

While it is not certain that Pinchas Sapir and his political colleagues, most of whom lived modestly, were fully aware of the negative implications of the system they crafted, it is clear that they did not expect this system to produce personal corruption and criminal mismanagement. Unfortunately, this is exactly what happened. Starting in 1968, Israel was stunned by scandals and economic collapses that involved some of Sapir's most favored enterprises. Companies such as Netivei Neft, Somerfin, Autocars, The Israel Company, Anglo-Israel Bank, Sollel Boneh, and Vered had either collapsed or were severely damaged by bad management and corruption. Public investigations revealed, for the first time, the magnitude of the "Sapir System" and its dynamics. They showed how callously money was granted, used and misused.[33] Most devastating were the cases of two top Mapai executives, Michael Tzur and Asher Yadlin. Tzur, a former director general of Sapir's Ministry of Commerce and Industry, cheated the government in the case of The Israel Company. In the process he helped himself to several million dollars. Yadlin, who was about to be nominated Israel Bank's chancellor, a position of high prestige and power, was convicted for embezzling the money of Kupat Holim, the Histadrut's powerful Sick Fund. What was typical of these individuals, and others who were caught, was their total surprise. All of them felt they were following old patterns of conduct and management that were legitimized by their elders, the founding fathers of Israel. In his book, *Testimony*, the most revealing document on the illegalistic practices of Mapai, Asher Yadlin wrote:

> I am not asking anyone's forgiveness. I do not apologize. I paid the full price—1217 long days and nights in jail. I do not argue that I am a victim of the regime. I am a victim in only one sense, that many, very many from the top administrative and political leadership of Israel could sit instead of me. I am also a victim in the sense that not Asher Yadlin the person but Asher Yadlin the symbol, sat on the accused bench.[34]

The truth expressed in Yadlin's book was shared by the people of Israel long before its publication. It played a major role in what was, for many years, unthinkable, the Labor defeat in the elections. No doubt, in 1977 a fifty-year-old organizational style was badly damaged. The only question was: how badly?

The Rediscovered Illegalism—The "Mapaization" of Likud

Most of the 1970s, the era that followed the 1973 Yom Kippur War, was dedicated in Israel to a sincere autocritique. The war shattered Israeli self confidence and caused many people to ask hard questions about themselves, about their leaders, and about what was called by the post-war protest movements "the poor quality of public life."[35] Most of these questions were asked, naturally, about the Mahdal (blunder), the intelligence failure to prepare for the war. A serious soul searching about many aspects of the illegalistic conduct of public affairs also took place. The post-war critical and moody spirit forced, in April of 1974, the prompt resignation of the entire gallery of Mapai top leaders: Golda Meir, Moshe Dayan, Pinchas Sapir, Abba Eban, and Israel Galili, all of whom were reelected only three months earlier. Never before had this party experienced such a shake up. The sense of new, and better, beginning was demonstrated by the free hand given to Aharon Barak, the dynamic state attorney general, to investigate and prosecute all the corruption scandals involving top Mapai men.[36] The effort, which did not save the party from its electoral debacle, was not renounced by the new administration. On the contrary, The Likud, which in the past suffered immensely from the old management methods of Mapai, vowed to change things and to create a better Israel. So did the successful Dash, Iga'al Yadin's Democratic Party for Change, whose entire platform called for institutional reforms and legalism.[37] While no major structural changes, such as an electoral reform, elimination of unnecessary government portfolios, or an introduction of a constitution took place, the first Begin administration demonstrated certain humility and civility. A clear separation existed between party business and government affairs. Many qualified Labor officials, who served the old regime, were asked to remain in their top positions and contribute from their experience and knowledge. The peace progress with Egypt, that was successfully initiated in 1977, further contributed to what appeared to be a new consensus of decency.

All the changes occurred in Begin's second administration. The electoral campaign of 1981 reshaped the political psychology of the Likud. All the early polls, which indicated a Labor comeback and the danger of losing power before they fully tasted it, created within the ruling party an immense anxiety. Likud activists, including the usually civic Begin, approached the electoral campaign as their Armagedon.[38] The previous consensus of public decency faded away. All the bitter memories of the past, from the *Sezon* (a 1946 violent Hagana operation against Begin's Irgun in collaboration with the British) to *Altalena* (an unauthorized Irgun arms ship sunk in 1948 under Ben-Gurion's orders), reemerged in great intensity. Likud charges of Labor discrimination against Oriental Jews added oil to the fire. Very few Israelis could recall a ruder and more violent electoral campaign. When it was all over, with a reinforced Likud in power, a new era started. All the early civility and humility were dropped and replaced by a brutal scramble for positions and influence. Both the party members of Herut and the Liberals behaved as if they had not been there for four years.

In fact, they conducted themselves like refugees who had just emerged from the desert of Judea, hungry and thirsty. None of the former non-Likud general directors of Likud Ministries was retained and a rat race by party loyalists to fill in much lower positions was begun. Many Herut activists, who were, in 1977–81, content with the great victory itself, wanted now to translate it to concrete rewards and jobs. They made it very clear that, in their opinion, inexperienced loyalists of greater Eretz Israel were better civil servants than experienced territorial minimalists.

Herut's junior partner, the Liberal party, was even worse. Its members, who had long given up their Liberal ideology or any ideology for that matter, lost, according to the polls, most of their constituency. They remained in public office only out of Herut's fear that if reduced to their deserved representation, the Liberal Knesset members would ally with Labor and help it regain power. One would have therefore expected them to be content with that political blackmail and behave properly in public. Not so. Confident of their political immunity, the Liberals managed to improve upon Herut's spoil system. Everything that was done by Herut in secret, was conducted by the Liberals in public, in front of the press and the T.V. cameras. The allocation of lucrative official positions became the best way to advance one's influence within this corrupt political party. Prospective supporters had to be shown in public what every party chieftain could offer. Akiva Eldar, Ha'aretz political corespondent was once told by a Liberal Minister that "every press report about political nominations [of his cronies-E.S.] gives him more power in his party's central committee and he would, consequently, never deny it even if it was false."[39]

The return, in 1984, of Labor to government and the initiation of the unity coalition did not curb the rejuvenated spoil system. There are many indications that it was, in fact, intensified. Each side tried to outdo the other by getting more of its loyalists to positions of power and influence. Almost the entire Israeli Civil Service became a battlefield between Likud and Labor. The division of Israel's Ministry of Foreign Affairs between two Labor general directors and the prolonged (three-years) battle for the nomination of the director of Israel's public television revealed a considerable deterioration. A rare evidence of the dynamics of the new politicization of the state's Civil Service was provided by Journalist Akiva Eldar, who obtained a confidential letter written to Israel's Finance Minister by Avraham Natan, Herut's controversial head of Israel's Civil Service Board:

> The root cause of the problem and its essence is the method according to which public people are chosen in their parties as potential

candidates for cabinet or Knesset seats. It is an open secret that these people need, in the various votes held in the party branches and central committees, the votes of their supporters, who, demand, according to the same methods, favors. This is the process through which that dependence is formed like a bill and an obligation to repay it later.

Some of these elected representatives are compelled, in the process of repayment, to turn to several government officials, among them the Civil Service Commissioner, and seek achievements lest their "record" be jeopardized.[40]

The reintroduction of the spoils system in the 1950s, was only one indication of Herut's *Mapaization*. It was soon supplemented by an innovative system of party finance. Herut was always weak financially; it never had a large and influential labor organization and did not have the skill and imagination to establish a Histadrut conglomerate of its own. The Tel-Hai Fund, Herut's poor financial arm, was almost always short on cash and in financial troubles. So after their recuperation from the first delirium of power, Herut's operators started to look for an opportunity to improve their party's lot. The opportunity presented itself in the form of the land trade in Judea and Samaria. Following the government's ideological decision to open all the West Bank for Jewish settlement, it further resolved to let individual developers buy Arab land and sell it in the free market. Had the West Bank lands been properly registered and readily saleable, there would have been no catch, but both conditions did not exist. The rural lands of the area were never properly registered, and all the potential land owners were warned by Jordan and the PLO that a sale of Arab land to Jews would result in a death penalty. Many poor Arab landlords could not resist the magic appeal of the Jewish money, and the situation created immense opportunities for smart businessmen who could maneuver among anonymous sellers, shadowy documents and encouraging authorities.

The issues at stake were attractive suburban lands bordering the green line, thirty minutes from Tel Aviv or Jerusalem. The developers who were ready to help Herut were promised a quick governmental approval of the only official license needed, a positive resolution by the settlement committee of the government. By the time the whole land issue was exposed, it was learned that under Herut's ideological umbrella of settling Eretz Israel a huge industry emerged. The promise of large sums of money drove many "idealists" to fake documents, cheat poor Arab peasants out of their land, improperly sell unavailable lots to future settlers and advertise the operation as a big Zionist project.

The process through which the legalism of the Israeli side of the old border was transformed to the illegalism of the West Bank was vividly criticized about by Yaari Rosen, a construction engineer who became a land merchant:

> The trouble today is that we play on their courtyard with our rules . . . We first had a problem with the lawyers who said "we cannot talk about that, we are not allowed to hear about that." We told them: "you cannot work here if you do not assume the Arab mentality. An Arab does not understand why should he do something for me without being paid. So I do not understand why are we so shocked by it? and they do not understand why we complain when somebody gives something to somebody else in order to get something done. This is the root cause of the problem.[41]

The involvement of several Herut officials with the land scandal has not become, for its leaders, an issue of grave concern.[42] When asked, they are quick to point out that the historical record of Labor corruption is so much richer that for every case that can possibly be brought against them they can provide dozens of opposite examples. They are, undoubtedly, right, but this form of *counterlegitimacy* is a sure recipe for a future persistence of Israel's illegalism.

Convenient and not unjust is a conclusion whereby the governing body of Israel and its leaders are blamed for all the recent miseries that tarnished the name of their country. No excuses mitigate the callous handling of the Pollard Affair or the obstruction of justice in the case of the top officials of Shin Beth, Israel's secret service, not even the security of the Jewish state. Other recent scandals, which demonstrated the total disregard of the Unity Government to the notion of the rule of law are also unforgivable, but the real issue is not personal. The problem of a whole political culture produced these gentlemen and has been extremely tolerant to many aberrations that took place long before they came to power. The political psychology of Itzhak Shamir, Shimon Peres, Itzhak Rabin, Rafi Eitan, and many other individuals involved in the recent scandals was shaped when almost everything was permissible. They all grew up in Palestine of the 1940s, when it was prestigious to cheat on the British and to engage in illegal settlement, illegal defense and illegal immigration. As goes the anecdote mentioned earlier, they did not notice that a Jewish state was established in 1948, and today we know why. They did not notice because their revered mentors did not notice either. The Zionist Founding Fathers of Israel were not vicious people or corrupt individuals. They were great idealists and enormous dreamers. They wished to build a better society and set an example for the rest of the world. Eager to do so as fast as they could, they did not care about legalistic details and procedures. All they wanted was political power, free of constraints, to make the dreams come true. They made only one mistake. None of them bothered to read Lord Acton and to stop at the page where it read: "power corrupts, absolute power corrupts absolutely." The real question about Israel is whether the time has not come for its present leaders to go back to Lord Acton and find out what some people around this globe have known for more than a century.

CHAPTER FOUR

Tehiya as a Permanent Nationalist Phenomenon

Aaron D. Rosenbaum

Polls indicate that Tehiya has emerged as the third largest political party in Israel. Founded in 1979 in reaction to the Egypt-Israel Peace Treaty, the party had three members of Knesset after the 1981 elections and five after 1984. The name Tehiya means revival, an adaptation of a liturgical reference to the miraculous raising of the dead. This in itself speaks volumes about the party and its purpose. Above all else, Tehiya is aware of its roots and sensitive to its place in history. This Jewish consciousness is central to the party's identity.

Roots

The walls of Tehiya's Knesset offices bear the portraits of Rabbi Avraham Yitzhak Kook, Avraham Yair (Stern), Vladimir Zev Jabotinsky and Yitzhak Tabenkin. Rabbi Kook, the Chief Rabbi of Palestine from 1921 to 1935, believed that Zionism would produce a religious and national renaissance for the Jewish people. He advocated reconciliation between religious and secular Jews. (His son, Rabbi Zvi Yehuda Kook, was an intellectual patron of the settlement movement and was also venerated by Tehiya.) Yair was a founder of Lehi (Stern Gang), an underground, nationalist fighting group that opposed Zionist accommodation with Britain during World War II. Jabotinsky was the leader of the Revisionist, non-socialist Zionists, now represented by Likud, who were committed to active Jewish self-defense and the international recognition of the Jewish homeland in all of pre-1922 Mandate Palestine. Yitzhak Tabenkin was the founder of Ahdut HaAvodah, a precursor of the Labor Party. Tabenkin was an opponent of partition and an advocate of kibbutz values and of massive settlement of the territories taken in the Six-Day War.

Though often described as "the true Herut," (the core party of Likud), Tehiya has extensive roots in Labor. It cites as inspiration not only Tabenkin, but Berl Katznelson, a foe of the Revisionists but an advocate of the HeHalutz pioneering movement and self-defense, Eliezer Livneh, Moshe Dayan, and Israel Galili, who backed settlement in the territories, and Yigal Allon, leader of the Palmach, Ahdut HaAvodah and Labor, who is increasingly viewed by many Israelis as the ideal, principled Zionist leader. The Allon for whom Tehiya feels an affinity is the "pre-political" Allon, the man who wrote in 1959, "If indeed the Arab rulers once again force upon Israel a total war, the existing borders will no longer bind the Israel Defense Forces. . . If the IDF should cross the borders of the divided land, it is forbidden to retreat again, but we must aspire from then on to stabilize the borders, which from the historical, economic and security aspect are the most natural."[1]

Tehiya sees itself as the inheritor and guardian of the principles espoused by these men. It believes that by returning to and implementing their ideas, Israel can renew itself and ensure its physical and spiritual security.

A Confluence of Three Components

Tehiya has integrated three separate political movements into one party. This makes Tehiya a sociological phenomenon as well as a political entity. Tehiya's adherents share the belief that a spiritual crisis threatens Israel both at home and abroad. They embrace an old-fashioned, uncomplicated Zionism, rooted in a romantic vision of the pioneering, pre-state Israel. They are committed to the idea of *Eretz Yisrael HaShlema* (The Complete Land of Israel), the belief that a geographically expanded, socially unified state can be a profound instrument of Jewish redemption and self-defense.

The Tehiya plexus includes:

(1) *Zionist Orthodox Jews who were part of the National Religious Party (Mafdal) and became active in Gush Emunim.* Many are activists who have settled in the West Bank; they are politically militant and hawkish, giving the highest priority to the idea of Eretz Yisrael HaShlema. Most have served in the IDF, and as a result believe in conciliation and cooperation between religious and what Tehiya calls "nonobservant"

Israelis. Originally led by Chanan Porat, the leaders of this group now are Rabbi Eliezer Waldman, head of a *yeshiva* in Kiryat Arba and Gush Emunim activist Gershon Shafat.

(2) *Second and third generation sabras, primarily from the Chug Ein Vered/Tzomet and Hityashvut (Settlement) movements of the Labor Party.* Included are people from the old Palmach Moshavim and Ahdut HaAvodah kibbutzim, many of them IDF career officers, plus urban Israelis born into the Labor Movement. They had become disenchanted with the corruption and insularity of Labor, with what they saw as its loss of ideals, and its loss of contact with its founders. They also believed in retaining and actively settling the land for strategic reasons and to fulfill traditional Zionist redemptionist ideals. Some formed the political group Tzomet, which joined Tehiya in 1984. Former IDF Chief of Staff Rafael Eitan (Raful) is the textbook example of this group, Professor Yuval Ne'eman somewhat less so.

(3) *Longtime Likud members, who defected from the party after the Camp David Peace Treaty.* They respected what Begin the Herut and Irgun leader had taught, and not what Begin the Prime Minister and his peace treaty had achieved. Historically mistrustful of both the established Zionist leadership and the non-Jewish world, they believe in military solutions and are suspicious of diplomacy. (This is especially true of those in Tehiya who are intellectual offspring of Lehi.) They are possessed of a religious, even mystical attachment to the ancient Jewish patrimony. This group is led by Geula Cohen, who like Prime Minister Yitzhak Shamir was once a member of Lehi.

Tehiya's leaders consciously share certain attitudes and characteristics:

• They are convinced that the philosophy espoused by Israel's founders should govern Israel's tactics and its view of itself as a nation.

• They are uncomfortable with certain aspects of modern Israel: what they regard as its Byzantine, consumerist economics; self-seeking, carnivorous politicians; bureaucratic obscurantism; loss of social cohesion, and doubts about national purpose.

• They believe their society faces real and present dangers.

• They believe that their positions are logical, pragmatic and objective, and that they conform to facts and historical experience.

• They employ, naturally and reflexively, the logic and intellectual processes of what might be called "the IDF experience." The

degree to which this approach resonates sympathetically throughout
Israeli society should not be underestimated.

• They favor as a matter of national identity and common sense
accommodation between religious and non-religious Jews.

• They have an almost adolescent belief in principled, open
governance.

• They risked careers and reputations to build Tehiya (yet they
remain part of Israel's social and political mainstream).

• They believe that the land of Israel itself can be a profound instrument of Zionist redemption.

Tehiya in the Eleventh Knesset had five members of Knesset, in
order: Ne'eman, Raful, Cohen, Waldman and Shafat. Ne'eman was
more than a figurehead (though that was one of the reasons he was
put forward at Tehiya's founding) but less than a political godfather.
Raful had standing and influence, but he had difficulty playing the
politician's role. Geula Cohen and Rabbi Waldman were operant
political powers in Tehiya; this was especially obvious when Ne'eman
was away doing academic work. Though there were strains between
Cohen and Eitan, there was considerable collegiality in Tehiya, in part
because of practical considerations (Tehiya is a synergy, and its individual parts might not be viable if they ran for Knesset separately)
and in part because the leaders didn't appear to have those kinds of
egos: Ne'eman and Waldman were naturally accommodating, Raful
was a team player, and Cohen, who gave up a leadership position in
Likud, was protective of her new power base.

Geula Cohen

Geula Cohen broke away from Likud in the aftermath of the
Camp David Accords. Her worldview begins with the presumption
that the non-Jewish world is incorrigibly anti-Semitic. She believed that
Begin was euchred by Sadat and the United States into risking Israel's
security. She objected to the loss of Sinai, to the precedent set by the
way in which the peace treaty was achieved and to the inequities and
imbalances of a peace process in which Israel surrendered physical
assets for paper treaties and external assurances. Geula Cohen gives
Tehiya its emotional center. In turn, she relies on Dr. Israel Eldad, a
former Lehi leader who is a columnist in *Ha'aretz* and *Yediot Aharonot*

and an exponent of right wing Zionism. Eldad is anti-Communist, radically nationalist, devoted to the idea of militancy as a virtue, and some would say anti-democratic.[2] He provided Cohen with an ideological framework for her opposition to the Camp David Accords.[3]

Cohen is direct, vociferous, a good legislative tactician. More than any other Israeli politician, she is the spiritual heir of the old Menachem Begin—the opposition leader, the Herut orator, the Knesset operator, the populist. She is one of those politicians who is a magnet for the victimized and the downtrodden. She does more ombudsman work than almost any member of Knesset, and the names of those to whom Tehiya provides services are given to local party branches for follow-up and recruitment for election work.[4]

Geula Cohen is of Yemenite extraction. She is a dedicated Jewish nationalist who advocates annexation of all of Judea and Samaria and Jewish settlement in Arab urban centers as well a outlying areas. In July 1986, she led Gush Emunim through IDF roadblocks to an ancient synagogue in Jericho, where the group prayed and announced hopes of establishing a settlement.[5] Her attachment to the territories is mystical and emotional; she is a particularly strong supporter of a Jewish religious presence on the Temple Mount (now occupied by the Dome of the Rock and the al-Aqsa Mosque and administered by the Jerusalem Wapf (Islamic Religious Endowment.)) She maintains close contact with the organizations that are finalizing plans for either a synagogue or a rebuilt temple on the Temple Mount.

In the Knesset, Geula Cohen has been the driving force behind Tehiya's push for military or alternative national service for yeshiva students and religious girls. She believes the experience of serving in the military creates an empathy between religious and nonreligious, which is essential for the psychological integrity of the state. She had taken the Agudat Members of Knesset to task for the hypocrisy of seeking dispensations from military service while relying upon IDF protection for yeshivot.

Professor Yuval Ne'eman

Yuval Ne'eman is a Nobel class nuclear physicist. He served in IDF Intelligence and as deputy head of IDF operations under the then-General Yitzhak Rabin. (The relationship between the two men is still close.)[6] Ne'eman's position is analogous to that of the American defense intellectuals who have emerged as stalwarts of American conservatism. His greatest contributions to Tehiya are his professional standing and his analytical thought process. His positions are empirical, supported by evidence, and constructed within a worldview that posits the cultural permanence of Arab hostility and diplomatic duplicity. Ne'eman broke with Labor over the Camp David Sinai Accords, and his reasons were almost wholly strategic.

He asserted that loss of the strategic depth afforded by Sinai would jeopardize Israel's security and make the mounting of an effective, casualty-conscious defense much more difficult. He also thought it ill-advised to surrender the advantages and investments Israel had in its three state-of-the-art airbases and its military infrastructure in Sinai. Ne'eman regarded Sadat as unstable and impermanent and Egypt's commitment to peace as transient, self-serving, duplicitous and weak. Ne'eman was also concerned with the psychological implications of Israel's entering into this agreement, specifically, that it would suggest an image of weakness, which Israel's adversaries would misjudge or exploit.

In a revealing 1985 interview, Ne'eman said that international law and peace treaties are "very low on my list of priorities, somewhere around fifth place."[7] He added, "I care about one thing and one thing only—Jewish survival. That sums up my political morality. The only reason for my entering the political world is to ensure Jewish survival. I am not a politician at all."[8] Ne'eman seeks to reinvigorate Israel's leadership. He believes that policymakers should be highly principled and not open to being coopted by transient considerations. He sees a lack of vision and an insular complacency of the Israeli leadership as the country's biggest concerns. He wants the youth of the country to have a consciousness of the quality and uniqueness of Israel; he believes that only this will give them a sense of purpose and will deepen and direct their commitment to the country.[9]

General Rafael Eitan

Raful brought Tehiya at least one additional seat, in part because he was compaigning even while he was chief of staff of the army.[10] He addressed soldiers with political intent for the last few months of his term, and this may explain why Tehiya did very well among IDF recruits. Raful draws better than any other Israeli politician at high schools; he is a key reason why Tehiya is by far the most popular party (40 percent) in polls of high school students. Tehiya thought Raful's base would be in development towns, but it has proven to stronger in the IDF, among young people and among the TAKAM kibbutzim."[11]

Like Geula Cohen, Raful is an ombudsman *par excellence*; as chief of staff, he was known as the advocate of the common soldier, especially Sephardim. Raful's appeal derives from this, not just his organizing for Tehiya during his last year in active service. As Professor Gregory Mahler has pointed out, Knesset members spend an inordinate amount of time on casework. A direct plea to a member of parliament frequently is the only way a citizen can get the bureaucracy to perform. Endeavors on behalf of "constituents" are a major way for factions and individual politicians to establish and validate themselves.[12] The fact that both Geula Cohen and Raful are known as ombudsmen suggests that Tehiya's support may be broader and more positive than might otherwise be thought.

Raful is anything but an intellectual, but as a former chief of staff and a stalwart of the old Palmach collective settlements, he is a member of two influential, prestigious social elites. However, some analysts believe Raful's attraction has passed its peak and will show a significant decline by the next election.

Rabbi Eliezer Waldman

Rabbi Eliezer Waldman's philosophical viewpoint is more developed and far-reaching than those of Tehiya's other leaders. He passionately believes in the concept that the "very touch" of the Jewish homeland would arouse the best in those who settled there and that living in a Jewish homeland would evoke communal feelings and create new institutions of Jewish life. Waldman credits both Rabbi Kook the elder and the younger, and he sees their analyses and prescriptions as being even more relevant to Israel today.

Rabbi Waldman holds that the acquisition of the Judea and Samaria reconnected the land of Israel, the state of Israel and the people of Israel with their roots. The very touch of the heart of ancient Israel transformed them, and the state itself, permanently. This vision of the state is based on a completion, the natural, logical fulfillment of that change. As evidence of this, Waldman cites the great spiritual impact the aftermath of the Six-Day War had upon all Israelis, including secular ones. In the universality of this spiritual transformation, he sees definitive evidence that the very touch of the land could show to both obsevant and non-observant Jews why the unifying things they have in common far outweigh the superficial divisions between them.

Rabbi Waldman's outreach to non-observant Jews, his cooperation with them in Tehiya and his advocacy of a reconciliation between observant and non-observant Jews derive directly from this. To him it is not only profoundly logical, it is precisely what is needed to fulfull Zionism and Jewish destiny. The descriptive phrase is *"Holchim b'yachad"* (Going it together), and Tehiya used it in 1984 as a campaign slogan.

Rabbi Waldman's spirituality and kindliness are a counterpoint to his political toughness. Some regard him as the shrewdest and most ambitious political operator in Tehiya's leadership. A leading authority on Tehiya and Gush Emunim cites evidence that Rabbi Waldman was an intellectual patron of the Gush Emunim terrorists who attacked West Bank mayors. Rabbi Waldman's son-in-law was among those indicted.[13]

The careers and operating styles of Tehiya's leaders illustrate the gap between Tehiya the Zionist ideal and Tehiya the Israeli party: Tehiya's leadership signed off on many of the legally or morally dubious actions of the National Unity Government; they worked ceaselessly to win amnesty for the Gush Emunim terrorists, sponsoring a bill in the Knesset to that effect; they have supported subterfuges to acquire Arab properties in the West Bank; they have fought the return of Arab villagers to the Baram and Ikrit, evacuated during the War of Independence; they have been indifferent, at best, to attacks upon Arab communities in the West Bank in reprisal for terrorist incidents. One can argue that Tehiya has been true to its constituency; alternatively, one may argue that Tehiya's constituency is still in the process of defining itself and its properties. Certainly, Tehiya's leaders, despite their invocation of the past, are modern politicians and practitioners of typical Israeli politics.

Tehiya's Zionism

In its platform, Tehiya asserts that yielding to the negative aspects of Western culture has weakened Israel: It has produced an unwillingness to struggle for abiding values, a willingness to compromise with terror, a shortsightedness about the future, a failure to apply the lessons of history and a paralyzing self-criticism, of which Tehiya sees Peace Now as the very embodiment. Tehiya believes that Israelis may be losing their national identity and Jewish distinctiveness, and thus run the risk of making decisions that are out of touch with those fundamental principles and the concomitant worldview. *As a social movement, Tehiya shares with Islamic fundamentalism the same atavism, the same reaction to the secular modern world, and the same feeling of powerlessness in the face of misguided change.* Tehiya calls upon the Jewish people to return to and strengthen Jewish culture and study the Jewish sources, in order to preserve an understanding of the Jewish purpose of the Israeli state and to arouse the faith and devotion necessary to fulfill the Zionist ideal.

The Zionist ideal, in this case, is one that seems almost pre-Herzl. It speaks of redeeming the land and the state, and in so doing, redeeming the Jewish people and Jewish civilizaton. It is an internal kind of Zionism the kind extant during the 1800 years after the Second exile. Waldman and Tehiya don't reject Herzl's Zionism, but Herzl, like the people who actually achieved Israeli statehood, was concerned with practicalities. The most important of those practicalities was winning the support and recognition of the non-Jewish world.

Given Tehiya's lack of concern for the opinion and good will of the non-Jewish world, it is not surprising that this strain of Zionism is consciously separate from that of Herzl and his political/spiritual legacy, the Zionism that actually produced the state. Not just the Chug Ein Vered types in Tehiya admire and invoke the hard-nosed pragmatism of the old Labor Party Zionists, but only part of that pragmatism apeals to Tehiya: the internal pragmatism of extending the borders of the state, of establishing settlements, of building the Haganah; of creating facts while operating above board or under the table, whichever was required. The externalized pragmatism of David Ben-Gurion and Chaim Weizmann in "Dealing with the Goyim" to get recognition of the state is unattractive to Tehiya. This party is capable of finesse, but not of self-effacement.

Those who came to Tehiya from Labor espouse traditional pioneering Zionism, the reform of national institutions that have lost their sense of vision and mission, and a recrudescence of the values of the Yishuv. Many of its members were in the Palmach, come from Palmach families or were founders of NAHAL settlements.[14] Pioneering in general, and the idealized Palmach and the NAHAL experience in particular have become inspirations for many Gush Emunim settlers and for many Jews who have chosen to settle in the territories or who actively support the idea. Across the political spectrum, many Israelis today share a desire to restore the values and practices of Israel's founders. In this context, NAHAL, along with the Palmach, Rabbi Kook and the pioneering Yishuv, have become Israeli icons.

Israelis whose primary concern is this vision of the state already are a central component of Tehiya, and the applied Zionism of the early Zionists and NAHAL is a central part of Tehiya's program and outlook. A confluence exists within Tehiya of the Laborites of Raful's Chug Ein

Vered and the religious settlers who comprise the bulk of Gush Emunim. This confluence is based on a shared regard for NAHAL, Palmach and the Old Yishuv—not so much as institutions but as *symbols* of the problems and potential of the modern Jewish state.

Tehiya's Likudniks join in the confluence with even less of an affinity for Palmach and NAHAL as institutions. Tehiya's Likudniks value selectively chosen characteristics, which they believe Palmach and NAHAL embody: a hard-nosed empiricism, a dedication to extending the borders of the state, a triumph over conventional wisdom, over compromise, and over "realism." They respect the power of these institutions as symbols and their capacity for evoking in Israelis a sense of the nation's full (and unfulfilled) potential. (Given all this, if one then recalls that at the heart of Revisionist ideology is a sense of historic, unfulfilled potential of Israel and the Jewish people, one can better appreciate the statement that "Tehiya is the true Herut.")

Tehiya also affirms that Israel must be a state conscious of its uniqueness. This consciousness in turn will ineluctably establish national values that 1) will keep Zionism alive in practice; 2) will protect the Jewish character of the state (just as the emphasis on the uniqueness of the Jewish people assures the specifically Jewish character of the Jewish civilization); and thus 3) *will protect the state from bad geopolitical decisions.* The foregoing sheds light on the reasons for Tehiya's surprising cohesion to date and suggests why in time the political appeal of Tehiya (or a party that truly subsumes Tehiya's ideas) might be much broader than the party's standing today seemingly would indicate.

The issue of national purpose and identity that underlies these symbols is one which touches most Israelis; the "Tehiya Argument is likely to become an increasingly important factor in Israeli politicial life in the years ahead. Like Libertarianism in the United States, the Tehiya Argument seems destined to become a permanent part of Israeli political cultures. *Tehiya, the party, might possibly break up or metamorphose, but Tehiya's worldview and agenda are now irreversibly established in Israel's political dialectic.*

Tehiya's Program

Tehiya held its 1986 party convention in Kiryat Arba, the settlement cum-city adjacent to Hebron. Tehiya's priorities in order of importance are:

(1) Annexation of Judea and Samaria. Retention of the territories as sovereign parts of Israel.

(2) More emphasis on aspects of "irreversibility." Tehiya's highest practical priority is the creation of more facts in Judea and Samaria: more population, more settlements (even small ones), increased viability of all settlements, and much more infrastructure, including roads, schools, facilities, an end to the separate Jerusalem Arab electric company, and a growing Jewish economic presence via targeted industrial development.

(3) The overall security problem and the Palestinian "dilemma," which would force Israel to validate the Palestinian claim to a homeland in (at minimum) the West Bank and Gaza. Articulating the concerns of its Gush Emunim constituents, Tehiya called for more police protection for West Bank settlers from terrorists attack and Arab harassment.

Tehiya believes that the government must do more to distinguish Palestinian self-expression from association of that expression with the PLO. Tehiya says that the PLO is fundamentally terrorist and out of bounds as a political entity with which Israel, or Israelis or Arabs in the West Bank should be in contact. Ne'eman has asserted that in the main, the Palestinian problem has to be solved outside Israel's borders. He has stated that this does not mean expulsion, that it has been Israeli policy since 1948. Ne'eman hedged on the issue of expulsion at the Kiryat Arba convention, then later qualified his remarks under pressure from the more politically astute Cohen and Rabbi Waldman.

(4) Uplifting of the nation, an admittedly nebulous concern. Tehiya called for national sacrifice and mutual concern, as opposed to parochialism and consumption. Tehiya also endorsed a return to (its idealized view of) traditional pioneering Zionist values, including accommodation between observant and secular Jews and between Jews and Arabs; it called for a return to traditional pioneering (as opposed to socialist/bureaucratic) Zionist values in practice. Tehiya believes this has a particular appeal to those who live in rural areas or in development towns or in certain old, mainline collective settlements, who went or were sent to those areas for specifically Zionist reasons and still feel committed or obligated to those values.[15]

Tehiya is correctly regarded as pro-American. Yet when pressed, party leaders reveal an ambivalence about the United States. To some extent, they distrust American diplomacy in the region. They are concerned about how Israel's dependence upon American economic and military assistance is affecting the nation. They have reservations about the impact of America's popular and political culture on Israel. Rabbi

Waldman, for instance, readily acknowledged the value of American aid, but added that it "subjugates us."[16] Tehiya's members of Knesset publicly criticized American pressure to investigate the Pollard spy scandal and American lobbying for the cancellation of the Lavi project. This reaction may be further in evidence if Israel joins a United States–sponsored peace conference.

Interestingly, Tehiya's economic outlook derives directly from its strategic outlook. It asserts that Israel's current economic difficulties are a product of the Sinai withdrawal: the loss of the oilfields, the costs of military relocation, and the assumption of tremendous debt. Tehiya has a formal economic program, but it is rudimentary. Most of Tehiya's stand on the economy is admittedly subsumed by Likud's platform.

Tehiya believes that military exemptions for the religious should be severely limited and service options flexibly expanded. Alternative forms of service have been suggested to ensure that all Israelis, even those who do not recognize the state, would be exposed to nationalist values and people from outside their own communities. More than anything else, this part of the platform has attracted centrist and liberal voters to Tehiya.

Tehiya also wishes to extend national service (not military) to Arabs, and make citizenship and voting dependent upon that.[17] Tehiya regards this as an obvious matter of pragmatism and common sense.

Though there has been some convergence between Tehiya and Rabbi Meir Kahane's Kach Party since 1986, Tehiya consciously separates itself from Kach. It cites three points:

(1) Tehiya does not believe in the expulsion of Arabs or that every Arab is a terrorist or a potential terrorist. Tehiya believes in severe and sure punishment for people who commit crimes—death penalties, expulsion, and heavy jail sentences.

(2) Tehiya is committed to the democratic system, and Kach is anti-democratic.

(3) Tehiya has its own interpretation of Jewish practice, principle and tradition, which is far more humane, cosmopolitan and tolerant than that of Kach.[18] Tehiya uses the Rosh Yeshiva, Rabbi Waldman, to articulate this. Waldman is kindly and intellectually polished; he contrasts well with the harsh, intellectually dubious Kahane. Waldman sees Kahane's view as pessimistic and intellectually simplistic. He has stated that Tehiya does not have all the immediate answers to Israel's problems, including retention of the Arab population, but he stresses that Zionism never conditioned its existence and its progress on immediate solutions for the problems at hand.[19]

Most Israelis regard Kahane as fringe elements, while Tehiya is perceived as being part of the mainstream. In part, the stature of Tehiya's leaders, especially Ne'eman and Raful, accounts for this. Kahane, a newcomer and a loner, is isolated from other Israeli politicians. In contrast, Tehiya's leaders are members of the Israeli elite. They have longstanding friendships and contrast with their counterparts in Labor, Likud, and the relogous parties. As noted elsewhere, Ne'eman has ties to Rabin, as Cohen does with Yitzhak Shimir (her son, Yitzhak HaNegbi, is the prime minister's political assistant.)[20] Finally, most Israelis sympathize with at least some elements of Tehiya's ideology. The same cannot be said of Kach.

Party Building and Election Prospects

In 1987, Tehiya opened more than fifty local party branches. Tehiya did a sophisticated neighborhood-by-neighborhood, voting booth-by-voting booth (polling station) analysis of the 1984 voting patterns. Each voting booth serves a maximum of 1,000 voters, therefore this gave Tehiya considerable fineness, specificity, and localization in its subsequent analysis of where its strength and potential strength were most heavily concentration.[21]

Tehiya is targeting youthful voters. Raful makes an average of two to three appearances at schools each week.[22] Many of Tehiya's voters are newly out of the army or just out of high school (where appearances by Tehiya Members of Knesset galvanized their sense of political identification). Their attitudes reflect lives lived exclusively in a post-1967 Israel and a typically Israeli pragmatism.

The very purity of Tehiya's vision is one thing that accounts for its appeal to youth: Young people are attracted not so much by Tehiya's ideology as by its direct logic and unambiguous positions. (For similar reasons, the liberal Shulamit Aloni of the Citizens Rights Movement is also popular among students.)[23] They are also attracted by the patriotism of the scientist Ne'eman and the soldier Raful and by the fact that they are not typical politicians. They are also attracted by the sense of purpose and identity that Tehiya's advocacy of settlement building gives them and by the connection to the idealism and adventures of Israel's past, which Tehiya's lionizing of the old values provides.[24]

In the Knesset election of 1988, many Tehiya voters cast ballots for the first time. Many were still doing their first army service, a profoundly nationalist experience that would sharpen their attachment to Tehiya. The party has been trying to build on this preexisting orientation to turn these people into reliable Tehiya voters and party members. Tehiya also has a strong presence in Israeli universities, and has been trying to build on that.

The Tehiya Secretary General is Gideon Altshuler, former head of an Israel Defense Force (IDF) brigade for Ariel Sharon. Shmuel Gorden, a former Lieutenant colonel, is head of organization for the party. Both have brought to Tehiya a military model for a structured, efficient, election-dedicated internal organization.[25] Tehiya is not yet a service party, coordinating social services and channeling patronage. In a sense, this simplifies its election tasks, and its promotes an image that the people attracted to Tehiya are dedicated, not self-interested.

In April 1986, the Hanoch Smith/Jerusalem Post/Davar Poll indicated that Tehiya would receive 8.5 percent of the vote in the next election; the Ma'ariv/Modi'in Ezrachi Research Institute Poll indicated that Tehiya would receive 9.0 percent. This would translate into ten Knesset seats. The pool showed Tehiya taking large numbers of voters from both Likud and Kach, and smaller amounts from Labor. A June 1986, Ma'ariv/Modi'in Ezrachi Research Institute poll showed Tehiya gaining nine seats if elections were held then. The poll indicated that Tehiya would draw votes away from Kach.[26]

An April 1987 Modi'in Ezrachi poll found that Tehiya would gain seven seats in Knesset if elections were held then. This poll suggested that Tehiya might be losing some of its religious supporters to the National Religious Party.[27] However, an April 1987 Hanoch Smith/Jerusalem Post poll showed Tehiya's support at between nine and ten seats. Smith wrote that Tehiya was drawing supporters from both Labor and Likud.[28]

Some analysts have suggested privately that because Israeli polls consistently undersample IDF conscripts, kibbutz and moshav members, and residents of West Bank settlements, Tehiya's electoral strength actually may be greater than the polls indicate. Alternatively, this may mean that compared with other small parties, Tehiya's support in the polls may be less vulnerable to voting day erosion.

Tehiya's continuing strength in the polls was somewhat surprising, because during the last year, the party actually hardened its image. Ne'eman became more outspoken in his anti-Arab statements. Geula Cohen aligned herself publicly with the radical, security-obsessed Levinger faction of Gush Emunim—an element that may be a minority within Gush Emunim itself.[29] Rabbi Waldman's intellectual patronage of the Jewish terrorist underground became a matter of public record. Yet, Tehiya's standing in the polls did not diminish. Both Likud and

Labor tried to minimize Tehiya's appeal to their supporters and its impact on the political debate, albeit without much success.

In mid-1987, factions within Tehiya linked to Gush Emunim and Tzomet, respectively, fought about the direction and leadership of the party. However, Gush Emunim activists still appeared likely to be given the next two positions on the Tehiya Knesset list. Tehiya was seeking to recruit other former generals like Raful and Members of Knesset (MKs) from Likud. If they were brought into the party, they probably would be given preferential positions on the Tehiya list.[30]

Near-Term Considerations

Tehiya does not put so high a priority on opposing or derailing the peace process, or on actively opposing American initiatives to reinvigorate the peace process, because Tehiya does not believe that a peace process actually exists. Until the Arabs make an unambiguous move, à la Sadat, Tehiya will not be reflexively in the forefront against American initiatives, as some American policymakers might expect. This analytical point can be expressed another way: only a genuine peace initiative from a Arab leader—not just moderate talk like that of King Hussein, or a symbolic action like that of King Hassan—will bring Tehiya out in force.

Tehiya, which was part of the Likud-led government coalition from 1981 to 1984, refused to join the 1984-1988 national unity government. Geula Cohen cited two reasons for this: 1) a distrust of Shimon Peres; 2) the fact that at the insistence of the Labor Party, the coalition agreement of the National Unity Government was ambigious on the fate of the territories and the possibility of trading land for peace.

Befitting its status, Tehiya has begun playing a pivotal role in Israeli politics. In July 1987, Tehiya's leaders met with Prime Minister Yitzhak Shamir and warned that they would vote to bring down the National Unity Government unless more settlements were built in the West Bank. Tehiya's leaders also threatened to support new elections if Israel tried to join the proposed international peace conference. Shamir responded by pledging to begin construction at two settlement sites. He committed the government to build new roads in Judea and Samaria and additional housing in existing settlements. Finally, he iterated his own opposition to the peace conference.

The fact that Tehiya could issue a credible threat demonstrates how much of a power in Israeli politics it has become. But the party's leaders do not want to be blamed for precipitating a Likud defeat;

Cohen, in particular, still feels concern for the political well-being of Likud and that of Shamir. Thus, Tehiya for several years refused to support new, early, elections, even though it would gain seats if elections were held. Annoyance with Shamir and the prospect of a breakthrough at the polls continue to weaken Tehiya's restraint on this score.

Tehiya is clearly contemplating a legislative coup of some sort, either the introduction of its bill on annexation of the territories or the introduction of a measure proposing the death penalty for terrorists. Its objectives are to raise Tehiya's public profile, to unsettle the coalition, and to get the Knesset on record on issues that Tehiya regards as essential and of interest to the public. Tehiya's private bill to grant amnesty to the Gush Emunim terrorists already had this effect in part. Though it was of doubtful legality, it gained forty votes in July 1987, including that of Shamir. Opponents were stunned by this result.

Tehiya's private bill for annexation has been placed on the table of the Knesset but has not been brought up because the proper political opportunity has not arisen. (Knesset procedure as usually interpreted requires that a six-month waiting period pass before a private bill that has been defeated can be reintroduced. This limitation includes private bills that are substantially similar. The six-month period can be circumvented by a special ruling by the Speaker of the Knesset that there has been a fundamental change in circumstances.) Tehiya has held its fire with this; Tehiya might bring up the legislation even if were apparent it could not pass. This option might be exercised 1) as a political device to cause the government trouble and/or 2) as a way to get the various factions and MKs on record on the subject of annexation.[31]

The political potential of such legislative initiatives should not be underestimated. In July 1985, four of the five Tehiya Members of Knesset (all but Raful) staged a sit-in in the Hebron *cashah* to promote greater settlement in the West Bank, particularly Arab urban centers, and to protest IDF restrictions on apartment purchases in the territories by Jews from Arabs. The protest aroused statements of implicit support from Likud cabinet members, including Sharon and Shamir, and touched off a fight within the cabinet between Likud and Labor ministers over settlement policy. Peres and Shamir acrimoniously argued the true meaning of Zionist redemption of the land. Tehiya clearly acted as a deliberate catalyst of a larger debate, and had been encouraged by its success in this affair.[32]

The possibility exists that either a synagogue or a rebuilt Third Temple will be established unilaterally on the Temple Mount.[33] Moslems have pledged to forcibly prevent this occurrence, but an attack would limit the government's options because internal political considerations would make it difficult for any Israeli government to defer to *pogrom* politics. Tehiya's Members of Knesset certainly will be among the outspoken supporters of the Temple builders, and it will be the political conduit for those Israelis who favor 1) a Jewish presence on the Temple Mount and/or 2) a riposte, as a matter of self-respect, to Moslem religious rioters. Cohen's political assistant, Yisrael Medad, has been involved with organizations favoring a return to the Temple Mount.[34]

Tehiya in its Political Context

Tehiya is politically adjacent to Likud, yet it is not a true outgrowth or satellite. To say otherwise would ignore the Jewish redemptionism of Gush Emunim, and the resonance of this idea among old Labor Zionists disenchanted with what they perceive as a loss of idealism and vision. From a functional point of view, Tehiya's emergence was inevitable. Tehiya is a major political representative of a new cohort in the Israeli body politic: the settlers in the West Bank. They are primarily religious and politically nationalist, therefore, a nationalist, religiously connected and/or motivated party or faction representing them was inevitable. However,

(1) It was not necessarily inevitable that this demographic reality would produce a formal, separate party, rather than a faction within a larger party. (Actually, it has, but the settler factions within Likud, Mafdal, and Labor are neither independent nor politically distinct.)

(2) It was not necessarily inevitable that the result would be a unitary party combining both secular and religious elements. The founders of Tehiya initially envisioned two parties, one religious, one secular.[35] The question then becomes, can Tehiya remain unified? So far, pragmatism and accommodation have governed both sides and tempered the judgments they've made. More important, most of the fractiously anti-secular religious settlers in the West Bank have remained in Mafal. This has decreased Tehiya's potential for breakup.

(3) It was not necessarily inevitable that Tehiya would attract some of the longtime Labor voters who supported the Democratic Movement for Change (Dash) in 1977. Some analysts have suggested that Tehiya is the latest party—but not the last—to attract those who have become disenchanted with the consumerist, bureaucratic, spiritually rootless

path the nation seems to have embarked upon. Some have suggested that Tehiya will go the way of Dash. Yet Dash was a reactive movement, catalyzed by Labor's corruption and complacency. Internally, divided, amateurishly led, failing in its mission, and eventually co-opted by Likud, Dash had little permanent appeal.

In contrast, Tehiya is rooted in concerns that are more permanent than Labor's shortcomings. While its agenda is narrow, the party's priorities are ordered and its vision of the state is well-thought out. The potential breadth of its appeal and its internal cohesion have enabled Tehiya to establish itself and grow into power: Unlike many small Israeli parties in the past, its influence has increased since the list was elected.

Yet having said this, one cannot deny that Tehiya constantly feels the influence of Likud, and responds to it. The party certainly is careful not to alienate or anger Likud's constituency. For this reason, Tehiya opposed the breakup of the National Unity Government and Peres' move for early elections in May 1987, even though Tehiya stood to gain additional seats if elections were held, and even though Tehiya had been on record as favoring elections.[36] As noted, the same reasoning motivated Likud in July 1987. Nor can one dismiss the possibility that Tehiya could integrate with Likud. Tehiya's leaders are divided about the wisdom and probability of this occurring.

Conclusion

For many Israelis, even those who do not support the party, Tehiya has a persuasive internal logic, the strongest component of which is the "logic of the land." This is both a thought process and a philosophical approach, which resonates at the very core of Zionist ideology and IDF doctrine, and permeates Israeli life and the national psyche. Tehiya is also a plexus of logic, a political expression of the natural confluence of the nationalist, pragmatic, utilitarian attitudes of its three constituent elements. Was Tehiya's institutional emergence due as much to the decline of Dash as to the signing of the Egypt-Israel Peace Treaty? Perhaps. Was its emergence (and growth) inevitable after public disenchantment with Egypt and the reality of the post-treaty era? Yes.

Tehiya's assumptions are pessimistic. The party does not trust the Arabs; it does not believe the Arabs are willing to make peace; it does not trust the Egypt-Israel treaties. Yet Tehiya is one of the most dynamic elements within Israeli politics today. The movement of true believers uses old symbols—Hityashvut, territory, land—to energize its appeal and resonate psychologically in a way no other party can match.

Events hurtful to Israel strengthen Tehiya's case, its ideological cohesion, its political standing and its influence upon society. What is perceived as Egypt's chiseling and its failure to live up to the letter and spirit of the Camp David Accords 1) bolsters the convictions of Tehiya's members (especially its leadership); 2) validates and legitimates the political position of Tehiya in the mind of the Israeli public; and 3) *moves Labor and Likud towards Tehiya's positions.* So do diplomatic pressure, assaults at the United Nations, unrest in the Occupied Territories, Islamic fundamentalism, Palestinian Liberation Organization (PLO) terrorism, and crises of national identity.

The collapse of the Camp David Accords or the overthrow of the current Egyptian regime would certainly elevate Tehiya and the so-called Tehiya argument. It would be proof positive of the claims that accompanied Tehiya's birth: Israel should not give away vital assets for a piece of paper; the constraints on even sincere Arab peacemakers are such that the diplomatic approach of "land for peace" always, ultimately will fail.

The issue of security is the *sine qua non* of Israeli political culture. The Israeli public is increasingly distrustful of ambiguity. Tehiya, which has fashioned itself as the embodiment of concerns about Israel's physical and spiritual well-being, now aims to redefine the very standards by which Israelis judge security and the nature of the state. In an Israel increasingly removed from its roots, buffeted by change and faced with hard choices, Tehiya's influence seems destined to grow. For now, Tehiya stands as a self-styled Jeremiah: often discounted, sometimes heeded, mindful of the past, obsessed with the future, tugging at the collective consciousness of Israel, not without honor, as yet a minor prophet in its own land.

Postscript

In the twenty months since this analysis was first drafted, there has been only one major change in Tehiya's status: the secession from the party of Rafael Eitan and elements of Tzomet. Eitan was never comfortable in the role of politician, and being in opposition was especially disconcerting. He chafed at Cohen's leading role in the party. Eitan stated that he wanted to broaden Tehiya's membership and increase democracy within the party. Other party leaders said that his real agenda was a merger of Tehiya with Likud and an increase in the Tzomet faction's influence within the party.[37]

In late November 1987, Eitan and Tzomet narrowly lost a vote on the compositon of the party's central committee. The next day, Eitan seceded from Tehiya and moved to establish himself as the one-man Tzomet faction in the Knesset.[38] Despite the frictions between Eitan and Tehiya's leadership, Tzomet and Tehiya are still politically and ideologically aligned. Many believe that any coalition government acceptable to Tehiya would also include Tzomet. Many Tzomet members with a Labor/Hityashvut background have remained in Tehiya.

As of May 1988, Tehiya's strength in the polls held steady. It appeared that in the November elections, Tehiya would take from six to nine seats, and Tzomet one or two.

[Editor's Note: The outcome of the election of November 1988 did not result in a level of representation for Tehiya predicted by the polls at the time Rosenbaum's essay was written. In the election Tehiya received 3.1 percent of the votes (compared with 4.0 percent of the votes in 1984) for a total of three Knesset seats (compared with five in 1984). Tzomet received 2.0 percent of the vote and two Knesset seats.]

PART TWO

Israel's National Security
and Foreign Policy

CHAPTER FIVE

Israeli National Security in the 1980s: The Crisis of Overload

Avner Yaniv

This may not have been Theodor Herzl's dream, but Israel's most spectacular achievements have been in the field of national security. The kibbutz, the establishment of a vibrant democracy, the integration of a complex and heterogeneous population of immigrants, sophisticated agriculture, science and technology, all these are fields in which Israel has made remarkable strides. In the final analysis, however, the Jewish state's most dramatic impact on the world has been as an effective warrior state.[1]

No event underscored this image more than the spectacular victory over Egypt, Jordan, and Syria in the Six-Day War. Paradoxically, since this dramatic watershed, Israel's national security policy has faced growing difficulties. In absolute terms, in the sheer magnitude of Israel's military capabilities, it has never been stronger. In relative terms, however, Israel's ever-growing national security effort has faced an acute problem of diminishing returns. The IDF may still be capable of defeating any combination of Arab forces, but it appears equally plausible that Israel's national security policy as a whole has been for some time in the throes of a deep crisis.

The malaise was identified even before the traumatic invasion of Lebanon. Thus, in an anguished letter that Major-General Avraham Rotem wrote to the minister of defense shortly before his retirement in 1981 he likened the IDF to

> a train with many cars carrying heavy and expensive duty but moving slowly on a side track, headed by an ancient locomotive which has lost its power, which rather than pulling holds back; and all it can

do is to honk and occasionally blow some smoke. The guards of the track are impressed from a distance by the semblance of the reality and by the expensive cargo, but they do not notice that the train moves by the inertia invested in the cars while consuming the energy which was gained by the previous trip....Hence, instead of replacing the locomotive by a new and powerful diesel, they replace some of the cars and add rusty old additional locomotives....Soon the energy will be spent, the inertial will dissipate and the train will come to a halt.[2]

The general's argument about the IDF can be easily expanded to a broader statement on the totality of Israel's national security. Once a coherent, spirited and tightly run system, it has become big, sluggish, expensive, operationally predictable, long on technology but short on ingenuity, an arena rife with anarchic power plays and cynical bureaucratic politics, a system that would rather maintain itself through consensus than run the risks, which may attend the making of hard decisions such as are called for by Israel's circumstances. As often is the case the popular tendency is to depict individuals as the "villains" whose actions or inactions have brought this about. Rafi Eitan has thus been blamed for the Pollard Affair; Amiram Nir was the villain of the piece in the Iran-Contra Affair; Avraham Shalom and Joseph Genosar were found guilty of a decline in the standards of the General Security Service; Arik Sharon was alone blamed for the failure of the war in Lebanon, and Moshe Dayan served as the lightening rod for the public rage over the costs of the Yom Kippur War.

Even the most cursory reflection suggests, however, that while individuals have made a great number of bad decisions, something deeper than this has been at play. Specifically, the malaise seems to stem from the conjunction of two structural problems: (1) a political crisis manifested by a general poverty of leadership amid unprecedented social, ideological, and political schisms; and (2) a staggering multiplication of critical problems in almost every facet of this policy.

Leadership and National Security

To be successful any policy requires a consistent and coherent intervention of a firm and visible hand. The task of leadership is not merely to define objectives but just as much to maintain the system on course as it grapples with the problems of implementation. This endeavor boils down to a constant, never-ending struggle to reconcile competing demands on the one hand and to strike a sensible balance between short-term and long-term desiderata on the other hand.

In this sense Israel's national security policy has experienced two broad periods of existence. The first, from independence through 1960, was distinguished by striking coherence and sense of purpose. David Ben-Gurion as prime minister and minister of defense throughout this period (excluding December 1953 to February 1955 when he retired to Sdeh Boker) demonstrated a clairvoyant grasp of both technical/tactical details and the larger context, and also enjoyed the immense advantage of an unchallenged personal authority. Thus, although structurally and constitutionally Israel's national security policy-making system suffered from major deficiencies, the impact of these shortfalls was attenuated by the sheer weight of the prime minister's authority and vision.

The second period in Israel's national security experience exhibited an almost diametrically opposed configuration of attributes. While the quality of leadership plummeted, the policy-making system became more institutionalized. The positive contribution of greater institutionalization, however, was offset by the negative impact of ever-weakening leadership. A taste of things to come could be observed during November 1953 through February 1955 when Ben-Gurion retired to Sdeh Boker. His powers were divided between Moshe Sharett (as prime minister and foreign minister) Pinhas Lavon (as minister of defense) and Moshe Dayan as IDF chief of staff. Though Ben-Gurion himself had chosen his successors, this division of labor proved so disastrous that Ben-Gurion had to be virtually rushed back from retirement in order to stem the ugly tide of chaos, which threatened to unravel the national security system.

Ben-Gurion was successful in restoring personal, bureaucratic, and political balance as well as conceptual coherence from 1955 to 1960. But the grand old man's pending retirement led to a struggle for succession, which sowed the seeds of enduring crisis even while he was still personally at the helm. Ben-Gurion retired finally in June 1963, leaving Levi Eshkol as his successor both as prime minister and as minister of defense. Before long, however, things were falling apart again. In fact the built-in crisis that Ben-Gurion's leadership had previously contained gradually resurfaced.

Under Eshkol the decline of strategic wisdom was manifested: in a failure to contain the escalation with Syria; in a failure to arrest the rise of the share of defense outlays in the Gross National Product; in a failure to maintain the high level of morale and self-confidence, which had been characteristic of Israeli society in the aftermath of the 1956 war; in a failure to employ Israel's considerable deterrence assets in order to manage the crisis that led to the 1967 war; as well as in a failure to prevent the expansion of the war into Jordan and Syria.

Under Golda Meir and Moshe Dayan the same tendencies continued to gather momentum. Military policy was often excessively
escalatory and failed to be synchronized with positive political incen-
tives for Arab governments. Arms procurement policies reflected a
shocking insensitivity to the long-term impact of the burden on the
Israeli economy. When all this went hand in hand with excessive self-
righteousness, a good deal of *hubris,* a self-congratulatory smugness,
and a myopic failure to address a significant rise in domestic unease,
the only surprising thing is that it did not lead to a greater calamity
than the 1973 war.

Golda Meir shared with Levi Eshkol a singular lack of political-
strategic vision. Both were also insufficiently versed with the minutiae
of both strategy and technology to be able to act as effective devil's
advocates to the advice that they were obtaining from the military. This
is not to suggest any excesses on the part of the IDF. Rather, what
should be underscored is that owing to the weakness of the political
echelon, the IDF was increasingly invited to offer policy advice on
matters in which its competence was in doubt. Eshkol was particularly
weak in this regard. Meir at least had formidable military experts such
as Dayan, Allon, Galili, Bar-Lev, and Rabin on her side. But the difference between Eshkol and Meir in this regard was more formal that
substantive. In the final analysis these two successors to Ben-Gurion
were grievously lacking in judgement on strategic and military affairs
and, therefore, were poorly prepared for evaluating politically the advice that their colleagues (Cabinet ministers with military background)
and subordinates (still in the IDF) were offering.

Under the Rabin-Peres Labor government (1974–77) this Israeli
variation on "the Peter Principle," namely, the promotion of military
and national security technocrats to their level of declining competence,
reached a new peak. Both men could draw on a formidable reservoir
of experience in virtually every aspect of national security. This great
advantage (which explains why they had been successful as subordinates and advisors) was undercut when leadership was entrusted
to them by their vicious personal feud, by a dismal inability to generate
public confidence, and by the weakness of their party political base.

During Menachem Begin's first three years in office (1977–80) a
semblance of a Ben-Gurion-style balance was restored to Israel's
national security policy system. Begin projected grandiloquent
authority, a rhetoric that could be easily mistaken for a historic vision
(of which in reality he probably had very little), and an impressive
ability to handle the domestic political dimension of national security.
Dayan (as foreign minister) and Ezer Weizmann (as minister of defense)

shared between them invaluable practical experience, a critical element of continuity with a past in the shaping of which Begin had virtually no part, as well as a good deal of authority.

This configuration of personality at the apex of Israel's national security machinary was, indeed, critical in turning Sadat's peace initiative into a contractual peace agreement. In turn, Egypt's withdrawal from the Arab war camp (especially when in conjunction with the Iran-Iraq war) implied that no viable Arab war coalition could be formed in order to initiate a coordinated surprise attack against the Jewish state. While this was one of the most important boosts ever to Israeli security, Begin's latter days in power had a catastrophic effect on the progress of peace. Without Dayan and Weizmann, Begin, an ignoramus in matters of national security, had to fall back either on the simple-minded, almost primitive, advice of Major-General Rafael Eitan ('Raful'), or on the counsel of the capable, powerful, experienced, but ruthlessly uninhibited Ariel Sharon.

This was a recipe for disaster. During this time (1980–83), the Israel Aviation Industry gradually nudged the government into the Lavi project. Also during these years, a far more repressive policy in the Occupied Territories greatly compromised IDF personnel and led to deep divisions within its ranks. This personality set up led the IDF into Lebanon where it performed a military operation whose objectives far exceeded what Begin's own Cabinet was willing to authorise.

Under the 1984–88 Peres/Shamir power-sharing, some of the wounds that the experience in Lebanon had inflicted slowly healed. The decisions leading to a phased-out withdrawal from Lebanon were clearly effective in toning down domestic divisions on the issue. Beyond this important achievement of the National Unity Government (NUG), its record on national security affairs has been dismal. In fact, although divisions on many critical national security issues did not correspond to the great divide between Labor and Likud, the pervasive, paralyzing, debilitating stalemate at the Cabinet led to a sluggish, cumbersome, acrimonious and for all these reasons damaging policy-making process.

The Overloaded Agenda

Gouvernent c'est choisir (To Govern is to Chose) was the political slogan (and title of a book) of Pierre Mendes-France. As French premier from June 1954 through February 1955, he acted systematically and, up to a point, successfully to implement this program. Three and a half decades later Israel seems to be in a situation which to a certain extent recalls the political, economic and moral crisis of the Fourth Republic during the Mendes-France era (the Occupied Territories offering a tragic analogue with Algeria). Much like France, Israel faces an urgent need for a clear and galvanizing reappraisal of national priorities. If the leadership that can do this is not available (which, at the time of writing, appears most unlikely), Israel's national security may be heading for fresh catastrophes. The full depth of the malaise can only be appreciated if the most salient policy issue areas in which hard decisions are urgently called for are briefly stated. Most salient among these have been the questions of doctrine, nuclear weapons, alliance management, regional orientation, arms production, arms sales, the Occupied Territories, and south Lebanon.

(1) *Doctrine:* Owing to Israel's perceived inferiority in the overall balance of forces with the Arab world, its strategy (at least since 1955) has been predicated on an overwhelming preference for interceptive, preemptive or even preventive wars. A war inititated by Israel would — in this view — permit the Jewish state to swiftly and decisively immobilize one central Arab adversary and thus deter other Arab states from joining. Such a war would be based on surprise, on a huge concentration of force (as a means of attaining local superiority) and on deep penetration maneuvers. In this manner Israeli planners felt confident that decisive battlefield victories could be achieved. The upshot would be substantially enhanced deterrence and ultimately, it was hoped, some sort of peace.

This scenario, which evolved between 1955 and 1967, was implemented with remarkable success in the Six-Day War. Since then, however, the entire edifice has been increasingly called into question. The last days before the outbreak of the Yom Kippur War revealed a deep reluctance to initiate war for fear of reaction by the United States. The 1982 war in Lebanon revealed that domestic opinion would be very reluctant to go along with the notion of an initiated war. Since 1982 the huge concentration of regular Syrian forces in the Golan has altered the strategic calculus altogether. Theoretically, the IDF can still break through Syrian fortifications, but this might cost so much in life and materiel that it no longer exists as a viable alternative. What, then, is to be done?

To the extent that can be judged, the IDF has been agonizing over this problem but (as during the last two years preceding the 1973 war) has not come up with any clear-cut solutions. The problem could be alleviated through a political reappraisal leading ultimately to some sort of an agreement with Syria that would reduce the risk of war.

Broadly speaking, what ought to be searched for in such negotiations is a state of nonbelligerency based on the denial to both parties of either the ability to launch surprise attacks or of the ability to employ tactics of protracted attrition. This, however, implies a substantial disengagement of forces, putting a distance between the armor of the two countries. Yet, not only the Syrian regime but also Israel would be most doggedly opposed to this. The sad truth is that the domestic political situation in Israel is not conducive to an imaginative search for a solution such as seems to be called for.

(2) *Nuclear Weapons:* Since the Egyptian-Czech arms deal of August 1955, Israel has been locked in a runaway arms race. Israel's own doctrine started from the maxim that the minimum requirement would be an Israeli force of sufficient strength to thwart effectively within not more than 21 to 30 days of sustained fighting a surprise attack by all Arab armies together. Each one of Israel's neighbors, however, has looked at the Jewish state's might as if it was mostly directed against itself alone. Thus, *structurally* a level of Israeli military strength that would be satisfactory from the Israeli point of view was bound to seem alarming from the Arab point of view. Conversely, what would be satisfactory from the Arab point of view would in all likelihood drive Israel to the conclusion that a preventive war had become inescapable. Added to this war trap was the impact on Arab arms build-up of their own neighbors (both Arab — i.e. Syria vs. Iraq — and non-Arab — i.e. Iran), and it all adds up to a recipe for catastrophe.

In economic terms Israel was successful up to roughly the departure of David Ben-Gurion in 1963 in keeping both an adequate ratio of forces and a ceiling of 6 to 8 percent of the Gross National Product (G.N.P.) on its defense outlays. For the next two decades (1963–83) the part of the G.N.P. allocated for defense rose almost uninterruptedly while (at least during the first half of this period) the G.N.P. itself was also growing. On the eve of the 1967 war Israel spent roughly 12 percent of the G.N.P. on defense. Following this war, and then the war of attrition, and, in particular the Yom Kippur war, the percentage of G.N.P. allocated to defense rose above 20 percent and that in an economy in which the government's budget is roughly two-thirds of the G.N.P.

This staggering rise in costs had its demographic corollary. The money spent on the expansion of conventional capabilities translated also (though not exclusively) into a colossal growth in size of the IDF. From an army of roughly twelve (mainly infantry) brigades in the 1950s the IDF had grown into an army of some twelve mechanized divisions (the equivalent of thirty-six brigades or roughly four army groups) at

the time this article was written. Already a decade ago it was forcefully argued by the late Moshe Dayan that this could not go on, that,
in fact, the IDF should stop its growth and turn to a different doctrine.
Dayan never made entirely clear what exactly he had in mind, but there
are indications that he intended a reduction in size and an undeclared
shift to nonconventional power multipliers.

Dayan's cryptic advocacy (which a number of academics subsequently explicated and adopted as their own[3]) was rejected by all Israeli
governments to date. The nuclear program, to be sure, continued apace
without interruption. With tacit American inducements (consisting of
threats of sanctions as well as promises that Israel's conventional needs
will be upheld come what may), Israel has desisted from going public
with the bomb.

A rather commonly held view is that Israel has opted for a posture
of deliberate ambiguity in this regard. The weight of the available
evidence, however, challenges this theory. Israel has not been
deliberately cultivating ambiguity as to its nuclear doctrine. Rather,
the thicket of ambiguity, which has evolved over the years, is the result
of an inevitable gap between the material development of significant
infrastructure and the policy preference for keeping discussion about
nuclear issues to a minimum. The development of a nuclear option,
especially when this has to be done secretly and against the wishes
of all world powers, takes decades. Therefore, even when a government has no intention of going nuclear in the forseeable future it cannot
escape the need for investing in the development of such a program.
These efforts are difficult to conceal; therefore, the result is a great deal
of speculation leading to inferences concerning intentions, which may
not at all be well-founded. This seems to have been the case of Israel.

However, the colossal Syrian build-up since the Egyptian-Israeli
peace, and especially after the Lebanon war, has placed enormous
strains on their doctrine. If Syria (in a worst-case scenario) succeeds
in bogging Israel down in an inconclusive war of attrition, the pressures
on other Arab states — chief of all Egypt and Jordan — to come to
Syria's aid by simply deploying forces in a way that would force Israel
to send forces to other theaters, might leave Israel in a position in which
it is unable to ''hold the line''. What should it then do? Should there
be a resort to nonconventional weapons? But that would surely force
the Soviets to extend a nuclear umbrella to their Syrian allies, which
in one fell swoop would offset any advantage to Israel as a result of
nuclearization. Worse still, if Israel were to go public with the bomb
it would inevitably create tremendous friction between itself and the
United States at a time at which it could ill afford such friction. Last,

but not least, what kind of nonconventional weapons should be developed and deployed to be effective against Syria without damage to Israel? After all, the distance between Damascus and Tel Aviv is barely 150 miles.

(3) *Alliance management:* One of the most important maxims of Israeli national security ever since independence has been that in the final analysis the imbalance between Arab power potential and that of Israel could only be redressed through a security guarantee with a great power, which would turn any attack against Israel into an attack against that great power. The position of *Ee Hizdahut* — nonidentification — maintained during the first few years of independence was never taken seriously by Ben-Gurion. He merely used it as a means of obtaining Soviet good will and weapons while keeping the U.S.S.R. at arm's length at a time when the United States was exceedingly aloof.

Taking a forty years' perspective, Israel has done very well in its constant efforts to obtain such a security guarantee. To be sure, the first years of independence were marked by inglorious isolation. This period gave way to a close alliance with France, and since the Six-Day War to an ever-tightening bond with the United States. Indeed, by 1988 Israel's security needs are all but automatically underwritten by the United States; the Jewish state already enjoys the status of a NATO ally, and the notion that Israel constitutes a strategic asset from the United States point of view is no longer brushed aside as was the case a decade ago. As a result, Israel's adversaries cannot help assuming that any successful military effort on their part against Israel would be met by a very vigorous American response.

Events such as the Iran-Contra and Pollard affairs suggest, however, that this close intertwining of Israeli and United States policies may also have its drawbacks. A formal treaty of alliance delineating exactly the lines of mutual obligation is still not a matter of practical politics. The United States will only sign such a treaty if and when the Arab-Israeli conflict has been fully, and formally, resolved. Israel, too, may be having doubts about the wisdom of contractual obligations when this might entail an explicit designation of the Soviets as adversaries and/or a commitment to consult the U.S. in advance of any act of significance. Meanwhile, however, the pressures of ongoing needs, issues such as intelligence sharing, Israeli logistic assistance to the United States in projecting power in the Persian Gulf, a Voice Of America relay station in Israel's Arava desert, or naval facilities for the Sixth Fleet at Haifa, Ashdod or Eilat, make it virtually impossible to simply postpone a decision on the principle. Should Israel continue its historic drive for a formal alliance with the

United States? Is this really in the Israeli national interest? If the answer is in the affirmative, what is it exactly that Israel should be seeking?

(4) *Regional orientation:* Israel's national security policy since the early 1950s assumed as a matter of course that the main menace came from a Sunni Moslem world surrounding the Jewish state from all directions. If these predominantly Sunni states were to unite under one leadership, their ability to convert their basic potential into realities of power would be greatly enhanced and Israel's basic inferiority would be underlined.

Assuming this, Israeli policymakers from Ben-Gurion to Shamir and Peres accepted without challenge the assumption that Israel should strive to weaken the Sunni Arab bloc through covert, and if possible overt, alignments with dissenting minorities in their midst, as well as with non-Sunni and/or non-Arab states on the "periphery" (as it was seen from Israel) of the Middle East. The main purpose of these links would be to force the Arabs to pay attention to potential theaters of military operations a long way from Israel. This would diffuse their military potentials and thus lessen the threat to Israel itself.

Such an orientation led to contacts with and support for the Kurdish minority in Iraq, the rebels in southern Sudan, the Druzes in Syria and, of course, the Maronites in Lebanon. The same philosophy also underscored, legitimized, and guided Israel's relations with Imperial Ethiopia, Imperial Iran and republican Turkey.

During the 1970s most of the main components of this scheme gradually unravelled. Ethiopian Emperor Haile Selasie was deposed by a revolutionary regime, which became closely aligned with the Soviet Union. Egypt broke ranks with the mainstream of the Sunni Arab bloc and moved toward peace with Israel and a lower profile in inter-Arab politics. The Shah of Iran was deposed by a pernicious regime of religious fanatics who, at least initially, were aligned with the PLO and a variety of other radicals in the Arab camp. Finally, the link with the Maronites in Lebanon proved to be far too problematic to be useful.

Despite all these changes Israel seemed to have persisted in the old "periphery" policy. Relations with Mengistu Meriam's regime in Ethiopia were maintained, albeit covertly. Relations with Iran were not restored to their level in the 1970s, but Israel continued to be involved in arms supplies to the Iranians. This policy has been the subject of growing criticism from important segments of professional and lay opinion both in Israel and in the United States. Critics argue that Iraq has completely reversed its attitude towards Israel and Zionism and that this offers an opportunity for another step in the peace process, which Israel should not sacrifice on the altar of the dubious connection with the Ayatollah's Iran. Whether or not these contentions are valid is not easy to determine. But one thing remains clear: Israel's regional orientation should be the subject of an open-minded reappraisal. What has to be determined is whether Israel should uphold its age-old "peripheral" doctrine or, alternatively, seek to establish closer relations with a Sunni Arab regional core bloc consisting of Egypt, Saudi Arabia, Jordan, and Iraq.

(5) *Self-sufficiency in weapons:* The French embargo on the eve of the Six-Day War and the tendency of various administrations in the U.S. to use the supply of arms as a lever with which to influence Israeli policy led to a strenuous Israeli drive for self-sufficiency in arms. An enterprise begun with the production of primitive mortars and the Uzi submachine gun moved to the assembly and subsequent modification of aircraft, the modification and then construction and design of tanks, and ultimately to an attempt to design and produce competitive all-purpose combat planes and missile boats.

The growth of the various industries which produced these weapons - the Israel Aviation Industry (IAI), the Israel Military Industry (IMI), and Rashut LeFituach Emtzaei Lehima (RAFAEL), as well as many privately owned industries that lived off contracts from these public corporations, attested to the important spinoffs to the Israeli economy and Israel's technological capabilities, which resulted from this drive for self-sufficiency. Their products were on the whole of very high quality, and unit costs were kept very competitive on the world market. This, however, was increasingly more difficult to maintain as Israel moved into the production of weapon systems that were dependent on foreign-produced components (such as jet engines); for the dependence on the supply of American-built components undercut Israel's ability to sell its weapons to the highest bidder (including pariah regimes in Latin America and Africa), which in turn threatened the ability of Israeli industries to keep down unit costs. Indeed, with the Lavi project this problem has become even more complex because the very financing of the project has become critically dependent on United States credits and grants.

The drive for self-sufficiency, then, has been called into question. If Israel insisted on completing the Lavi it would have to do so at the expense of military preparedness (which the IDF and the IAF greatly resent) as well as of development efforts in other areas (such as Sa'ar 5, the new missile boat for the Israeli Navy) and under conditions in which expected overseas sales would be too limited to ensure an affordable unit cost. Given these calculations it is clear that the Lavi has ceased to be a viable policy option. But what are the alternatives? Israeli governments had debated this complex issue for several years while allowing the Lavi project to continue uninterrupted. But by 1987 the moment of decision had come. Recognizing all these constraints, the National Unity Government made a decision in August 1987 to stop the Lavi project. This led to a great deal of rancor, to massive layoffs, but not to a clear decision about the future of Israel's independent effort in the domain of arms production such as has been called for since the middle of the 1970s.

(6) *Arms Exports:* Israel's Global Reach, as Aron Klieman described it[4], has had both critical rewards (about $1.1 billion worth of exports annually, which is the equivalent of close to 25 percent of the direct costs of defense) and very negative repercussions, too. In particular it has tarnished Israel's image not only with the Soviet Bloc and the Afro-Asians (who were hostile in any case) but also with Israel's traditional sources of public support in Western Europe and the United States. With the recent trends in Congress as regards South Africa and Latin America, Israel may well be running into a very difficult situation in which it will either have to stop its arms sales to those regimes which Congress will (or will have already) declare unqualified, or, alternatively, suffer a major eclipse in its relations with the United States.[5] What makes this dilemma particularly painful is the fact that the fight against arms sales to pariah regimes is led by prominent Jewish leaders, enjoys a great deal of support in Jewish intellectual circles, and, above all, has a real domestic constituency in Israel. (Even the most die-hard supporters in Israel of ignoring the criticism and pushing on with the sales to the highest bidder do not exalt the virtues of Apartheid.) Again, as with some of the other issues mentioned above, the moment of decision is approaching. Should Israel continue to sell weapons indiscriminately in Africa and Latin America or is a fundamental reorientation both warranted and feasible?

(7) *The Occupied Territories:* Twenty years after the Six-Day War it appears increasingly less controversial to see the occupation of the West Bank, Gaza, and even the Golan as a huge liability from the point of view of Israel's long-term security. In the late 1960s an Israeli writer could still present this result of the June war as "a cursed blessing."[6] The same writer today has probably dropped the blessing and underlined the curse. To be sure, the occupation of the West Bank, Gaza, and the Golan may have greatly enhanced Israel's ability to deter Jordan from any thought of direct military confrontation. In the final analysis, however, it has compromised Israel's self-image, undermined

Israel's domestic cohesion, escalated the conflict with Syria, stimulated the growth of an assertive and self-conscious Palestinian political entity, driven a painful wedge between Israel and world Jewry, and exposed the Jewish state to new but vicious security risks, which in the long run appear to defy an easy solution.

Prior to the Six-Day War the pockets of Zionist territorial maximalism, which had existed in both the right and the left, had been effectively contained. Ben-Gurion ruthlessly disciplined Begin's Herut (in which Stern Gang leaders such at Yitzhak Shamir found political refuge, too) and then succeeded in remorselessly affixing on this political movement a stigma of infantile, rash, and verbose irresponsibility. Though relying on more subtle methods, Ben-Gurion was just as adamant and effective in isolating, demoralizing and weakening the followers of Yitzhak Tabenkin within the left chauvinist Ahdut HaAvoda.

This campaign against Jewish extremism went hand in hand with an effort to stamp out all remnants of Palestinian nationalism. The main objective of this strategy was accommodation with a Hashemite Jordan based on Israel's recognition of the latter's control of the West Bank. If Ben-Gurion's objective is defined in this way, it is not surprising that he later saw the 1967 War as a calamity of historic proportions. For what this astounding military victory essentially did was to salvage from oblivion the twin ghosts of Jewish maximalism and Palestinian particularism.

The full impact of this "alliance" of Arab and Jewish militants has only begun to be widely appreciated in recent years. Israel's first decade in control of the West Bank and the Golan (but not of Gaza, which proved to be a "hornet's nest" from the very beginning) logically nurtured a great deal of self-congratulating myopia. Palestinian leadership on the West Bank as represented by mayors such as Ali Ja'abri and Hamdi Kna'an was cooperative enough to give Dayan's policy of "carrots and sticks" a temporary lease on life. Consequently, Israel could boast that its military occupation was the most humane in world history (as if a humane occupation is less of an occupation that a repressive one).[7]

During the interval between the 1973 and 1982 wars, this idylic scene began to unravel under the impact of a complex change in most of the particulars of the situation. Dayan's sensitivity and wisdom was not matched by his heirs as members of the cabinet in charge of the Occupied Territories. Israel's weakness in the opening phases of the Yom Kippur War, and the Arab world's ascent with the rise in oil prices, combined to stir opposition in the Occupied Territories. The rise of the PLO to international prominence added impetus to the process, because it weakened the traditional pillars of society in the West Bank and Gaza, and provided a focal point of identification and for the first time since 1967 (to some Palestinians since 1948) a tangible hope of political deliverance.

Moreover, in Palestinian eyes Israel was forced out of the Sinai by Egyptian and Syrian military pressure in conjunction with American political pressures and inducements. This seemed to offer a recipe for easing Israel out of the West Bank, Gaza, and the Golan. While the population in these areas did not have conventional weaponry, it could resort to mass protests. The protests elicited repressive counter-measures and thus drew Western attention and sympathy.

None of these factors escaped the attention of the Israeli right. Noting, too, that the 1973 war led to Israel's phased withdrawal from the Sinai, and confirmed in these anxieties when even Begin proved willing to sign away the Sinai in exchange for peace with Egypt, these circles joined forces under the overall political umbrella of the Tehiya movement. Spearheaded in the Occupied Territory by Gush Emunim and articulating their case through an impressive (and very heterogeneous) gallery of parliamentarians, this movement incessantly forced the hand of successive governments and scored a remarkable success in its effort to transform the face of the Occupied Territories by extensive settlement right in the heart of densely inhabited parts of the territories. Not surprisingly, this added fuel to the rising tide of Palestinian resentment and restiveness and thus accelerated the pace of the protest/repression cycle.

Since the early 1980s, all hell seems to have broken loose. Sharon's experimentation in colonial repression on the basis of Professor Milson's naive/Machiavellian theories, and the blind violence of the Jewish underground, succeeded in uniting the otherwise divided population in a wall-to-wall front. Israel's unsuccessful war in Lebanon, in particular the ejection of the once proud IDF from south Lebanon by means of Shiite terrorism, spurred the hope of Palestinians that the same methods could work in the West Bank and Gaza, too. Indeed, the Shiites's success in this regard made a mockery of Palestinian resistance and forced the latter to show that they too could achieve the same result through similar means.

Thus, twenty years after the Six-Day War Israel is faced by a nightmare consisting of a breakdown of law and order in the West Bank and Gaza (and to a lesser extent the Golan) as a result of both Jewish and Arab terrorism. The ugly pattern is, alas, only too familiar from comparable tragedies elsewhere. The Arabs have evolved an extensive network of underground cells. They have evolved a sophisticated method of using strikes and demonstrations for larger political ends. While refraining from the use of extensive fire power (which requires weapons that are difficult to obtain and hide), Palestinians have turned rocks, knives, and Molotov cocktails into formidable weapons. These were used sporadically and indiscriminately against chance targets of opportunity before the *intifada* (uprising) beginning in winter 1987–1988, but became used in a sustained and widespread way after that time.

The IDF's countermeasures are all familiar: arrests, curfews, and the blocking or demolition of homes in which suspects were hidden. While increasing the resentment of the population, such measures do not adequately deter further chance attacks. The response of the Jewish settlers/vigilantes consists of calls on the government to employ harsher measures, which ultimately lead to unauthorised, blind pogroms by Jews against Arabs. This has forced the military government to take sides: IDF units were ordered to protect Arabs against Jewish vengence. The Jewish hands that press triggers in West Bank Arab streets are ultimately linked to the centers of power in the very heart of the Israeli political system; therefore, these measures for countering and controlling Jewish terrorism could hardly be effective enough to stem this tide of rebellious Arab action/provocative Jewish reaction. In the final analysis, the methods that are most likely to achieve this range from the unfeasable to the unthinkable: either the wholesale expulsion of the Arab population (which parts of the Jewish right hopes for) or unilateral Israeli withdrawal from any responsibility in the occupied areas (which is the vain hope of the Israeli left).

(8) *South Lebanon:* In June 1985 Israel completed the third and last stage of the IDF's withdrawal from Lebanon. During the two-year phased withdrawal, the government of Yitzhak Shamir and — following the 1984 elections — the National Unity Government under Shimon Peres were at pains to arrive at some understanding with Syria and with the Shiites. Sensing apparently that Israel was leaving Lebanon because it could no longer tolerate the cost of the occupation of that country, Syria would not enter into any serious dialogue. All it did was to allow Lebanese President Amin Gemayel to enter into protracted and ultimately fruitless negotiations with Israel concerning the restoration of the pre-1967 Armistice regime. Indeed, this, too, was only acceptable for the Syrians if Israel abandoned General Lahad's South Lebanon Army (SLA), gave up its security belt in south Lebanon, and in fact enabled a complete return to the intolerable pre-1982 status quo ante bellum.

The Syrian proposals as presented to Israel by the Lebanese delegation to these talks impaled Israel on the horns of yet another dilemma for which it has not found a satisfactory solution. If the Shiites of South Lebanon had been united under a moderate leadership accepting the notion of a 'live and let live' accommodation with Israel, a return to the international border would be ultimately acceptable to Israel even without a formal peace treaty. Indeed, if this were the case the return of the PLO to this area would have been prevented by the Shiites for their own reasons.

The Israeli government was fully aware that the al Amal movement under Nabih Berri's leadership was struggling to establish itself as the sole legitimate and effective spokesman for the Shiites in Lebanon. Realizing that Amal's prospects for winning this struggle against the Hezbolla radicals were not clear and, therefore, that open support from Israel could jeopardize al Amal's position, the Peres government in fact confined itself to sending al Amal discreet signals of good will. Al Amal, however, was too weak to reciprocate.

To be sure, Nabih Berri must have realized that there was no conflict of interests between the Shiite community in south Lebanon and Israel. He had also been as opposed as Israel to the return of the PLO to the area, but Berri faced tough opposition from Hezbollah. At stake was nothing less than the leadership of close to one million Shiites in Lebanon. The winner in the struggle would not only deliver the Shiites from their underprivileged and underrepresented position in Lebanon, but might even ultimately become a Lebanese national leader (with the inter-Arab and international significance that this could entail). The alternative, however, could be a complete loss not only of an attractive political position but even, perhaps, of the life of the loser (and possibly the life of his family, too). Such a choice breeds a vicious game of outbidding in which the militants invariably have the upper hand.

For these reasons Berri could not enter into any dialogue with Israel, not even a mute one. In fact he was impelled to demonstrate to the Shiite masses in Lebanon that he could be at least as tough vis-a-vis the Israelis as the Hezbolla. In turn Israel could not trust al Amal to play the role of a buffer between the Galilee and the turmoil of north Lebanon. A buffer based on an Israeli-supported militia (the SLA) was the very least Israel could do to insulate itself from the Lebanese quagmire.

If Berri was thus rationally impelled to be militant against Israel even before the establishment of the SLA, once this militia was set up its undoing became al Amal's supreme test. If Berri was successful in removing the SLA and sending the IDF back across the border, his chances for winning the contest with Hezbolla would improve. Conversely, Berri's failure would be Hezbolla's (and indirectly the PLO's) success. Israel was thus thrust into an inherently self-defeating posture, which may have been inescapable in the short run. In the long run, however, Israel's maintenance of the SLA could undermine the moderates in al Amal. This would be a boon to the Hezbollah radicals and thus conceivably plant the seeds of further confrontations between Israelis and Shiites. The only thing that could adequately solve this problem would be an Israeli-Syrian understanding leading to the support of both to al Amal and the resistance of both to the PLO on the one hand and the Hezbolla on the other hand. Short of such a complicated understanding, the situation left behind the IDF since its withdrawal from Lebanon thus contains a dangerous time bomb. This was underscored during the Israeli action in Mayadun early in May 1988. If not defused somehow, this complexity could lead to the reengagement of the IDF in Lebanon, a proposition that, after Israel's bitter experience during 1982–85, has few supporters.

Like any other issue discussed above, the problem of south Lebanon would pose a major challenge even to a very capable leadership. Together, however, the eight clusters of issues discussed above constitute a formidable hurdle which no Israeli government in the forseeable future — be it Labor-based, Likud-based, or a power-sharing coalition — will be able to resolve satisfactorily. This can only have very grim implications. What lies ahead, in all likelihood, is an Israeli national security policy of muddling through, of incremental and fragmented decision making based more on political consensus building than on operationally sensible thinking. This could perhaps do under normal circumstances. But given the scope of the issues and, indeed, the nature of the stakes, the results are almost certain to be further mishaps, blunders, "rogue operations," setbacks, *mechdalim*, and quite likely tragedies.

CHAPTER SIX

Israeli-Soviet Relations Under the National Unity Government

Robert O. Freedman

When a new leader takes power, especially in a country that had witnessed a stagnation bordering on immobilization in both its foreign and domestic policies for more than half a decade, a review of policies and policy options should be expected. Therefore, it should come as no surprise that soon after Mikhail Gorbachev took over as first secretary of the Communist Party of the Soviet Union in March 1985, a change in Moscow's relations with Israel took place. In order to fully understand the thrust of Gorbachev's policy toward Israel, which involved the issue of Soviet Jewry, it is first necessary to examine Soviet policy toward the Middle East as a whole, because Soviet policy toward Israel can best be understood if it is seen as part of Moscow's overall policy toward the Middle East.

Observers of Soviet policy in the oil-rich and strategically located Middle East are generally divided into two schools of thought as to Soviet goals in the region. While both agree that the Soviet Union wants to be considered a major factor in Middle Eastern affairs, if only because of the USSR's propinquity to the region, they differ on the ultimate Soviet goal in the Middle East.[1] One school of thought sees Soviet Middle Eastern policy as being primarily defensive in nature, that is, as directed toward preventing the region from being used as a base for military attack or political subversion against the USSR. The other school of thought sees Soviet policy as primarily offensive in nature, as aimed at the limitation and ultimate exclusion of Western influence from the region and its replacement by Soviet influence. The opinion of the author is that Soviet goals in the Middle East, at least since the mid-1960s, have been primarily offensive in nature; and in the Arab segment of the Middle East, the Soviet Union appears to have been engaged in a zero-sum game competition for influence with the United States.

In its efforts to weaken and ultimately eliminate Western influence from the Middle East, and particularly from the Arab world, while promoting Soviet influence, the Soviet leadership has employed a number of tactics. First and foremost has been the supply of military aid to its regional clients.[2] Next in importance comes economic aid; the Aswan Dam in Egypt and the Euphrates Dam in Syria are prominent examples of Soviet economic assistance, although each project has had serious problems. In recent years Moscow has also sought to solidify its influence through the conclusion of long-term Friendship and Cooperation Treaties such as the ones concluded with Egypt (1971), Iraq (1972), Somalia (1974), Ethiopia (1978), Afghanistan (1978), South Yemen (1979), Syria (1980), and North Yemen (1984), although the repudiation of the treaties by Egypt (1976) and Somalia (1977) indicates that this has not always been a successful tactic. Moscow has also attempted to exploit both the lingering memories of Western colonialism, and Western threats against Arab oil producers. In addition, the Russians have offered the Arabs diplomatic support at such international forums as the United Nations and the Geneva Conference on an Arab-Israeli peace settlement. Finally, Moscow has offered the Arabs aid of both a military and diplomatic nature against Israel, although that aid has been limited in scope because Moscow continues to support Israel's right to exist both for fear of unduly alienating the United States with whom the Russians desire additional strategic arms agreements and improved trade relations, and because Israel serves as a convenient rallying point for potentially anti-Western forces in the Arab world.[3]

While the USSR has used all these tactics, with greater and lesser degrees of success over the last two decades, it has also run into serious problems in its quest for influence in the Middle East. First, numerous inter-Arab and regional conflicts (Syria-Iraq; North Yemen-South Yemen; Ethiopia-Somalia; Algeria-Morocco; Iran-Iraq, etc.) have usually meant that when the USSR has favored one part, it has alienated the other, sometimes driving it over to the West. Second, the existence of Middle Eastern Communist parties has proven to be a handicap for the USSR, as Communist activities have, on occasion, caused a sharp deterioration in relations between Moscow and the country in which the Communist party has operated. The Communist-supported coup d'etat in the Sudan in 1971, Communist efforts to organize cells in the Iraqi army in the mid and late 1970s, and the activities of the Tudeh party in Khomeini's Iran, are recent examples of this problem.[4] Third, the wealth that flowed to the Arab world (or at least to its major oil producers) since the quadrupling of oil prices in late 1973 has enabled the Arabs to buy quality technology from the West and Japan, and this has helped weaken the economic bond between the USSR and a number of Arab states such as Iraq and Syria. Fourth, since 1967 and particularly since the 1973 Arab-Israeli war, Islam has been resurgent throughout the Arab world, and the USSR, identified in the Arab world with atheism, has been hampered as a result, paticularly since the Soviet invasion of Afghanistan in 1979 where Moscow fought against an essentially Islamic resistance force. Fifth, only the United States has been able to talk to both sides of the Arab-Israeli conflict and, as a result, has dominated the Middle East peace process since the 1973 Arab-Israeli war. Finally, the United States, and to a lesser extent, France and China, have actively opposed Soviet efforts to achieve predominant influence in the region, and this has frequently enabled Middle Eastern states to play the extraregional powers off against each other and thereby prevent any one of them from securing predominant influence.

To overcome these difficulties, Moscow has evolved one overall strategy — the develpment of an "anti-imperialist" bloc of states in the Arab world. In Moscow's view these states should bury their internecine rivalries, and join together along with such political organizations as the Arab Communist parties and the PLO, in a united front against what the USSR has called the "linchpin" of Western imperialism in the Middle East — Israel. Under such circumstances the Soviet hope is that the Arab states would then use their collective pressure against Israel's supporters, especially the United States. The ideal scenario for Moscow, and one that Soviet commentators have frequently referred to, was the situation during the 1973 Arab-Israeli war when virtually all the Arab states supported the war effort against Israel, while also imposing an oil embargo against the United States.

As is well known, not only did the oil embargo create domestic difficulties for the United States, it caused serious problems in the NATO alliance, a development that was warmly welcomed by Moscow. Unfortunately for the USSR, however, this "anti-Imperialist" Arab unity was created not by Soviet efforts, but by the diplomacy of Egyptian President Anwar Sadat, and when Sadat changed his policies and turned toward the United States, the "anti-imperialist" Arab unity sought by the USSR fell apart. Nonetheless, so long as Soviet leaders think in terms of such Leninist categories of thought as "united fronts" ("anti-imperialist" Arab unity, in Soviet parlance, is merely another way of describing a united front of Arab governmental and nongovernmental forces) and so long as there is a deep underlying psychological drive for unity in the Arab world, Moscow can be expected to continue to pursue this overall strategy as a long-term goal.

The primary Middle Eastern concern for Moscow when Gorbachev took power was the formation of an Arab alignment consisting of King Hussein of Jordan, Yasser Arafat's wing of the PLO, and President Hosni Mubarak of Egypt. The Soviet problem was that Egypt's isolation in the Arab world was ending; as a signatory of the Camp David peace process, which Moscow strongly opposed, Egypt would move further out of diplomatic isolation in the Arab world as a result of Mubarak's ties to Arafat and King Hussein, while Moscow's main Arab ally, Syria, would be further isolated.

As 1985 began, the Arab world could be said to be divided into three main camps. On the one hand was what might be called the Egyptian camp consisting of Egypt, Sudan,[5] Somalia, and Oman. All four states had either openly, in the case of Egypt, or tacitly supported Camp David; all had denounced the Soviet invasion and occupation of Afghanistan; all had major military relationships with the United States, which included joint military exercises.

On the other end of the spectrum was the so-called Front of Steadfastness and Confrontation, which bitterly opposed Camp David and was generally supportive of Soviet foreign policy. Syria, Libya, and South Yemen were the main countries in this alignment, although elements of the PLO and Algeria also shared some of its policy perspectives, and received arms from Moscow. Nonetheless, there were serious divisions within the Steadfastness Front, with both Algeria and most of the PLO opposing Libyan and Syrian aid to Iran in the Iran-Iraq war; Algeria clearly unhappy with Libya's signing of an alliance with its enemy, Morocco, in 1984; and Arafat and Assad bitter enemies.

In the middle of the Arab spectrum were such countries as Saudi Arabia, Jordan, Kuwait, Tunisia, Morocco, Iraq, the United Arab Emirates, and the Yemen Arab Republic (North Yemen). Receiving weapons from East and West, they had in common with the Egyptian-led camp an aversion to the Soviet invasion of Afghanistan, but they shared with the Steadfastness Front an opposition to Camp David, although they seemed more willing to ultimately sign a peace agreement with Israel than were Steadfastness Front members Syria, Libya, and South Yemen. Moscow's worry was that this centrist grouping was moving toward Egypt, and Jordan's decision in September 1984 (just as Shimon Peres was becoming prime minister of Israel's National Unity Government) to resume diplomatic relations with Egypt and the frequent meetings between Mubarak and Hussein (which led to such cooperative projects as a ferry service and even military maneuvers)[6], as well as between Arafat and Mubarak, seemed to indicate that such a movement had begun. Egypt's readmission to the Islamic Conference in 1984 and to the Islamic Development Bank in early February 1985 (and later to the Arab Sports Union in August 1985)[7] were further indications of such a trend.

Consequently, the Soviet reaction to the mid-February announcement in Amman of the Hussein-Arafat agreement on a joint negotiating strategy for the Middle East peace process, and its rapid endorsement by Mubarak, was a very negative one. While not immediately attacking Jordan or Egypt directly — Moscow still had hopes of ultimately weaning both away from the United States, (a Soviet-Jordanian arms agreement had just been signed)[8] — the Soviet displeasure was clear as Moscow feared that the United States would again be able to engineer a Middle East peace settlement without the participation of the USSR, and that Moscow's long-hoped-for Middle East peace conference, where it would sit as an equal with the United States, would not take place.

This was the rather negative Middle East situation that greeted Gorbachev as he took power in March 1985. The new Soviet leader's signals to Israel, therefore, should primarily be understood as an attempt to gain entry for Moscow in a Middle East peace process, which by March seemed well underway. In addition, the new Soviet leader much wanted a summit meeting with the United States, and given both Moscow's overestimation of Jewish influence in the United States and the close American Jewish tie to Israel,[9] a major Soviet gesture toward Israel was probably viewed in Moscow as a means of improving its image in the United States prior to the summit, where Moscow hoped such key issues as strategic arms agreements, and trade and technology exchanges would be discussed.

The signals sent by Moscow covered two central areas: the reestablishment of diplomatic relations between the Soviet Union and Israel, and an increase in the number of Soviet Jews allowed to leave the USSR. Interestingly enough, the Soviet gestures to Israel were to come despite a series of Israeli actions that bound the Jewish state even more tightly to the United States, including its signing of strategic cooperation and free trade agreements with the United States and its professed willingness to allow the United States to build a Voice of America transmitter on Israeli territory and to enter into the American Star Wars defense scheme.

The first major Soviet gesture came in mid-May, two months after Gorbachev took power. The signal came in the form of *Izvestia's* publication of Israeli President Chaim Herzog's congratulatory message to the

USSR on the fortieth anniversary of the allied victory over Nazi Germany. What was significant about the *Izvestia* publication was not only that it was the first time such a message from an Israeli leader had been published since relations were broken in 1967, but also that the message itself contained a denunciation of the Nazis as Herzog declared that the Jewish people "will never forget the huge contribution of the Red Army in the final destruction of the Nazi monsters in Europe and her assistance in the freeing of Jews who survived the concentration camps."[10] Given the fact that Soviet propaganda media had long equated Israeli and Nazi activities, and had even accused Zionists of actively aiding the Nazis,[11] the publication of this message seemed to be a major reversal of Soviet policy on this issue.[12]

Following a late May visit to Washington by King Hussein who, perhaps both as a sop to Moscow, and as a means of diplomatically protecting his flank, continued to call for an international conference on a Middle East peace settlement with Moscow's participation, State Department spokesman Edward Djerejian listed a number of specific actions that Moscow could take to show that it was ready to play a "constructive role" in the Middle East peace process. These included resuming full diplomatic relations with Israel, ending Soviet anti-Semitic propaganda, improving the treatment of Soviet Jews, and ending arms aid to militias in Lebanon.[13] Interestingly enough, however, while Soviet Middle East specialist Yevgeny Primakov, director of the Soviet Institute of Oriental Studies, in an interview in Moscow predicted that the USSR would not accept "one side setting preconditions for the other to meet," and stated that it was premature to ask the USSR to recognize Israel as a condition for holding an international conference on the Middle East,[14] Gorbachev was to move in just such a direction.

In mid-July with Arafat and Hussein calling for an Arab summit, and with a review session commemorating the tenth anniversary of the signing of the Helsinki agreements due to open at the beginning of August — a session that was likely to see the issue of Soviet Jewry raised — Gorbachev apparently decided that a major discussion between Soviet and Israeli diplomats on the subject of both renewing diplomatic relations and increasing the emigration of Soviet Jews to Israel was in order. The meeting took place in Paris at the home of Israeli-born pianist Daniel Barenbaum between the Israeli Ambassador to France, Ovadia Sofer, and his Soviet counterpart, Yull Vorontsov. Sofer's description of the meeting was leaked to Israeli radio, which promptly broadcast it. Given the importance of the Israeli radio broadcast — even though Moscow publicly denied any deal was made[15] — it is reprinted here in full:

There has been a signal — and not just a minor one — from the Soviet Union. This time it is a real flashing light. The Israeli ambassador to Paris recently met with the Soviet ambassador to France. The Soviets, under a fresh, new administration, are hinting about a package deal for the emigration of Jews. They are ready for a compromise over the Golan Heights. There is a hint about the renewal of diplomatic relations, and a genuine chance for high-level meetings. Our political correspondent Shim'on Schiffer has the details of this disclosure:

[Schiffer] I should say at once that reference is to a Soviet initiative — not a coincidental meeting at a cocktail party, but a lengthy meeting that lasted for more than two hours and took place on Monday of this week. It was full of political content and genuine signals. Ambassador Sofer went to the meeting, which was held in Daniel Barenboim's residence, provided with directives he had received from Israel. The Soviet ambassador, Yully Vorontsov, admitted that he is the candidate to replace his country's ambassador to Washington. He is leaving for Moscow next week and will be prepared to convey to the Kremlin leaders the details of the Israeli position.

When will relations between the two countries be renewed, Sofer asked? The Soviet ambassador said the relations had been severed following the Israeli conquest of the territories, and so Israel would have to do something about this. I quote: There must be some sort of movement on the matter of the Golan Heights; negotiations with Syria would supply the Soviet Union with a pretext for the renewal of relations. We will not oppose a section of the Golan Heights remaining in Israeli possession, if this is achieved through negotiations with Syria. Ambassador Sofer asked if it was a coincidence that the Soviet speaker was not mentioning Judea and Samaria. No, it is no coincidence, the Soviet ambassador said. In any event, he added, the severance of relations with Israel was a grave error and a sensitive, ill-considered move that harmed the Soviet Union.

It seems that the clearest and most amazing things were said on the issue of Soviet Jewry. The problem of Jewish emigration from the Soviet Union can be solved within the framework of a package deal, in return for an end to the anti-Soviet propaganda Israel is conducting in the United States and Europe, the Soviet speaker said. We would be prepared for the Jews to leave if we are promised that they will emigrate to Israel, not the United States. The Soviet Union fears a brain drain to the West. The Soviet ambassador admitted that mistakes had been made by the authorities in their attitude toward refuseniks. Those errors, he said, originated in the behavior of Soviet Jewry and the pressures applied to the Soviet Union. As for the continuation of the political process, the Soviet ambassador again raised the proposal regarding the convening of an international conference with the participation of the Soviet Union. My country, he said, cannot agree to negotiations under the sole aegis of the Americans. On the Palestinian Issue, the Soviet ambassador said it was hard to see how it would be possible to find a solution to the Palestinian problem while also satisfying Israel's security demands. Vorontsov repeated his emphasis on the Soviet Union's commitment to Israel's existence, while expressing concern at the continued freeze in the peace process. Ovadya Sofer asked the Soviet ambassador to organize an urgent meeting between Vice Prime Minister Yitzhak Shamir and his new Soviet counterpart, as early as the U.N. General Assembly session in New York in September.

The report on the meeting was received with satisfaction and amazement in Jerusalem, while, at the same time, it confirmed earlier evaluations that Mikhail Gorbachev's rise to power in the Soviet Union presages a change in the relations between Israel and the Soviet Union. However, and this is yet another evaluation, the policymakers here will — after having studied the material — have to deliberate and make far-reaching decisions on these issues.[16]

In evaluating the Israeli ambassador's description of the meeting, it is of course necessary to treat it with some skepticism, given the normal tendency of ambassadors to portray themselves and their countries in the best light in such dispatches. Nonetheless, the fact that Dobrynin was soon to leave Washington (although he was not replaced by Vorontsov) and that Vorontsov repeated a number of Soviet Middle East positions, including the call for an international conference with Moscow's participation, does lend some credence to the report. In any case, the most interesting aspect of Vorontsov's discussion is that he seemed to indicate that diplomatic relations could be restored if there was at least a partial Israeli withdrawal on the Golan Heights, and that large-scale emigration of Soviet Jews could take place if they emigrated to Israel and not the United States, and if Israel ended the anti-Soviet propaganda it was undertaking in the United States and Europe.

Yet, the Soviet hint of renewed relations, while welcome in Israel, was received in a highly negative way by Moscow's Arab allies, especially Syria. Syria, the USSR's main bastion in the Arab world, was incensed that the USSR would consider renewing ties with Israel while even part of the Golan Heights seized during the 1967 war remained in Israeli hands. As a result, the USSR in both official visits and radio broadcasts to the Arab world repeated the old Soviet position that diplomatic relations would not be restored until Israel gave up all the land conquered in 1967.[17] At the same time, however, Moscow continued to hint to Israel that relations could be restored if

Israel agreed to Moscow's inclusion in a Middle East peace conference.[18] For his part, Israeli Prime Minister Shimon Peres expressed a keen interest in improving ties with the USSR, although he fluctuated in his comments, one day demanding restored diplomatic relations as the price for Moscow's entry into the Middle East peace process, but on the next stating that it would be enough if the USSR allowed large numbers of Soviet Jews to emigrate to Israel.[19]

Moscow's primary concern at the time of the Sofer-Vorontsov meeting was that the Arafat-Hussein agreement might receive acceptance from the centrist Arab states, and this concern was heightened in late July when an Arab summit was scheduled for Casablanca in early August. While Syria and its Steadfastness Front allies (the PDRY, Algeria, and Libya) and its protectorate, Lebanon, boycotted the session, the fact remained that both Hussein and Arafat were actively seeking support for their agreement at the conference, while Egypt was also hoping that the summit would restore it to full membership in the Arab League.[20] Meanwhile, the United States continued to play an active role in the Arab world; on the one hand it continued its efforts to form a Jordanian-Palestinian negotiating team acceptable to Israel, and on the other hand it sought to reinforce its ties to Egypt, Jordan, Oman, and Somalia by carrying out joint military exercises with them.

The summit, however, did not meet the needs of Hussein and Arafat, or the United States. While it did not denounce the Amman accord, neither did it endorse it. The absence of both King Fahd and Saddam Hussein (lower-ranking Saudi and Iraqi figures took their places) were factors limiting the effectiveness of the meeting. The most the summit would do in its final communique was to "take note" of the Amman agreement by stating that the summit "viewed with understanding the explanations it has been given by King Hussein and Yasser Arafat who consider that the Jordanian-Palestinian Initiative is in conformity with the resolution of the 1982 Arab Summit of Fez."[21] Moscow may also have been pleased that the summit established a committee to seek reconciliations between Iraq and Syria, and between Syria and Jordan,[22] thus indicating not only that the centrist Arabs attending the summit did not want to alienate Syria by endorsing the Amman accord, but also that the Arabs were again trying to restore a semblance of unity, which Moscow hoped would be the "anti-imperialist" unity it had long sought. Finally, the fact that Egypt was not readmitted to the Arab League by the summit was also pleasing to Moscow.[23]

Nonetheless, the Soviet media continued to express concern that United States efforts to obtain an accord between Israel and a Jordanian-

Palestinian negotiating team might succeed.[24] Perhaps for this reason, Moscow made yet another gesture to Israel, this time in the form of an agreement between its close Eastern European ally, Poland, and Israel, whereby the two countries agreed in principle to establish "Interest sections" in foreign embassies in each other's capitals — the first stage in the process of reestablishing diplomatic relations.[25] While Moscow was not yet resuming diplomatic ties itself, this was a clear gesture that it was prepared to do so, and Gorbachev, during his visit to Paris in early October, noted "as far as reestablishing relations (with Israel) is concerned, I think the faster the situation is normalized in the Middle East, the faster it will be possible to look at this question."[26] The announced resumption of low-level diplomatic relations with Poland, World Jewish Congress President Edgar Bronfman's visit to Moscow carrying a message from Peres, Peres's meeting with Soviet Foreign Minister Edward Shevardnadze at the United Nations in October, and Gorbachev's visit to Paris reinforced the rumors circulating in Israel that Moscow was about to release 20,000 Soviet Jews and allow them to be flown directly to Israel on French planes.[27]

The momentum toward even a partial Soviet-Israeli rapprochement — if that indeed was Gorbachev's goal — was slowed and then stopped, however, as the peace process fell by the wayside in the face of an escalation of Middle East terrorism. While Moscow itself was to suffer both embarassment and physical loss as a result of the Middle East terrorism (one of its diplomats was murdered in Beirut), the end result was that the peace process, centered around negotiations between Israel and a Jordanian-Palestinian delegation, was halted, a development from which Moscow was to profit diplomatically.

The root of the problem lay in the fact that Arafat, in an effort to maintain credibility with the hard-liners in his organization, stressed the escalation of "armed struggle" (terrorism) soon after concluding the Amman agreement with King Hussein.[28] For his part Peres was vulnerable politically for even considering negotiations with Palestinians close to the PLO, and he was frequently attacked by the Likud party, his rival in the National Unity Government, for being "soft on terrorism" and "soft on the PLO." As a result, when a wave of terrorist murders struck Israel during the spring and summer of 1985, Peres not only found it increasingly difficult to negotiate with any Palestinian closely linked to the PLO, he also came under increasing pressure to retaliate. When three Israelis were murdered in Cyprus at the end of September by terrorists who proclaimed they were fighting for the Palestinian cause, Peres authorized an attack on PLO headquarers in Tunis on October 1, 1985, perhaps signalling to Arafat that if the PLO leader wished to fight while he was negotiating, Israel could play the same game.

Moscow lost little time in exploiting the Israeli attack to try to undermine the United States position in the Middle East, and once again appealed for Arab unity against Israel and the United States, as anger in the Arab world erupted over the attack, for which the United States, as well as Israel, was blamed in a number of Arab capitals. Even before the uproar over the Israeli attack had died down, another event from which Moscow was to profit diplomatically took place. This was the hijacking of the cruise ship Achille Lauro and the murder of a Jewish passenger, Leon Klinghoffer, by a PLO faction headed by Mohammed Abbas, a hard-line PLO leader who was linked to Arafat because of their mutal opposition to Syrian leader Hafiz Assad.[29] The hijacking had two major diplomatic benefits for Moscow. In the first place, the action of the United States in forcing down an Egyptian plane carrying the hijackers and Abbas inflamed United States relations not only with Egypt but also with Italy, where the plane was forced to land, when Italian Premier Bettino Craxi allowed Abbas to leave his country. While subsequent United States aid to Egypt when one of its aircraft was hijacked to Malta somewhat smoothed over the strain in United States-Egyptian relations, there was no question that serious diplomatic damage had been done, a development that Moscow evidently hoped would lead to a weakening of United States-Egyptian relations.

In addition to profiting from the strain in United States-Egyptian relations, Moscow also obtained diplomatic benefit from Shimon Peres's policy change on the Middle East peace process. Apparently concluding that Arafat and the PLO had discredited themselves badly in the United States by the Achille Lauro episode[30] as well as by Arafat's failure to go ahead with a previously arranged agreement with British Prime Minister Margaret Thatcher,[31] under which British Foreign Secretary Sir Geoffrey Howe would meet in London with a joint Palestinian-Jordanian delegation that contained PLO members if it agreed to recognize Israel, Peres sought to sidestep the PLO and make a direct deal with Jordan. Realizing that Hussein had become displeased with Arafat because of the diplomatic debacle in London, but also that the king needed some sort of diplomatic cover for his dealings with Israel, at the United Nations on October 21 Peres proposed Israel—Jordanian talks under "international auspices."[32] Unfortunately for Peres, however, King Hussein was not to opt for the Israeli offer and moved instead to improve relations with Syria; as the king in a major speech at the opening of Jordan's parliament on Novermber 2nd noted, the Saudi-sponsored meetings between Jordanian Prime Minister Zaid

Rifal and Syrian Foreign Minister Abdul Raul Qasim over the past two months had marked a "good beginning" toward improving Syrian-Jordanian relations.[33] Indeed, relations were to rapidly improve in November and December with Hussein publicly apologizing for Moslem Brotherhood attacks on Syria, which had used Jordan as a base of operations, and visiting Syria at the end of December in the first meeting between the two leaders in Damascus in six years.

As the chances for a Middle East peace settlement brokered by the United States receded, Moscow took a much harder line with Israel as the mid-November summit between Reagan and Gorbachev in Geneva apprached, despite reported calls by Egypt and Jordan for Moscow to restore diplomatic relations with Israel as a way to advance prospects for Middle East peace talks.[34] Indeed, on the eve of the summit, a Soviet government spokesman, Albert Vlasov, demanded as the price of renewed relations that Israel agree not only to allow the USSR to participate in the international peace conference, but to allow the PLO to participate as well — clearly something Peres was unwilling to accept.[35] Perhaps because of this condition, Peres shifted his position, and now stated that the resumption of Soviet Jewish emigration from the USSR was much more important than the restoration of diplomatic ties. "If they agree to renew Allya," he stated, "we shall waive our objections to their taking part in an international conference on the Middle East."[36]

Peres thus presented Moscow with an interesting choice. As far as its position in the Arab world is concerned, it is far less costly for Moscow to release Soviet Jews than it is for it to reestablish ties with Israel, and Moscow has long wanted to participate in an international conference on an Arab-Israeli settlement. On the other hand, however, it was doubtful whether the USSR would settle for just a symbolic role in an international conference — the most Israel seemed to be ready to concede — in return for sharply increasing the number of Jews allowed to leave the Soviet Union. Indeed, Moscow took an increasingly hard line toward Israel after the summit.

Yet, Moscow's harder line policy toward Israel may have had additional causes as well. Arab leaders, perhaps remembering the 1972 Nixon-Brezhnev summit, seemed concerned that a superpower deal might be worked out at their expense;[37] and Reagan's presummit demand for linkage between an arms control agreement and Soviet behavior in the Third World, may have heightened Soviet determination to prove that no such deal had taken place.[38] Indeed, in a spate of articles appearing in the Soviet media at the time of the summit, including Arabic language radio broadcasts and *Novosti* statements distributed in Beirut, the USSR dismissed as "fabrications and lies" claims that Arab interests would be compromised at Geneva.[39] An Arabic language broadcast, by a senior Soviet commentator, Alexander Bovin, sought to put an end to Arab concerns about any such deal:

> Themes are put forward on the possibility of a new Yalta for the sharing of influence in the Middle and Near East during the Geneva summit meeting. These fabrications and accusations are aimed at giving rise to the idea of a possible Soviet-U.S. collusion at the expense of the Arabs' interests. Despite the fact that the Soviet Union has firmly refuted all this, more unfounded rumors are being spread on the possibility of a Soviet-Israeli resumption of relations even if Israel does not relinquish its expansionist and aggressive line.

> Western propaganda is spreading rumors to the effect that the Soviet Union is ready to allow 500,000 Soviet Jews to immigrate to Israel upon a request from the United States. All these fabrications and accusations are aimed at making the Arabs no longer sure of Soviet support and thus compelling them to relinquish the struggle against the conspiracies of imperialism and Zionism and for the achievement of the Arabs' interests. This is the aim of Washington and Tel Aviv, who are trying to cast doubts between the Arab and Soviet leadership and are planning schemes of separate deals with the Israeli invaders under U.S. aegis. It should be pointed out that the weakening of the struggle of the Arab front against imperialism by way of making fabrications against the Soviet Union and thereby rupturing Soviet-Arab friendship is a well-know method of imperialism, Zionism, and Arab reactionaries.[40]

Nonetheless, despite Moscow's hardening rhetoric, and the slow pace of the negotiations between Israel and Poland on the setting up of interest sections, Peres did not give up hope. Indeed, the attendance of Israel's President Chaim Herzog at the National Convention of Israel's Communist party in early December, the first time an Israeli President had ever attended such a function, was a clear gesture to Moscow that Jerusalem was interested in continuing a dialogue with the USSR.[41] The head of the Soviet delegation to the party conference, Mikhail Menashev, stated, however, that Herzog's attendance at the convention would not influence Russia's policy on the exit of Soviet Jews or hasten the renewal of diplomatic ties.[42] Then, when King Hussein, in mid-February 1986, denounced the PLO leadership for failing to move ahead in the peace process, the split between Arafat and Hussein intensified and Soviet fears of an American-orchestrated Arab-Israeli peace agreement receded further, at least for the short term.

Under the circumstances it appeared unlikely that Moscow would have to satisfy either of Israel's demands because the possibility of a Middle East peace conference greatly diminished.

Meanwhile, notwithstanding Moscow's flirtation with Israel, the condition of Soviet Jewry worsened during Gorbachev's first year. Despite the release of such well-know Soviet refuseniks as Anatoly Shcharansky, Grigory and Isal Goldstein, and Ilya Essas, the number of Soviet Jews allowed to leave the USSR plummeted, reaching a low of 47 during March 1986 — the anniversary of Gorbachev's coming to power. At the same time, Soviet pressure on Jews seeking to emigrate was stepped up and nine Jewish activists were arrested and imprisoned.

The drop in the Soviet Jewish exodus in March 1986 may have reflected the decline in Soviet interest in the Middle East, as did Gorbachev's speech to the 27th Party Congress of the Communist Party of the Soviet Union. If one takes Gorbachev's speech as a programmatic listing of his priorities, the Third World was low on his list and the Arab-Israeli conflict barely mentioned. This was in clear contrast with Brezhnev's speeches at previous party congresses, where the Middle East received a great deal of attention and certain Arab countries, such as Syria, were singled out for praise. Gorbachev did, however, refer to the Middle East as one of the world's "hotbeds of the danger of war."[43]

Nonetheless, if Gorbachev was seeking to downplay the importance of the Middle East, the region, and particularly the Arab-Israeli conflict, soon demonstrated its importance for Moscow again. In the first place, Syrian-Israeli relations again heated up in 1986; an increasing number of press reports indicated that war would break out between the two countries. Contributing to the heightened tension were the Syrian decision to construct a series of artillery and tank emplacements near Israel's security zone in South Lebanon, Israel's forcing down of a Libyan plane that contained high-ranking Syrian Ba'ath party officials (instead of the PLO terrorists Israel was seeking), and perhaps most important of all, the direct Syrian linkage to terrorist attempts to blow up Israeli civilian airplanes in London and Madrid.

The Syrian linkage with terrorism was not the only circumstance that posed problems for Gorbachev. After a minicrisis in January 1986, when the United States blamed Libya for terrorist attacks in Rome and Vienna in late December 1985, two military confrontations between the United States and Libya took place (in March and April 1986). During the United States-Libyan crisis of January 1986, the then-Soviet Foreign Ministry spokesman, Vladimir Lomeiko, in refusing to answer a press conference question on what the stand of the USSR would be if the United States attacked Libya, noted only that Soviet actions were aimed at "preventing conflicts," not at "constructing scenarios for their escalation."[44] The same Lomeiko, at a Moscow press briefing on March 25 after the first United States attack on Libya, noted only that the USSR had provided "moral and political support" to the Libyan people, and would take "all measures appropriate within the framework of existing treaties."[45] The absence of any promised *military* support in Lomeiko's statement and the fact that the USSR and Libya still had no formal treaty pledging Moscow to come to Kaddafi's aid, demonstrated, however, that the USSR was not willing to back up Kaddafi with more than words, and this was again shown during and after the more extensive American raid on April 15. Indeed, the most that Moscow would do at the time was postpone (and only temporarily) a scheduled Shultz-Shevardnadze meeting — a minimal action that could not have impressed many Arab states.

In the aftermath of the United States bombing of Libya for its alleged terrorist activities, Moscow could not be certain the United States would refrain from taking action against Syria, another sponsor of terrorism. An American — or an American-backed Israeli — punitive strike against Syria, would again raise serious questions of Soviet credibility if Moscow did not aid its Middle Eastern ally in such a situation (especially after its failure to aid Libya). On the other hand, if Moscow went to Syria's aid, there would be a very real possibility of a superpower confrontation. Given these unpalatable alternatives, Gorbachev seems to have decided to move diplomatically to avert the possibility of such a clash by publicly cautioning both Libya and Syria against terrorism in order not to give "the imperialists" any pretexts for attacks, and also by negotiating seriously with Israel to arrange consular-level talks in Helsinki, Finland and also acceding to Israel's demand to make the talks public.[46] The latter diplomatic ploy, Moscow may well have felt, would deter an Israeli attack on Syria, lest it harm a possible improvement of Soviet-Israeli relations, which in turn held out the possibility of an increase in the number of Soviet Jews being allowed to leave the USSR.

A second Middle East development, which may have contributed to Moscow's decision to initiate public contacts with Israel, was the USSR's efforts to play a role in the Middle East peace process. Following Jordanian King Hussein's split with Arafat in February 1986, Moscow sought to exploit the new diplomatic situation by calling for a preparatory committee made up of the United Nations Security Council's five permanent members to prepare for an international conference on the Middle East.[47] When in late July, however, Israeli Prime Minister Shimon Peres and Moroccan King Hassan had a surprise meeting in Morocco, Moscow may have become concerned that it would one again be left on the diplomatic sidelines as a major peace initiative unfolded. (The last surprise summit, it will be recalled, was Sadat's visit to Jerusalem in November 1977, which led to the Camp David agreements less than a year later.) To avert this possibility, therefore, Moscow may also have agreed to public diplomatic talks with Israel.

A third contributing factor behind Moscow's request for consular talks may have been the Soviet desire to improve ties with the United States. The Soviet announcement of consular talks with Israel on August 4 coincided, apparently not accidentally, with the announcement of the scheduling of the September 19 and 20 meeting between United States Secretary of State George Shultz and Soviet Foreign Minister Edward Shevardnadze to prepare for a United States-Soviet summit. (The earlier meeting had been postponed by Moscow, it will be remembered, because of the American bombing of Libya in April.) The nuclear disaster in Chernobyl, the precipitous drop in world oil prices (more than 50 percent of Soviet hard currency earnings come from oil and natural gas sales), Gorbachev's efforts to restructure the Soviet economy, and the major eonomic difficulties facing the USSR were all factors moving the Soviet leadersip toward an arms control agreement that would prevent another expensive spiralling of the arms race. For this reason Gorbachev sought a second summit with the United States, and, given Moscow's tendency to overestimate Jewish influence in the United States, the new Soviet leader may well have felt that the gesture to Israel would help pave the way for the summit.

Nonetheless, the Soviet-Israeli talks in Helsinki, the first such official diplomatic negotiations between the two countries since the 1967 war, did not immediately produce the results either side said it wanted, although the symbolic significance of the talks was probably much more important than their content. While the Soviets wished to send a team of officials to inventory Soviet property (primarily owned by the Russian-Orthodox church) in Israel, the Israeli delegation, under heavy domestic pressure from such individuals as Moshe Arens and Anatoly Sharansky, raised the issue of Soviet Jewry at the talks, and the meeting ended after ninety minutes.[48] Nonetheless, the very fact that the talks were held, and the fact that one month later Israeli Prime Minister Peres and Soviet Foreign Minster Shevardnadze held detailed (and apparently cordial) negotiatons at the United Nations,[49] as well as subsequent meetings between the Soviet and Israeli ambassadors to the United States, all indicated that the Soviet Union was keeping alive its contacts with Israel.

Following the Shevardnadze-Peres meeting came the Reykjavik summit between Reagan and Gorbachev, the second summit between the Soviet and American leaders in less than two years. Although no arms control agreement was reached, primarily because Gorbachev linked such an agreement to the termination of the American Strategic Defense Initiative, nonetheless the issue of Soviet Jewry was emphasized by Reagan at the summit,[50] thus reminding the Soviet leader that one of the ways Moscow could demonstrate its desire for an improved relationship with the United States was to permit an increase in the number of Soviet Jews allowed to leave the USSR. Secretary of State Shultz's participation in a Seder with Refuseniks during his Moscow visit in mid-April 1987 made the same point.

Soon after the Reykjavik summit, for which Reagan was severely criticized both in the United States and western Europe for inept planning and insufficient consultation, came another blow to the Reagan Administration — the Iran-Contra scandal. This scandal, among other things, put the United States on the diplomatic defensive in the Middle East; many of the Arab states which had looked to the United States for protection against Iran became bewildered at the "arms for hostages" diplomacy carried on by the United States with Iran. This created somewhat of a vacuum in Middle East diplomacy, and Moscow sought to exploit this situation by stepping up its efforts to achieve an international conference on the Middle East, to be arranged by a preparatory conference of the five permanent members of the United Nations Security Council. By early 1987, the USSR had received support for its position from such diverse groups as the nonaligned movement and the United Nations General Assembly; at the end of January 1987, Moscow also received the endorsement of the Islamic Conference.

The idea of an international conference was also increasingly welcome to Shimon Peres, who after stepping down as prime minister from the National Unity Government in October had now become Foreign Minister and vice prime minister. In addition, the United States, with an Irangate-weakened administration, came under increased pressure from Arab states such as Egypt and Jordan to agree to an international conference. In part to deflect such pressure, Prime Minister Shamir traveled to the United States in mid-February; he branded the idea of an international conference "a Soviet-inspired notion supported by radical Arabs."[51] (Shamir also, unsuccessfully, sought to get the United States government to deny refugee status to Soviet Jews so as to deter them from coming to the United States.) At the same time, however, Peres went off to Cairo, where he and Egyptian President Hosni Mubarak called for an international conference in which Israel would have the right to approve the participants. Their call for an international conference was reinforced by the European Economic Community, which also called for such a conference.[52]

For his part Shamir stepped up his criticism of the international conference further as his office, on March 11, published a formal statement repudiating the idea of such a conference. In this document he was particularly critical of Soviet efforts to achieve an international conference, claiming that rumors of Soviet efforts to improve Soviet-Israeli relations were essentially "disinformation" and noting that Moscow's goal all along had been a total Israeli withdrawal from territories captured in the 1967 war.[53]

As the internal Israeli debate on an international conference heated up, Moscow began to step up its signals to Israel to demonstrate its desire for improved ties. Although a more restrictive emigration decree went into effect on January 1 that limited emigration to first degree relatives (mother, father, sister, brother, child) of people abroad, statements by a number of Soviet officials indicated that emigration would rise, and indeed after averaging less than 100 per month in 1986, emigration shot up to 470 in March 1987 and 717 in April, with a *Novosti* official, Sergei Ivanko, predicting an exodus of 10-12,000 by the end of the year.[54] In this context two major non-Israeli Jewish leaders, Morris Abram, president of both the National Conference on Soviet Jewry and the conference of Presidents of Major Jewish Organizations, and Edgar Bronfman, president of the World Jewish Congress, journeyed to Moscow in late March and met with a number of Soviet officials, including Anatoly Dobrynin, the former Soviet ambassador to the United States, who was now the director of the International Department of the CPSU Central Committee. According to Abram, they received "assurances" from the USSR in a number of areas pertaining to Soviet Jewry in return for their willingness to consider changes to the Jackson-Vanik and Stevenson amendments. Given the importance of this meeting, the text of the "assurances" in the Abram report is listed below:[55]

1. Soviet Jews with exit visas for Israel will travel via Rumania on flights to be established.

2. All Refuseniks and their families will be allowed to emigrate to Israel within a one-year period, except for legitimate national security cases. A procedure will be established, however, to review previous visa denials on national security grounds. This procedure may involve officials on a level as high as the supreme soviet.

3. First degree relatives may emigrate for family reunification within an established time frame. There may be flexibility within the framework of the current narrow interpretation of "first degree relative."

4. Cases of those Refusniks recently placed in a "never allowed to emigrate" category will be reviewed.

5. All Jewish religious books may be imported into the USSR, and a recommended list of books will be submitted.

6. Synagogues will be opened in all sites where there is a demonstrated need.

7. Soviet Jews will be allowed greater access to rabbinical training. Some may even be allowed to study in the United States.

8. The teaching of Hebrew in school or synagogue settings will be considered together with similar restrictions applied to other religious groups.

9. A kosher restaurant will be opened in Moscow, and liberal provisions will be made for ritual slaughter.

The Bronfman-Abram mission got a mixed reaction in Israel. While Peres warmly endorsed it, Shamir deprecated its value, and Soviet Jewry activists such as Anatoly Sharansky, Lev Elbert and Yurl Shtern, fearing that once the 10,000 refusniks were allowed to leave the gates would close permanently, denounced it. Elbert claimed it was a "trade of 3,500 families for 2 million people waiting to leave."[56]

In arranging the meeting with Abram and Bronfman (although subsequently denying that any "deal" had been made)[57], Moscow apparently had two goals. In the first place, with a new summit on the horizon because Gorbachev had "decoupled" SDI from other arms agreements, and with the Soviet leader now energetically pushing his plan for an intermediate-range nuclear arms agreement, the sharp increase in the number of Soviet Jews allowed to leave the USSR, the promise of a still greater exodus inherent in the Bronfman-Abram visit, and the Soviet decision to free almost all the jailed prisoners of Zion (those imprisoned for wanting to go to Israel) all clearly had major public relations value in the United States. In addition, however, it also gave political ammunition to Peres, who saw in the increase emigration the price that Moscow was paying to qualify for attendance at an international conference, a price Peres had cited back at the time of the first Reagan-Gorbachev summit in 1985. For his part, Shamir sought to counter this development by formally separating the issue

of Soviet-Israeli relations from the Soviet Jewry issue, a development
that angered Soviet Jewish activists in Israel.[58]

Meanwhile, however, Peres pursued his efforts for an international conference. Meeting for the first time publicly with pro-PLO
Palestinians, Peres claimed that the Palestinians expressed the desire
for Palestinian representatives acceptable to Israel.[59] At the same time
China, also evidently interested in an international conference, began
formal diplomatic talks with Israel at the United Nations.[60] As the
momentum for the conference built, the Soviets announced they again
wanted to send a consular delegation to Israel (albeit without any
reciprocal visit by an Israeli delegation)[61], and Peres stated that Moscow
had already requested visas for the delegation.[62]

In early April, as Peres set out for visits to Spain and to the
Socialist international meeting in Rome, he was actively pushing for
an international conference, and Shamir, who was just as actively opposing the conference publicly stated that he hoped Peres's efforts to
arrange an international peace conference would fail.[63] In an atmosphere of the beginning of a domestic political crisis in Israel, Peres
met with two high-ranking Soviet officials in Rome, Karen Brutents,
deputy director of the International Department of the CPSU, and his
Middle East advisor, Alexander Zotov, in what Peres was later to
describe as "the first serious direct dialogue between the two nations."[64] The meeting created a major political stir in Israel with Peres,
who agreed to keep the details of the six hours of discussions secret,[65]
giving the impression of major progress in the negotiations both in
terms of the exodus of Soviet Jews and in the improvement of Soviet-
Israeli relations. Peres went so far as to assert that "if there is no international peace conference within the next few months, the chance for
peace could slip away."[66] He also leaked the information that the USSR
had spoken against any "coercion" by the superpowers in the context of an international peace conference, or by the conference itself,
that Moscow had agreed to the idea of bilateral talks as part of the
international conference, and that they had spoken of Palestinian
representation at the conference in more general terms than just the
PLO.[67]

The Likud political counterattack was not long in coming. Even
as Peres was meeting with the Soviet officials in Rome, the Likud
chairperson of the Knesset subcommittee on immigration, Uzi Landau,
accused Peres of creating the impression that moves toward an international conference were a condition for Jewish emigration from the
QSSR.[68] Shamir was even sharper in his criticism on April 10, when
he denounced the idea of an international conference as "national

suicide.''[69] The Labor party, in a formal meeting several days later, responded by stating that it would not accept any reduction in the pursuit of the peace process and the resumption of emigration from the USSR, and asserting that Shamir's statement that the idea of an international conference was conceived by Peres during a nightmare, might deal a blow to Israel's vital interests and the government's performance. The Labor party also stated that Peres would submit a ''practical proposal'' for convening an international conference to the government within a few weeks.[70] For its part, the Likud party through a spokesman, Yosi Ahimeir, issued a statement that Israel's stated willingness to take part in the Geneva talks (the international conference planned for 1977) became null and void with the signing of Camp David. The statement also noted that Likud was the first to start the struggle for the sake of Soviet Jewry, and that the (Labor) alignment's claim that Likud is curbing the emigration of Soviet Jewry ''is astonishing and ridiculous.'' Ahimeir also stated that ''there is no connection whatsoever and there should be no connection between emigration and the concession of Judea and Samaria.''[71] Shamir himself, seeking to rally the Soviet Jewish activists in Israel in his political battle to torpedo Peres's plan for an international conference, deprecated Peres's efforts to show there had been a real change in Soviet policy by asserting that

> there are only rumors and piecemeal reports about a few hundred Jews who have been allowed out, but this does not represent a change. If the Soviet Union wants to improve its image and attain a different attitude from the West by changing its policy on Jewish emigration, it must open its gates and allow hundreds of thousands of Jews out without imposing any restrictions and qualifications. We must not sell the Jewish cause cheaply.[72]

While the internal Israeli debate raged in April, Moscow was not idle. On the one hand it was active in helping the PLO achieve a semblance of unity; both PFLP leader George Habash and DFLP leader Naef Hawatmeh agreed once again to cooperate with Arafat at the Algiers meeting of the Palestine National Council, albeit on condition that the PLO break with Jordan and Egypt. (Moscow was apparently rewarded for its efforts with a seat on the PLO executive committee for the pro-Soviet Palestine Communist Party.) While the return of the extremist Habash to the PLO would appear to have lessened the chances for the PLO participating in the peace talks, Gorbachev sought to reemphasize Moscow's interest in improved ties with Israel and to reinforce the idea of a Middle East conference. During his talks with visiting Syrian leader Hafiz Assad in late April, the Soviet leader implicitly warned Assad against going to war because of the danger of nuclear escalation, and asserted that the absence of relations between the USSR and Israel "cannot be considered normal." He went on to say, however, that the reason Soviet-Israeli relations were broken was Israel's "aggression against the Arabs." After repeating Moscow's recognition of Israel's right to a "secure and peaceful existence," Gorbachev also noted that changes in Soviet relations with Israel were possible only if there was a Middle East settlement.[73] Moscow also invited a group of blind Israeli athletes to the USSR as yet another signal of its desire to improve ties.[74]

By now a full-fledged political crisis had erupted in Israel with Peres using the issue of an international conference to try to bring down the National Unity Government. Indeed, Peres went so far as to claim that Israel had "an opportunity that we have not had since the creation of the State of Israel."[75] In using such hypebole, however, he left open some very basic questions about the international conference, such as 1) who would represent the Palestinians (Peres claimed Jordan had agreed to abandon the PLO, which had broken with it at the PNC conference in Algiers, but Jordan denied this.);[76] 2) the role of the USSR at the conference (In none of its public statements had Moscow agreed to the basically ceremonial role Peres had stated for it.); and 3) whether or not the conference as a whole would have to confirm the decision of the bilateral committees (The USSR had continued to indicate it wanted the conference as a whole to approve all bilateral agreements.). In any case, the debate, at least in the short run, became academic; Peres found he did not have sufficient Knesset votes to bring down the government on the issue of an international conference, and by mid-May he announced he was not going to submit the plan for the international conference to the Israeli cabinet.[77] Nonetheless, the Israeli debate about the international conference is a useful point of departure for examining Soviet-Israeli relations and their impact on Soviet Jewry in the first two years of the Gorbachev regime.

Conclusions

In examining Soviet policy toward Israel in the first two years after Gorbachev took power, two central conclusions can be drawn. First there were clearly changes in Soviet policy, although the significance of these changes remains open to debate. Thus, there was a sharp upsurge in Soviet Jewish emigration, reaching 871 in May 1987, the highest monthly total since 1981. In addition, almost all the prisoners of Zion were released from jail, and a number were permitted to go to Israel. Finally, Moscow stepped up its level of contacts with Israel on the formal diplomatic level. This process began in July with a secret meeting between the Israeli and Soviet ambassadors to France, continued in 1986 with public consular-level talks in Helsinki, Finland in August and an extended meeting between Peres and Soviet Foreign Minister Shevardnadze, at the United Nations in September. The pace of contacts increased in 1987 with numerous meetings between Soviet and Israeli officials, and culminated in April with a six-hour meeting between Peres and the Soviet delegation to the socialist international conference, headed by the deputy director of the CPSU's International Department, Karen Brutents, and with Moscow's announcement that it was interested in sending a consular delegation on a visit to Israel. In yet another sign of its interest in improving relations with Israel, Moscow permitted its Warsaw Pact ally, Poland, to reestablish diplomatic relations with Israel, albeit at the low level of diplomatic interest sections.

In seeking to explain these changes under Gorbachev, there appear to be two major factors to consider — Middle East politics and Soviet-American relations. When Gorbachev took office, the Middle East peace process appeared to be well underway as a result of the Hussein-Arafat agreement of February 1985 and United States efforts to broker a Palestinian-Jordanian negotiating team acceptable to Israel. Consequently, Gorbachev, a far more flexible leader than his predecessors, felt an opening to Israel was necessary for Moscow to enter the peace process from which it had been excluded since 1973. While the peace process came to a halt because of the rise in Middle East terrorism and the break between Hussein and Arafat, Moscow continued its contacts with Israel, in part because it was seeking Israeli support for an international peace conference, which Gorbachev, as his predecessors, felt was the best way to resolve the Arab-Israeli conflict (and enhance the Soviet position in the Middle East in the process), and in part because Moscow, seeing an escalation of Syrian-Israeli tension due to Syria's involvement in terrorist attacks against Israeli aircraft, wished to deter a possible Israeli attack on Syria.

By the fall of 1986, the threat of a Syrian-Israeli War had receded, but Moscow now saw the opportunity to go on the diplomatic offensive in the Middle East as the Iran-Contra scandal dealt a major blow to the United States position in the region. Consequently, Gorbachev stepped up Soviet efforts to convene an international conference on the Middle East, and these involved expanded contacts with Israel. Fortunately for Moscow, Soviet interests in convening an international conference were reciprocated by Peres, who saw in such a meeting, particularly after he stepped down as prime minister, a means of bringing down the National Unity Government and moving Israel to new elections.

In advocating such a conference, and claiming important changes had taken place in Soviet policy, such as the increased exodus of Soviet Jews, Moscow's professed willingness to allow the Refuseniks to leave (as noted in the Bronfman-Abram visit to Moscow in March 1987), and the release of the prisoners of conscience, Peres left open a series of questions to which the Soviets, in speaking to various audiences (Arab, Israeli, NATO) had given very ambiguous answers. These included 1) whether Moscow would resume diplomatic relations with Israel once an international conference got underway (what Moscow had hinted to Israel and NATO states), or whether it would refuse to do so until Israel withdrew from the territories captured in 1967 (what it told the Arabs); 2) whether Moscow would be satisfied with merely a formal role at the international conference or whether it would demand the right for the conference as a whole to approve any agreements reached in bilateral talks between Israel and her neighbors; and 3) whether the PLO would participate in the conference. (It appeared unlikely that Moscow, having invested a considerable amount of effort in helping to bring some of the disparate factions of the PLO back together, would throw away the political capital it had gained in the organization by excluding it from such a conference.) To be sure the ambiguity of the situation fitted Moscow's goals perfectly; so long as there was no conference, it could continue to pursue a number of policy options simultaneously (Israel, PLO, Arab states) without having to commit to any one, while giving the impression of being actively involved in the peace process, a policy that was calculated to bring Moscow dividends not only in the Middle East but in the United States, as well. This was the case because Moscow's opening to Israel, along with its policy toward Soviet Jews in 1987, seemed aimed at influencing public opinion in the United States.

Following the CPSU party conference in February 1986, with his position in the party reinforced, Gorbachev set about to undertake major economic and political reforms in the USSR. To succeed in his program, however, particularly at a time of declining hard currency earnings due to the drop in oil prices, Gorbachev clearly wanted to slow down the arms race to free resources for Moscow's lagging economy. He was also interested in getting credits from the United

States, as well as investments in joint enterprises, and this necessitated changes in the Jackson-Vanik and Stevenson amendments. Given the fact that Moscow has long overestimated Jewish influence in the United States, and that it understands the close tie between American Jewry and the State of Israel, Soviet gestures to Israel, coupled with the increase exodus of Soviet Jews, seemed aimed at improving the Soviet image in the United States for arms control purposes and positioning Moscow for United States trade benefits. Indeed, the very fact that National Conference on Soviet Jewry President Morris Abram was invited to Moscow, and that he indicated a willingness to support changes in the Jackson-Vanik and Stevenson amendments if the Soviet Jewish exodus increased, indicated that Moscow was actively using the issue of Soviet Jewry (as well as the appearance of an improved relationship with Israel) to improve its standing in the United States.

A second major conclusion that can be drawn from this study is that the issue of Soviet Jewry has become an important one in Israeli politics. Prior to the advent of Gorbachev, it had been a peripheral issue, with only such fringe politicians as Geula Cohen actively embracing it. By 1986, however, a key Likud leader, Moshe Arens, was involved in the issue, and he and ex-Refusenik Anatoly Sharansky, along with other former Soviet Jews, effectively pressured the Israeli government at the time of the Helsinki talks in August 1986 to take a harder line on Soviet Jewry than it might other wise have done. Then, in March 1987, the issue became even more sailent in Israeli politics; Peres sought to link the issue of the Soviet Jewish exodus to an international peace conference with Moscow obligingly increasing the exodus, and he spoke out more and more forcefully for the conference and even sought to bring down the National Unity Government on this issue. Shamir sought to exploit the rising tide of discontent among Soviet Jewish activists living in Israel by claiming that Peres (and Bonfman and Abram) had "sold out" to Moscow for too few Jews.

In sum, therefore, the first two years of the Gorbchev regime were eventful ones for Israel and the Soviet Jewry movement. Moscow increased contacts with Israel, yet formal diplomatic relations still appeared to be a long way off unless an international peace conference could be unexpectedly convened, and even then Moscow's reestablishment of ties with Israel would by no means be assured. In addition, there was a sharp increase in the exodus of Soviet Jews; a continuation of this increase was hostage to both the diplomatic situation in the Middle East and progress in the arms control negotiations between the United States and the USSR. Thus Gorbachev's first two years offered the appearance of change insofar as Soviet-Israeli relations and the fate of Soviet Jewry were concerned. Whether Gorbachev's endeavor will lead to a genuine change or turn out to be merely a temporary phenomenon is, however, for the future to tell.

[Editor's Note: Professor Freedman adds that in the period since May 1987, while there has been a small improvement in the formal diplomatic relationship between the Soviet Union and Israel with the establishment of consular delegations in the capitals of each country, and a growth in the number and quality of people-to-people exchanges of a cultural, religious, and athletic nature, nonetheless the Soviet Union remains far from establishing full diplomatic relations with Israel, and has exploited the apparent warming of Soviet-Israeli relations primarily to score propaganda points in the Soviet-American relationship.]

CHAPTER SEVEN

Israel in the Middle East

Laurie Mylroie

The year 1988 held promise of the resolution of major conflicts throughout the world—in Afghanistan, the Persian Gulf, the Western Sahara, Cambodia, Namibia, and Angola. Yet no comparable promise of the Arab-Israeli settlement appeared on the horizon, it seemed to have a unique intractability.

Still, important changes were seen in the Arab-Israeli arena. In recent years it almost seemed that the conflict had resolved into a tacit undeclared settlement. Israel enjoyed peace with Egypt and a working relationship with Jordan. A highly effective cease-fire kept the quiet along the Syrian-Israeli frontier, while unilateral Israeli action buffered its northern border from Lebanon's turmoil. Indeed, the apparent premise of United States diplomacy after America's own fiasco in Lebanon was to rely on those developments to maintain a minimal goal—stability.

Yet, sustained Palestinian unrest, beginning in December 1987, put the lie to any complacency about the stability of an undeclared settlement. The Palestinian uprising spurred new diplomatic efforts, while seemingly thwarting chances of their success and threatening to erode the long-term normalization of Israeli-Arab relations.[1]

Thus, Israel's position in the Middle East can be understood in terms of two contradictory trends: 1) the quiet normalization of Israeli-Arab relations; and 2) the continued resistence by some parties to any settlement of the conflict. For, increasingly, the Arab-Israeli conflict is not accurately described as a conflict simply between Arabs and Israelis. After all, Iran is as hostile to Israel as any Arab state.

Rather, the conflict, or at least its intractability, is better understood if a distinction is drawn between two kinds of states—

137

"moderate" status quo regimes, and self-styled revolutionary regimes.[2] The former—Egypt, Morocco, Jordan, and others—have little interest in sustaining the conflict. They tend to seek its resolution and have contributed to the de facto normalization of dealings with Israel. The latter—Syria, Iran, Libya, and other—have every interest in maintaining a state of confrontation with Israel. Their anti-Zionism helps justify their claim to rule and provides a rationale for their ambitions.

This phenomenon is not unique to the Middle East, and is better recognized outside the area. For example George Kennan's 1947 "The Sources of Soviet Conduct," which helped shape United States postwar containment policy, explained Soviet foreign policy as a function of domestic politics.

> The stress laid in Moscow on the menace confronting Soviet society from the world outside its border is founded not in the realities of foreign antagonism but in the necessity of explaining away the maintenance of dictatorial authority at home.[3]

In the Middle East self-styled revolutionary states tend to postulate a Zionist threat "not founded in the realities of foreign antagonism." The perceived threat generates their commitment to maintaining a confrontation with Zionism, while blocking the attempts of others to reach a settlement with Israel.

The Normalization of Arab-Israeli Relations and the Erosion of the Periphery Theory

The periphery theory, the strategic doctrine of Israel's founder, David Ben-Gurion, entailed a view of the Middle East conflict as one between Arabs and Israelis. Fully articulated in the late 1950's, after the rise of Gamal Abdul Nasser, the periphery theory posited the unceasing enmity of the Arab core. The theory called for alliances with the non-Arab states on the "periphery" of the Middle East—Iran, Turkey, and Ethiopia—and alliances with the non-Moslem or non-Arab minorities within the Arab states—the Kurds of Iraq, the Maronite Christians of Lebanon, and so on.[4]

Yet, as will be argued here, the circumstances under which that view was valid have changed in subtle but significant ways. Since the disengagement agreements that followed the 1973 war, there has been a marked erosion of Arab hostility toward Israel. At the same time, new threats to Israel's security have arisen from non-Arab states, while some minorities, long considered key elements in the periphery strategy have proven too weak to be useful allies. Israel's situation, and the persistent intractability of the Arab-Israeli conflict, are better understood as the reflection of the ambitions of radical regimes in the region as they pursue an unceasing rivalry with the moderate states.

Egypt

The 1979 Egyptian-Israeli peace treaty marked a watershed in Israeli-Arab relations. It was Israel's first peace treaty with an Arab state, the Arab state that had long been champion of the confrontation with Israel. As Israel made peace with Egypt, it sacrificed ties with a periphery state that had become radical, Ethiopia, where in 1974 Emperor Halie Selassie had been overthrown.

In the fall of 1977, while hosting the secret talks that led to Sadat's trip to Jerusalem, Morocco's King Hassan complained to Foreign Minister Moshe Dayan of continued Israeli arms sales to Ethiopia.[5] Dayan soon made them public, bringing Israel's dealings with Ethiopia to a sudden halt.[6] In retrospect, it seems Dayan sabotaged the increasingly problematic ties with Ethiopia to promote the peace with Egypt.[7]

A decade after it was concluded, Israel's peace with Egypt still holds. Although Israelis expected more from it, their worst fear was not realized, namely that one of the area's many crises would lead to the treaty's demise. The treaty has survived a host of difficult and unexpected challenges—the punitive Arab ostracism of Cairo, the assassination of its Egyptian author, Israel's invasion of Lebanon, and the Palestinian uprising.

Nor was the Egyptian-Israeli peace always as cold as it is today. The chill set in with Israel's June 1982 invasion of Lebanon. The invasion, which came three months after the implementation of the final stage of the peace treaty, was a major embarrassment for Cairo. The war in Lebanon seemed to vindicate the radical Arab charge that Israel had neutralized Egypt in order to pursue ambitions against the other Arab states more effectively.

Cairo also seemed to believe that Israel's action raised the opportunity to advance its reentry into the Arab world by downgrading ties with Israel. In September 1982, following the massacre of Palestinians in the Beirut camps of Sabra and Shatilla by Israel's Lebanese allies, Egypt withdrew its ambassador from Tel Aviv. High-level meetings were suspended and other aspects of normalization virtually ceased.

The conflict with Israel tends to be manipulated to serve "realpolitik" interests, and Egypt's distance from Israel had little impact on its Arab relations. Those who proceeded to deal with Egypt did so because they needed Cairo's support anyway. PLO Chairman Yasir Arafat, for example, paid a highly controversial visit to Cairo in December 1983 on the same boat in which he fled Lebanon under fire from Syrian-backed forces. Similarly, Iraq's ties with Egypt grew increasingly close after the summer of 1982, when Baghdad found itself evermore on the defensive in its long war with Iran. King Hussein renewed ties with Egypt in the fall of 1984, in conjunction with his own diplomatic efforts in the Arab-Israeli arena.

Radical Syria, however, continued to insist that renewal of Arab relations with Egypt be contingent on Cairo's abrogation of the peace treaty, and the timorous Gulf states long remained fearful of crossing Damascus. The Arab decision to sanction the reestablishment of relations with Egypt, which was taken at the November 1987 Amman summit, was due to particular developments in the Persian Gulf. The massive deployment of the United States Navy in the area after July 1987 offered some assurance to the Saudis, while Iranian provocations during the pilgrimage that summer had taxed Riyadh's considerable willingness to conciliate its foes. Under those circumstances, the Arab states voted to endorse the renewal of diplomatic relations with Egypt. The endorsement amounted to *de facto* acceptance of the peace treaty. The decision, however, had little to do with the state of Egyptian-Israeli relations, which had improved considerably since their low after the Lebanese war.

Nor was Egypt's cool posture toward Israel simply a play for Arab reacceptance. Cairo had complaints about three elements of Israeli policy: its invasion of Lebanon; its intensive program of West Bank settlements; and its claim to a small stretch of the Gulf of Aqaba coast. The Likud government, arguably, did not negotiate in good faith on the Palestinian autonomy provisions of the Camp David accords, preferring to maintain control over the West Bank. Moshe Dayan resigned as foreign minister in October 1979 in frustration with his government's position, as did Ezer Weizmann as defense minister the next spring. The team that replaced them, particularly after the 1981 elections, was even less accommodating on the issues that divided Israel and Egypt.

One question came to stand out particularly. As Israel completed its withdrawal from Egypt, a dispute arose over Tabah, "a 700-yard strip of sand in Northern Sinai with a five-star hotel and a topless beach."[8] The fact Jerusalem allowed such an issue to impede relations with the only Arab state to sign a peace treaty with it was more testimony to its unease with the new relationship and disappointment over the evolution of the peace than to the importance of the beach.

The Likud government made no progress on these questions. Israel could not bring itself to leave Lebanon despite the high cost of staying there; the government remained committed to a program of West Bank settlement; and it was uncompromising on Tabah, although Israeli title was far from clear.[9] After the formation of the National Unity Government in September 1984, progress was made on all three issues, and Egyptian-Israeli relations slowly improved.

The building of new West Bank settlements virtually ceased, if only as part of the austerity program necessary to halt the hyper-inflation loosed by the second Likud government. The Unity government soon completed the painful task of withdrawing unconditionally from Lebanon. Finally, in the summer of 1986 Egypt and Israel reached agreement on procedures for resolving the Tabah dispute.

With a procedural agreement on Tabah, Prime Minister Shimon Peres visited Cairo in September, marking the first Egyptian-Israeli summit since the death of Anwar Sadat. President Hosni Mubarak announced the return of Egypt's ambassador to Tel Aviv, and some of the chill came off Egyptian-Israeli relations. When the Palestinian uprising began a year later, Egypt took certain measures, such as cancelling its usually lavish National Day reception in Tel Aviv and discouraging Israeli participation in the Cairo book fair. Egypt did not alter the basic relationship with Israel, however, and the country's ambassador remained in Tel Aviv.

In the end, maintaining the peace treaty is important to the Egyptian government. The treaty is necessary for Egyptian-American relations. Perhaps, too, Cairo came to see that its Arab problem could not be solved by manipulating its relationship with Israel. The Arab states that continued to oppose Egypt's reentry did so because it served to diminish a potentially powerful rival. Egypt could do nothing, consistent with its own interests, to meet their conditions, because they formulated conditions that could not be met.

Morocco

The Moroccan monarchy has long held a benign attitude toward Israel. Although Morocco is distant from the scene of the Arab-Israeli conflict, King Hassan has been active in efforts to resolve the dispute. In 1976, Itzhak Rabin visited Morocco as prime minister. The next year, secret Egyptian-Israeli negotiations, sponsored by Morocco, helped pave the way for the Camp David accords.[10]

Five years later, in November 1982, King Hassan hosted the Fez Arab summit. That summit approved the first Arab plan for a settlement with Israel. The Fez Plan (a slightly modified version of a proposal raised the year before by Saudi Arabia's King Fahd) was acceptable neither to Israel nor the United States; the plan called for an independent Palestinian state while only implicitly recognizing Israel's right to exist. Yet, the plan allowed individual Arab states to articulate their commitment to a peaceful resolution of the conflict and make other gestures toward Israel when they chose.

Most dramatically, the Fez Plan was the ostensible basis for the July 1986 summit between King Hassan and Prime Minister Peres. Although nothing substantive came from the meeting, it was highly symbolic. King Hassan was then chairman of both the Organization of Islamic Countries and the Arab League. With the title of both, the king became the second Arab leader to meet publicly with Israel's prime minister, ending Egypt's isolation on that score.

After the summit, King Hassan delivered a long speech explaining why he had met Peres. In it, he reflected on the history of the Arab-Israeli conflict, describing the Arabs' rigidity and hinting at the darker reasons behind it,

> I will tell you about the 1965 'Summit'. ...Since (the Arab leaders) requested my opinion, I said, provoking an indescribable outcry among the audience: 'You have no choice, either you make war now (I was talking about Israel), you are 80 million and they are only two million...'
>
> 'Or, I continued, 'you should take another path: Recognize Israel, integrate it into the League of Arab States. It will merge into the 80 million souls.'
>
> My remarks were received with much tumult. What prevented us from recognizing Israel, which at that time, was only a tiny territory?
>
> The Israelis would have accepted recognition with joy. Instead of such a measure, there were only wild remarks regarding a certain Shukary [PLO chairman] ('Let's throw them into the sea') and finally, it was we who have been thrown out of our land.
>
> After that, men dare attack us. But they are so flighty, so irresponsible.[11]

In fact few attacked King Hassan; only the radical states did. Syria broke diplomatic relations. Palestinian hardliners issued a quick denunciation.[12] Iranian-backed Hizbollahis stormed Morocco's embassy in Beirut, while Iran's foreign minister condemned

> the visit of the Zionist regime's Prime Minister Shimon Peres to Morocco and stressed that Muslim Moroccan people will not allow their treacherous ruler to continue such treasons.[13]

Now known is the fact that Iran had already approached Israel as an intermediary for the covert purchase of United States arms, and Peres, whose meeting with Hassan Iran so strongly denounced, had supported those dealings. Iran's reaction to the summit reflected a typical feature of radical policy—hostility toward Israel unwarranted by objective circumstances. How, after all, could Iran, with consistency, denounce Hassan's meeting with Israel's prime minister when Tehran was dealing with Israel itself?

The Hassan-Peres summit also reflected the *de facto* normalization of Israeli-Arab relations. King Hassan's speech was retelevised in Saudi Arabia, a sign of Riyadh's sympathy. That impression was reinforced by the fact that Saudi Crown Prince Abdullah had visited Morocco two days before, and thereby gave rise to speculation that he was informed of Hassan's plans.[14]

In the end, nothing much happened to the Moroccan king. No one shot him. He did not suffer domestically. By the often brutal standards of the area, it was a small step.

Lebanon

Israel's war in Lebanon at first seemed to mark one more element in the *de facto* normalization of Israeli-Arab relations. Later, it only entailed one more element of the unravelling of the peripery theory by discrediting a minority traditionally aligned with Israel.

Initially, it seemed that the war would bring Israel some gain. At one point, under United States auspices, a Lebanese-Israeli agreement was concluded, the accord of May 17, 1983. While the May 17 accord fell short of providing for the full peace of the Egyptian-Israeli treaty, it called for the abolition of the state of war and agreement on a series of normalization measures and security arrangements. The accord thus marked the second formal political agreement between Israel and an Arab state, and constituted one more step in breaching the wall of Arab hostility.

Unfortunately, the government of Lebanon, more specifically, the Maronite community, which had allied with Israel, proved to be a weak and unreliable reed. Already during the war Israel's protegé, Bashir Gemayel, had shown himself unwilling to provide the military support Defense Minister Ariel Sharon expected. Once active hostilities were over, Gemayal raised unexpected resistance to Israeli plans for a formal reconciliation,[15] before he was assassinated by Syrian agents in September 1982.

Negotiations with the new Lebanese government headed by Bashir's brother dragged on for eight months before the accord was signed, the terms proved impossible to implement. Mired in its own "Vietnam," Israel, after much debate, hesitation, and delay, withdrew in September 1983 to more defensible lines south of Beirut. The withdrawal already reflected recognition of the high cost in any attempt to secure political gains from the war. When, in March 1984, the Lebanese government bowed to Syrian pressure and abrogated the agreement, Israel did nothing to prevent it.

The Likud government never fully reconciled itself to an unconditional withdrawal; it took the election of the National Unity Government to implement such a plan. The new government settled for achieving a minimal goal about which there was a national consensus—insuring the safety of Israel's northern border. In the end a narrow "security zone" was established in Southern Lebanon, patrolled by a local militia backed as necessary by the IDF. Although the effort still entailed intermittent clashes with Lebanese opposition forces, the final arrangements succeeded in bringing tranquility to the north with minimal casualties for the IDF.

The Lebanese war put paid to the grandiose ambitions of the second Likud government. Israel's military might could not re-order the political map of the Middle East, as the defense minister seemed to have aspired to do. The attempt at a war in Lebanon, which would simultaneously install a friendly government there and, by ousting the PLO, allow Israel to impose its own terms on the West Bank, proved a fiasco.

Among the war's repercussions was the emergence of Hizbollah, the radical Shiite fundamentalist organization, backed by Iran. Hizbollah's leading role in the war of attrition against the IDF should have alerted Israeli officials to the danger posed by Tehran. Through the Lebanese door, a threat from the "periphery" suddenly appeared on Israel's borders.

Lebanon also undermined the periphery strategy by demonstrating the futility of a policy based on alignment with the Maronites. Although the Maronites were traditionally seen as part of the periphery, there had long been question about the value of relying on them.[16] Israel's experience proved beyond question that the Maronites could not serve as very useful partners in an increasingly Muslim and fragmented Lebanon, and Israel largely disengaged from political involvement in the evermore chaotic situation there.

Jordan

Jordan's posture toward Israel was one more aspect of the *de facto* normalization of Israeli-Arab relations. Although in the summer of 1988

King Hussein announced the decision to cut ties with the West Bank, he had spent the previous six years constantly, if cautiously, maneuvering to find a path for negotiations. Yet, the king never felt strong enough to negotiate on the basis of platforms that the United States was willing to endorse, given the American view of the situation, including the desire to exclude the Soviets and a complacency about the region's stability.

In September 1982, when the United States offered its first peace proposal since the Camp David accords, the Reagan initiative, Hussein sought to negotiate on its basis. Aware of his weakness vis-a-vis Syria and the internal constraints imposed by Jordan's large Palestinian community, Hussein felt the need for support. He looked first to the PLO, designated by the Rabat Arab summit eighteen years before as the offical representative of the Palestinians. For six months Hussein sought some agreement with Arafat, but in the end, Arafat proved unable or unwilling to bring his organization along, and in April 1983, having failed to secure a green light from the PLO, Hussein reluctantly announced his inability to accept the United States plan.

Israel's expulsion of the PLO from Beirut followed by Syria's expulsion of the PLO from Tripoli the next year had weakened the organization and increased King Hussein's flexibility. Soon after turning down the Reagan plan, the king began a long effort to establish Jordan as a credible party for West Bank negotiations. In January 1984 he revived Jordan's parliament, suspended after the 1974 Rabat summit. The parliament included representatives from the West Bank, and its reconvening implicitly revived the king's claim to speak on behalf of that territory. In September Jordan reestablished relations with Egypt to enhance Egypt's ability to help mediate an agreement. Finally, in November Amman hosted its first meeting of the Palestinian National Council (PNC). As its purpose was to advance a joint Jordanian-PLO initiative, the seventeenth PNC was vehemently opposed by Damascus and the radical Palestinian factions.

The February 11, 1985 Hussein-Arafat accord, which followed the PNC meeting, represented the high point of the king's efforts to reach an understanding with the PLO. From the beginning key differences were papered over, however, and at the end of the year the accord began to unravel. The precipitating event was the failure of the meeting planned for October between a Jordanian-PLO delegation and the British foreign minister. Both the Jordanian and British governments expected that after such a meeting the PLO members of the delegation would issue a statement opposing terrorism and recognizing Israel, but when PLO representatives balked, the meeting was cancelled. That initiated a new phase in the deterioration of PLO-Jordanian relations, culminating in Hussein's suspension of the accord four months later.

Hussein then began to turn to Syria. For a variety of tactical reasons, Damascus was open to his approach. Syria ceased its activities of the year before, which had included the assassination of a number of Jordan's ambassadors, while King Hussein dropped his support for Muslim fundamentalists in opposition to the Syrian regime. Damascus also agreed in principle to the idea of an international conference on the Arab-Israeli conflict.

Most likely, Damascus believed that such a conference would not materialize. If it did, Syria would likely still be able to block any real progress, as it had done in 1977, the last time an attempt had been made to hold such a conference. Yet Asad's agreement in principle provided King Hussein the flexibility he needed to pursue the option of negotiations.

In April 1987, the king and Israeli Foreign Minister Peres reached a semi-public accord on the format for such a conference, which was to be held under United Nations auspices. The agreement provided for bilateral committees with the authority to reach bilateral agreements.[17] It was hoped that that would provide a means around any Syrian or Soviet veto. The next month, Peres came to Washington expecting to garner United States support.

The support was not forthcoming. The administration did not like the Soviet presence; it hesitated over the consequences of the possible failure of the conference; and deferential to Likud's opposition, Washington was reluctant to take action that would raise problems with half the Israeli government. Yet those considerations had not stopped the United States before from involvement in Arab-Israeli negotiations. Other reasons must be sought for its passivity. Ultimately, it seems Washington believed that the status quo would remain viable for some time, and therefore no urgency attended a resolution of the conflict.

When the Palestinian uprising soon disproved that, the United States was quick to rush forward with a new initiative, but what was possible before the uprising was not possible afterwards. Indeed, had there been negotiations in progress, the sense of motion, if not movement, might have alleviated some of the despair, which gave rise to the uprising in the first place.

Another opportunity to explore a settlement was, arguably, lost. King Hussein had maneuvered to create maximum flexibility for himself, in cooperation with the Labor party, which was, after all, half the Israeli government. Washington mistook the very quiescence that had contributed to Hussein's maneuverability for a longer-term stability, which rendered serious diplomatic efforts unnecessary. Consequently, it did not act.

Iraq

The erosion of the periphery strategy was also reflected in a revision of revolutionary Iraq's attitude toward the Arab-Israeli conflict. In that respect, there was some parallel with Egypt, where successive wars and sustained hardship had, after 1967, caused the regime to subordinate the rhetorical aspects of its policy, which had been an element in the failed pursuit of regional hegemony. In both cases the policy revisions involved a subordination of their anti-Zionist posture.

Baghdad had long held one of the most rejectionist positions of any Arab state toward the Arab-Israeli conflict, namely that armed struggle was the only legitimate way to recover Palestine. In the sometimes abstruse lexicon of the Arab-Israeli conflict that meant that any political settlement, no matter how favorable to the Arabs, was illegitimate. That position was tantamount to the demand for the destruction of Israel.

Ambiguous as it was, Iraq's shift began soon after it was forced on the defensive in the Gulf war. Speaking to a United States congressman in August 1982, Saddam Hussein acknowledged the need for a "secure condition for Israelis" while asserting that "there is not a single Arab official now who believes it is possible to remove Israel and has this in his policy."[18] Similarly, in January 1983, the foreign minister explained that Iraq was encouraging a PLO-Jordanian rapprochement aimed at negotiations with Israel, the first time Baghdad explicitly stated its support for such negotiations.[19]

The shift in Iraq's posture was long given short shrift in Jerusalem, which continued to look toward Iran. Only after the November 1986 revelation of the covert United States-Israel arms sales did Israel's Persian Gulf policy become the subject of much public discussion. The result of that extended debate was that by the spring of 1988, when Iran agreed to end the war, Israel had essentially adopted a posture of neutrality between Iran and Iraq, even described as a response to various signals from Iraq.[20] Khomeini's surprise acceptance of a ceasefire, however, seemed to end any Iraqi interest in covert dealings with Israel, even though the Israeli interest, or at least neutrality, remained.[21]

Although nothing seems likely to come from the belated shift in Israel's position, the idea that Israel would consider an approach to Iraq was a new indication of change in the Arab-Israeli conflict. Above all, the animosity of the Arabs and, conversely, the friendliness of the "periphery" could no longer be taken for granted.

Persistent Intractability; The Legitimization of Radical Regimes

If there was a normalization of Israeli relations with key Arab states, hostilities remained as fixed as ever with others. States whose animosity toward Israel was unabating included Syria and Iran; the PLO's position was perhaps best described as quasi-paralysis. Other parties also remained antagonistic—Algeria, Libya, and South Yemen— but they were too distant from the conflict to have much impact, and the latter two had little political importance in any case.

What distinguished these governments was their self-description as radical, revolutionary regimes. They regularly proclaimed their commitment to the liberation of territory occupied by Israel and to the restoration of Palestinian rights, but they did not necessarily follow policies directly geared to achieving those goals. Iran, for instance, spent more effort trying to liberate Baghdad than Jerusalem, while Syria sided with Iran against Iraq.

Nor did Israel's attitude toward them necessarily determine their attitude toward Israel. Israel might be friendly, as it was to Iran, or it might be hostile, as it was to Syria. Both were still strongly anti-Zionist. Nor was proximity relevant. Libya is very far from the Arab-Israeli conflict, as is Tunisia. Israel even bombed Tunis in 1985, but never did a thing to Libya. Yet Libya is far more antagonistic to Israel than is Tunisia.

The factor that correlated most closely with the hostility of a Middle Eastern state toward Israel was whether that state deemed itself a radical regime or not. Governments that professed a harsh, uncompromising anti-Zionism generally considered themselved revolutionary states. Their anti-Zionism can be understood ultimately as a function of their domestic politics.

Their anti-Zionism helps justify their domestic rule and their regional ambitions; there is great resistance to abandoning it, even when the posture may seem counterproductive or unrealistic. Such a perspective helps explain the persistent intractability of the Arab-Israeli conflict, and why, even if some governments have moved toward a *de facto* accommodation with Israel, others strongly resist it.

Syria

Syria maintains a strong posture of anti-Zionism and opposition to reconciliation with Israel. Damascus claims that Zionism is the greatest threat to the "Arab nation." By standing in the vanguard of confrontation with Zionism, Syria is defending the Arab nation. That posture leads Damascus to oppose any settlement with Israel, or at least one remotely acceptable to Washington or Jerusalem. The stand also leads Damascus to block the efforts of other parties to achieve a settlement.

As Syrian President Hafez el-Assad explained at the last Islamic Conference summit in January 1987,

> The main topic to be discussed is the issue of the Arab-Israeli conflict, which has been the principal Arab and Islamic issue. . . . The importance of this conflict (is due) to the grave dangers it poses. . . . In their endeavor to achieve the expansionist/Torah scheme, the Zionists are defying the international community. . . We must put an end to the existing relations between Israel and some Arab brothers.[22]

However, as gunfire from the Iran-Iraq war echoed in Kuwait, the host of the conference, and Shi'a fundamentalists launched an arson campaign in the shaykhdom's oil fields, many summiteers probably felt Iran was the greater danger to them.

Damascus' position was that Zionism was the real threat because it is expansionist and racist; any settlement must be resisted. Syria remained adamantly opposed to the Camp David accords, and not only the accords of a decade ago; it attacked any attempt to reach a settlement outside a consensual Arab position. The demand for the simultaneous resolution of all aspects of the Arab-Israeli conflict was a recipe for stalemate. Evidently, that was an outcome acceptable to Syria.

Damascus consistently opposed Egypt's readmission into the Arab fold. Nearly a decade after the Arabs broke relations with Egypt, at the November 1987 Amman summit, Assad faced the determination of a number of key Arab states to reestablish those ties. Although he made a surprise reverse and relented to their demands, a gesture was still made to him. Egypt's membership in the Arab League remained suspended, as Assad insisted.

Although Syria's position was formally based on opposition to the Camp David accords, its posture was indistinguishable from the calculated "realpolitik." As Tehran noted in pique at the anti-Iranian tenor of the summit, which Syria either could or would not block, "The main opposition (to Egypt's reentry) came from Syria. Syria knows well that Egypt is its main rival for leadership of the Arab world, so it opposed this plan more than anyone else."[23]

In fact, contradictions between Syria's declaratory stance and its actual policy abounded. Damascus has posed as the champion of the Palestinians, even as it has attacked them. The government forced the PLO out of Northern Lebanon in 1983, completing the job that Israel

set out to do the year before. After the PLO later succeeded in infil-
trating back into Beirut, Damascus supported the Amal militia in a
siege, lasting on and off for three years, of Shatilla and Burj al-Barajnah,
the same Palestinian camps that had witnessed the Phalange slaughter
several years before.

Similarly, since the Egyptian-Israeli peace treaty, Damascus has
sought to achieve "strategic parity" with Israel. Syria has argued that
negotiations from a position of weakness would lead to an "imposed
peace," but parity for the sake of negotiations is indistinguishable from
the requirements of war. In any case, the consequences of Syria's stand
is to put off both to some indefinite future date.[24]

If Damascus sought parity with Israel, it should have aimed to
consolidate an "Eastern Front," including Iraq. That is the scenario
most feared by Israeli defense planners, but Assad's policy secured
the opposite. Even with the Gulf war's end, Iraq seems unlikely to
join Syria against Israel.[25] Formally, Syria opposed the Gulf war. In
practice, however, it promoted the war's continuation, insuring that
its rival, Iraq, remained tied down with Iran. Not surprisingly, Syria—
not Israel—was the first to feel Iraq's wrath when the Gulf war ended,
as one of Iraq's first moves was to support the Lebanese Forces in
opposing Syria's candidate for the president of Lebanon.

Despite Syria's pan-Arab posture, the effect of its policy has been
to divide the Arabs. In practice, Damascus places higher priority on
excluding its rivals, Iraq and Egypt, than either liberating Palestine by
force, which Iraq could help achieve, or recovering it through negotiations, with which Egypt could help. As long as Egypt and Iraq were
constrained in one way or another, only relatively weak states remained
in the Arab heartland, vulnerable to Syrian domination. While Syrian
policy is carried out in the name of confronting "the Zionist threat,"
it does not serve to meet any Zionist threat. In the end that works well
enough because the Zionist threat is much less ominous than Syria
portrays it to be.

Rather, Syria's position becomes a rationale for its ambitions at
local hegemony, while enhancing the regime's domestic legitimacy.[26]
Small wonder, then, that Damascus has little interest in a resolution
of the Arab-Israeli conflict on terms acceptable to any other party and
is satisfied with the stalemate that results.

Iran

Since the revolution, Tehran has maintained the most anti-Zionist
posture of any state in the Middle East. Tehran claims that Zionism,
along with imperialism, is engaged in a conspiracy against Islam, as
represented by the Islamic Republic.

Israel sold arms to Iran for many years and provided Iran political support, long arguing that the West should not abandon Tehran, lest it turn to Moscow.[27] Thus, Iran's claim that Zionism was engaged in a conspiracy against the Islamic Republic is without foundation. That sort of discrepancy suggests that the rigid anti-Zionism of some regimes in the Middle East cannot be explained on objective grounds.

The most tangible aspect of Israel's continuing attachment to Tehran was arms sales. Military relations were close under the shah, and after the revolution Israel continued to sell Tehran arms. Although arms sales were interrupted for some periods, they basically continued until perhaps as late as the fall of 1987.[28] The rationales for such sales shifted—to protect Iranian Jews; to promote a pro-Western miliary coup; to establish ties with "moderates"; to avoid driving Iran into the arms of the Soviet Union; to rescue American hostages in Lebanon.[29]

Ultimately, the changing rationales amounted to the conviction that Iran would one day return to the Shah's pro-Israeli policy. That belief was forcefully stated by Israel's defense minister as late as October 1987,

> for 28 out of 37 years Iran was a friend of Israel. If it could work for 28 years...why couldn't it once this crazy idea of Shiite fundamentalism is gone?[30]

The gap between Israel's friendliness toward Iran and the Islamic Republic's hostility toward Israel, and Jews, was immense. From the beginning the regime stirred up anti-Jewish feeling as part of a general approach to inflame mob passions and revolutionary fervor.[31] The Protocols of the Elders of Zion, with venomous anti-Semitic charicatures, appeared in the Iranian press. Prominent members of the Jewish community were among those executed during the first years of the revolution. To be sure, a distinction, which was not always clear, was drawn between Judaism and Zionism. Unremitting hostility was reserved for the latter.

The Islamic Republic adopted a demonstrative anti-Israeli posture from the very start. In February 1979, two weeks after Khomeini returned to Tehran from exile in Paris, Iran severed its relations with Israel and turned over its embassy to the PLO. Tehran soon denounced the Egyptian-Israeli peace treaty and broke relations with Cairo for it.[32] Particularly after 1982, when Iran took the offensive in the Gulf war, it claimed that its goal was the liberation of Jerusalem. Like Syria, Iran rejected any political settlement of the Arab-Israeli conflict; Iranian officials regularly called for Israel's elimination. When the Amman summit sanctioned the reestablishment of Arab relations with Egypt, Tehran denounced that, too.

In fact, it would be hard to conceive of any regime more hostile to Israel than the Islamic Republic. Yet Israel remained attached to Iran. Key officials believed that the regime would fall in the relevant future. Meanwhile, Tehran's hostility was to be endured as a tactical problem, until that day when the strategic prize, Iran, reverted to its earlier friendliness toward Israel.

The strength of Israeli conviction was astonishing. Perhaps that rigidity could only be understood as an attitude induced by the long conflict with the Arab states. The fact that it confused the tactical and strategic, and otherwise suffered grave flaws became apparent once the policy was exposed to meaningful public discussion. The revelation in November 1986 of the covert United States-Israeli arms sales to Iran precipitated a prolonged debate over Israel's Gulf policy. Official policy did not survive that debate.

Academic experts and a number of journalists attacked the government's premises. They argued that it was absurd to support a regime that was so hostile and had caused Israel grave harm. Furthermore, even if Iran never broke through Iraqi lines—which at times seemed possible—the ideology it sought to export was very dangerous. Egypt's government faced an Islamic opposition. What would have been more disastrous for Israel than the overthrow of the only Arab government to have signed a peace treaty with Jerusalem?

The public criticism led to a change in Israel's position, beginning the next year. In September 1987 Peres declared Israel's support for a "durable cease-fire in the Persian Gulf," while denouncing Khomeini and his "militancy of hatred and backwardness."[33] Prime Minister Itzhak Shamir soon joined in condemning "the crazy war."[34] Not until June 1988, however, was the key shift made. Then Defense Minister Itzhak Rabin, declared "I've changed my mind. The Iran-Iraq war no longer serves Israel's interests." At that point, the "prime minister's club" no longer insisted that Iraq's hostility was unremitting, while Iran's eventual sympathy was assured. Israel was tacitly backing away from the unthinking adherence to the "periphery strategy" in the Persian Gulf.

The PLO

The PLO differs from the radical states, even if the consequence of its policy, so far, has, like theirs, been stalemate. The PLO is not a government-controlling territory. Rather, it is a highly fractured organization consisting of eight groups, each with ties to one or more Arab governments, which provide financial support and a territorial base.[35] Intra-Arab divisions are reflected in PLO politics, even though a premium is put on maintaining Palestinian unity. That translates into a lowest-common-denominator consensual position and diplomatic rigidity.

While some elements within the PLO would seemingly gladly accept a compromise settlement with Israel, others maintain a hard-line position. The leadership's inability or unwillingness to confront them, has, so far, left PLO policy hostage to extreme elements, often more beholden to the states whose support they receive than to any significant Palestinian constituency.

Intensifying the divisions is an element of brutality in regional politics. More than one Palestinian has been assassinated for articulating a compromise position, including Dr. Issam Sartawi during 1983 in Portugal and later Said Hammami in London. Other prominent figures were killed as rejectionist states, particularly Syria, sought to thwart a settlement.[36] Those Palestinian leaders ready to advocate compromise with Israel faced great personal risks just for saying so.

The PLO had failed, so far, to articulate a policy that might bring tangible gain to the Palestinians, particularly those living in the West Bank and Gaza. Although its position has moderated over time, a significant gap always remained between its position and that which would be an acceptable basis for negotiations, particularly for the United States and Israel. While rigidity exists on both sides, the consequences differ. Trying to promote Palestinian participation in the latest United States initiative, Egypt's president argued

> We waste many opportunities, and this is not confined to us. (The Israelis) also waste many opportunities, but the difference between us is that they have the land. They have the land, so it does not matter for them if opportunities are wasted. As for us, if we waste an opportunity, we will be the losers. The more opportunities we waste, the more we lose.[37]

Like King Hassan two years before, Mubarak complained of the Arab's rigidity and its consequence. Yet from a radical perspective the stalemate is not counterproductive. That helps explain why so many "opportunities" were wasted. Divisions within the PLO have, so far, left it by default in the rejectionist camp.

The Palestinian uprising, more than any other event, has put the PLO on the spot. The unrest is generating an indigenous West Bank and Gaza leadership. While that leadership still looks to the PLO, it is also expressing frustration at the PLO's inability , after a long period of local protest, to translate that protest into a credible political program. West Bank pressure is being exerted for such measures as the establishment of a provisional government and the explicit recognition of Israel, measures that might facilitate the start of negotiations.

If the uprising produces a Palestinian leadership with which it is possible to negotiate, then it will have marked a sea change in the Arab-Israeli conflict. That, development, too would mark one more step in the erosion of the periphery theory. The uprising has also changed Israeli opinion in ways that are not yet known. While the uprising has not reduced the obstacles to peace, it may change them in important ways. In any event, it has demonstrated the consequences of complacency and inaction.

[Editor's Note: Professor Mylroie adds that four major developments worthy of note have taken place in the Middle East since the conclusion of this article. One significant event was the establishment of an official United States-PLO dialogue when Yassir Arafat met the Kissinger terms of 1985 as modified by the Reagan administration. The initial meetings of American and PLO negotiators received a great deal of attention, although progress remains limited. A second significant event was Egypt's return to the Arab League in May of 1989, an indirect outcome of the cease-fire in the Iran-Iraq war reflecting Iraq's enhanced position in Arab politics and its ability to exert pressure on Syria. A third event was the decision of the International Tribunal that the settlement at Tabah belonged to Egypt, with Israel's subsequent withdrawal from that territory. Finally, there was an intensification of Iraqi support for the Christian government in Lebanon.]

CHAPTER EIGHT

Israel and Morocco: The Political Calculus of a 'Moderate' Arab State

Mark A. Tessler

An understanding of Israel's present and future relations with various states in the Arab world requires a proper analysis of the way in which the leaders of these countries calculate their political interests. Whereas it is sometimes assumed that the behavior of Arab political elites is motivated principally by an unswerving hostility toward Israel, or by a cynical desire to use the Israeli-Palestinian conflict to deflect attention from pressing domestic problems, the reality in most instances is far more complex. Arab leaders, like all leaders, take a wide variety of domestic factors and international relationships into consideration when making foreign policy decisions. Even with respect to Muammar Qaddafi, who is frequently said to be driven almost exclusively by his own particular brand of ideological militancy, scholars have shown that it is more productive to focus on strategic thinking and assessments of interest than on ideology when seeking to analyze his behavior toward other states.[1] A similar approach is needed to understand the way that Arab rulers perceive and attempt to deal with Israel, and, at least in general, this holds whether the Arab leader is more moderate or more militant in his posture toward the Jewish state.

The preceding is not intended to suggest that ideological considerations should be neglected by those seeking to explain or predict interstate relations, in the Middle East or elsewhere. On the contrary, ideology, including attitudes toward Israel in the Arab case, does play

Author's Note: The author acknowledges with gratitude the very helpful comments provided by Ambassador Richard B. Parker. A slightly modified version of this chapter was published in *The Jerusalem Journal of International Relations* (May 1988).

a role in the shaping of foreign policy. While unidimensional analyses of Arab political behavior are not uncommon, especially among some whose experience in the Middle East is limited to Israel, the result has frequently been an inclination to attribute a sort of intrinsic intransigence to Arab rulers. Such analyses are not only inappropriate from a scholarly point of view, they also discourage serious thinking about the conditions that will promote Arab-Israeli accommodation. To the extent that Arab leaders are seen as irrational political actors, driven by passions they are unable or unwilling to control and even, when necessary, working against their own country's welfare for the sake of ideological purity or symbolic satisfaction, Israel and its supporters will to that extent be unwilling to propose compromises, which reasonable men would be expected to accept, and will be inclined to dismiss as propaganda any such proposals put forward by the Arabs themselves.

The case of King Hassan II of Morocco, who has long been receptive to contact with Israel, offers an opportunity to combat the stereotypes about Arab political behavior that some may hold. In addition, and more fundamentally, it permits undertaking an assessment that puts Arab attitudes toward Israel into their proper analytical perspective by focusing on the political calculations of an important Arab head of state. Seen from this perspective, the present investigation aspires to make a scholarly and political contribution that goes beyond describing the character of King Hassan's dealings with Israel. The chapter also seeks to encourage and illustrate an approach to inquiry, one that may be useful to those seeking to shed light on Arab attitudes and behavior toward Israel more generally. This approach should be particularly helpful to those who have a strong interest in Israel but who also wish to understand the foreign policy behavior of Arab states.

The application of this approach could provide information that will be useful to those desiring to promote in other Arab countries the kind of receptivity to contact with Israel that has been displayed by Morocco during the last decade or so. More plausibly and immediately, however, the value of the approach to inquiry pursued in this chapter lies in its recognition that the international behavior of any Arab state, whether more or less open to relations with Israel at the present time, cannot be satisfactorily comprehended without attention to the costs and benefits associated with particular foreign policy options, to the political dynamics that determine these costs and benefits, and to the strategic thinking that governs their evaluation by national leaders. These are the ingredients of the "political calculus" that the present investigation seeks to discover in the case of King Hassan II, and which must be brought to light in any serious analysis of the formulation and conduct of foreign policy.

Moroccan-Israeli Contacts

On July 22 and July 23, 1986, King Hassan II of Morocco and Prime Minister Shimon Peres of Israel met in Ifrane, a Moroccan resort town known for its mountain air, pine forests, and Swiss-style chalets. The Hassan-Peres summit was historic in significant respects. With the exception of Egypt, which agreed to negotiate with Israel in 1978 and which signed a peace treaty with Jerusalem the following year, no Arab country had either recognized Israel or been willing to permit public meetings between its own leaders and officials of the Jewish state. Hassan's invitation to Peres was thus a bold and dramatic gesture, one that was made with very specific objectives in mind. Nevertheless, the Ifrane summit was by no means the first time that Hassan had welcomed Israelis to his kingdom. On the contrary, it was rather the most recent in a series of Israeli-Moroccan encounters stretching back more than a decade.

Israeli-Moroccan contact might in fact go all the way back to 1965. Although never confirmed, there are reports that Israeli operatives in France assisted Moroccan security agents in abducting Mehdi Ben Barka, a leader of the opposition that was challenging King Hassan's government in the mid-1960s. Ben Barka at the time headed the Union Nationale des Forces Populaires (UNFP), a left-oriented political party that was rapidly gaining influence among the country's urban poor. The king's concern with the UNFP and the left opposition increased after young men from the slums of Casablanca rioted in March 1965; late in the year Ben Barka was kidnapped and murdered in Paris as part of the regime's crackdown on opponents. A full and authoritative account of the "Ben Barka Affair" has never been made public, but it is widely believed that French police officers took part in the operation. Rumors of Israeli collusion persist as well.

Most contacts between Israel and Morocco have happily been of a different sort. Of particular interest is the role King Hassan played in forging the connection between Israel and Egypt that eventually led to the Camp David Accords of 1978. Yitzhak Rabin, the current minister of defense and prime minister of Israel from 1974 until mid-1977, reports in his memoirs that Hassan began to mediate between Jerusalem and Cairo in 1976. According to Rabin, the king attempted initially to involve Syria as well.[2] Rabin made a secret trip to Morocco at this time as part of a process in which Hassan held separate talks with each of the parties and, interestingly, sought to avoid any involvement by the superpowers.

The culmination of the king's effort came in September 1977, at a secret meeting between Hassan and Moshe Dayan. Dayan, at the time foreign minister in the government of Rabin's successor, Menachem Begin, had to disguise himself to enter Morocco. He wore a wig, sunglasses, and a false mustache. Dayan also followed a complicated itinerary before being received by Hassan in a 600-year-old palace in Marrakesh. He traveled from Paris on a commercial Moroccan airliner, which landed at Fez, and was then driven to Ifrane for the night. The next day he returned to Fez for a flight to Marrakesh, and finally began his meeting with the king late in the evening. Despite the strict secrecy surrounding his visit, Dayan later reported that the encounter had been informal and relaxed. "Don't worry," Hassan is said to have told his guest, "I won't be overthrown if it becomes known that you are here."[3]

Dayan was impressed with the hospitality he received and, especially, with Hassan himself. He reported that the king saw himself as having a special role to play in bringing Arabs and Jews together, and that the monarch had accordingly spoken at length both about his own warm relations with the Jews of Morocco and about his commitment to Arab-Israeli reconciliations. Dayan then told Hassan that Israel was interested in direct and high-level contact with Egypt, to which Hassan replied with a promise to investigate the matter. Israel's answer was not long in coming; just eleven days later Dayan was invited to return to Morocco for a meeting with General Hassan Tohami, deputy prime minister of Egypt and personal emissary of Anwar Sadat. These events led to Sadat's dramatic visit to Jerusalem two months later, which in turn spawned the Camp David accords and the Israel-Egypt peace treaty of 1979.

Peres himself had met with King Hassan prior to the 1986 summit. In July 1978, Peres spent two days with the Moroccan monarch in Rabat; and then in March 1981, during an election campaign in which he hoped to lead the Labor Alignment back to power, he visited Morocco again and was received in the same Marrakesh palace where Hassan had welcomed Dayan. These meetings, like those involving Rabin and Dayan, were held in secret; neither Hassan nor Peres discussed them publicly. Nevertheless, a few Israeli sources give accounts of the encounter.[4] Among the topics of conversation in the 1981 meeting were Labor's chances of defeating Menachem Begin's Likud bloc in the forthcoming election and the ways that America's Middle East policy might change under the new administration in Washington.

Peres placed emphasis on the behavior of the Arab states in his discussions with Hassan. He reportedly spoke of the need for enhanced cooperation among the conservative and moderate states of the Arab world, most notably Saudi Arabia, Jordan, Egypt, Sudan, Morocco, and Tunisia. This alliance, he argued, would cooperate with the United States — and tacitly with Israel — in order to enhance the stability of the Middle East. Peres also stressed the need to deepen Israeli-Egyptian cooperation. Normalization, he told the king, would promote the eventual acceptance of Israel by other Arab states. Hassan, by contrast, sought to focus attention of the Palestinian dimension of the Middle East conflict, asking his guest whether a Labor-led government would agree to amend United Nations Resolution 242 so as to include a reference to Palestinian rights. Peres showed no interest in this line of thought, however, stating that attempts to modify the resolution would only lead to more conflict and confusion; it would, in his judgment, open a Pandora's box. The king was apparently disappointed by this response, but the two men nonetheless discussed other possibilities and later parted amicably.

Moroccan-Israeli contacts continued and, in contrast to these early meetings, some took place in the public arena. In May 1984, for example, Morocco permitted thirty-five prominent Israelis to attend a conference of Moroccan Jewry in Rabat. The Israelis were flown to Morocco from Paris by the Royal Air Force. Hassan did not meet the visitors personally, but the crown prince, the prime minister, and other senior officials did attend a reception in honor of the conferees. Another instance of Moroccan-Israeli contact took place in May 1985, when Israel's deputy minister of agriculture, Avraham Katz-Oz, visited Morocco and explored the possibility of agricultural cooperation between Rabat and Jerusalem. Katz-Oz stated that Israel could assist Morocco not only in the domain of agricultural technology but also with respect to marketing, especially because Rabat was seeking to establish closer agricultural ties with the United States and could make use of Israel's contacts in the United States.

*****

Although the Hassan-Peres summit caught observers by surprise, there were indications late in 1985 and early in 1986 that the king was beginning to think about a new gesture toward Israel. In November of the former year, Hassan told French journalists that he would be willing to meet Shimon Peres. This statement was particularly significant because the king made it in public, and in this respect it contrasted sharply with previous overtures toward Jerusalem. For this reason, too,

Hassan's declaration drew much more criticism from Arab sources than
had his earlier gestures toward Israel.

Hassan invited Peres to Morocco in December, but the intensity
of Arab complaints showed the king that he had moved too quickly,
without having first laid a foundation for his action. Therefore, rather
embarrassingly, he abruptly retracted his offer to meet with the Israeli
prime minister. Yet the king did not abandon his plan; he instead
sought to gain legitimacy for his scheme by involving other Arab
countries in it. At an Arab summit meeting in March, Hassan urged
that steps be taken to explore Israel's willingness to negotiate on the
basis of peace proposals acceptable to the Arabs, meaning the plan
adopted at the Fez summit conference of September 1982. The Fez Plan
calls for creation of an independent Palestinian state in the West Bank
and Gaza, with East Jerusalem as its capital, and for mutual recognition between this state and Israel. The March 1986 summit took no
action in response to Hassan's suggestion about contacts with Israel.
In retrospect, however, it is clear that the king was laying the
foundation for a renewal of his own invitation to Prime Minster Peres.

Arrangements for Peres's visit were worked out on July 11 during
a secret meeting in Paris between Moroccan and Israeli officials. The
prime minister and his party arrived in Morocco ten days later, traveling on an Israeli Air Force plane, which flew directly to Fez and landed
at about 11 p.m. on the night of July 21. The Israelis were taken in
a motor convoy to the luxurious villa, which had been reserved for
them near Hassan's palace in Ifrane, and in a highly unusual gesture
of cordiality the king drove to the Israelis' residence to welcome his
guests personally. All of the visitors were profuse in their praise of
the hospitality they received. Uri Savir, Peres's media advisor and
spokesman, compared it to a story out of "A Thousand and One
Nights." Lavish eight- and nine-course meals were served, he reported.
"We were lodged in a fabulous hilltop villa, and three or four ministers
were constantly on hand to host us."[5]

Hassan and Peres held two days of substantive talks, beginning
shortly before noon on July 22. Present at this meeting were two other
Israelis: Savir and Rafi Edri, a Moroccan-born member of Knesset. Savir
and Edri had traveled to Paris earlier in the month to make arrangements for the trip. Peres also received counsel from two additional
officials who had come with him to Ifrane. One was Cabinet Secretary
Yossi Beilin, and the other was Dr. Nimrod Novik, the prime minister's
foreign policy advisor. Hassan was accompanied in the discussions by
Foreign Minister Abdel Latif Filali, Interior and Information Minister
Driss Basri, and Ahmed Reda Guedira, the king's closest political
advisor.

As he had done in his secret talks with Peres in 1978 and 1981, Hassan focused his attention on the central Palestinian dimension of the Arab-Israeli conflict. Specifically, after he and Peres had both set forth general analyses of the current Middle Eastern situation, the king told Peres that he had two questions to ask. First, in return for peace with the Arab world, would Israel agree to withdraw from all Arab territories captured in the 1967 war? Second, would the Israeli government agree to negotiate with the Palestine Liberation Organization? By asking these questions, Hassan deliberately placed his dialogue with Peres squarely within the framework of the Fez Plan. Indeed, the king was quite explicit about this, emphasizing that the Fez Plan endorsed the Palestinians' right to self-determination and recognized the Palestine Liberation Organization as their sole legitimate representative. According to Hassan, acceptance of these points was the price that Israel must pay for peace with the Arab world.

Peres answered both of Hassan's questions in the negative, which, according to some Israeli analysts, is what the king should have expected. As Israeli journalist Hirsh Goodman asked rhetorically, "Could Peres, without cabinet consultation, without party approval, without the presence of a legal advisor or non-partisan senior government official, and without any national mandate, have committed Israel to any of the basic assumptions of the Fez Plan — direct negotiations with the PLO; a pre-commitment to return all of the territories; the creation of an independent Palestinian state; and the renegotiation of the status of Jerusalem?"[6] Every one of these elements of the Fez Plan was unacceptable to the overwhelming majority of Israelis. Had Peres yielded on any one of them, Goodman wrote in the *Jerusalem Post*, he would have needed Dayan's wig and sunglasses to return to Israel.

Nevertheless, the Israeli prime minister may have found it helpful to be asked these questions by Hassan. Peres's Labor Alignment is distinguished from its major political rival, the Likud bloc, by a willingness to withdraw from some of the territory that Israel has held since 1967 and by a more moderate approach to the question of Palestinian rights. While Labor's position on these issues stops far short of the Fez Plan, Peres can now tell the Israeli electorate with more credibility that Arab leaders will respond to moderation on the part of the Jewish state and that Labor's advocacy of territorial compromise does indeed hold some promise of movement toward peace. The ability to make these arguments when campaigning against Likud and other right-wing parties in elections is an important political benefit that Peres and his party may have reaped from the meeting in Morocco.

Peres also hoped to derive political benefit from his visit to Ifrane in another way. Jews of Afro-Asian origin now make up a majority of the Israeli population, and Jews of Moroccan origin are the largest subset among them. These so-called Oriental Jews have traditionally voted for Likud rather than Labor, and anti-Alignment sentiment runs especially high among those whose families came from Morocco. Moreover, Peres in particular is disliked by this category of the Israeli population. He has, for example, been shouted off the podium on several occasions when attempting to address audiences composed of Israelis of Moroccan origin. Labor's obvious interest in improving its image in this community was made even greater by the internal power struggle that was taking place within Likud. The struggle broke into the open at the Likud party convention in March 1986 and, because of the personalities involved, its outcome could have affected the degree to which the party continued to be seen as responsible to Afro-Asian voters. The net result of all this was that the Alignment in general, and Peres in particular, was in a position to derive political capital from the Ifrane summit.

Whatever the eventual political fallout back in Israel, Peres's negative response to Hassan's inquiries produced some tense hours during the Ifrane summit. According to the king's own account, he told the prime minister that because Israel was unwilling to recognize Palestinian rights and establish a dialogue with the PLO, there was nothing more to discuss and it remained only to say goodbye. Hassan agreed that the Moroccan and Israeli advisors present should nevertheless be given a chance to formulate a communiqué, the official version of which was in French, read as follows:

His Majesty King Hassan II has, on July 22 and 23 of 1986, received at his palace in Ifrane Shimon Peres, prime minster of Israel. During the talks marked by frankness and devoted essentially to the study of the Fez Plan, the Moroccan sovereign and the Israeli prime minister analyzed, in depth, the situation in the Middle East and the conditions, in form and in substance, likely to contribute efficiently to the establishment of peace in this region.

His Majesty King Hassan II gave a presentation of the Fez Plan, explaining his views concerning the merits of each of its elements and suggesting that this plan has the double merit of, on the one hand, constituting the sole document which is objectively valid to serve as a basis for a just and durable peace and, on the other, being the object of an Arab consensus, in contrast to any other plan or peace proposal.

In his turn, Mr. Shimon Peres clarified his observations on the Fez Plan, putting forth propositions pertaining to conditions he deems necessary for the installation of peace.

As the meeting was of a purely exploratory nature, aiming at no moment at engaging in negotiations, His Majesty King Hassan II will inform the Arab leaders, and Prime Minister Peres his government, of the points of view developed during the talks.[7]

*****

The Hassan-Peres summit is significant in the context of the Arab-Israeli conflict in at least four respects. First, it was marked by openness, in contrast to Hassan's previous encounters with Israeli leaders. It had originally been planned to keep the talks secret, leaving it to Hassan and Peres, once in Ifrane, to decide whether and in what context to announce their meeting to the public. When Rabat told Jerusalem that Israeli journalists were welcome, however, it became clear that the summit was not to be kept secret after all; and indeed the world learned of the meeting while the Israeli prime minister and his party were still in the air on their way to Morocco. Furthermore, Hassan reinforced the public nature of the summit by giving a lengthy report to his own countrymen in a nationally televised address. The king defended the legality of his action, insisting that "no one can say the Fez resolutions forbid contact with Israel, within the framework of the plan," and then added that "no decision of the League of Arab States, since it has existed, has forbidden an Arab leader to meet with an Israeli leader." Even more significant, however, was the king's claim that his action was helpful and courageous, as well as legal. He told the Moroccan people, *inter alia:*

> My brothers will be the judge of what is proper to do, now that they have grasped the tenor of the conversation. I did not accept this meeting in order to negotiate or to decide on anything. In my mind, this was an exploratory effort. I personally think it cowardly not to listen to an adversary, an enemy. We have, dear people, been educated in courage. The newspapers have written: "The courageous action of Hassan II..." But my action, essentially, was not courageous, it merely was the fruit of our common civic education... We have learned that it is necessary sometimes to sit at the negotiating table rather than demonstrate in the streets.[8]

Second, and of related significance, Hassan consulted with other Arab actors. Although he stated in his speech that "I did not notify a single Arab head of state about this," in fact it appears that the king consciously sought to operate and exercise leadership within a moderate Arab consensus. To begin, as reported, he urged the Arab League at its summit in March 1986 to explore Israeli willingness to negotiate on the basis of the Fez Plan. Although he ostensibly hoped that the initiative would come from others, he undoubtedly realized that the league would not respond to his suggestion and thus was laying a foundation for his own subsequent action. Further, it appears that Hassan did contact key Arab states about his intentions. Jordan radio reported that a high-level Moroccan envoy was in Amman on the night of July 21, delivering a message from Hassan and consulting with King Hussein, the Jordanian monarch. In the wake of this development, there were rumors that Hussein himself might soon join Hassan and Peres in Ifrane, or that he might at least take steps to sound out other Arab leaders about their attitude toward such a possibility. King Hassan also briefed the leaders of Saudi Arabia and Egypt; it is particularly significant in this connection that Saudi officials permitted Hassan's forty-five minute speech to his countrymen to be broadcast live in their own country as well. Finally, the Hassan-Peres communiqué committed the king to report on Israel's position to other Arab leaders.

Third, moderate Arab leaders reacted wtih comparative restraint to the Hassan-Peres summit. While Syria, Algeria, Libya, and some elements within the PLO denounced the king forcefully, the Saudi decision to broadcast the king's speech was indicative of the tolerant attitude that key Arab regimes took toward the meeting. Egypt, the only Arab state that has made peace with Israel, praised Hassan's action. Egyptian President Hosni Mubarak called it "a good initiative," adding that "everybody who likes peace would be happy about it."[9] Initial reaction among some Palestinian nationalists in the Occupied Territories was also encouraging, although admittedly cautious as well. For example, Hanna Siniora, editor of the East Jerusalem daily, al-Fajr, which is usually sympathetic to the Arafat wing of the PLO, said he welcomed the meeting and hoped it would lead to negotiations between Israel and the Palestinians.

Among the Arab analyses favorable to the meeting were those advanced by Jeune Afrique, a Paris-based French-language weekly with strong North African connections. The journal argued that Arab rejectionism played into the hands of Israeli extremists, enabling them to deflect attention from Jerusalem's own intransigence by pretending that there are no Arabs willing to negotiate. Hassan's initiative, on the other hand, offered the Arabs a significant public relations victory; it demonstrated to all the world that there are Arabs willing to make peace and that Israelis can also say "no." The magazine added that Hassan had also succeeded in reopening the file of the Palestinians, an important development in view of PLO troubles in recent months.[10]

With the exception of Egypt, none of these Arab sources offered unconditional praise of Hassan's initiative. Some expressed skepticism, and most said that they would ultimately judge the summit on the basis of its results. Nevertheless, this was hardly the militant condemnation that was hoped for by Arab rejectionists or other critics of the Moroccan monarch, or by hard-liners in Israel who are also opposed to compromise. Some Arab states, like Tunisia, did not comment on the summit at all, and observers judged the condemnation of others, such as Iraq and Kuwait, to be restrained and to some extent perfunctory.

A fourth point of significance is the existence of the communiqué, which reinforced the public nature of the meeting. The statement issued at Ifrane also records Hassan's concern that the meeting, though exploratory, be understood as part of an effort to foster a broader Arab-Israeli dialogue.

Moroccan-Israeli contacts continued after the Ifrane summit. In August, Israeli newspapers reported visits by Moroccan agricultural specialists and by Moroccan journalists. The papers also reported in August that Israeli Transport Minister Haim Corfu had been invited to attend a transportation convention in Morocco. This marked the first time an Israeli cabinet member had been asked to attend a conference in an Arab country other than Egypt. In October, the king himself met several Israeli officials when he received members of the World Association of Moroccan Jewry at his palace in Rabat. Those with whom he met included four Moroccan-born Israeli members of Knesset, among them Rafi Edri, who had accompanied Peres to Ifrane. Finally, four Moroccan businessmen and agriculturalists visited Israel in March 1987. The Moroccans met with a number of Israeli officials, including Deputy Minister of Agriculture Avraham Katz-Oz and Yitzhak Peretz, a Morocan-born member of Knesset affiliated with the Labor party. Katz-Oz told reporters that he had met the men during his own visit to Morocco two years earlier and expressed the view that, despite denials from Rabat, the delegation would not have been possible without the approval of Moroccan authorities.

The United States Contribution

Three kinds of explanations have been advanced by those who seek to account for King Hassan's receptivity to contact with Israel.

First, some argue that Hassan is motivated by a desire to demonstrate the strategic value of a Moroccan connection to the United States and other Western powers and, in so doing, to acquire tangible benefits in return. Second, some suggest that Moroccan calls for Arab-Israeli reconciliation are not totally cynical but, rather, that the king genuinely regards himself as a bridge between Arabs and Jews. Third, some assert that Hassan is pursuing a strategy that he sincerely believes to be in the interest of the Arabs in general and the Palestinians in particular. These three explanations are not mutually exclusive.

Morocco depends heavily on United States military and economic assistance, which is essential for the conduct of the war in the Western Sahara and, more generally, for the nation's economic survival.[11] As shown in the acompanying table, Washington currently provides Rabat with about $130 million annually in economic and military assistance. The amount of overall foreign assistance to Morocco declined somewhat between 1983 and 1986, and this is naturally a source of concern to Rabat. More generally, however, United States aid has more than doubled since the Reagan administration came to power and the percentage of assistance given as a grant has increased steadily since 1982. Even though these expressions of American friendship toward the regime in Rabat are hardly adequate to offset Morocco's deepening economic troubles, they represent significant sums of money, which King Hassan's government would find it extremely difficult to do without.

The king may be hoping that his gesture toward Israel will lead to a substantial increase in assistance from the United States. After all, Egypt currently receives about $2.5 billion in United States aid annually, a figure that assumed such proportions only after the Camp David Accords of 1978. Thus, were his meeting with Peres to generate serious movement toward Arab-Israeli accommodation, Hassan might find it reasonable for Washington to show its appreciation by helping to meet the economic needs of a valuable Arab ally. In all probability, however, Hassan's objectives and expectations were less grandiose. The king's immediate concern in 1986 was to limit the aid cuts expected to result from United States efforts to reduce its budget deficit. He also hoped, if possible, to see American foreign assistance restored to its 1985 or 1984 level.

In calculating that an overture toward Israel might help him to acquire more United States support, the king has not only been influenced by the example of Egypt. Hassan is also aware that several black African countries, most notably Zaire and Liberia, have been able to shore up United States aid packages by reestablishing diplomatic

Table 1
United States Foreign Assistance to Morocco, 1980–1986
(millions of U.S. dollars)

Fiscal Year	1980	1981	1982	1983	1984	1985	1986
Development Assistance (grant)	9.1	12.1	10.7	13.5	19.0	19.5	20.0
Economic Support Funds (grant)	0	0	0	0	7.0	15.0	11.5
Public Law 480 Title I (loan)	5.8	25.0	35.0	27.5	45.0	55.0	40.0
Public Law 480 Title II (grant)	9.9	16.	13.5	10.5	14.9	8.8	5.6
Foreign Military Sales (guaranteed loan)	25.0	33.4	30.0	75.0	38.75	8.0	5.0
Military Assistance Program (grant)	0	0	0	25.0	30.0	40.0	45.0
International Military Education & Training Program (IMET) (grant)	0.9	1.0	1.1	1.3	1.5	1.47	1.85
TOTAL	50.7	87.6	90.3	152.8	156.15	147.77	128.95
TOTAL GRANT	19.9	29.2	25.3	50.3	72.4	84.77	83.95
PERCENT GRANT	39%	33%	28%	33%	46%	57%	65%

Source: U.S. Department of State

relations with the Jewish state. Yet another indication that Hassan hopes his moderate stance towards Israel will contribute to increased United States aid is the fact that he has sought to generate support for Moroccan interests from Jewish and Zionist groups in the United States. For example, it is no accident that he chose David Amar and Jo Ohanna to lead a high-level mission to the United States in the spring of 1985. Amar, the king's personal business manager, is also head of the Moroccan Jewish community. Ohanna is the only Jewish member of the current Moroccan parliament. More recently, when a new Moroccan ambassador to the United States was named early in 1987, he made it a point to meet with American Jewish leaders and a number of Jewish Congressmen. For example, the new ambassador, M'hamed Bargach, met in April with Stephen Solarz (D-N.Y.), an outspoken supporter of Israel who several years earlier had been critical of United States aid to Morocco, and Howard Wolpe (D-Mich.). Indeed, reports of the meeting, including pictures, were printed in the weekly newspapers serving a number of American Jewish communities.

Rabat not only seeks direct economic assistance from the United States. Extremely important, too, is World Bank and International Monetary Fund (IMF) policy toward Morocco, which to a considerable degree is shaped by the attitude of the administration in Washington. Since 1983, the World Bank has almost doubled its lending to Morocco, the amount having increased from roughly $250 million to more than $400 million annually. The International Monetary Fund has also played an increasingly important role in the financial affairs of the country. As Rabat's current accounts deficit worsened and contributed to an external debt approaching $13 billion, the IMF in September 1985 granted Morocco 18 months access to $230 million in standby credit and an additional $132 million for the financing of overseas grain purchases. In August 1986, with another half billion dollars added to the external debt, and with Morocco unable to pay either its bill for imports or its debt service obligations, the IMF agreed to negotiate a new loan package and to reschedule the country's debt yet again.

Morocco is receiving this assistance through its incorporation into the "Baker Plan," named for United States Treasury Secretary James Baker. Fashioned at the 1985 World Bank-IMF Conference, the plan offers fifteen countries a total $20 billion in commercial credit in return for austerity measures and economic policy reforms. Morocco is one of the countries included in the plan, and in part the World Bank and the IMF have been responsive to Rabat's needs because Morocco has indeed carried out many of the belt-tightening and reform measures demanded by its international creditors. For example, the country has reduced subsidies on foodstuffs and other basic commodities and cut public spending during the last eighteen months. Morocco has also begun to limit state intervention in the economy and to expand the private sector.

Rabat's ties with the United States are critical, too; Morocco would not likely have been included in the Baker Plan had it not been seen as a team player and a valuable ally by the Reagan administration. Thus, IMF and World Bank assistance to Morocco — whatever its long-term value, and this is a matter of debate — is also in large measure a function of Moroccan-American relations.

*****

Although Morocco has long enjoyed a cordial relationship with the United States, events of the last few years have led some in Washington to wonder about the value of a close alliance with King Hassan,[12] and this in turn has caused Rabat to seek opportunities to assure the United States that it is indeed a useful and reliable ally. To begin, internal unrest and domestic challenges to Hassan's rule have raised questions about the long-term stability of the monarchical regime in Morocco. In 1979, for example, in the wake of the Iranian revolution, the Central Intelligence Agency issued a report indicating that the government of King Hassan could be overthrown in the near future. Thereafter, concern intensified as a result of major rioting in Casablanca in 1981, postponed elections in the same year, a military shakeup following allegations of a plot against the monarchy in 1983, and blatantly rigged local elections in the latter year as well. A watershed of sorts was reached in January 1984, when widespread rioting left the nation badly shaken and brought a government crackdown that added to the climate of tension and uncertainty.[13] The combined weight of these developments led some in Washington to suggest that United States interests were not well-served by close identification with the government of King Hassan.

Comparisons between Morocco and Iran were common at this time and reinforced doubts about the future of Hassan's government.[14] These comparisons were encouraged, in the first instance, by structural similarities between the shah's regime and that of King Hassan. Both were traditional monarchies supported by the military and governing in association with a small and privileged elite. Symbolic factors also suggested commonalities between the government in Rabat and that in Tehran prior to the revolution. These included both the pomp and extravagance of palace life, and the opposition of Islamic movements claiming that monarchies are alien to the true spirit of the religion. Relevant, finally, was the fact Hassan received the shah after his overthrow while opponents of the Moroccan monarch visited Tehran following Khomeini's ascent to power.

Whether justified or not, all of this contributed to concern about the long-term prospects of King Hassan and his government and lent credibility to the view of those who argued that the king might soon be incapable of containing the challenges confronting him. Even if the regime did survive, some added, repression would inevitably increase and this would make the Rabat government a less desirable ally. Senior officials of the Reagan administration were not themselves overly preoccupied with concerns of this sort. On the other hand, criticisms and doubts were expressed in Congressional and State Department circles and could not be ignored by authorities in Rabat.

Rabat's worries about its ties to the United States have also been shaped by past disputes over the delivery and use of American weapons. Beginning in 1977, there were complaints that Morocco was violating a 1960 security assistance agreement between the two countries and this brought opposition, both in Congress and by the Carter administration, to the continued provision of certain weapons to Morocco. The charge was made, in particular, that Rabat was using United States-supplied aircraft in the Saharan war, even though Washington had made them available with the understanding that they would not be employed outside of Morocco's internationally recognized borders. The administration announced in November 1978 that it was limiting arms sales to Morocco because of this situation;[15] and the following spring, both because of the arms question and because of growing strains in Moroccan-American relations more generally, Rabat asked President Carter to withdraw the United States ambassador in Rabat.

Washington modified its arms policy toward Morocco late in 1979 and, significantly, a key factor in overcoming congressional opposition was the support that Rabat received from a number of representatives known for their sympathies toward Israel. A full account of the role that pro-Israeli political action groups played in this episode is not available, but it does appear that these groups encouraged their friends on Capitol Hill to be responsive to the needs of King Hassan's government.

Changing attitudes and perceptions within the Carter administration also had much to do with the change in policy. The revolution in Iran led to charges that the shah had fallen because of inadequate United States support, and Washington was thus sensitive to the contention that it might no longer be perceived as a strong and reliable ally. In this connection Assistant Secretary of State for Near Eastern and South Asian Affairs Harold Saunders, in January 1980, made the following statement to Congress about the need to assist Morocco: "With Southwest Asia in turmoil, we need to nurture our relations as never before with all Islamic and nonaligned states, but we particularly need to stand up for and support our avowed friends and supporters.''[16] Rabat's case in the American capital was further helped by the fact that Polisario forces carried out attacks inside Morocco in 1978 and 1979. These raids added validity to Rabat's insistence that it was not fighting a "foreign" war in the Sahara and that the use of United States weapons against Polisario thus was not a violation, or at least not a serious violation, of the security assistance agreement it had signed with the United States.

The political orientation of the Reagan administration predisposed it to be less critical of Rabat, and Washington accordingly agreed in 1981 and 1982 to increase the flow of arms to Morocco. Morris Draper, who replaced Harold Saunders as assistant secretary of state for Near Eastern and South Asian affairs, stated in March 1981 that "it would not be in the spirit of this Administration's policy if support for America's traditional and historical friends. . . were to be withheld.''[17] Moreover, a number of senior United States officials visited Morocco at this time, including Secretary of State Alexander Haig who traveled to Rabat in February 1982. One result of this new warmth in Moroccan-American relations was the establishment early in 1982 of a joint military commission. Another was a dramatic increase in the amount of military assistance that Washington proposed to provide to Morocco. The administration in April asked Congress to authorize $100 million in military sales credits for the 1983 fiscal year, an increase of more than 300 percent from the 1982 level of $30 million. The joint maneuvers that Moroccan and American armed forces carried out in April 1983 was an additional manifestation of the deepening military cooperation between Washington and Rabat.

In 1984 a new and potentially more serious complication emerged in Moroccan-American relations, the formation of a political union between Morocco and Libya. In August, Hassan met with Muammar Qaddafi in Oujda and signed a treaty establishing the Arab-African Union. Moreover, though the Oujda Agreement envisioned only a loose confederal structure linking the two states, the Arab-African Union was not limited to symbolic pronouncements professing an intention to work for unity in the future. On the contrary, it was marked by expanded economic and cultural cooperation and by the actual creation of federal political institutions, some of which had begun to function by the end of 1984.[18]

The agreement between Hassan and Qaddafi was eminently reasonable from the Moroccan point of view.[19] Rabat's motivation for the accord was to end Tripoli's support for Polisario guerrillas, Morocco's adversary in the eight-year-old war in the Western Sahara; to offset a 1983 Treaty of Fraternity and Concord between Algeria,

Tunisia, and Mauritania, which reduced the influence of both Morocco and Libya in the North African political arena; and to gain a variety of economic benefits, the most important being the opportunity for unemployed Moroccans to find work in Libya. Furthermore, although there had long been serious strains in the relationship between Rabat and Tripoli, a rapprochement between the two governments had been in the making for over a year, which meant that Washington and others might properly have anticipated the Hassan-Qaddafi alliance of August 1984.

The formation of the Arab-African Union nevertheless took the United States by surprise and brought bitter denunciations from American officials. The Reagan administration felt betrayed by its allies in Rabat and was particularly angry that the initiative for the new alliance had come from Hassan. One of Washington's fears was that the union might enable Qaddafi to exploit domestic opposition in Morocco, or perhaps move Morocco away from its traditional moderate and pro-Western foreign policy. The principal United States concern, however, was that the union with Morocco would enhance the legitimacy and reduce the diplomatic isolation of the Muammar Qaddafi, whom the United States considers an international outlaw. Equally important, Washington worried that under the mutual defense provisions of the unity agreement, United States arms made available to Morocco might find their way to Tripoli, perhaps even to be used in Qaddafi's foreign adventures.

Hassan insisted that United States fears were unfounded and suggested that his association with Qaddafi would actually moderate the Libyan leader's behavior. The United States remained skeptical, however, and the United States-Moroccan relations were accordingly strained during the latter part of 1984. Moreover, these strains were intensified, and any hope that the Moroccan connection might moderate Qaddafi's own behavior dashed, when Egyptian police apprehended Libyan agents seeking to carry out a campaign of terror and assassination late in the year. United States determination to take action against Qaddafi intensified during 1985 and 1986, culminating with bombing raids on Tripoli and Benghazi in April of the latter year. These developments caught Hassan in the crossfire between his Libyan and American allies and created considerable tension in relations between Washingon and Rabat, all of which helps to explain Hassan's desire to appear sensitive to United States ties to Israel and supportive of American peace-making efforts in the Middle East. Fearful that his Libyan connection might bring an end to the American support his government enjoyed, and on which it had in fact become heavily dependent, the Moroccan monarch sought opportunities to demonstrate to the United States the utility of his friendship.

*****

An example of Hassan's effort to make himself useful to the United States was his responsiveness to Washington's desire to gain access to Moroccan military bases for use, if necessary, by the United States Rapid Deployment Force. The RDF is a strike force that had been created specifically for use in the Middle East. In the spring of 1982, on the eve of Israel's invasion of Lebanon, Washington and Rabat were involved in intense negotiations over the question of American access to Moroccan military facilities, and the Reagan administration almost certainly signaled that a return was expected on its investment in Morocco. The matter was a major topic of discussion when Hassan visited the United States in mid-May, and a week later the two countries concluded an agreement whereby American military planes would be permitted to use Moroccan airfields in the event of an emergency in the Middle East or Africa. Facilities were to be made available to the United States at several Moroccan airfields, most notably the military section of the Casablanca international airport and the military air base at Sidi Slimane. This arrangement would continue for six years, with the possibility of renewal in 1988.

Although Rabat recognized the need to satisfy the Reagan administration, and hence concluded an agreement with Washington, the matter of United States access to Moroccan military installations was highly sensitive for the Moroccans. Negotiations were intense. Hassan's government at first played down the importance of its talks with the United States and then, for a time, sought to conceal the fact that a facilities access accord had been concluded. Washington, for its part, respected Moroccan concerns to the extent of agreeing that the text of the accord not be made public. There are also reports that Morocco retains a right to reject requests for access to its facilities if the United States is taking action against an Arab country with which Rabat has friendly relations.

Morocco's military cooperation with the United States in general, and the facilities access agreement in particular, gave much ammunition to King Hassan's critics. Both domestic and foreign opponents of the king charged that Hassan had subordinated Moroccan and Arab interests to those of the United States and Israel. The purpose of the Rapid Deployment Force, they insisted, was to protect American interests in the Middle East, adding that these interests often ran counter to those of the Arabs. Israel and a few conservative and

unrepresentative Arab regimes might benefit as well, but the projection of United States military power into the region nonetheless ran
counter to the true interests of the Arab world; on this basis they condemned Hassan for betraying the cause of the Arab nation. Such
arguments were forcefully advanced by the king's critics at home and
abroad, including both those on the left and those associated with
militant Islamic movements. Algeria, in particular, sought to embarrass
Morocco by calling on all Arab governments to deny the RDF access
to their military facilities.

Making all this even more sensitive from the Moroccan point of
view was the fact that Washington and Rabat were conducting negotiations and concluding an agreement at a time when Israel's invasion
of Lebanon was widely expected. Following numerous Israeli denunciations of PLO activity in southern Lebanon, the Israel Defense Forces
had mobilized in April for a possible sweep across the country's
northern border. Many observers predicted that an invasion was
imminent; and, even though the operation did not immediately take
place, there was no doubt about the determination of Menachem
Begin's government to neutralize PLO forces in Lebanon. Moreover,
many in the Arab world believed that the United States was taking
a tolerant attitude toward Israeli designs, and perhaps even giving
Jerusalem active encouragement. At the very least, the United States
at the time shared the Israeli government's belief that instability in
Lebanon was primarily the result of the PLO's presence in that country.
Reinforcing the perception of United States-Israeli collusion was a visit
to Washington by Defense Minister Ariel Sharon. Sharon met with
Secretary of State Alexander Haig several weeks before the actual
invasion, which took place early in June. Although it is denied in both
Washington and Jerusalem, many believe that Haig at this time gave
tacit and perhaps even direct approval for the invasion.

While these developments gave King Hassan reason to put some
distance between himself and the Reagan administration, he in fact
judged it in his interest to do just the opposite. The conclusion of a
facilities access agreement between the United States and Morocco
accordingly indicates the degree to which Hassan attaches importance
to his American connection and is willing, if necessary, to take stands
that are unpopular in the Arab world in order to preserve it. Furthermore, the king not only went forward with the military cooperation
accord he had concluded with the United States, he also involved
himself deeply in the diplomatic activity that followed Israel's invasion
of Lebanon, and he did so in close collaboration with the United States.
This, too, shows the king's priorities and strategy in the defense of
Moroccan interests.

After the invasion, Morocco helped to organize a meeting of the Arab League in order to respond to events in Lebanon and, also, to the evolution of the Arab-Israeli conflict more generally. Then-Foreign Minister Boucetta visited a number of Middle Eastern countries in August to canvass Arab opinion and to lay the ground work for an Arab summit, to be held in Fez in September. About this time, on September 1, the American president put forward a peace initiative designed to resolve the critical Palestinian dimension of the Arab-Israeli conflict. President Reagan proposed that Israel relinquish control of the West Bank and Gaza, Arab areas which it had occupied since 1967, and that the Palestinians who live in these territories be permitted to achieve their self-determination in association with the Kingdom of Jordan.

Although the Reagan Plan was not entirely satisfactory to the Arabs, Hassan praised it and, along with a few other Arab leaders, attempted to see that it was favorably reviewed at the Fez meeting. Clearly, Israel's expulsion of the PLO from Lebanon, invading a sovereign Arab country and laying siege to its capital, did not weaken the king's desire to ally hmself with Washington on matters affecting the Middle East and did not erode his willingness to work for an accommodation with the Jewish state.

The Arab summit viewed the Reagan Plan as a positive development but urged the United States administration to go farther. It proposed its own alternative, which was Arab recognition of Israel in return for creation of an independent Palestinian state in the West Bank and Gaza, with East Jerusalem as its capital. Washington's response to the decisions taken at Fez was mixed. On the one hand, the administration was disappointed that the Reagan initiative received only a lukewarm endorsement. On the other, although the Arabs' own peace plan was not acceptable to the United States, Washington recognized that it was an expression of Arab moderation, one which moved the Arab world closer to acceptance of Israel's right to exist. Equally important in the context of the present analysis, Washington acknowledged that Hassan had played an important role in formulating and securing approval for the Arab peace plan, and the administration took note as well of the king's response to those who complained that the plan did not unambiguously express a willingness to make peace with Israel. With an eye toward observers in the United States, Hassan issued public statements making it clear that Morocco was prepared to recognize the Jewish state and affirming that this was also the position of the other Arab countries that endorsed the plan adopted at Fez.

In October, Hassan led a delegation to the United States to explain the plan and urge support for it. He also sought to discuss with administration officials concrete steps that might be taken to promote peace. Six Arab states participated in the mission. Hassan had originally sought to add a representative of the Palestine Liberation Organization but abandoned this proposal when the United States objected. While in Washington, Hassan again praised the Reagan Plan and stated that peace with Israel was possible. In one public declaration he expressed confidence that peace and coexistence could be achieved "on the basis of the American and Arab proposals and the United Nations Security Council resolutions." In another he stated that "the Arab nations will recognize Israel if it returns to its pre-1967 borders."[20]

King Hassan, an important head of state, led an Arab delegation to the United States and publicly affirmed in the American capital his willingness to make peace with Israel. This action demonstrates once again that Hassan believes it is in his interest to seek an accommodation with the Jewish state and to coordinate his policies closely with the United States. Indeed, Hassan has considerable freedom to maneuver; Morocco is far from Israel, and the country has no Palestinians among its population. Nevertheless, while he may therefore have fewer constraints than some other Arab leaders, the critical point in the present context is Hassan's judgment that he can maximize the economic and political benefits his country receives from the United States by attempting to move Arab attitudes toward Israel in a direction pleasing to Washington.

*****

Under Hassan's leadership, Morocco has adopted a position toward the Arab-Israeli conflict that will win it favor in the United States. The country has in recent years pursued this policy with consistency, even during periods when Arab-American relations were strained. Hassan has also been willing to pursue this policy in a visible manner, not only in the United States but in the Arab world as well and, to a reasonable degree, inside Morocco itself.

Therefore, it is not surprising that the king would regard a new overture toward Israel, and even a gesture as bold and dramatic as his public summit with Shimon Peres, as a useful device for easing the strains that entered into Moroccan-American relations following the 1984 treaty between Hassan and Muammar Qaddafi. Washington was disturbed and perhaps even offended that one of its closest allies in the Arab world would offer legitimacy to a man whom the United States considers an international outlaw. The Reagan administration also worried that Moroccan resources, and especially weapons supplied to Morocco by the United States itself, might become available to Qaddafi and actually enhance the Libyan leader's ability to make trouble. As the confrontation between Washington and Tripoli deepened during 1985 and the first part of 1986, Hassan experienced growing pressure to cut his ties with Qaddafi and concluded that action to smooth out his relations with the United States was necessary. Seen in this context, and against the background of his past contacts with the Jewish state, his invitation to Peres became less of a surprise.

United States praise for Hassan was not long in coming. In glowing statements, the White House and State Department lauded the king for his "courageous initiative" and "potentially very important" contribution to the Arab-Israeli peace process. As expressed in a State Department press release issued the day after the summit, "This is a historic opportunity to further the cause of peace in the region and the United States Government urges all governments to support these leaders." The United States admitted that it had been consulted in advance about the meeting and explained that Washington appreciated Hassan's initiative all the more in view of the importance it attaches to face-to-face contacts between Israeli and Arab leaders. For several years, the Reagan administration has taken the position that any revival of the peace process must involve direct talks between Israel and its neighbors. One State Department official interviewed immediately after the summit called this an "absolutely fundamental" element of Washington's Middle East policy, strongly endorsing the Hassan-Peres meeting in this context and adding that "this is the way in which serious work can get started."[21] Two days later, United States Secretary of State George Shultz described the summit as "an important step forward in creating an atmosphere in the region that will foster a broader peace."[22]

Richard Murphy, assistant secretary of state for Near Eastern and South Asian affairs, summed up United States reaction in the following statement before a subcommittee of the House Foreign Affairs Committee in October.

> The growing realization in the Arab world that direct contacts with Israel are acceptable and beneficial was clearly exemplified by King Hassan's meeting with Shimon Peres and the muted reaction to it, including in the Arab world. The Moroccan monarch joined those who forthrightly declare to the world that they are willing to take risks for peace — to face threats from rejectionists who all too often resort to cowardly terrorism and intimidation to block peace. We applaud Morocco's action.

Murphy's statement, entitled "Supporting U.S. Interests in the Middle East," also listed other "positive developments that we have seen in the region over the past several months," and at the top of this list was Hassan's abrogation in August of the treaty of union with Libya.

In sum, Hassan's calculations appear to have been sound so far as Moroccan-American relations are concerned. The public pronouncements of State Department and other United States officials should not be taken too literally, and the administration in Washington was certainly under no illusions about Hassan's various motives. Nevertheless, the king had succeeded in demonstrating his desire to end the strains in Moroccan-American relations and in showing that his country might have something to offer the United States in return for its support. Thus, as an Israeli commentator, Asher Wallfish, wrote on the day of the summit, the Moroccan monarch had staged "a *coup de theatre* for the guest as well as the host" but "Hassan will probably gain more from the visit than Peres." The king "constantly needs to prove to the United States administration that he deserves to keep on getting the financial and military aid he receives. What better way than by mounting a fresh initiative for dialogue?"[23] And indeed, Hassan's meeting with Peres, followed by his announcement five weeks later that Morocco was terminating its union with Libya, brought about a significant improvement in relations between Rabat and Washington. The Hassan-Peres summit also received very favorable notices in Europe.

Other Contributing Factors

The preceding might suggest that Hassan's interest in Arab-Israeli accommodation is insincere and manipulative. In fact, however, it may reasonably be argued that the king is motivated not only by a concern for the preservation of good relations with the United States but also by a belief that he has a special role to play in bridging the gap between Arabs and Jews and, further, by a conviction that he is rendering a genuine service to the Palestinian cause. Consideration of these arguments is not intended to challenge the view that Hassan's political calculus is based above all on a desire to be recognized and rewarded by the administration in Washington. Rather, the arguments are presented to identify and assess some of the other factors that contribute to the king's receptivity to contact with Israel. These additional perspectives on the Hassan-Peres summit will also contribute to an understanding of the king's self-image and of moderate Arab views about solutions to the Palestinian problem.

The situation of Morocco's own Jewish community sheds important light on Hassan's attitude toward the Jews and Israel.[24] Even though the number of Jews in Morocco has shrunk from over 250,000 at independence to less than 18,000 at present, the Moroccan Jewish community remains the largest and most secure in the Arab world. Members participate actively in the nation's economic and political life. Although many are poor, many others are quite prosperous, and there is a bureaucratic and professional Jewish middle class. A recent election brought a Jew into parliament. Further, because most Jews today live in Casablanca, the regime has in the past been responsive to their needs by including a Jew among its candidates for the Casablanca Municipal Council. Finally, and perhaps most important, Jews retain control of their community and its institutions, including schools, courts, social services, and administrative councils. In each of these areas, the Jews of Morocco enjoy considerable autonomy, permitting them to maintain a level of communal solidarity and coherence that is unknown among the Jewish minority in any other Arab country.

Hassan takes personal pride in this situation, regarding himself as the protector of Moroccan Jewry; as a result, most of the latter believe the king is sincerely concerned about their welfare. Moreover, Hassan is carrying forward an established historical tradition, which encourages the view that the king's attitude is neither aberrant nor cynical but, rather, deeply rooted in the Moroccan monarchy's conviction that it is responsible for the well-being of all citizens of the country. For example, Hassan's father, Mohammed V, was admired for his refusal to deliver Jews to the Nazis during World War II, and for this a public square was recently dedicated to his memory in the Israeli city of Ashkelon. No other Arab leader, not evan Anwar Sadat, has been so recognized by the Jewish state.

These are among the considerations that led Moshe Dayan to write that King Hassan genuinely believes himself to have a special role to play in bringing Jews and Arabs together. This is the view that Hassan has of himself as leader of Morocco, a view he sees as totally consistent with the projection of Morocco's Islamic identity as a nation; an extension of this explicit and visible commitment to Arab-Jewish cooperation within Morocco is the contribution the king aspires to make to Arab-Jewish reconciliation in the international arena. Hassan has decreed, for example, that Moroccan-born Jews living in Israel have not forfeited their Moroccan citizenship and are welcome to return. Indeed, he has issued statements inviting them to do so on a number of occasions.

Even before the round of secret diplomacy that led up to the Camp David Accords of 1978, the king encouraged visits to Morocco by prominent American Jews and even by some Israelis who were not of Moroccan origin. Visitors were often told that, under Hassan's guidance, Morocco conceives of itself as a bridge, as a point of meeting and transition. The country's history and geography show it to be a link between Europe and Africa. Similarly, with respect to ideology and culture, it is a place where East and West intersect. In the context of this global and internationalist perspective, it is perhaps natural that the king should also see himself and his country as a point of reconciliation between Muslims and Arabs on the one hand and Jews and Israelis on the other. To be sure, there are elements of romanticism and even propaganda in such images of Morocco. In other circumstances, Hassan stresses that his nation's core is Arab and Islamic and that all other aspects of its identity are of secondary importance, and indeed this is the case. In the king's view, however, being Arab and Muslim is perfectly consistent with the international vocation that he has assigned to himself and his country.

All of this leads to the conclusion that Hassan takes seriously his image as protector of the Jews in Morocco and views himself as a leader capable of transcending local quarrels and of working for Arab-Jewish accommodation on the international level. Accordingly, the king's attitude toward Israel and toward Jews is motivated not by self-interest alone but also by a genuine sense of historic and personal responsibility, the latter reflecting both a sincere ideological commitment and a healthy measure of egoism. As expressed by an American diplomat at the conclusion of the Ifrane summit, the king "really does see himself as playing a role in resolving the conflict. . . . He has long portrayed himself as a leader in the Arab world, as someone worthy of international attention."[25]

*****

Another part of the explanation stands in partial opposition to theories of self-interest by placing emphasis on the contribution to the Palestinian cause that Hassan aspires to make. This, too, may reflect a degree of egoism. Further, Palestinians and others may legitimately debate whether Hassan's initiatives in actuality advance the realization of Palestinian rights, and the king's actions have in fact been condemned by many Palestinians. Nevertheless, it remains probable that Hassan's motivations include a sincere desire to solve the Arab-Israeli conflict in a way that respects and responds to the Palestinians' demand for a homeland.

Hassan's contribution to shaping and winning support for the Fez Plan is consistent with this analysis. Although the plan remains unacceptable to Arab rejectionists, who refuse to accept the existence of Israel as a Jewish state, it is nonetheless firmly based on the national and political rights of the Palestinian people, above all the right to self-determination. As stated, the plan calls for creation of an independent Palestinian state in the West Bank and Gaza with East Jerusalem as its capital. Further, the Fez Plan is an attempt by moderate Arab states to win support for the Palestinian cause in the United States and Europe, and to persuade the Western powers in turn to exert pressure on Israel. Put forward in response to the September 1 peace initiative of President Reagan, the plan offers recognition of Israel in return for the creation of a Palestinian state; and indeed this two-state solution has already been endorsed by most European nations.

Even if the Fez Plan has not won as much support in the United States as Hassan and other moderate Arabs might have hoped, it stands as a constructive and reasoned response to the Reagan administration's own peace proposals. The proposal also contrasts sharply with Israel's uncompromising attitude toward the American initiative of September 1, 1982. While the Arabs indicate a willingness to make peace with Israel in the context of a two-state solution, the Israeli government, then under the leadership of Menachem Begin, totally rejected the Reagan initiative and stated that it is not even an acceptable starting point for negotiations. Under such circumstances, Hassan and other Arab leaders might logically conclude that Arab moderation would strain relations between Washington and Jerusalem and produce greater American support for Palestinian rights. At the very least, it should have led the Reagan administration to act on its calls for Israeli withdrawal from the Occupied Territories and for the exercise of Palestinian self-determination in association with Jordan.

Hassan's subsequent activities have not strayed from either the Fez Plan or the moderate Arab consensus it represents. This was evident when he urged the Arab League in March 1986 to test Israeli willingness to negotiate on the basis of the plan and also when he himself took the initiative by inviting Peres to Ifrane. Moroccan officials commenting on the Hassan-Peres summit placed particular emphasis on this point. For example, Foreign Minister Filali told the *Jerusalem Post* in an interview, ''The most positive result, in my opinion, is that Peres understood the fundamentals of the Fez plan, which Israel has always opposed.''[26] The following excerpts from this interview are also indicative of Morocco's desire to make progress towards solving the Israeli-Palestinian conflict.

It is clear that if Peres had arrived with concrete proposals the king would have been happier.

We thought the Israelis were ready to take a step toward the Palestinians. In any event, we feel it was necessary to do what we did, that is to start a dialogue.

It is my feeling that the Israelis must be less intransigent. We (ourselves) are realistic and believe that this conflict has gone on much too long.

Peres cannot return to Morocco if he does so only to tell us the same thing. But he promised in a document he gave us that Israel would not impose its sovereignty on the Occupied Territories.

I also want to stress the warmth radiating from the meeting. There was a kind of electric current flowing between the king and Peres and between the members of the Moroccan delegation and the Israeli team — in which was included a Jew of Moroccan origin. When the king appealed to Shimon Peres, he used the word "brotherhood."

Some of these same points were expressed by Hassan himself when he reported to the Moroccan people on his meeting with Peres. The king stated, for example, that he had resisted all attempts to move the talks beyond the context of the Fez Plan. He accepted Peres's determination to present his own proposals; but he insisted that the meeting be exploratory, not part of a negotiating process, and repeatedly stated that he himself was interested only in exploring Israel's attitude toward the Fez Plan. Also, in his speech and elsewhere, Hassan emphasized his responsibilities within the Arab League, including the chairmanship of its committee on Jerusalem. Here, again, he reaffirmed his determination not to modify the established Arab position on the Palestinian question, insisting that his sole purpose was to give Israel an opportunity to narrow the gap between itself and Arab moderates.

The king also indicated in his speech that two sets of considerations had influenced the timing of his initiative. One had to do with the circumstances of the Arab world, and of the Palestinians in particular. The other had to do with the domestic political environment in Israel.

In the former context, it is significant, although Hassan did not say this explicitly in his address, that the PLO had asked the king for assistance in the wake of its growing internal fragmentation and its split with King Hussein of Jordan in February 1986. Details of Morocco's contacts with the PLO are not available, but it is known that in the spring of 1986 there were discussions between Moroccan officials and representatives of the PLO and that the latter asked the former for diplomatic support from the king. In June, for example, a high-level PLO delegation visited Rabat for consultations with senior Moroccan officials and, presumably, with Hassan as well. The timing of this visit was important; it took place five weeks before the summit and after several months of Moroccan statements about the need to encourage Israel to negotiate on the basis of the Fez Plan.

In the latter context, Hassan sought to test Israel's political waters before Peres turned the premiership over to Yitzhak Shamir of Likud. Likud represents that segment of the Israeli electorate that is committed to territorial maximalism. For example, the Likud-led government of Shamir's predecessor, Menachem Begin, rejected the peace initiative put forward by Ronald Reagan in 1982 because it called for Israeli withdrawal from the West Bank and Gaza. The Labor Alignment led by Peres, on the other hand, reacted favorably to the Reagan initiative, even though not all of its provisions are acceptable to Labor and even though the alignment shares with Likud a rejection of the Fez Plan. Despite their political and ideological differences, Labor and Likud had shared power in a government of national unity since 1984, agreeing to rotate the premiership between the leaders of the two parties. Under this arrangement, Peres had taken the first turn as prime minister and was scheduled to relinquish the position to Shamir in October 1986.

Hassan hoped to exploit the political divisions between Labor and Likud and to provide Peres with a reason to withdraw from his agreement with Shamir. Aware that Peres's popularity among Israelis had risen substantially in recent months, and also that some Alignment insiders were urging the prime minister to break the coalition agreement and call new elections, the king hoped to give Peres an opportunity to translate moderation toward the Arabs into domestic political capital. Should a breakthrough be achieved at Ifrane, Peres might decide to campaign on a peace plan, which he and Hassan had fashioned and, with this additional momentum, he might achieve a large enough victory to permit Labor to form a government without the participation of Likud. Such a development would, of course, be in interest of Hassan and other moderate Arab leaders. Even if the Ifrane summit did not accomplish enough to have this kind of immediate impact on the Israeli political scene, it could nonetheless give Zionist advocates of territorial compromise ammunition to use in more distant elections. Israeli moderates consistently complain that the credibility of their political platform is limited by the absence of Arab leaders willing to state explicitly and publicly that they are ready for peace with the Jewish state.

A final point stressed in Hassan's own analysis is the fact that the meeting was held in Morocco. The king reported that Israeli officials had requested that the summit be convened in the United States during a visit Hassan had planned. A meeting in Washington also appears to have been the preference of the Reagan administration. Both Jerusalem and Washington, it can be argued, would actually get more mileage from an Arab leader welcoming the Israeli prime minister to his own country. Nevertheless, while they welcomed the summit, some of the president's advisors in fact complained that they had gone to considerable trouble to accommodate Hassan's wish to be received in the United States capital. They were accordingly displeased when the meeting with Peres required the king to cancel his trip to the United States. As a result, Hassan would almost certainly have agreed to a meeting in Washington had he been motivated solely by a desire to score points with the Reagan administration.

Hassan apparently was pursuing other goals as well, and his motivations included a genuine wish that the fruits of his encounter with Peres be substantive as well as symbolic. He sought to maximize his control over the meeting and his leverage over the Israelis, which could be accomplished by hosting rather than attending a meeting with the Israeli prime minister; his purpose in this was almost certainly to increase the chances of striking a bargain, one which would be politically advantageous to Peres but which would also advance the cause of the Palestinians.

In the short run at least, none of this made much difference so far as the Israeli-Palestinian conflict is concerned. Moreover, there were attempts by Egypt, Jordan, and others to foster movement toward a resolution of the conflict during 1986, and these, too, had few practical consequences. The diplomatic activity that characterized 1985 and 1986 thus came to an end and, from the Palestinian point of view, the prospects for an end to occupation appeared more remote than ever. In late 1986 and throughout 1987, the Arab world increasingly turned its attention away from Israel and the Palestinians, to the perceived threat from Iran; Israel, with Yitzhak Shamir now serving as prime minister, not only continued to reject any negotiation based on the Fez Plan, it displayed, at the official level at least, a diminishing interest in any form of territorial compromise in the West Bank and Gaza. Against this background the *intifada*, the Palestinian uprising in the West Bank and Gaza, began to take shape at the end of 1987. The uprising is an attempt by the Palestinians to send a message to both Israel and the Arab world, to the effect that continued occupation is unacceptable and that there will be no peace unless Arabs and Israelis address themselves to the Palestinian problem.

On the other hand, Hassan's vision, which is the vision of Fez, is by no means dead. Indeed, it was powerfully revived during 1988, first by the *intifada* and, even more, by PLO declarations accepting United Nations Resolutions 242 and 338 and endorsing a two-state solution to the Israeli-Palestinian conflict. As a result, the United States has moved in the direction advocated by Hassan, entering into a substantive dialogue with the Palestine Liberation Organization. Senior United States officials have made statements to the effect that Israel will have to resign itself to eventual withdrawal from the Occupied Territories. Further, the events of 1988 gave rise to the discussion and debate inside Israel that Hassan had hoped his own diplomatic initiative would produce. Israelis increasingly regard the Palestinians, rather than Jordan, as the appropriate negotiating partner for any peace talks that might take place in the future. Also, several public opinion polls taken in 1988 and 1989 showed a majority of Israelis to be willing to negotiate with the PLO under certain conditions. Indeed, more than one-third expressed the view that a Palestinian state would be established in the Occupied Territories within ten to twenty years.[27] Although any serious and sustained movement toward peace is still quite remote, the Palestinian problem has returned to a central place on the Middle East's political agenda, and Israel is debating its options with respect to the territories much more seriously and realistically than it has in years.

Hassan cannot claim much credit for these developments. Like President Mubarak of Egypt and King Hussein of Jordan, he has continued to work through quiet diplomacy to encourage movement in this direction. Nevertheless, the Palestinians themselves are responsible for the changes that have begun to take place. By telling Israel and the world that occupation is not cost-free, and by then adding that mutual recognition and peace is a viable and available option, the Palestinians have produced the debate inside Israel that Hassan had earlier hoped his own initiative would generate. While he was unable to achieve his objective, the implications of recent events so far as Rabat's overtures to Israel are concerned are that the king's reasoning was sound and that he was on the right track. The cards he had to play were simply much weaker than those available to the Palestinians; he could not disrupt Israeli lives as the Palestinians have done through the *intifada,* and his advocacy of the Fez Plan fell flat, perhaps inevitably, so long as Israel was convinced that the PLO was unwilling to make peace.

While the limits of what could be accomplished should have been, and perhaps were, known to Hassan from the beginning, the events of 1988 and 1989 lend additional weight to the argument that a genuine search for Arab-Israeli accommodation is among the considerations that have shaped the king's attitude toward Israel. Within the limits of his ability, he has endeavored to say to the Israelis, and perhaps to the Americans as well, what it turns out needed to be said to generate movement toward peace; accordingly, both his reasoning and his motivations, in effect his calculus, have to a significant degree been vindicated. The Hassan-Peres summit of 1986, as well the king's favorable predisposition toward the Jewish states more generally, should therefore not be seen entirely in the context of Rabat's desire to win favor with the United States. Hassan sought to help the Palestinians as well as himself, and although this was not his only motivation, or even his principal one, it is necessary to conclude that the king's invitation to Shimon Peres was not an entirely cynical and manipulative political act.

CHAPTER NINE

The Guarded Relationship
Between Israel and Egypt

Ann M. Lesch

In the ten years that have passed since the signing of the peace treaty between Israel and Egypt, the relationship between the two countries has suffered severe strain. The Israeli invasion of Lebanon in June 1982 and the uprising of the Palestinians on the West Bank and Gaza Strip during 1988 complicated Egypt's ability to deepen the ties with Israel. Israelis, in turn, were disappointed by the lack of warmth in relations and were disturbed by the killing of Israeli tourists and diplomats in the mid-1980s. The promise and hope offered by Camp David have not been realized; yet the accord has not been annulled. Reverting to the prior condition of hostility does not serve the interests of either state and therefore the terms of the treaty are adhered to, albeit in a guarded and circumscribed manner.

Egyptian-Israeli relations can be divided into three distinct phases. From the fall of 1977 through the spring of 1982, both parties concentrated on negotiating the peace treaty and implementing its terms. They exchanged ambassadors in 1979, signed accords in the fields of trade, tourism, and culture, and completed Israel's withdrawal from Sinai, despite complications raised by Israeli negotiators over the status of Tabah.

Even though the bilateral components of the treaty were fulfilled with minimal discord, the wider aspects of the accord remained subject to dispute.[1] Israeli Prime Minister Menachem Begin argued that there should be no linkage between implementation of the bilateral treaty and forward movement on the status of the West Bank and the Gaza Strip. After the Knesset resolved that unified Jerusalem should be the eternal capital of Israel, negotiations over autonomy for the Palestinians

187

in the Occupied Territories virtually halted. Israel's bombing of the partially complete nuclear reactor in Iraq in June 1981, hours after Begin
and Egyptian President Anwar Sadat had met in Sinai, was an acute
embarrassment to the Egyptian government.

The final summit between Begin and Sadat, held in Alexandria
in August 1981, was a bitter experience for Sadat. Begin was unwilling to make any moves on the Palestinian issue and continued to insist on Israel's right to sovereignty over the West Bank and Gaza Strip.
Sadat was confronted with protests in the streets and mounting
demands by opposition politicians that he sever relations and recall
the Egyptian ambassador from Tel Aviv. Faced with those contradictory pressures, Sadat reacted by lashing out at his internal critics. He
arrested more than 1,500 in early September, drawn from all parts of
the political spectrum.

Following Sadat's assassination in October, the new president,
Hosni Mubarak, had to contend with the same contradictory forces.
On the one hand, Israel wanted him to prove that he would not change
Egypt's existing policy toward the peace treaty. On the other hand,
he had to mollify Sadat's internal opponents and prove that he would
not treat Egyptian political forces in the cavalier manner of his
predecessor. Mubarak responded by financing several bilateral accords
during the winter of 1981–82. He allowed Israel to participate in international fairs in Cairo that spring and let Israel open an Academic
Center in May. Nevertheless, he refused to accede to Israeli requests
that he visit Jerusalem: he was willing to go to Israel itself, but not
Jerusalem, following the Knesset-mandated annexation. At home,
Mubarak released politicians and intellectuals from detention and
ended pressure on them to cooperate with Israel. By opening the
political process slightly and allowing the opposition parties to resume
publishing their newspapers, he gained considerable public support.
Egyptians perceived him as following the legally correct path vis-a-vis
Israel without displaying the effusiveness and recklessness of Sadat.
Nor was he held responsible for his predecessor's errors. The tone,
if not the substance, of the relationship began to alter in 1981–1982.

The dramatic change occurred in June 1982 when Israel invaded
Lebanon in order to break up the military and political infrastructure
of the Palestine Liberation Organization, to link up with Lebanese allies
who might control the war-torn country, and to enhance the security
of Israel's borders. The invasion marked the initiation of the second
phase in Egyptian-Israeli relations, generally termed the "cold peace."
That phase lasted until September 1986 and was punctuated by an

initial two years of bitter and acrimonious contact, followed by two years of a slight and gradual thaw.

Soon after the Israeli army entered Lebanon, the Egyptian government decreed a freeze in the normalization process. Existing agreements were honored but no new accords were signed. The invasion, which took place exactly six weeks after Israel completed its withdrawal from Sinai, was perceived by many Egyptians as a slap in their face. The few who had been willing to have contact with Israelis felt undermined: their hopes were dashed that human relations would lead to a broader peace process and less militant Israeli policies. Following the massacre of Palestinians at Sabra and Shatilla refugee camps near Beirut in mid-September 1982, by Lebanese Phalangist militiamen under the eye of Israeli troops, public anger compelled the Cairo government to respond by recalling its ambassador from Tel Aviv.

For the next two years, the relationship was distinctly cool. The Egyptian government sharply criticized Israeli practices in the Occupied Territories, its continued military presence in Lebanon, and its insistence that the West Bank and Gaza Strip should ultimately come under Israeli sovereignty. Only in 1984 did Cairo's attitude begin to shift. In the hope that the hard-line Likud party would lose control over the government to the Labor party, Egypt allowed a delegation from the Labor party to visit Cairo in the spring and expressed in somewhat veiled terms its willingness to improve relations if the political climate in Israel should change.

The Israeli elections, however, were disappointing to Egypt for they demonstrated the polarization of the electorate and forced Labor and Likud to form a National Unity Government. Prime Minister Shimon Peres, therefore, lacked a clear mandate to improve relations with Egypt and renew the peace process. His hands were tied by his Likud partners. Peres managed to persuade the cabinet to withdraw from Lebanon by June 1985 and, in January 1986, to agree to arbitration over Tabah. He maintained a tough stance on the Occupied Territories and did not endorse the PLO-Jordanian agreement of February 1985, which Mubarak had helped to foster. Nevertheless, Egypt allowed ministerial exchanges to take place in the spring and summer of 1985 and began to talk about resuming the normalization process.

Those gestures came to naught. In the fall of 1985, the Israeli bombing of the PLO headquarters in Tunis, the killing of Israeli tourists by an Egyptian soldier in Sinai, and the uproar over the "Achille Lauro" hijacking led to renewed tension between the two countries. The machine-gun attack on Israeli diplomats outside the international fair grounds in Cairo in March 1986, and continued popular resistance to normalization, apparently convinced the government that a low

profile should be maintained. The ongoing stress involved in negotiating the terms for arbitration over Tabah also took its toll on the
relationship.

Nonetheless, a significant shift occurred in 1986, which ushered
in the third phase. An eleventh-hour accord on Tabah enabled Peres
to meet with Mubarak on September 11 and convince Egypt to return
its ambasador to Tel Aviv.[2] For Peres, the summit was a personal
triumph at the end of his term as prime minister. For Mubarak, the
meeting was more ambiguous. He had worked hard to restore Cairo's
credibility in the Arab world and had benefited from the Iran-Iraq war,
which had compelled Baghdad to seek Egyptian arms and manpower.
Arab states had begun to ignore, if not condone, the presence of the
Israeli ambassador in Cairo. If the summit meeting with Peres did not
lead to substantive diplomatic moves toward resolution of the Palestine
problem, Egypt could be placed in an awkward situation once again.

Thus, the emphasis at the September summit and at the follow-
up meeting in February 1987 was on restoring diplomatic momentum.
The two leaders agreed to support the concept of an international conference in which the Palestinians would be represented by a joint
Palestinian-Jordanian delegation. That approach was frustrated,
however, by Peres' inability to win support for it from his Likud partner
and the new prime minister, Yitzhak Shamir. As Peres was visiting
Cairo in early 1987 to discuss the international conference concept,
Shamir was in Washington doggedly opposing it. By the summer
Shamir had clearly checkmated Peres, and the possibility of negotiations was stalled.

The tenth anniversary of Sadat's visit to Jerusalem was marked
not by celebrations with Israel but by an Arab summit conference that
tightened the Egyptian-Iraqi ties and led to the restoration of diplomatic
relations between Egypt and most of the Arab governments. The third
phase in Egyptian-Israeli relations has thus been characterized by complexity and cautiousness: Egypt has balanced the slight improvements
in its relations with Israel by far more extensive improvements in its
relations with the Arab world, and Egyptians have continued to keep
Israelis at arm's length. Even this degree of contact could be jeopardized by the *intifadah*, the Palestinian uprising that began in December
1987.

Normalization

Ever since the peace treaty was signed, Israel and Egypt have
defined normalization differently.[3] From the start, Israel sought a

special relationship with Egypt. Israelis wanted more than a formal peace: they aspired to be accepted totally by Egyptians. In contrast, Egyptians grudgingly accepted the reality of Israel's existence but questioned its right to exist, often rejected its Zionist political philosophy, and sought to support the Palestinian struggle for statehood. Egyptians did not want to remain on a war footing with Israel, but that did not mean that they would embrace the Israeli people.

As Israelis pressed for friendship, Egyptians reacted warily. Officials in Cairo maintained correct contacts but refused to accord Israel a privileged position in relation to other countries. Egyptian tour agents, hotel managers, and merchants dealt with Israeli visitors, but the intellectual community refused overwhelmingly to meet with Israelis, much less to visit Israel itself.

The treaty provided for negotiations on trade, cultural, and civil aviation accords to begin within six months of Israel's interim withdrawal from Sinai, which took place in January 1980. Under Sadat's prodding, bilateral agreements in each of those areas were completed and signed and arrangements were made for oil to be sold to Israel. Nonetheless, signs of public hostility were soon evident. When Israeli President Yitzhak Navon visited Cairo in November 1980, his address to the Peoples Assembly was cancelled because of criticism by the opposition Socialist Labor Party, and his visit to the Helwan iron and steel factory was called off because workers threatened to demonstrate in protest.[4] All the major professional unions — law, medicine, journalism, and university professors — voted to boycott Israelis and to censure any Egyptian who visited Israel.

The freeze on normalization in 1982 gave official sanction to those private attitudes. Tourism and trade were significantly reduced, planned visits by Israeli ministers were cancelled, and scientific contacts were minimized. Even after relations improved in 1984, contacts remained limited between private citizens, and the optimism of 1979 did not return.

Tourism

Tourism has been the most visible arena for normalization. Israelis, isolated since 1948 from the neighboring Arab countries, were eager to break out of their claustrophobic confines. Their right to travel freely to Egypt was viewed as a prime indication of Cairo's intention to establish an open relationship.

Direct travel by bus and air began in 1980, well before the Memorandum of Understanding on Tourism was signed on 17 December 1981. El Al airline opened an office in Cairo, and Egypt established a new airline to handle its reciprocal flights. That maneuver was designed to avoid subjecting the national airline, Egyptair, to boycott by other Arab states. Israelis could obtain visas relatively easily from the Egyptian embassy in Tel Aviv, and the consulate in Eilat was authorized to issue special permits for Israelis to visit Sinai for up to one week.

The eagerness with which Israelis sought to travel to Egypt was indicated by the statistics: 14,000 went there in 1980; 38,000 in 1981; and 45,000 in 1982. Despite the subsequent freeze, 63,000 Israelis visited Egypt in each of 1983 and 1984.[5] The killing of a group of Israeli tourists in Sinai in October 1985 and the wave of anti-Israeli demonstrations in Cairo that autumn caused a sharp drop in late 1985 and 1986. Nevertheless, in 1987 the number swelled to 72,000.[6]

Many provisions of the Memorandum of Understanding were never implemented once Egypt froze relations. Egypt never held a "tourism week" in Tel Aviv, joint charter flights were not arranged, and there was no joint promotion of tourism. Few Egyptians traveled to Israel. One estimate maintained that the total over seven years was only 16,000, of whom an unknown number were traveling in an official or semi-official capacity.[7] Israeli spokesmen expressed their disappointment: "We wanted Egyptians to come here, to see we don't have horns."[8] Bureaucratic red tape, coupled with official and public disapproval of such visits, has accounted for the unwillingness of private citizens to travel there. The Coptic Orthodox Pope Shenuda II has even instructed his community to stay away from Jerusalem so long as its diplomatic status is not resolved and the Christian holy places lie under foreign occupation.[9]

Despite talk of easing restrictions in mid-1985 and visits to Israel by the Egyptian minister of tourism that year, new protocols for joint charter flights to Sinai and cooperative publicity were not implemented. The *intifadah* further cooled Egyptian interest in Israeli tourism. For Egypt, the importance economically of their business remains minimal: the 60,000 Israeli visitors in the first eleven months of 1987 are balanced against the 90,000 Americans, 600,000 Arabs, and 750,000 Europeans.[10] At present, there are indications that the government has quietly advised Israel to reduce the numbers traveling to the Nile valley, in part out of concern that angry Egyptians could harm them in the volatile political atmosphere caused by the *intifadah*.[11]

Trade

Israelis were initially optimistic that they could establish extensive commercial ties with Egypt. Egyptians, however, generally responded by voicing fears of Israeli economic penetration and domination. Over time, Israelis realized that opportunities were more limited than they had anticipated, and the Egyptian public became less anxious that Israeli goods and entrepreneurs would overwhelm them. Contacts remain low-key, with trade often laundered by third-party firms and banks.

Egypt began supplying oil to Israel in November 1979, and the bilateral trade protocol was signed during the Israeli trade minister's visit to Cairo in April 1980. The agreement was ratified by the Peoples' Assembly a year later. Israel participated in the Cairo International Trade Fair in 1981 and 1982, an act that triggered boycotts by most Arab firms. Several Israeli businesses opened offices in Cairo, notably Histadrut's conglomerate Koor Industries and the leading agricultural marketing cooperative, Agrexco.[12] Transport costs were reduced in 1982 when Israeli trucks were allowed to drive all the way to Cairo, rather than reloading their goods onto Egyptian vehicles at the border.

Thus, within a short time, a variety of Israeli products were exported to Egypt. They were valued at $10 million in 1980, $13.7 million in 1981, and $22 million in 1982, and included baby chicks for poultry farms, pipes for drip irrigation, consumer goods such as T-shirts and sports shoes, and even agricultural products such as eggs, butter, and chocolate. Egypt sold little in return: an estimated $700,000 worth in 1982, largely in textiles and construction materials, in addition to oil valued at $500 million.

Egyptian entrepreneurs resisted trading with Israel, in part because goods such as textiles and fruit could be obtained more cheaply internally and high-fashion clothes were sought from Europe. Moreover, they had well-established ties with European, Japanese, and American firms in electronics and technical fields. Egyptian public sector factories particularly opposed dealing with Israel. Nationalist feeling was strongly embedded in that sector; the factories had long-standing contracts with Arab countries, and many of their products were designed for internal consumption.

After the Israeli invasion of Lebanon, Egypt honored trade agreements that had already been signed, but no new accords were made and old agreements were not renewed. Israeli sales to Egypt dropped to $5.5 million in 1983. Egypt did not allow Israel to participate in the trade fair in 1983, although it did participate in 1984 and sold $13 million worth of goods in Egypt that year.[13] In 1985, the ministers of energy and oil exchanged visits and a new agricultural cooperation accord was concluded. Agriculture Minister Yusif Wali encouraged Israel to help introduce plastic greenhouses and drip irrigation, and he sent a special delegation to Israel in 1986 to study its agricultural techniques. As a result of the upturn in trade, Israel placed an economic attaché in its Cairo embassy for the first time in June 1986.[14] Nonetheless, most deals continued to be made through third parties, to reduce risk of an Arab boycott and to deflect internal criticism, even though costs increased as a result of the middlemen's fees and added transportation expenses.

Overall, trade relations are limited and are likely to remain that way. The competitiveness of their products, administrative and financial restrictions on foreign trade, and political constraints combine to inhibit contacts. Agricultural equipment and petrochemical products such as pesticides are likely to be the main Israeli exports to Egypt, and Egyptian firms will continue to prefer Arab and European sources and outlets for their production. With the *intifadah*, Israel has once again been banned from the Cairo trade fair.[15] In fact, today it is Israel that needs the opening to Egypt most: sixty percent of its oil comes from Egypt, making Egypt its number one supplier of petroleum.[16] Israel can ill afford to jeopardize that source of indispensable energy for its economy.

Cultural Accords

The bilateral cultural agreement, signed on 8 May 1980, spoke in sweeping terms of promoting understanding and friendship. The executive protocol was signed seventeen months later and specific subaccords followed in early 1982. The radio and television accord provided an opportunity for each country to assist visiting correspondents, exchange programs and films, and engage in joint production of TV programs. Exchanges of students and sports teams were envisioned, and exhibits of contemporary art and performances by folklore groups were specified. Israel would participate in the annual international book fair in Cairo, and each country could open an academic center in the other state.

Israelis considered the cultural accords vitally important means to affect Egyptian attitudes toward Israel. They hoped that increased contact would alter Egyptians' negative images of Israel and that interactions among young people would foster positive feelings that would deepen the peace process. Some Egyptians agreed that psychological barriers and negative stereotyping were important components of the conflict. Human contact, they felt, would reduce Israelis' feelings of isolation and encirclement and would make them realize that peace was possible with their neighbors.

Nonetheless, little was achieved prior to Israel's invasion of Lebanon. Israeli newspapers were sold in Cairo; some Israeli journalists visited Egypt; the Israeli Academic Center opened in Giza, and Israeli films and books were exhibited at the annual fairs. The one joint production involved coverage of Israel's evacuation of Sinai on 25 April 1982. Only a handful of Egyptians traveled to Israel: an art counselor to the government held an exhibit in Jerusalem; three medical professors went there, and one delegation of university students and professors.[17] The doctors were vociferously criticized by their fellow academics. Moreover, the few academic meetings with Israelis in Egypt had a semiofficial flavor: two seminars at the Center for Political and Strategic Studies of *al-Ahram* newspaper, held at the urging of the foreign ministry; a gathering with Labor party leaders on the premises of the governing party's *October* magazine;[18] and a conference sponsored by the Washington-based Political Psychiatry Institute.[19]

After Sadat's death, the government stopped pressing academics to meet with Israelis. By mid-1982, all pretense of cultural cooperation ended. Planned trips to Israel by an Egyptian folklore group and an art exhibit were cancelled. Israel was not permitted to join in the Cairo book fairs in 1983 and 1984. An Egyptian diplomat noted bitterly: "How can we talk about sending musical bands and artists to Israel when they are massacring people?"[20]

The Israeli Academic Center remained the only locale for intellectual contact during the freeze.[21] The center assisted Israeli research projects, organized seminars, and provided Egyptians with information on Israeli research and references in Judaism, Hebrew literature, and contemporary economic issues. The center assisted Hebrew language and literature classes at Ain Shams University and, for awhile, held language classes on its own premises. Nevertheless, its director was not invited to lecture at any Egyptian university, and he could not establish any formal institutional contacts. A narrow range of intellectuals and students were willing to risk contacting the center.

Since the partial thaw, cultural contacts have remained strained. Virtually no Egyptian intellectuals or scientists have visited Israel, and the academic boycott remains strong in Cairo. The government has resisted pressure from Israel to open a cultural center in Tel Aviv, using budgetary constraints as an excuse. Demonstrators burned the Israeli flag at the book fair in 1985 and handed out leaflets denouncing the peace treaty. In 1988 Israel was absent from both the book fair and the film festival. Thus, the general public in Egypt has no contact with the Israeli media and culture. Both at the official and popular levels, those inhibitions are likely to continue. Only in the area of scientific cooperation has there been any substantive, long-term interaction.

Scientific Exchanges

Egyptian and Israeli scientists have been curious about each other's scientific research for an extended period of time. Before the peace treaty, some met informally at international conferences and exchanged papers through the good auspices of third parties. Afterwards, Israelis began to explore the possibility of scientific cooperation. One senior physicist ascertained that Egypt would set certain conditions for contact: joint research was feasible so long as it took place in fields remote from ideological and political issues, included third-party institutions in Europe and the United States, and stayed clear of Sinai.[22] Sinai was particularly sensitive for Egypt because researchers had used it as a laboratory for a dozen years. The government wanted to emphasize that Israelis no longer had the right to work there.

Specific research programs were established under two related rubrics, the bilateral Memorandum of Understanding between the two Ministries of Agriculture, and the USAID Regional Cooperation Project. Concrete research included the Gemiza Project, approved in 1980 by the Egyptian minister of agriculture and funded by a $57 million USAID grant.[23] That five-year grant supported studies on improving grain crops at a government research center in the Delta. Israel provided an expert in drip and sprinkle irrigation, who supervised the growing of experimental vegetables. Gemiza II, which concluded in December 1985, added Israeli expert assistance for arid zone agriculture in the Western Desert, also with USAID funding. Related American-funded projects have promoted innovative techniques in growing field crops, medicinal uses of desert flora, and solar heating of soils.[24] Egypt and Israel also conduct parallel field trials and exchange visits and expertise concerning the growing of crops in brackish water and the development of drought-resistant shrubs that sheep and goats would eat.[25] Joint meetings have been held in San Diego in 1981, where the coordinating third-party university is located, and also in Egypt in 1984 and Israel in 1985. Twelve Egyptians attended the latter meeting, including senior agricultural ministry officials, and scientists from Ain Shams University and government agricultural research stations. A workshop was held in Alexandria in 1986, which fifteen Israel scientists attended, and an Agricultural Ministry official praised the "Israeli know-how (gained) within the framework of our joint study."[26]

Despite severe diplomatic tension, considerable cooperation was established between the scientific communities in the field of agriculture. One outside evaluator of the USAID project noted that the Egyptians viewed this contact as a major achievement under difficult circumstances, whereas the Israeli participants were impatient for more.[27] He commented that sending two students to Israel "is considered a great step forward for the Egyptians. In contrast, Israelis consider it a small step and ask 'when will a professor be transferred to study in Israel?' " At joint meetings, participants found their personal feelings and national sensitivities involved: project leaders conceded that "a good part of their energies and emotions are at times sapped by...political jostling" rather than by scientific debate. Nevertheless, the scientific and practical benefits of the research have outweighed political considerations and have kept the projects functioning.

Similar scientific efforts in the field of marine science — focused on the efforts to counter erosion of the Mediterranean coast — and infectious diseases have also made headway.[28] The latter involves studies on three illnesses that threaten humans and livestock: Rift Valley fever, malaria, and leichmaniasis. The $5 million joint program has been managed by the National Institute of Health in Washington, D.C. One Israeli scientist alluded to the common concern: "Mosquitoes have a flight path that recognizes no international borders."[29] Israelis participated in workshops at Ain Shams University, and international conferences were held in Egypt and Israel in 1985. But only two of the twelve Egyptians scheduled to go to the Israeli-based conference actually went; the Egyptian Medical Association takes an especially strong stand against such cooperation. In fact, the association censored a senior professor from Ain Shams University for inviting Israelis to a conference in Egypt.[30] The principal Egyptian investigator for the health project noted the caution with which such research must be approached:[31]

> Bearing in mind the sensitivities and complexities involved, scientific cooperation should not be pressed too hard....The scientific communities should not be imposed on one another but should naturally seek out one another when given the proper opportunity....Cooperation is needed to solve common health problems as well as to...solidify a lasting peace.

Normalization remains a term without an agreed definition. Egyptian officials see normalization as adherence to the letter of the peace treaty and strongly reject the idea that normalization means special ties to or a preferential status for Israel. According to them, Egypt has behaved correctly: Israeli tourists travel freely in Egypt, frequent air and land transport is available between the two countries, oil is sold in substantial quantities at an agreed price, and the Israeli Academic Center functions openly. The government argues that it cannot compel its citizens to cooperate with Israelis and that trade, tourism, and cultural relations must evolve gradually and voluntarily. Where there are mutually beneficial interests, as in the field of agriculture, contact will develop of its own accord. Where there are political, economic, or psychological barriers, relations cannot be forced.

That definition is unsatisfactory to most Israelis. They criticize Egypt for reneging on the spirit of normalization and accuse the government of fostering popular hostility. Some Israelis fail to connect Egypt's coolness toward them with their own government's actions in Lebanon and the Occupied Territories. Other Israelis, however, perceive that linkage clearly. Shimon Shamir, the first director of the Israeli Academic Center, who returned to Egypt as his country's ambassador in 1988, lamented as his term as director ended: "Seeing my own country from Egypt through the eyes of Egyptians was not a very pleasant experience...(I could see) Jewish terrorism, racism and...expansionism...(along with Israel's failure to make) this peace the cornerstone of a whole structure of peace in the region."[32]

In the current environment, few positive signs can be discerned. Without a fundamental change in the official Israeli approach to the Palestine issue and serious efforts to achieve a comprehensive peace, the bilateral relationship will remain circumscribed. Normalization will remain abnormal.

Attacks Against Israelis

In the decade of diplomatic relations, Israeli officials and tourists have generally been able to visit and travel in Egypt without fearing for their personal safety. That is a major achievement, given the depth of antagonism that preceded the accord. Nonetheless, three sets of incidents have marred the record. One centered on the series of attacks on Israeli diplomats by an organization called Egypt's Revolution. The second involved the death of a group of Israeli tourists in Sinai. The third resulted from the arrest of an Israeli drug smuggler in Cairo. Sensitive questions of security and jurisdiction were raised by those incidents.

The protection of Israeli diplomats has been a continual concern. The initial site of the embassy in a villa on a busy commercial street was deemed too vulnerable.[33] Soon, the embassy was moved to the top floors of a high-rise building near the Nile. The street to the embassy was blocked to traffic and special communications equipment was installed on the roof. Although a rocket was fired from the adjacent bridge at the embassy in early 1985 — damaging a nearby apartment — no other attacks on embassy property have been reported.

Given the Egyptian anger at the Israeli invasion of Lebanon and its policy in the Occupied Territories, it is striking that no known attacks on Israelis took place until 1984. The series of three attacks were carried out by Egypt's Revolution, a tight-knit group that sought to annul the Egyptian-Israeli treaty and protest against the limits that were placed on Egyptian sovereignty in Sinai. The group's manifestoes denounced the government for allowing Israel to participate in the trade fair and letting the Israeli flag fly "in the sacred skies of Egypt."[34] It called on Egypt to return to its Nasserite heritage.

On 4 June 1984 an Israeli administrative attaché was wounded by gunmen as he approached his home, late in the evening. On 20 August 1985, three embassy staffers were shot as they drove to work in the morning. The driver, administrative attaché Albert Atrakchi, was killed immediately. Both attachés were security officers in the embassy, and neither had requested protection from Egyptian security forces. On 19 March 1986, a carload of Israeli diplomats was ambushed as they left the grounds of the Cairo International Trade Fair. Despite tight security and the presence of numerous bystanders, the attackers sped away leaving one Israeli dead. (In a fourth attack in May 1987, the chief of security at the American Embassy and his assistant were wounded as they drove to work.)

The Israeli government's reaction to the attacks was strangely subdued. In each instance, it stated that the murders would not affect bilateral relations. Nonetheless, there was concern about the inability of the Egyptian, Israeli, and American security forces to find the group. Attempts to trace the gunmen's vehicles led to dead ends, and the only firm evidence linking the attacks were ballistic tests that indicated that the same gun was used in the attacks. The case was only cracked when one member of the group contacted the United States Embassy in the summer of 1988, apparently in the hope of gaining asylum, funding, and immunity from prosecution. Embassy officials questioned him for fifty days before they turned him over to the Egyptian police. Key members of Egypt's Revolution were arrested in September, and their trial began on 1 November 1988 before the Emergency Supreme State Security Court with the prosecution demanding the death penalty.[35]

According to published statements, the organizer, Mahmud Nuriddin, has worked as an intelligence officer in the Egyptian Embassy from 1964 to 1977, when he resigned in protest against Sadat's visit to Israel.[36] He had remained in London until 1984, prospering in real estate. Upon his return to Cairo he formed a small, select group that included at least five military officers, who provided weapons, ammunition, intelligence information, and training; some professionals, and the son of the former Vice President and Revolutionary Command Council member Hussein al-Shafei. Connections were also reported to the eldest son of Nasser, who took asylum in Yugoslavia and was included in the indictment. Given the structure of the members of Egypt's Revolution, it was not surprising that journalists and politicians of varying views expressed sympathy for their nationalist motivations, if not for the method that they used. The trial promised to heat up the political atmosphere inside Egypt and to cause increased tension between the two countries.

The sole attack on Israeli tourists — but one which had a searing impact — was the death of seven tourists, including four children, in Sinai on 5 October 1985.[37] Suleiman Khater, a military conscript at a guard post at Ras Burka, shot the tourists as they climbed up a sand dune on the beach. Khater claimed that he had orders to prevent anyone from approaching the post at night and that he called to them to stop before he shot. He also maintained that he did not know their nationality or ages. The Egyptian government claimed that Khater had gone berserk.

The incident touched off a storm of protest. Israelis charged that Egyptian authorities had prevented the wounded people from being transferred to a hospital in Eilat for a crucial eight hours and had meanwhile blocked Israeli doctors from treating them on the spot. Egyptian students, intellectuals, and opposition politicians turned Khater's act into a cause célèbre. Some argued that Khater had shot the Israelis as a patriotic gesture. Others maintained that he was repulsed by the immoral behavior and dress of Israeli tourists on the beach. Huge demonstrations were staged at universities during the trial.

The Egyptian government reacted defensively to the criticism. On the one hand, it rejected Israeli pressure to issue a formal report concerning the behavior of Egyptian officials at the site and also refused to let Israel become directly involved in the trial. On the other hand, it set up a special tribunal to award compensation to the victim's families and held the trial of Khater in camera before a military court. Many Egyptians concluded that the government was engaged in a cover-up and criticized the sentence of life imprisonment with hard labor. Khater's death in a military hospital ten days later caused an outburst of protests. Although officially stated to be a suicide, Egyptians tended to believe that Khater had been killed either by military officers or by the Israeli intelligence service. The death left a bitter aftertaste, widening the credibility gap between the government and the public. The Israeli government remained dissatisfied with Egypt's handling of the case, and the issue of compensation is still not completely resolved.

The third incident, involving an Israeli drug smuggler caught at the Cairo airport, raised sensitive questions of sovereignty. Yosef Tahan was caught on 18 August 1985 as he traveled from Bombay to Israel with 2.75 pounds of heroin.[38] The arrest came just as Egypt was beginning a high-profile campaign aganist trafficking in narcotics, which included warnings that smugglers could be sentenced to death. Tahan was convicted on 5 February 1986 and sentenced to death by hanging. Citizens of Sri Lanka and Pakistan as well as a dozen Egyptians also languished on death row.

The Egyptian government was irritated by Israeli press coverage of the case, which gave the impression that Tahan had been singled out. The Israeli embassy involved itself in the case, by obtaining an Egyptian lawyer to handle his defense and seeking to prevent his execution. Egyptians bristled at Israel's effort to gain preferential treatment for Tahan. The idea that Israel will want to jeopardize bilateral relations over the defense of such an unsavory citizen remains doubtful.

Egypt is understandably anxious to assert its rights of sovereignty and legal jurisdiction in the three sets of cases. The government is pressed, on one side, by Israel, which has sought severe sentences for Egyptians who have killed Israelis but a lenient sentence for its own drug smuggler. On the other side, it must take into account the views and demands of the Egyptian public, which sympathizes with the political aims of the Egyptian attackers and fears the pressure that Israel and the United States bring to bear on the Egyptian government. The cases have been the subject of behind-the-scenes diplomatic bargaining, which only makes the public more critical and more wary of their country's dependence and susceptibility to pressure.

The Controversy Over Tabah

The acrimonious disagreement over the status of Tabah irritated bilateral relations for more than six years. Its resolution through arbitration represents a landmark case in successful recourse to international legal instruments.

Tabah had not posed a problem before December 1981, when the deadline approached for Israel's final withdrawal from Sinai.[39] A 250-acre triangle of land south-west of Eilat, Tabah juts into the Gulf of Aqaba, commands a clear view into Sinai, and contains sweet-water wells and pleasant beaches. Tabah adds three-quarters of a mile to Israel's five-mile-wide coastal strip, marginally improving its naval and tourist holdings along the Gulf. Although possession of Tabah would enhance Israel's strategic and economic position slightly, Israel had abandoned far more significant assets in Sinai already, notably oil fields and tourist resorts.

Defense Minister Ariel Sharon, however, claimed that Tabah lay within Israel and that boundary pillars had not been sited properly along the international border a half century ago. Sharon evidently sought to use the issue as a means to delay evacuation from Sinai. Nonetheless, Egypt finessed the issue by agreeing that it should be resolved diplomatically. Meanwhile, Israel would withdraw its forces behind the line claimed by Egypt, and Egypt would not move into the zone claimed by Israel. The Multinational Forces and Observers (MFO) would be stationed in the disputed area. That accord prevented Sharon from blocking evacuation, but left Israel with leverage over Egypt.

Many Egyptians believed that retaining Tabah signaled that Israel rejected the concept of total territorial withdrawal in return for peace. By insisting on even a minor border change with Egypt, Israel could justify more significant alterations of the lines with Jordan and Syria. Thus, withdrawal from Egypt would not serve as a precedent for the other occupied lands.

Tabah soon became a national issue in Egypt, as a symbol of the continued alienation of Egyptian soil and the lack of full sovereignty in Sinai. In the meantime, Israel consolidated its hold by constructing a five-star hotel within the disputed zone. A tourist village had opened after the peace treaty but prior to the 1982 withdrawal. However, the Aviya Sonesta hotel was only in the early stages of construction and did not open until November 1982. By encouraging its completion, in violation of the commitment to not make changes within the zone, the Israeli government apparently believed that the presence of such a major investment would reinforce its own claim to Tabah.

Article VII of the peace treaty stated that, in the event of a dispute over implementing the treaty, the two sides should first negotiate and then turn to either conciliation or arbitration. Conciliation would lead to a recommended solution that would not be binding upon the parties and might take into account historical events, contemporary economic realities, and other non-legal aspects of the claims. Arbitration would be binding and would be based solely on considerations of international law.

Israel preferred conciliation, recognizing that its weak legal case would be balanced by the "acquired rights" and equity represented by the hotels. The Egyptian government favored arbitration on the grounds that the issue was purely technical, involving a disagreement over the location of border markers on Egyptian sovereign territory. Moreover, arbitration would compensate for Egypt's relatively weak position in the military balance of power with Israel and would preclude consideration of the presence of the hotels in Tabah.

When the two countries began to discuss the problem in 1982, they failed to agree over the proper role of the MFO, and Israeli police remained within the zone. Egypt objected strongly to the completion of the Sonesta hotel. With the overall freeze in relations, neither side made a serious effort to resolve the problem until late 1984, when the National Unity Government was formed under Shimon Peres. Peres was anxious to hold a summit meeting with Mubarak and to ease relations, and thus had an incentive to resolve the festering sore caused by Tabah. Egypt, moreover, insisted that the summit could not be held and the ambassador could not return to Tel Aviv until Tabah reverted to Egyptian control and Israeli forces withdrew completely from Lebanon.

Peres' efforts resulted in the reconvening of Tabah talks in January 1985. In March, as Israel prepared to withdraw from Lebanon, Mubarak moderated his stance. The ambassador would return, he indicated, when Israel would accept a timetable for arbitration. Peres welcomed the shift but could not win the backing of Likud ministers to resolve the problem through binding arbitration rather than conciliation. Shamir appeared to prefer to maintain the "cold peace" rather than enhance Peres' prestige by an accord on Tabah and a probable summit meeting with Mubarak. Only when Peres threatened to bring down the government and call new elections did Shamir concede, in an all-night meeting of the inner cabinet in January 1986.[40]

Each side tried to link resolution to Tabah in the context of normalizing relations, returning the Egyptian ambassador, opposing terrorism, and ceasing hostile statements in the press. Egypt articulated its own package, linking Tabah to progress on the Palestine issue and holding an international conference to achieve a comprehensive peace. In order to prevent the linked issues from derailing resolution of the Tabah problem, they formed two working groups: one to deal with Tabah and the other to discuss normalization and peace.

By mid-August 1985 the two countries agreed to the wording of the question concerning the location of the boundary pillars that would be presented to the arbitration panel.[41] They still had to agree on the three international members of the panel and on the mapping of the area. Peres was anxious to resolve those issues quickly so that he could hold a summit with Mubarak in early September — the last possible moment before he would relinquish the premiership to Shamir. That handed considerable leverage to the Egyptian team, which used it effectively to ensure the neutrality and stature of the international arbitrators and to uphold Egypt's definition of the marker site. Moreover, Egypt ensured that a fixed timetable would be set for the presentation of evidence to the panel and completion of its procedures, so that neither side could willfully delay the proceedings or postpone implementing the panel's ruling.

Peres left office with the satisfaction of placing the Tabah issue on a course toward resolution, meeting with Mubarak in a summit in Alexandria on September 11–12, and gaining the return of the Egyptian ambassador to Tel Aviv. The arbitration panel convened in Geneva from late 1986 until the fall of 1988. Each party submitted three sets of memoranda to the panel, in May and October 1987, and February 1988. The panel members visited the site in mid-February 1988 and convened defense hearings in March.[42] On 29 September 1988 the panel ruled in Egypt's favor concerning the placement of the marker on the north side of Tabah.[43] (Of nine markers along the border, the panel ruled in Israel's favor on five). However, the panel did not settle the angle that the 190-yard line would take from the last boundary pillar to the Gulf of Aqaba. Joint discussions would also be required over compensation for the owners of the two hotels, which would fall under Egyptian sovereignty.

The Israeli government had sought to sidestep the panel and reach a separate compromise with Egypt, particularly when the evidence accumulated suggested that it would lose the case. United States diplomats had tried to mediate, suggesting that Israel concede Egyptian sovereignty over Tabah but retain special privileges.[44] Israeli tourists might be allowed to enter the zone without a visa, Israeli courts might have jurisdiction over Israeli nationals violating the law within Tabah, and Israel might retain a 49% share in the ownership of the hotels. Shamir rejected those compromises, not wanting to voluntarily concede sovereignty to Egypt. In the end, however, he had to accept the binding ruling of the panel, which was far less satisfactory for Israel.

When the ruling was issued, Shamir blamed Peres for having agreed to international arbitration and asserted that the results proved that Israel should never become involved in international negotiations on vital issues, an allusion to his opposition to an international conference to resolve the Palestine problem. Peres retorted that the outcome proved, instead, that by stubbornly refusing any compromise, Israel lost everything: by demanding everything, Israel lost the entire terrority. That, too, was an allusion to Shamir's refusal to consider any territorial change on the West Bank and Gaza Strip.[45] Nonetheless, the acrimony over the outcome on Tabah did not become an issue in the elections. Egypt also tried to smooth over the results: the government urged the press to tone down its reactions to the ruling and agreed to postpone bilateral discussions over the remaining issues until late November, well after the Israeli parliamentary elections on November 1.[46]

The dispute over Tabah has moved from being a point of contention and acrimony to being resolved. On February 27, 1989, the two governments agreed that Israel would evacuate the encalve on March 15. Subsequently, Israelis could continue to visit Tabah without an Egyptian visa, Israeli currency would be accepted at the hotels, and Israel would supply their water and electricity. The Egyptian government will reportedly pay $40 million for the Sonesta hotel. Despite this mutually acceptable resolution, the dispute has left a sour taste on both sides because so much energy was expended over an essentially minor issue. Egypt saw Tabah as an artificial problem, created by the Israeli government in order to delay evacuation and retain leverage over Egyptian behavior. Within Israel, Tabah became a pawn in the contest for power between Peres and Shamir. Resolution of the status of Tabah is important in removing a tension point between the two countries. However, it is neither likely to mark a major shift in their relationship nor serve as a precedent for resolving other outstanding Arab-Israeli issues by neutral arbitration. The success or failure of the quest for a comprehensive peace in the region is apt to be the key factor determining the nature of the bilateral ties.

Assessment

The promise inherent in the peace between Egypt and Israel has not been realized. Energy has been expended excessively on subsidiary issues such as Tabah, Coptic properties in Jerusalem, and Canada Camp near Rafah.[47] Egyptian sensitivity over its national sovereignty has been aroused over those issues and others involving the trials in Cairo of citizens for killing Israelis. Israeli sensitivity over its isolated status has been aroused by the cool response of Egyptians to the treaty and the lack of warmth in the relationship.

The basic problem, however, has been that the bilateral relationship cannot be separated from the broad regional context. Begin evidently thought that was possible, and allowed Sharon to take advantage of the neutralization of the Egyptian armed forces by invading Lebanon, consolidating Israel's hold on the West Bank and Gaza Strip, and annexing the Golan Heights. Sadat had accepted a bilateral treaty in anticipation that it would be the first step toward a comprehensive accord, and was dismayed by the subsequent Israeli actions as well as by the Arab governments' immediate isolation of Cairo. Ezer Weizmann, a prominent Israeli politician who moved from a hard-line to a dovish position during the 1970s, underscored Egypt's dilemma. Egypt made a "giant move" by signing the peace treaty, Weizmann averred, but "we didn't take the autonomy issue seriously; we said 'no more war' and went ahead and made war; we went into Lebanon. . .and we killed and bombed — and then we have the effrontery to complain that Egypt is returning to the Arab world."[48]

By 1988 Egypt had engineered a significant shift in its diplomatic orientation. The return to the Arab fold was signaled by Mubarak's trip to the Arab states along the Persian Gulf in early January, prior to his visit to Washington. Egypt also managed to assert an independent role in the ongoing effort to resolve the Palestine problem. Mubarak swiftly condemned the Israeli forces' "unjust and oppressive measures"[49] against the Palestinian *intifadah* and offered to help broker an accord. The government pressed for the inauguration of an international conference and for the United States and Israel to include the Palestine Liberation Organization in the negotiations. Egypt even recognized the state of Palestine, which the PLO declared in November 1988, and brushed aside Israeli charges that such recognition violated the bilateral accord.[50]

Nonetheless, Cairo was compelled to quell demonstrations and protests that erupted among Egyptian students and the broader public, which expressed both their anger at Israeli behavior on the West Bank and Gaza and their frustration at the inability of Egypt to significantly affect Israel's policies. Egyptian diplomats commented that relations with Israel were "as delicate as during Sabra and Shatilla,"[51] and expressed their dismay at Israel's lack of response to their mediating effort:[52]

> We had high hopes that during the *intifadah*, the Israeli-Egyptian relation could play a role in easing the situation. We hoped that we could talk more sense to the Israelis about Palestinian rights. People are shocked this hasn't happened.

Egyptian-Israeli relations have survived the shocks of Israel's invasion of Lebanon and the ongoing *intifadah*. Egypt has also been able to restore ties with the Arab world while maintaining its accord with Israel. Nevertheless, normalization and fruitful interchange remain impossible. Without broading the peace to include the Palestinians, only a guarded and carefully circumscribed relationship can be maintained.

[Editor's Note: Professor Lesch adds that the Egyptian government is trying to use its unique position as the only Arab country having diplomatic relations with both Israel and the PLO to enhance its stature as a mediator. Moreover, Cairo provided the venue for a meeting between the Soviet and Israeli foreign ministers in the Spring of 1989. Egypt recently proposed measures to guarantee fair elections in the West Bank and Gaza, such as Israeli military forces withdrawing from the population centers during the voting, freedom of expression for candidates, and international supervision. Although the bilateral relationship remains limited and the prospects for Israeli-Palestinian negotiations are remote, Egypt has carefully positioned itself to play a constructive role and to promote the peace process.]

CHAPTER TEN

The Not-so-Silent Partnership: Emerging Trends in American Jewish-Israeli Relations

George E. Gruen

In the past several years there has developed within the American Jewish community an increasingly restive mood and a more assertive posture with regard to actions and policies of the government of Israel. While solidarity with the State of Israel remains high, American Jews have started to reexamine the traditional boundaries between legitimate involvement and improper interference by one community in the affairs of the other.

Some basic rules governing the relationship between the State of Israel and the Jewish communities of the Diaspora that seemed to have been long settled, have again become the subject of intense discussion and controversy. For some American Jews, the Pollard Affair raised the specter of dual loyalty. Periodic Knesset debates over "Who is a Jew?" have pitted the American Conservative and Reform movements and the leaders of American Jewish philanthropic and intergroup-relations agencies against the Orthodox religious establishment in Israel. Should American Jews accept the Israeli view that Russian Jews with Israeli visas are no longer "refugees" if they choose to come to the United States, since they can immediately become full citizens of the Jewish state? Or should American Jews continue to urge Washington to provide special assistance to all Russian Jews who wish to come to the United States, in accordance with the principle of freedom of choice?

Do American Jews have a right, or even a duty, to speak out if they disagree with aspects of Israeli foreign policy, or should they remain silent and passive, for example, in the face of the furious debate within Israel on the issue of territorial compromise? Complicating this question futher, Israel's uneasy National Unity Government made up of the rival labor and Likud blocs, has since 1984 spoken with two voices on crucial elements of Israel's peace policy toward Arab nations and on its ultimate borders. Both Prime Minister Yitzhak Shamir and former Prime Minister Shimon Peres, who shared power in the last coalition, have solicited support for their respective foreign policy stances from American Jews.

Basic Principles of the Relationship

The basic principles of Israel's relationship with the American Jewish community bear reexamining. These principles were enunciated by Israel's first prime minister, David Ben-Gurion, and reflect his worldview. Ben-Gurion, who always displayed a profound sense of history, knew that the establishment of a Jewish state created a new and unique situation. Jewish sovereignty had not existed for some nineteen centuries. Moreover, the concept of the modern, democratic nation-state in which Jews were accorded full and equal participation in political life, as in the United States, was also a relatively recent phenomenon. Prime Minister Ben-Gurion therefore welcomed the initiative of Jacob Blaustein, a leading American industrialist then president of the American Jewish Committee, to discuss and clarify the relationships between the new state and the American Jewish community.

Blaustein had been working hard in Washington to enlist American political support and economic assistance for the new Jewish state. Yet he always made a point of stressing that he advocated a pro-Israeli policy "as an American citizen and a Jew." In the face of continuing opposition in State Department circles, he argued that strengthening Israel would advance American national interests by creating "a stronghold of democracy in an area where liberal democracy is practically unknown." It was therefore essential, Blaustein maintained, that Israeli statements or actions not undermine this sense of common interest or raise the specter of dual loyalty for American Jews.

The extensive Blaustein-Ben-Gurion discussions, which were considered by Israel's cabinet, led to an exchange of public statements at a luncheon held at the King David Hotel on August 23, 1950. The prime minister declared that it was "entirely clear" to him that "American Jews, as individuals and as a community, have only one political attachment and that is to the United States of America. They owe no

political allegiance to Israel." He noted that in his first speech following Israel's admission to the United Nations, Foreign Minister Moshe
Sharett had stressed that "Israel represents and speaks only on behalf
of its own citizens and in no way presumes to represent or speak in
the name of the Jews who are citizens of any other country."[1]

Mayor Teddy Kollek, addressing a delegation from the Conference of Presidents of Major American Jewish Organizations in
Jerusalem in march 1987, noted the relevance of the Ben-Gurion
declaration to the Pollard Affair, which was then causing shock waves
among American Jews. Kollek, who had been the director-general of
the prime minister's office at the time and closely involved in the
Blaustein-Ben-Gurion discussions, recalled that Ben-Gurion had stressed that "any weakening of American Jewry, any disruption of its communal life, any lowering of its sense of security, any diminution of
its status, is a definite loss to Jews everwhere and to Israel in particular."

Those who had recruited Pollard to spy on behalf of Israel, Mayor
Kollek said, had been insensitive to these considerations. "We have
to go back to basic principles," he told the Presidents' Conference
delegation, "and not to try to be overly smart." In an interview with
a *Jerusalem Post* reporter a few days earlier, Kollek had already expressed
the hope that Israel would quickly reaffirm that although it sought the
sympathy and support of American Jewry, "their loyalty belongs to
the United States."[2]

The basic principles of the Ben-Gurion-Blaustein exchange included an Israeli promise of noninterference in American Jewish affairs.
Ben-Gurion declared: "We, the people of Israel, have no desire and
no intention to interfere in any way with the internal affairs of Jewish
communities abroad... Our success or failure depends in a large
measure on our cooperation with, and on the strength of, the great
Jewish community of the United States, and we, therefore, are anxious that nothing should be said or done which could in the slightest
degree undermine the sense of security and stability of American
Jewry."[3] On the American side, Blaustein agreed that "Jewish communities, particularly American Jewry in view of its influence and its
strength, can offer advice, cooperation and help, but should not attempt
to speak in the name of other communities or in any way interfere in
their internal affairs."[4]

When Prime Minister Yitzhak Shamir was asked at a meeting with
American Jewish leaders on March 18, 1987, whether in light of the
Pollard Affair these principles were still valid, he assured the
Presidents' Conference delegates: "We don't want to interefere in the

life of the Jewish people in the Diaspora. We want to talk with them, to consult, to agree if we can, on all the issues on the Jewish agenda. We are one people... we don't impose our views, we try to convince, when we believe we are right."[5]

Yet while there may be ostensible agreement on these principles, problems arise in applying them to specific situations. For example, during the 1988 Israeli electoral campaign both major Israeli parties, as well as many of the smaller ones, actively solicited contributions from American Jews. Estimates of the total were as high as $10 million. Ironically some of those who regard public criticism of Israeli policies by American Jews as unwarranted interference are nevertheless eager to receive foreign money to strengthen their own party and its political positions. Those who believe that it is appropriate for citizens of one democracy to seek to influence the outcome of elections in another cite as a precedent the action of Americans of Italian origin in providing financial support for the Christian Democrats in the Italian elections after World War II. The United States Government encouraged this intervention in order to help prevent a Communist victory, which seemed a very real danger at the time.

Stimulating Aliyah or Freedom of Choice?

Israeli leaders from Ben-Gurion to Shamir have sought to convice the Jews of the Diaspora of the importance of *aliyah* (Jewish immigration) to Israel. Most American Jews acknowledge this and understand the deep disappointment felt by Israelis over the fact that the great majority of Jews have chosen to remain in the Diaspora. American non-Zionists as well as Zionists have increasingly been sensitive to these concerns. For example, the Institute on American Jewish-Israeli Relations, which was established by the American Jewish Committee in 1982, issued a statement in October 1986 encouraging and recommending practical steps to increase *aliyah*. The statement by the Institute's American Advisory Board noted:

> Over and above the ideological motivations that individuals may have for deciding to go on *aliyah*, namely the wish to live a full Jewish life in a Jewish State, it is recognized that decisions to go on *aliyah* are frequently the result of positive experiences in Israel, particularly by young people, such as extended study periods, work or service programs, frequent visits, or investments in Israel. Accordingly, the Institute should stimulate and in some instances undertake programs of study, research and education that would have as their objective

increasing and enhancing all such opportunities for American Jewish-Israeli interaction... The Institute should also work with Israeli leaders to improve their educational programs dealing with *aliyah* and to remove those barriers which impede successful absorption of the immigrants into Israeli society.

What has irked American Jewish leaders since Jacob Blaustein's time are Israeli declarations that negate the legitimacy of Jewish life in free societies such as the United States. They have also objected to the use of what they consider questionable methods to stimulate *aliyah*. The most recent of these has been the unsuccessful attempt by Israeli officials to change United States immigration policy so as to prevent Russian Jews with visas for Israel, who opt to go to America instead, from benefiting from current United States refugee aid provisions. This has become a pressing matter now that the Soviet Union is again permitting substantial numbers of Jews to leave. In the early months of 1988, more than 80 percent of Russian Jewish emigrants chose to go to the United States rather than to Israel. In May, out of a total of 1,169 with Israeli visas, 1,059, or 91 percent, chose the United States.[6]

The Israelis have also been negotiating with the Soviet Union and Romania to arrange direct flights for Jewish emigrants from Moscow to Tel Aviv via Bucharest. This would, in effect, close off the American option for those Jews who now go to Vienna, where they choose whether to go on to Israel or to the United States. The Israeli Cabinet announced on June 19 that Israel would use all "legal means available" to insure that Russian Jews with exit visas for Israel "would indeed reach Israel directly."[7] American officials continue to support freedom of choice. In an attempt to help resolve the legal and ideological issues, eight major American Jewish groups active in human rights, Soviet Jewry, philanthropy, and immigration announced on June 8, 1988, that they supported a two-track approach: while welcoming direct flights for those wishing to settle in Israel, they also called for a quick and effective program whereby Russian Jews in North America would issue direct invitations for family reunification to their relatives in the Soviet Union. The American Jewish groups noted that "the Soviet government has indicated its readiness to respond to such direct invitations for family reunification," and they urged the United States government to continue its advocacy "on behalf of family reunification in Israel and the West."[8]

In developing guidelines for dealing with this painful controversy, the authoritative statement issued by Israel's first prime minister in August 1950 and reaffirmed by him in the joint Ben-Gurion-Blaustein statement in April 1961, is worthy of note:

We should like to see American Jews come and take part in our effort. We need their technical knowledge, their unrivalled experience, their spirit of enterprise, their bold vision, their "know-how"... The tasks which face us in this country are eminently such as would appeal to the American genius for technical development and social progress. But the decision as to whether they wish to come — permanently or temporarily — rests with the free discretion of each American Jew himself. It is entirely a matter of his own volition. We need *halutzim*, pioneers too. *Halutzim* have come to us — and we believe more will come, not only from those countries where the Jews are oppressed and in "exile" but also from countries where Jews live a life of freedom and are equal in status to all other citizens in their country. But the essence of *halutziut* is free choice.[9]

That *aliyah* must be a matter of individual free choice, therefore, was recognized as an immutable principle by the founder of the Jewish state. To be sure, Israel might do more to make aliyah an attractive and viable alternative for Diaspora Jews. Natan Sharansky, whose heroic twelve-year struggle to make *aliyah* captured the minds of millions, recently offered a far-reaching criticism of Israeli immigration priorities. Warning Israeli leaders that they must radically overhaul their cumbersome bureaucracy and improve the absorption process if Israel is to attract and keep significant number of *olim* from the Soviet Union, he criticized the Aliyah and Absorption Ministry and the Jewish Agency for their failures on a number of bread-and-butter issues, particularly housing, job programs, and loans.

"After struggling in the Soviet Union with the KGB, what are we doing in Israel?" he asked. "We are struggling for this mortgage or that mortgage, with this bureaucrat or that bureaucrat."[10] To emphasize his dissatisfaction, Sharansky rejected a request by the United Jewish Appeal to make a fundraising tour in America, saying that the money raised would only be used to strengthen bureaucracy. Together with other Soviet Jewish leaders in Israel, he formed a new Zionist Federation of Soviet Jewry to advocate his views.[11] This organization, intent on changing the bureaucratic status quo, mirrors a trend that has been emerging in the Diaspora.

Those Who Pay the Piper Wish to Call the Tune

One area of increasing contention between Israeli leadership and the leadership of Diaspora Jewry has been the management of the network of worldwide Jewish and Zionist organizations that link together the sovereign Jewish state and Jewish communities. American Jewish leaders have been manifesting a greater sophistication and assertiveness in their joint endeavors with Israelis in several areas where they were previously content to follow the Israeli lead. Nowhere is this more apparent than in the field of philanthropy.

Leaders of American Jewish philanthropic organizations, who every year raise nearly $500 million for Israel, began in the 1980s to demand a more direct role in determining where and how their money would be spent. An organization called "The New Israel Fund" (NIF) was created in 1979 to subsidize indigenous efforts in Israel that promote Jewish-Arab coexistence, further civil rights and intergroup relations, and deal with social problems, such as battered women and rape victims, that its founders felt had not been adequately addressed by the Israeli bureaucratic establishment. During the fiscal year ending June 30, 1987, the NIF collected $2,574,000. While this is still a relatively small sum, it represents a 35 percent increase over the previous year and 20 times what it had raised in 1980.[12]

In 1987, the Jewish Community Federation of San Francisco diverted $100,000 of its funds to its own Israeli programs, sparking condemnation by the United Israel Appeal, the central channel for UJA funds for Israel. This development, like the growth of the New Israel Fund, presage a more activist and creative role for American Jews in Israel-related philanthropy.[13]

The main focus of displeasure for American benefactors was the Jewish Agency and the World Zionist Organization, the central institutions that control allocation and disbursment of funds raised abroad for Israel. Israeli Conservative and Reform institutions — local branches of movements to which the majority of affiliated American Jews belong and from whose members most contributions to Israel originated — claimed the right to equality of status and public funding. These movements are virtually unrecognized by the Orthodox religious establishment in Israel, which retains a near monopoly on government funding for religious charities.

The Orthodox establishment has even sought to extend abroad its predominant control over laws relating to the personal status of Jews in Israel, and this has provoked resistance from the organized American Jewish community. A proposed change in the Law of Return, the legislation governing Jewish immigration to Israel, was once again debated in the Knesset in July 1987. Ultra-Orthodox legislators, backed by the Likud, were agitating for changes in the law requiring that all conversions be according to *halakhah*, Jewish religious law, and that the Israeli rabbinate pass on the validity of foreign conversions. These amendments, in effect, would have barred from automatic Israeli citizenship individuals converted to Judaism by non-Orthodox rabbis. An ad-hoc coalition of mainstream American Jewish organizations, including the American Jewish Congress, the American Jewish Committee, the Anti-Defamation League, leaders of the conservative and Reform movements, and various local Jewish federations, sent messages to Israeli government officials and Knesset members opposing the changes.

While similar messages had been sent in the past, there was now a greater activism, signaled by a special delegation of leaders of the council of Jewish Federations and Welfare funds who flew to Jerusalem to lobby Knesset members to vote against the bills. They were joined by local Jerusalem representatives of the American organizations. The Jewish leaders warned that changes in the law that would delegitimize Reform and Conservative conversions would rupture Jewish unity and might seriously harm American Jewish support for Israel. Their lobbying effort helped to convince a narrow majority to defeat the bills.[14] It should be noted that the initiative for the amendment had also come from the United States — the supporters of the Lubavitcher Rebbe in Brooklyn were responding to his request to assure that *halakhah* be strictly observed. Other American ultra-Orthodox groups added their support.

At a meeting with the Presidents' Conference in New York on June 6, 1988, Prime Minister Shamir assured the group that he believed the issue of conversion should be handled ''by cooperation, mutual consultation, and by agreement'' among those concerned. Nevertheless, on June 14 he not only voted for the two amendments, which would have given the Orthodox authorities in Israel exclusive authority to determine who is a Jew, but also imposed party discipline on members of his Likud bloc to do likewise. The American groups opposed to the changes once again contacted the Knesset members who had appeared to be wavering the week before the vote. In the end, the amendments were defeated.[15]

Efforts to Reform the Bureaucracy

American philanthropists also demanded a greater share of the positions in the Jewish Agency directorate and reform of the highly politicized patronage system that distributes jobs and funds in that organization and the World Zionist Organization. Because of the extensive patronage inherent in the Israeli party system, the Agency's departments often duplicate some of the functions of Israel's ministries, particularly Aliyah and Absorption, providing jobs for the party faithful who do not find their way into the government bureaucracies. The Americans charged that this duplication led to waste and mismanagement, and insisted on change.[16]

In December 1987, the American participants staged a full-scale revolt at the 31st World Zionist Congress in Jerusalem, where they managed to implement part of their program. A candidate favored by the Americans, Simcha Dinitz, a former Israeli ambassador to the United States, was elected as head of the Jewish Agency, defeating the candidates initially proposed by the two main Israeli political groupings. Gideon Patt, a cabinet minister, had been the Likud favorite for the post, while the Labor Alignment had first considered 70-year-old Akiva Lewinsky, who was rejected because of his age, and then Nissim Zvilli, a young Agency department head, rejected because of lack of experience. The Americans hailed Dinitz's election, considering it a victory for the depoliticization of the Agency, and asserting that the other candidates had little to offer except their party credentials. They hoped that Dinitz, with his long experience in the United States, would elevate relations between the Israelis and the Diaspora representatives to a true and meaningful partnership.

Although the Americans' efforts to restructure the Agency exasperated some Israelis, including Uzi Narkiss, head of the Agency's Information Department, they were underterred. After defeating two of the Labor candidates for head of the Agency, they did join with Labor to address their other concern: the hegemony of the Orthodox establishment and its hold on certain Agency budgets. Against the best efforts of the Orthodox parties and the Likud bloc, a resolution was passed calling for "complete equality for all streams of Judaism." Many Israelis resented the Americans' power play at the Zionist congress, arguing that if Diaspora Jews wanted to assume a primary role in the Jewish Agency's machinery they should, in the words of an Israeli delegate, "fulfill the supreme command of Zionism and make aliyah. They cannot sit in New York, or Paris and simply pay up." Dissatisfactions boiled over into rancor. The 31st Congress ended on an undignified note, with delegates throwing flower pots at each other and exchanging blows.[17]

Despite these momentary bad feelings, the thrust of the Americans' message was taken to heart. One measure of their success has been the Katz Report, a document submitted to the Board of Governors of the Jewish Agency in the fall of 1987 that called for major changes in the bureaucracy. The report recommended that the

Agency's aliyah and absorption departments be streamlined, transferring many direct immigrant services to the Israel government, and also suggested that the absorption department transform itself into an advocacy center, which would work closely with existing immigrant groups, such as the Association of Americans and Canadians for Israel, as well as the one formed by Sharansky. Indeed, Shoshana Cardin, Chair of the Agency's long-range planning committee, said at the time of Sharanskys challenge to the Agency that his remarks were "unfortunate" because major changes would be taking place within the organization within six to twelve months, "changes which we have been working towards for years in a thoughful and serious manner."[18]

Professor Daniel J. Elazar, president of the Jerusalem Center for Public Affairs, criticized the Israeli media and various public figures for engaging in "an orgy of Zionist bashing" and failing to acknowledge the real achievement of the World Zionist organization in bringing about a Congress based upon "open, democratic elections in the Diaspora" that resulted in significantly broadening the base of the WZO to include the Conservative and Reform constituencies. He expressed the hope that the elections would be only the first step toward "a major structural reform of the Zionist movement to make it a real instrument of world Jewry." He noted that "those of us who see the state as an instrument of the Jewish people rather than an end in itself, do not see the pursuit of partnership with the Diaspora as diminishing Israel's political sovereignty." Such partnership, he stressed, requires power-sharing. In practice, that meant a measure of overlapping structures among the government, the WZO, the Jewish Agency, and other institutions. That power-sharing tends to promote efficiency was well demonstrated, he said, in Project Renewal "where Diaspora intervention on the side of the local residents [in distressed neigborhoods] was vital to overcoming the bureaucracy at the center." Elazar added that the Diaspora involvement could also improve the aliyah process.[19]

Two current proposals pushed by UJA activists are arousing opposition from some veteran Israeli Zionist functionaries. One is a plan to create a joint Jewish education authority to coordinate the dozen or so bureaus and departments dealing with education in the World Zionist Organization and the Jewish Agency. The other, proposed by the New York UJA-Federation, would set up a panel to study the total merger or separation of the WZO and Jewish Agency. The philanthropists saw the Zionists' objections as less of an ideological issue than a struggle over turf.[20]

Growth of Debate and Dissent in Diaspora-Israel Relations

As the Ben-Gurion-Blaustein correspondence shows, the issue of advice or "interference" in the affairs of the other community were matters of some delicacy between Israel and Diaspora Jewry in 1950. Today as well, the most sensitive and contentious issue in this relationship is the legitimacy and function of advice or public dissent from Israeli government policies, particularly those involving the peace process or the security of the state.

This issue has once again come to the fore since 1987, when several American Jewish organizations, notably the American Jewish Congress and the American Jewish Committee, made public statements supporting the convening of an international peace conference under United Nations auspices to initiate direct negotiations leading to a settlement of the Arab-Israeli conflict on the basis of Security Council Resolution 242. This resolution is understood by the United States and Labor governments in Israel to require an exchange of substantial West Bank and Gaza "territory for peace." Prime Minister Shamir opposes the conference, while Foreign Minister Peres has frequently spoken in its favor. Beginning in 1987, both Shamir and Peres have lobbied American Jews in support of their views, sowing confusion and division in American Jewish ranks, because their activities have challenged a powerful communal predisposition to support whatever government is in power in Israel.

In the traditional view, it was not considered appropriate for Diaspora Jews to question the wisdom of the democratically elected Israeli government on matters relating to the security of the state, publicly or otherwise. Some have argued that because Israel is in a state of permanent war and beleaguered by hostile neighbors, questions of life-and-death importance can be decided only by those who pay taxes in Israel, serve in its army, and die in its wars. In this view, held by many Israelis and American Jews alike, American Jews are "armchair generals," lacking the personal commitment, credentials and expertise necessary to advise Israel on vital decisions. The Israeli holders of this view, echoing Ben-Gurion, often repeat the familiar refrain of exasperated Zionists: "Don't advise us, join us."[21]

Other arguments against Diaspora Jewish criticism of Israel on defense and foreign policy issues maintain that any such activity, especially when launched publicly, is inherently harmful, because one key objective of the Arab propaganda assault on Israel is to drive a wedge between Israel and those liberal, democratic countries — especially the United States — that form the basis of its diplomatic support. Thus, anything less than total Jewish solidarity with Israel, whatever its policies, can lead to a reduction of American economic and military assistance and dangerously increase the political isolation of the Jewish state.

Prime Minister Shamir made this assertion categorically when he addressed the Conference of Presidents of Major American Jewish Organizations in Jerusalem on March 2, 1988, in the middle of some of the worst weeks of the continuing turmoil in the West Bank and Gaza. "The American Jewish community has always been regarded as a bastion in Israel's defense. This source of power has expressed itself many times and in many sectors of the American scene," he said. "It is inconceivable that, God forbid, American Jews would permit themselves to be used in this campaign against us, even if they have criticism or doubts of their own with regard to some of Israel's policies and practices." Jews abroad have a "moral duty," he declared, to "support the Israeli government, never a foreign government against Israel. It is absolutely un-Jewish and very dangerous to join an anti-Israel front with non-Jews." Shamir expressed hope "that the great American Jewish community will have sufficient strength to put an end to this criticism," saying "it's up to you. Every critical statement of a Jewish leader does much more harm than many violent demonstrations in Gaza and elsewhere."[22]

The prime minister's remarks were greeted with stunned silence by the Presidents' Conference members. Some members whose organizations had been critical of Shamir's policies and had openly supported the Peres approach of territorial compromise and an appropriate international conference, seethed inwardly. When Shamir reiterated the same views at a meeting in New York on March 20, adding, "When Israel decides, the Jews of America must support it," Albert Borspan could remain silent no longer. The senior vice president of the Union of American Hebrew Congregations, which comprises more than 800 Reform synagogues in the United States and Canada, rose up to challenge the prime minister:

> Jews are united in a commitment to Israel and its security, but we do not serve you or Israel by telling you whatever you want to hear. Given the fact that the people and the Government of Israel are divided right down the middle, isn't it obvious that American Jews are going to be divided as well? And if Israelis are embroiled in debate over these issues, isn't it to be assumed that American Jews will be debating these issues as well?

And, Mr. Prime Minister, isn't it the worst way to build unity by equating disagreement with a particular policy with disloyalty to the Jewish people, and to Israel?

Shamir responded that while there could, of course, be arguments, the government of Israel would have to make the decisions, and American Jews had no right to contribute to American governmental pressure on Israel. Vorspan noted that he felt like Daniel in the lions' den as Shamir's response was greeted by a "stormy, sustained ovation." Yet Vorspan remains convinced that many American Jews agree with him.[23]

Those who disagree with Shamir's position have stressed that the ties between Israel and the Jews of the Diaspora confer on Diaspora Jews a special responsibility to offer advice and constructive criticism to the Jewish state, even concerning alternative approaches to peace. In this view, Israel, as the spiritual, cultural and emotional center of the Jewish people, should accept advice and criticism as evidence of the Jewish world's sincere concern. If Israelis expect Diaspora Jews to be partners in terms of raising funds, gathering political support, and promoting aliyah, a reciprocal airing of views should be a healthy part of this relationship. Indeed, some Israelis have argued that it is a crucial part. Authors Yehuda Amichai, Amos Elon, Amos Oz, and A.B. Yehoshua, four of the most prominent writers in Israel today, wrote a letter to the *New York Times* dated February 15, 1988, expressing their heartfelt plea to the American Jewish public to discuss openly the issues raised by the Palestinian uprising.

We refuse to believe that the Jews of the United States are indifferent to whether there shall be war or peace. We cannot believe they are indifferent to whether Israel will remain a democracy. We ask them to speak up. By their very silence, they are massively intervening in Israeli politics and silently but effectively supporting one side in the debate, the tragically wrong side. We implore them to speak up.[24]

Another argument put forward in favor of an independent stance by American Jews identifies a danger to American Jewry itself, and ultimately to Israel, if Jews in the United States identify automatically and unqualifiedly with Israeli government policy. While this concern is now voiced primarily by the "minimalist" critics of the successive governments' negotiating posture, such as the Israeli Peace Now movement, in the past it came from right-wing "maximalist" critics both in Israel and the Diaspora. Such an example is Shmuel Katz, an Israeli author who was one of the founders of the Greater Land of Israel Movement, which maintains the essential "wholeness" of Israel within its historic boundaries and opposes any territorial concessions.

In 1976, at a meeting held at American Jewish Committee headquarters in New York, Katz warned American Jewish leaders that if they did not adopt a somewhat independent stance from that of the Israeli government — then controlled by the Labor party — and were perceived as automatically falling in line with Jerusalem's dictates, they would soon by regarded by the American government and the general public as nothing more than agents for a foreign power and their loyalty would come into question. Not only would this threaten their own security, but it would ultimately hurt Israel, because the views of American Jews would be discounted and dismissed in advance as simply another example of special pleading by a foreign group. The basic strength of American Jewish support for Israel depends on the ability of American Jews to convice the 97 percent of the American public that is not Jewish that support for Israel is in the highest national interest of the United States itself, Katz maintained. Only if American Jews adopt an independent stance, including occasional criticism of Israeli policies and actions, would they be able to maintain their credibility with the American public.[25]

Another bone of contention pertains to the kinds of forums deemed appropriate for airing criticism of Israel. If American Jews voice their advice and criticism, should they do it publicly or should they address Israeli leaders through private channels? Some American Jewish and Israeli leaders maintain that public criticism of Israel, particularly in the American media, becomes a *hekhsher* — an official stamp of approval — for slanderous attacks by Israel's enemies. American Jewish criticism of Israeli policies and Israeli society emboldens those who wish to pressure Israel, reasoning that they will not be accused of anti-Semitism, since the Jewish state is being criticized by Jews themselves.

Many others argue, however, that refraining from constructive criticism of Israel in the world press abandons this field to Israel's enemies. Israel will be strengthened, in this view, if criticism is voiced by responsible Jewish leaders in a judicious manner, allowing non-Jews to see that Jews are naturally not all of one mind or cowed and afraid to speak up. Some American non-Jews have recently indicated gratification that they did not feel obligated to express their misgivings about Israeli actions in the territories publicly because authoritative voices within the Jewish community were speaking up and conveying similar concerns directly to the Israelis.[26]

Reasons for the Increased Questioning of Israeli Policies

Diaspora Jewish dissent from various Israeli policies has mounted since the ascent to power of Menachem Begin's Likud bloc in 1977. To be sure, some debate began shortly after the Six-Day War of June 1967, which raised the possibility of using the newly captured territories as bargaining chips. However, in view of the Arab league's policy of rejection of any negotiations with Israel, adopted at the Khartoum Summit in August 1967, this discussion remained largely theoretical.

Another factor inhibiting criticism of Israeli government policy on matters of defense and foreign policy was the standard response of officials, "We have access to secret information that we can not share with you, so trust us, we know what we are doing." However, in the United States, the Vietnam War and the Watergate scandal served to erode public confidence in government, especially among the younger generation. In Israel, the negligence and failures in intelligence that led to the surprise Arab attack on Yom Kippur of 1973 (*he-mechdal*) had a similar effect in shattering public confidence in the wisdom and infallibility of the government.

According to historian Arthur Hertzberg, American Jewish dissent from Begin's and Shamir's policies arises from Diaspora opposition to the aspect of Likud's ideology that calls for the permanent retention of Judea and Samaria (the West Bank and Gaza) and massive Jewish settlement there to accomplish de facto annexation of these areas to Israel. " Begin's victory in 1977 made it inevitable that the question of the 'undivided land of Israel' would, before long, divide the Diaspora," Hertzberg wrote. He went on:

> From the very first moment, the Likud Prime Minister, a man of honor, refused to pretend that his interest in the region, which he insisted on calling Judea and Samaria, was based on security considerations. He told all and sundry, including President Carter at their first meeting in July 1977, that his prime task was to reeducate the Jews of the world, and all of the concerned political powers, about the true meaning of Zionism: The claim to Jewish sovereignty over the land west of the Jordan was not negotiable.[27]

For the reasons Hertzberg outlines, observers of the American Jewish scene perceived a growth in dissatisfaction that threatened to result in increasing estrangement from Israel. On January 9, 1982, David Polish, a well-known Reform rabbi and Zionist, urged Israeli leaders to pay attention to the "changing mood" of the American Jewish community. Speaking at the 25th convention of the Labor Zionist Alliance in New York, Polish declared that "Jews are not yet openly critical, but in contrast to their former undeviating assent, they are strongly dissenting in private." He decried the lack of a "proper forum for the discussion of controversial issues in our communities and on a national level," and expressed opposition to the idea that "'Diaspora Jews must always approve of Israel's policies, even when they are being bitterly fought in Israel."[28]

Then came the war in Lebanon. Like most Israelis, American Jews generally supported Israel's entry into Lebanon in June 1982, when it was thought that the operation was a limited foray to knock out the Palestine Liberation Organization's bases and infrastructure within the forty-kilometer rocket range of Israel's northern border. As the war went on and fighting extended to the outskirts of Beirut in July, a painful ambivalence arose within the American Jewish community. "We all cherish Israel," said Roland Gittelsohn, a Reform rabbi in Boston, but he added that the invasion "threatens to tear us apart... We worry, agonize, fear, and also doubt." Leonard Fein editor of *Moment* magazine, and a supporter of the Peace Now movement in Israel, stated the problem succinctly: "Our powerful communal disposition has always been to rally round the flag. The problem is that the flag now is in a suburb of Beirut, and that's a long way to go for a rally."[29]

Fissures began to appear in the organized Jewish community. The question of how to respond to events in the Middle East evoked impassioned debate at the annual meeting of the Central Conference of American Rabbis (Reform) in New York at the end of June 1982. Rabbi Robert Marx of Chicago offered a resolution declaring that "the tragic loss of human life and the tremendous destruction of property" in the Lebanon war "leave us concerned, not only for the people in Lebanon but for the soul of Israel and the Jewish people... The current Israeli leadership interpreted American Jewish support for Israel as support for its policies in Lebanon. This is not so." Rabbi Ronald Gittelsohn, who had just returned from Israel, stated the basic dilemma: "Was Israel right in pushing beyond its forty-kilometer objective? I don't know. I have been among Israel's severest critics... I have criticized Israel in the past and I shall criticize again... but not now, my friends, not now... The house is on fire and my brothers and sisters whom I dearly love are in that house... For the sake of Zion, I will hold my peace."[30] But such admonitions to withhold judgement were not to last.

The general press gave attention to the impact of the war in Lebanon on traditional American Jewish solidarity with Israel. The *Christian Science Monitor* ran a front-page story in July 1982 entitled, "Some American Jewish Leaders Voice Anguish Over Lebanon." The story noted that former World Jewish Congress presidents Philip Klutz-nick and Nahum Goldmann, the veteran Zionist leader, and former French premier Pierre Mendes-France, had called on Israel to lift the siege of Beirut and to declare its readiness to negotiate with the PLO on the basis of mutual recognition. Most of the organized American Jewish community, however, denounced the statement.[31]

In September 1982, the Phalangist massacre in the Palestinian refugee camps in Beirut sent waves of shock and revulsion through the American Jewish community, where numerous organizations and individuals were quick to issue expressions of sadness and regret. The dismay was intensified when the Begin government, in the face of Labor party demands for its resignation, seemed to stonewall all attempts to conduct an inquiry. Major American Jewish organizations, including the American Jewish Committee, B'nai B'rith, and the American Jewish Congress, as well as many prominent individuals, called on Israel to conduct an independent judicial inquiry to discover what acts of omission or commission by Israeli military officers and government officials might have facilitated the massacre. The impact of the American Jewish influence on the government's decision to appoint the independent Kahan Commission is difficult to measure because it followed a massive demonstration of some 400,000 Israelis in Tel Aviv calling for such government action.

These and other contentious incidents caused some observers to argue that a split was developing between the American Jewish leadership and the broader membership of Jewish organizations on the issue of the scope and conduct of the war. Hans Jonas, professor of philosophy at the New School for Social Research, claimed that "the official Jewish organizations cannot bring themselves to say this, but in the rank and file I can assure you there is a feeling of disgust, of shame. I know rabbis who feel exactly as I do, but who cannot express it because their congregations would be up in arms."[32]

Despite the shocks to American Jewish opinion engendered by some aspects of the Lebanon war — particularly the Sabra and Shatilla massacres — public opinion polls showed that American Jews still staunchly supported Israel. When Gallup asked (Sept. 22-23, 1982) whether United States aid to Israel should be suspended to force an Israeli pullout from Lebanon, 75 percent of American Jews said no, compared with 38 percent of the broader American public. The same poll asked American Jews what they believed to be the most appropriate role for American Jews concerning Israel. Thirty-six percent of the sample claimed that American Jews should take an active role in trying to affect Israel's policies; 24 percent said they would support

Israel's government regardless of its actions; and another 30 percent
thought that the best stance for American Jews would be to maintain
neutrality.[33]

Clearly, the question of dissent — which issues, which forums
— had become an issue in Israel-Diaspora relations well before the current disputes on how to respond to the Palestinian uprising that
erupted in December 1987.

Reaction of American Jews to the Palestinian Uprising

The continuing disturbances in the Occupied Territories trouble
American Jews greatly, according to a *Los Angeles Times* poll that
measured the opinions of both Jewish and non-Jewish American in
early April 1988. the results suggest that the violence dismayed both
Jews and non-Jews, writes Robert Sheer of the *Los Angeles Times*, but
also engendered views that are far more nuanced, contradictory, and
complex than most analysts have thought. Specifically, American Jews
are not so preoccupied with Middle East issues, nor as homogeneous
in their thinking, nor as different from their non-Jewish neighbors as
is usually assumed.

The portrait of American Jewry that emerges from the survey —
based on a random national sampling of 1,018 Jews drawn from over
200,000 names, and 1,100 non-Jews — shows "an active, committed
Jewish community increasingly polarized and concerned about the
direction of events involving Israel." This polarization could be discerned on a wide variety of issues, from conclusions about the nature
and acceptability of Israeli actions in the Occupied Territories to perceptions of the strength and durability of United States-Israeli ties.

For example, 35 percent of the Jews surveyed felt that the continued occupation of the West Bank "will erode Israel's democratic and
humanitarian character," while 45 percent did not (non-Jews responded
by a ratio of 35 to 32, with a third not being sure). This suggests that
agruments stressing the demographic problem find resonance among
a solid third of the American Jewish polulation.[34]

The formula "land for peace," which is the basis of the Shultz
peace plan, generated a similar split. thirty-one pecent of Jews agreed
that Israel should "give up the Occupied Territories in exchange for
Arab recognition... as part of a settlement of *the* Middle East conflict,"
while 43 percent disapproved (emphasis added; presumably a higher
percentage would agree to trade *some* territory for peace). Despite what
seems to be ambivalence on pressing the "land for peace" formulas,

over 60 percent of the Jews favored the Shultz initiative, including an international peace conference, as did a similar percentage of non-Jews. Only 17 percent of the Jews were opposed. Strongest opposition came from the Orthodox, but even they supported the Shultz initiative by 41 to 23 percent. the remainder of the Jews said they were unaware or unsure.

These numbers suggest that many Jews favor American diplomatic solutions to the Arab-Israeli conflict by virtue of their being advocated by a secretary of state and a president who are noted for their firm support for Israel. They may also reflect the general American confidence in the value of negotiations to solve disputes. This conclusion is buttressed by the results of a poll conducted by Penn and Schoen Associates in mid-January 1988. They concluded that "even though the American people view the PLO negatively and believe it remains committed to the destruction of Israel, they still overwhelmingly favor negotiations. Americans have a bias towards trying a reasonable approach; they feel you can discuss anything, no matter how intractable or emotional the issues may be."[35]

Jewish respondents to the *Los Angeles Times* poll were sharply divided over the issue of public dissent from Israeli policies. A majority (54 percent) of Jews who defined themselves as Conservative Jews felt that Israel should be given public support even when they disagreed with policies in private, as against 36 percent who disagreed. For the Orthodox the figures were 49 to 43. A majority (51 percent) of Reform Jews felt that Jews should not publicly support policies of which they disapproved, as against 42 percent who felt they should. Interestingly, Jews who regarded themselves as "nonaffiliated" were somewhat more ready to criticize Israel than non-Jews expected them to be. Among the nonaffiliated, 58 percent believed they should not support Israel when they disagreed with its policies, in contrast to 29 percent who said they should. When this question was asked of non-Jews, 30 percent thought Jews should publicly support Israel despite their private misgivings, while 49 percent said they should not. However, one-fifth of the non-Jewish sample were not sure, as against 10 percent for the nonaffiliated and roughly 5 percent for affiliated Jews.[36]

Attitudinal Differences Based on Age and Religious Affiliation

There were interesting generational differences in the willingness to criticize Israel. Younger Jews claimed a greater right to voice criticism of Israel's policies. They disagreed with a statement saying that "Jews should support Israel in public even when they disagree in private," by a margin of 3 to 2. Younger Jews also tended to be somewhat more sympathetic toward the Palestinians. Twenty-seven percent of Jews under the age of 41 said they felt themselves equally or more sympathetic to the Palestinians than to the Israelis, as compared to only 17 percent of the older Jews who felt that way.

This suggests that Jews born after the Holocaust and who were not personally aware of the difficult struggle to achieve Israel's independence in 1948 view the Middle East situation from a different perspective than their elders. When they started school, Israel was already in existence, a fact that colors their perceptons about its strength and permanence. They have a less romantic view of Israel, know less about it, and do not appreciate the precariousness of Jewish existence as much as their elders. Nonetheless, support for Israel among them is still broad-based.

Three-fourths of all Jews still feel close to Israel. More of the Orthodox feel close (88 percent), but even two-thirds of the nonaffiliated continue to feel some closeness. There has been an increase in attraction to Israel among the Orthodox and Conservative over the past few years, but a sense of somewhat greater alienation among the Reform and nonaffiliated.[37] The following table gives the statistical breakdown, in percentages, of responses to the *Los Angeles Times* question: "Compared to three or four years ago, do you feel closer to Israel now, or about the same, or do you feel more distant from Israel now than you did three or four years ago?"

	Orthodox	Conservative	Reform	Nonaffiliated	Total
Closer	25	25	13	15	19
Same	71	64	69	61	65
Distant	4	10	16	19	14
Not sure	-	-	1	4	1
Refused	-	1	1	1	1

A third of both younger and older Jews agreed with the view that the Palestinian unrest that began in December 1987 consists primarily of acts of civil disobedience, not acts of war against Israel, as the Israeli government maintains. Dissatisfaction with Israeli positions also surfaced in response to a question about whether Arabs or Israelis would have to change their attitudes before peace can come to the Middle

East. Eighty-six percent of Jews said that the Arabs would have to change their attitudes, but a full 65 percent registered their conviction that Israeli attitudes must also change (80 percent of non-Jews agreed). Forty-one percent of Jews also agreed with the statement that "there is an element of racism involved in the attitudes of Israelis toward Arabs."

Twenty-seven percent of Jews said that the foreign and domestic policies of Israel have become less acceptable to them over the last several years, more than twice the number, (11 percent) who maintained that those policies are now more acceptable. A fourth of the Jews surveyed believed that the current unrest in the West Bank and Gaza may lead to a weakening of Israel-United States relations.

Basic Solidarity with Israel Continues Despite Diaspora Uneasiness

Is the current widespread American Jewish uneasiness being translated into practical dissociation from Israel? Martin F. Stein, chairman of the Board of Trustees of the United Jewish Appeal, reported on May 19, 1988 that the UJA Campaign was "still progressing positively" even though Israel continued "to be plagued with internal problems." As of April 30, 1988, UJA had raised $548.6 million in pledges, an increase of 10.6 percent over the previous year. Cash collections were down somewhat from the previous year, $115.6 million as against $128 million on April 30, 1987, but this was regarded less as an expression of dissatisfaction with events in Israel than a reflection of the changes in United States tax laws and the stock market crash of October 1987. Indeed, Mr. Stein noted that on UJA "Super Sunday," which this year fell on February 7 — two months into the Palestinian uprising — the UJA received pledges of $43 million from the 280,000 persons called, an increase of $8 million over the previous year.

Stein tentatively concluded: "Perhaps our donors — whom I believe are concerned about what they are hearing, reading and seeing — realize that Israel is not to blame for the current situation and that the solution requires that the Arabs not resort to war, terrorism, or mass civil disobedience and rioting, but rather to an acceptance of the reality of Israel and the need for dialogue based on that reality."[38]

But what of the reaction of the 56 percent of American Jews, who, according to the Los Angeles Times poll, said that they had not contributed $100 or more to the UJA/Federation in the past year?

On the whole, despite their dissatisfaction with specific Israeli policies, American Jews do not want the United States to take punitive action against Israel. The *Los Angeles Times* poll asked, "Do you think the United States government should step up its military aid to Israel, or keep it at about the same level, or do you think the government should cut down military aid to Israel?" Foreign aid generally has virtually no constituency among the public at large and there is a receptiveness to suggetions to cut it, especially in times of budgetary constraint. Moreover, Israel is the largest single beneficiary of United States foreign aid. Among the non-Jews, 34 percent said they favored cutting down military aid to Israel, yet a majority still favored keeping it at the current level (47 percent) or even increasing it (8 percent). In contrast, the Jews overwhelmingly supported maintaining or increasing the level of United States military support. Some 90 percent of all affiliated Jews, irrespective of denomination, backed continued or increased aid. Even among the unaffiliated, more than three-fourths were for current levels (64 percent) or increased (12 percent) aid to Israel. Only 10 percent favored some cuts. (The poll did not ask about a total cutoff of aid.)[39]

There were also significant distinctions between attitudes to the government and to the people of Israel. Among non-Jews, the current Israeli government was viewed favorably by only slightly more (33 percent) persons than those who viewed it unfavorably (29 percent), although 39 percent said they were uninformed. Among the Jewish sample, favorable responses ranged from 76 percent among the Orthodox to 60 percent among the nonaffiliated. Unfavorable views ranged from 12 to 25 percent, respectively.

The good news is that despite their misgivings about certain governmental policies, most American still have a favorable opinion of the Israeli people. Of those who had an opinion, the ratio of favorable to unfavorable views was 50 to 14. Israelis are still seen as "people like us," who share our backgrounds, interests, and values. Conversely, while there is growing sympathy for the Palestinians, the Arabs in general and the PLO in particular still suffer from a generally negative image. As was to be expected, among the Jews positive feeling toward the Israelis was strikingly higher, ranging from 89 percent positive to 2 percent negative among the Orthodox to 84 to 4 among the reform and 78 to 5 among the unaffiliated.

Disagreement Does Not Mean Divorce

Clearly, although there is a good deal of agonizing and soul-searching within American Jewry about the news coming from Israel, basic feelings of solidarity with the Jews of Israel remain strong. Of course, this is subject to change, especially if Israel were to adopt policies viewed as inimical to American interests or to basic Jewish and democratic values.

For the time being, however, American Jews seem to have instinctively understood the distinctions suggested by Israelis from across the political spectrum. David Grossman, the author of *Yellow Wind*, who harshly criticized current Israeli policies in the territories before a meeting sponsored by the New Israel Fund in New York on May 10, 1988, drew a sharp line between such criticism and advocating American economic and political pressure to force Israel to change those policies.

Similarly, Ehud Olmert, a leading young Likud member of the Knesset, told a visiting American Jewish Committee group in Jerusalem in February: "Of course you have a right to express your views and we even welcome your criticisms, because we know they come out of love and a shared concern for our common future." What he could not stand, however, were those American Jews who in response to Israeli actions in quelling the riots were saying, "Well, if Israel is going to be that kind of a country, I will have nothing more to do with it." Mr. Olmert gave the example of a family that discovers that a son is involved with drugs or has committed a crime. "If you are really part of a family, you don't walk away and disown the member who is in trouble," Mr. Olmert said. "You try to work together to cope with your common problem."

[Editor's Note: The major themes raised by George Gruen in his chapter were clearly illustrated following the election for the Twelfth Knesset in November 1988. At that time both Likud (winning forty seats) and Labor (winning thirty-nine seats) were competing for the support of the religious parties in the coalition-formation process. The return sought by the religious parties in exchange for their support was a commitment relevant to the "Who is a Jew?" question, seeking policies regarding conversion standards closer to those positions advocated by Orthodox doctrine.

In the end, the reaction of the American Jewish community played a significant role in the outcome of the conflict. Lobbying by American Jews contributed to both the Likud and Labor parties resisting the demands of the religious groups, and eventually another National Unity coalition was formed between Likud and Labor, without the government agreeing to the demands put by the Orthodox parties. The political fallout on both sides of the Atlantic was quite significant, however. In a manner very similar to that which Gruen illustrated here, Israeli politicians resented the clear and direct pressure put upon them by American Jews strongly opposing the demands of the religious parties. On the other hand, American Jews responded that if their support was regularly sought by Israel, they had a right to express their opinion in areas of such fundamental importance.]

PART THREE

The Domestic Political Environment

CHAPTER ELEVEN

The Party's Just Begun:
Herut Activists in Power and After Begin*

Alan S. Zuckerman, Hanna Herzog, and Michal Shamir

> Now, I sometimes ask myself, "Who? What? What
> have we become?" On Sunday, I attended the
> meeting of the Party Center in Jerusalem. Of the
> two thousand persons there, maybe one hundred
> could sing the *Betar* hymn or the song of *Etzel*....
> So I ask: Where is my movement?
>
> *A veteran of sixty years, who first joined the Revisionist*
> *Movement in Vilna.*

> Today, there are all kinds of new members in the
> party and everyone has his own ideas. That's not
> the way it was in Begin's time. Then, when he
> spoke, everyone relied on Begin. Today, Begin is
> no more and everyone wants to take his place,
> and so they fight.
>
> *A former resident of Bet Shean, now living in Tel Aviv,*
> *and no longer very active in the party.*

> I go to party headquarters, at Metzudat Ze'ev,
> every Thursday. We sit there, see friends, meet

*The Department of Political Science, Tel-Aviv University, The Pinchas Sapir Institute
for Development Studies, The Jerusalem Institute for Israel Studies, and the Faculty
Development Fund of Brown University provided research support. Asher Arian, Stanley
Feldman, Yitzhak Galnoor, Calvin Goldscheider, Michael Rich, and Darrell West provided
crucial assistance at various stages of the research, and Raphael Cohen-Almagor and
Ilan Ben-Ami were very able research assistants. We are pleased to be able to thank all
these persons and institutions and to note that we remain responsible for our analyses.

235

people, exchange ideas. You know.... "How're
you doing? How're things? What happened to that
guy, who became so-and-so's assistant." We check
to see who's advancing and who's losing ground.
Hundreds are there every Thursday. The big shots
are there to be seen. They come to meet
members.... There's an open door, and cabinet
ministers and Knesset members sit there, and
whoever wants can go and talk with them.... Arik
Sharon and David Levy come too. All the guys
who go there sit in the cafeteria with them, laugh
with them.... You know, show how they are
friends of the big shots.

*A young activist, born into a political family of Iraqi
origin.*

In August 1983, Menachem Begin ended his political career. He
resigned as prime minister, closed himself behind the door of his apartment, and disappeared from public life. While Begin was active, he
embodied the Herut party. He inherited the leadership of the Revisionist movement from Jabotinsky, its founder, and directed Etzel, the
prestate military organization, that fought for independence from the
British. Begin transformed the Revisionist movement into the Herut
party, and then attracted other parties into the Likud, forming one of
the two largest political blocs in Israel. When he stepped down, the
Herut Center, for the first time in nearly four decades, had to choose
a new leader. Herut and Begin were no longer synonymous.

Begin dominated his followers through personal magnetism and
the adroit use of political symbols. Unlike the Labor movement, Herut
had neither an elaborate ideology nor a large-scale political machine.
Instead, Begin offered rhetoric and direct appeals to voters. In the early
years, Herut activists were volunteers, committed to an expansive
vision of the Land of Israel and opposed to Labor. Intimate friends
and former comrades in arms, Herutniks were veterans of Etzel or its
counterpart, Lechi. Begin's closest followers were "the fighting
family"; he was their "Commander." The party's activists appeared
only at elections and occasional conventions. They worked through
large bodies with diffuse authority, not committees with defined
responsibilities. The most active, those in the movement's center,
helped Begin design the party's platform and nominate candidates to
the Knesset.[1] Begin controlled the movement through a web of personal attachments, friendships, loyalties, and shared dreams.

As Begin and his followers moved from the fringes of Israeli politics to an electoral plurality and dominance over the governement, Herut activists changed. Reflecting movement in the electorate, Sephardim, those Jews whose origins lay in Asia and Africa, filled the party's organization. Controlling the government, the party's ministers and deputy ministers commanded powerful bureaucracies and began to use their positions to mobilize support for their own as well as their party's goals. New activists, seeking the spoils of office, have joined Herut. They acquire and retain jobs through political connections, spend much of their time working for the party, and find that most of their friends and family members are active in Herut as well. Increasing numbers of Herutniks have become political professionals.

Herut politics is now the conflict of party factions. Careerists and newcomers battle the remnants of "the fighting family." Interests associated with political jobs and appointments complete with ideological demands in structuring party policy. Party meetings attract political professionals searching for contacts, aid for constituents, and support in contests over positions. The outcome of conflict among the factions determines who is chosen to run for office and where candidates are placed on the ballot, appointments to government agencies, and the control of positions within the party's organization.

Opportunities to expand political careers and threats to positions already controlled account for the emergence of faction politics in Herut. Ethnic grievances and ideological commitments do not explain why activists attend meetings or join factions. The "Commander's" departure exacerbated the budding tensions within Herut. The jobs of growing numbers of political professionals depend on the outcomes of party contests. Joining a faction ensures the success of one's political position. In turn, conflict among the factions exacerbates the need for the support of allies and strengthens the ties among faction members. Begin's retirement has joined with electoral victories and patronage politics to transform Herut into a political party.

The Data

We draw our analysis of Herutniks from a survery of delegates to the Labor and Herut conventions held in the spring of 1986. Both groups were elected and appointed from local branches of their parties.While Labor conventions occur every few years, the several thousand delegates to the Herut congress were attending the first conclave since 1979. Following the literature on party activists, we take these delegates to be a reasonable representation of the general category of party workers.[2] Despite some problems of exclusiveness and exhaustiveness, the delegates are "party members not part of the party leadership who are substantially more active than other members and the party's voters"[3]

Our data come from two interwoven sources: a telephone survey of a large sample of the delegates and wide-ranging discussions in the homes and offices of a subgroup selected from the general sample. We drew a random sample from the list of delegates for each party's congress. The 399 surveyed on the telephone, 200 from Herut, and 199 from Labor, amount to approximately 8 pcercent of all the delegates (10 percent of those in Herut and 6 percent of the Laborites). We tried first to obtain permission to interview the delegates on the floor of the Herut congress. When our request was denied, we turned to the use of a telephone survey, conducted by the Modiin Ezrahi research group. We provided them with a list of 600 delegates, 300 from each party, so as to reach the target of 200 from each of Herut and Labor. Difficulties in locating phone numbers and addresses of some of the delegates account for almost all those who did not respond to the survey. The nature of telephone surveys allows for relatively few questions, all with very precise meanings. As a result, we conducted directed discussions with fifty of these delegates. We chose the second group so as to maximize our ability to investigate the place of ethnicity in Israeli politics.[4] In addition, because of a dearth of studies on Herut relative to Labor, we oversampled Herutniks especially those whose origins lay in Asia and Africa. We were especially interested in the extent to which those who control governing positions use them for political ends; therefore, we also made sure to interview a relatively large number of those who occupy government positions. In all cases, the two forms of information mesh with and do not contradict each other. The open-ended interviews supply the color and details that help us to elaborate the quantitative analysis of the activists. Together, the two sets of data allow us to draw a portrait from complementary perspectives on the party activists.

Joining the Party: Ethnic Networks and Political Ties

A massive influx of support from Israelis of Asia-African origin spurred Herut's expansion in the electorate and growth as a political organization. Activists born in Morocco, Yemen, and Iraq joined those, like Begin himself, whose origins were in Poland and other countries of Europe and America. Indeed, so many Asia-Africans enlisted that they now form the majority of the party's activists: Orientals (so defined, if the delegate's or his father's country of origin is in Asia or Africa) compose 53 percent of the Herutniks; Westerners (so defined if the delegate or his father was born in Europe or America) are 34 percent of the activists, and native Israelis (those born in Israel of a father born in Israel) are 14 percent.[5] In the Labor party, Westerners account for 59 percent of the activists; Orientals, 33 percent; and native Israelis, 10 percent. Similarly, the ethnic groups, in our sample, have an unequal distribution in the parties. Sixty-five percent of the Orientals and the native Israelis are in Herut, and 65 percent of the Westerners are in Labor. In addition, children of those born in Europe or America are much more likely to be in the Labor party (75 percent of them as compared one-third of the others). They contrast sharply with the children of Orientals, three-fourths of whom are in Herut. There is a skewed relationship between ethnicity and recruitment into the two political parties.

Differences in ethnic origin, however, do not distinguish the social identifications and friendship networks of Labor and Herut activists. Nearly two-thirds in both parties with no differences according to ethnicity defined themselves as either an Ashkenazi or a Sephardi (the names associated with Europe-American and Asia-African ethnicity respectively).[6] Similarly, three-fourths of the activists in both parties reported that the same proportion of their friends came from the two ethnic categories. Rather, most of the activists' friends and family members link them to their own parties. Nearly 60 percent claimed that a "large part or all" of their friends and family members are in their party. Nearly two-thirds of the Laborites and half of the Herutniks, with no ethnic differences, reported very high levels of friends in their respective parties. Approximately three-fourths of the Asia-Africans share party membership with members of their families compared to two-thirds of the Europe-Americans in labor and half the Westerners in Herut. Native Israelis, especially those in Herut, are much less likely to have friends and families in their parties. Differences in ethnic origin neither increase the likelihood that an activist claims an ethnic identification nor affect how the activist chooses his friends. most of their intimate social ties connect them to political comrades.

Asia-Africans in Herut and Labor show no significant differences in their perceptions of ethnic issues and in the extent that their ethnic origin affects their political lives. Most of the activists deny the current significance of ethnic prejudice in Israel. Labor Orientals have the highest perceptions, and Westerners in Herut have the lowest. More than 80 percent encountered no more than a "very small" and 10 percent "a small" amount of personal discrimination. Both sets of delegates agree that ethnic discrimination was once more prevalent. A Herutnik summed up the responses of most of his colleagues: "There used to be ethnic discrimination, but today, because the Sephardim were strong and pushed ahead, there is none. And Begin was the one who gave the big push to the change.... A little remains of the prejudice, but not like it once was.... I haven't felt any discrimination in years." A young labor activist of Asia-African descent maintained that his party is open to all ethnic groups. "I don't see any ethnic discrimination at all in Labor. I know the party well in my area and less well at the national level. But, when I see the workers, for example, when I go to the meetings of the Central Committee, I don't see fewer Orientals...." Almost all of the delegates in both parties contend that ethnic discrimination is not an important issue in contemporary Israel.

Family loyalties, personal experiences, and obligations associated with jobs and careers led most Herutniks to their party. Many had parents and other relatives already involved in the Revisionist movement. A Herut veteran told us:

> I joined Betar [the Revisionist youth organization], in Poland, when I was eight. My teacher's son was a Commander in Betar. I had experienced problems with the Gentiles.... I had heard of Jabotinsky, and I was excited. My father was a member of the Brit Hahayal and my brother later joined Betar. Here in Israel, we joined Etzel. We were a family of Revisionists, all of us."

Another reported: "I'll tell you. I saw politics in my father's house. He worked for Herut, even before the establishment of the state. Those are my roots.... I joined, because I believe. That is my belief, that this is the right way." Yet another echoed this theme: "I joined in the simplest possible way.... My father was a member of Etzel. I absorbed politics at the dawn of my youth."

In the early years of the state, many of these families suffered at the hands of the Labor party's political machine:

> We lived in Ramat Gan, and my father simply had no work. they wouldn't give him work. I remember this myself, when I was a boy. I remember too one of Bialik's lines: 'Even the Devil cannot create the revenge of a little child.' I can never forget, what they told him: 'You are a Revisionist. You have no work.'

Others were new immigrants who experienced the might of the Labor movement:

I got involved in politics, soon after I finished the army, in 1952, and I began to work in an engineering company attached to the army. One day, a member of the Workers' Council came up to me and asked: "Listen. have you been let go yet?" I asked him, "What's this, 'Have I been let go?' " I didn't know anything at all about politics. I had just finished the army. He said, "O.K. scram, get out of here." Two hours later, I received a letter of dismissal, just like two days earlier I had received a letter telling me that I was promoted. I thought that I was getting another raise, instead I was fired. I had a friend, who had brought me to the job, who was also a member of the council, and I asked him, "What's happening, here?" He looked and was shocked, so he went to ask why I was fired. The Council told him that I was fired, because I hadn't joined the Mapai party. He asked me why hadn't I joined, and I replied, "Chaim, What is this joining?' What does joining mean?" Then he said, "Don't you know?" I said, "No." I really didn't know, and he believed me, because he knew me well. I told him that I don't get involved in that kind of thing.... I had never thought of getting involved in politics. I asked him, "Which party do I have to join?" He said, "Don't you know? Mapai" I told him, "I don't know Mapai. I don't know anything about politics." I said, "O.K. Go to the office." He said, "There's no choice, Yehuda, go home. We'll find a way to get back your job, but for now you're fired. They're afraid that you're wise to things and that you will get angry, when people are fired illegally, so they fired you."

The respondent reported other such encounters with Mapai politicians. "Today, I hate the Labor Alignment, and I do so for just this reason, their arrogance, the slaps in the faces that they handed out." Several others related similar tales of mistreatment and nastiness at the hands of Mapai politicians and clerks at the Histadrut and the Workers' Councils, all affiliates of the Labor movement. Only among these delegates do we hear echoes of ethnic resentment by Orientals directed at Labor activists, who were Ashkenazim. The dominance of Labor's political machine during the early years of the state drove activists to Herut.

Some of those who joined as children did not have deep ideological roots in the movement:

When I was a boy, they would always get neighborhood kids to distribute campaign flyers and leaflets. I remember that not only did I give out the pamphlets, but I was something more. I was what could be called a 'broker.' It seems that I was a precocious child. They used to give me a sack of leaflets and tell me to give them out. Then I would gather a group of younger children, give them each an ice cream or promise an ice cream, and they did the work for me, while I remained with a large portion of the remaining money. That's how I started. We kids used to fight over who would distribute the leaflets. I remember how the older guys received tickets to the cinema, and I was really jealous....

Others come to politics, because of their jobs. A Herutnik, who had been a career officer in the Israel Defense Forces for more than 20 years, reported that he first considered joining a political party, when he left the military. Recruitment into Herut grew out of his first civilian job as an advisor to a cabinet minister and the personal friendship that developed between his family and that of the minister. Joining the party, he said, was like, "many things in life, which happen without planning for them." His military credentials made him attractive to the party. Entering Herut was part of his new job. He is not alone. Eighty percent of the Laborites work for the government or brances of the Histadrut, economic spheres long colonized by the Labor movement, and half the Herutniks are located in jobs with patronage connections. Family connections, career demands, and policy concerns draw activists into Herut.

Admiration for Begin drew several Herutniks to his party. One told us:

> I loved the Herut movement from the time that I was a child in Morocco.... In truth, I don't remember if there was Betar there, but I had heard of it, and what I had heard even more was the name of Begin, who really touched my heart. I knew that there existed a man named Begin, who really moved me.

This respondent joined Herut, in 1963, after immigrating to Israel and serving in the army. "There was very little news about Herut then, but as that changed, and Begin gave speeches, he touched me. I loved that man, and that moved me to join. When they announced that they were ready to accept members into the movement, I jumped at the chance." Another, already involved in political work, described a similar experience. "My shift to Herut came from Begin, not my home which had not been involved in politics at all.... But you can say that it began with the Liberal Center party, where I used to work. It started from the time I began to pay attention to Begin's articles or when I heard him at gatherings, and they pulled me in his direction. The man himself did it. I listened to his speeches and that pulled me." Begin's personal magnetism attracted Herut activists.

Finally, many of the activists in both parties see the Herut as less hierarchical, more open to new members, and so loosely organized so as to make it easy to rise quickly within the party. "In Herut, everything is open," a young Herutnik told us. "You can stand for an office. There is no appointments committee. If you want to compete, you can. The opportunities are wide open. Everyone has the same chance. A professor at Tel-Aviv University and a garbage worker are equal." Two Labor activists, both young Sephardim, who were recently recruited into the party, agreed:

> It is easier for Orientals to advance in the Likud [i.e., Herut]. They let them. One of the Likud Ministers told me, 'Anyone who can sign his name, I will appoint as an Assistant Director [of a Ministry].' That's funny, but it gives you a sense of how aware they are of the need to advance.

An activist from a poor neighborhood of Jerusalem described how he and his friends had been recruited into Labor as a separate group. "They gave us a small budget too, but the really important things, like access to the Ministry of Education, areas where we can really make policy, they keep from us. We are still fighting them." Perceiving a relatively open Herut organization, new activists moved easily into the party.

Ashkenazi predominance in the rigid and hierarchical organization of Labor and the openness of Herut made it relatively easy for Asia-Africans to enter the expanding Herut. In turn, the social networks of Orientals magnified the likelihood that they would enlist new orientals into Herut. Opportunities for political advancement more than Sephardi grievances as such produce different patterns by which the two parties attract activists.

The Emergence of Conflict within Herut

The entry of new members and activists into Herut, the control of patronage positions, and Begin's retirement have inserted a high level of conflict into Herut. The relatively open organization provides access to positions in the national and local leadership, appointment to government positions, and nominations to run for office to those who amass the most votes in contests within the party. The months preceding local and national elections and the party conventions, therefore, are periods of intense politicking. In Herut, no committee on appointments selects candidates. As a party veteran reflected, "Here, the branches live. No one sends a letter from Metzudat Ze'ev, that these ten men should be picked.... or those five should be chosen and you can pick another five. In our party, the brances send their own people." He went on to link this openness and the emergence of conflict within Herut. "Certainly, this would cause a crisis for the veterans. All of a sudden, they see that we, the fighting family are a only few." Recent party history has been characterized by an expanding organization and intense conflict.

The buds of the internal power struggle appeared soon after Herut came to control the national government. David Levy was the first to gather his own following. At the fourteenth convention in 1979, he and Ariel Sharon traded verbal blows over the election of the Herut executive (*Jerusalem Post*, 8 August 1979). Two years later, they battled over placing candidates on the party's list for the Knesset. After the election, Levy induced Begin into naming him deputy premier (*Jerusalem Post*, 12 August 1981). Control of the national government, and access to patronage that comes with national power, was followed by the emergence of political maneuvering among Begin's lieutenants.

As long as Begin led the party, his decisions carried the day. In the words of one of the Herut veterans:

> In Menahem Begin's time, there ....was no need for conventions. There was one leader, one camp, organized, unified, and strong. There were occasional conventions. They were like festivals. Everyone rejoiced with their friends. It was a celebration. Ever since Begin left — then we have had problems — but we will survive them.

At the 1979 convention, Begin easily dampened the conflict between Levy and Sharon. "Two short meetings" was enough time to decide who would run the party's organization, select the party's center, and, thereby, pick the candidates for the Knesset: "Herut is both marionette theatre and chorus cum band, with Begin pulling all strings and orchestrating every sound.... It was something of a religious event, far beyond the usual admiration accorded to party leaders." (Mark Segal, in the *Jerusalem Post*, 8 June 1979). While Herut's electoral success and control of governing offices led to internal competition, Begin could limit the extent internal conflict.

When Begin retired, the richest position of all, leader of the party and candidate for prime minister, became the object of conflict. On September 2, 1983, the Herut Center, by a vote of 436 to 302, chose Yitzhak Shamir over Levy to replace Begin as prime minister. A year later, Sharon challenged Shamir, capturing 40 percent of Herut Center's votes. In subsequent votes, the center selected Moshe Arens, Shamir's closest ally, to the second position on the list of candidates, Levy to the third, and relegated Sharon to the ninth slot. A delegate bemoaned the factional conflict that has followed Begin's departure. "I don't believe that there should be factions in the Herut movement. In Begin's time, there was no such thing. No one knew of camps (i.e., factions).... There was a leader, and the Herut movement was one unit." In Begin's absence, contests in Herut begin with conflict over the party's leadership.

The delegates who form the basis of our study attended the most sharply divided convention in party history. A week before it opened, Levy gathered one thousand followers, behind his banner: "David Levy, for the unity of the Herut Movement." (*Ha'aretz*, 5 March 1986). Moshe Arens likened Levy's and Sharon's factions to the Mafia, claiming that it, "will destroy the party." (*Yediot Aharonot*, 3 March 1986). The factions battled first over the procedures for selecting delegates. According to the regulations, 1,200 delegates were to be elected by the branches; 191 were nominated by a special personnel committee that assured the inclusion of party veterans; 200 delegates were from La'am, a now defunct party incorporated into Herut, and the party's court chose the remainder (approximately 200). This arrangement favored the new activists, who are especially active in the local branches. Shamir and Arens cried foul. "[Levy] complains about personal deprivation. He presents himself as someone who has been deprived, but for seven years, he has controlled the party's organization, and 'organized' the branches to help himself." (*Yediot Achoronot*, 3 March 1986). Once convened, the convention erupted in violence. Delegates cursed each other and threw punches, bringing the convention to an abrupt and early adjournment. Distrust and enmity divided Levy, Sharon, and Shamir.

Herut Factions

Responding to the spiraling level of conflict, Levy, Sharon, Shamir, and Arens have formed three well-organized camps. Each faction has a dominant leader, frequent meetings, and an organization. Each runs its own candidates for the key positions in the party organization. Conflict over patronage controlled by the party feeds their competition for dominance (see for example, *Yediot Acharonot*, 28 November 1986 and *Ha'aretz*, 2 January 1987):

> I don't belong to any of the factions and I will tell you why. What does 'belonging' mean? .... It's thinking only about what you can get. There is no crisis of ideology. There is a crisis of seats [of power]....

All of them are for settlements in the territories; all are for social justice,
and that's everyone, everyone. They all play the same tune. But what
is it? Everyone wants the seats [of power]....

The struggle for political power not ideology or policy divides Herut.
We sought to assess the delegates' identification with a faction
by asking them two questions. The first was who they supported for
party leader: Shamir, Levy, Arens, or Sharon. Because all the faction
leaders proclaim their support for Shamir's leadership and maintain
that the competition was really over who should lead when he retires,
we asked a second question: If your first choice cannot serve, who
would you prefer to take his place and listed the same four leaders.
Based on our substantive knowledge of Herut party politics, we defined
those who did not answer both questions as not supporting any faction
(15 percent); those who mentioned Levy in either answer as being in
his faction (22 percent); those who mentioned Sharon in either answer
as a member of his faction (16 percent), and the remainder, 47 percent
of the activists, as members of Shamir's faction, whose second in command is Arens. Our data correspond rather well to the estimates of
informed observers and the one vote that took place at the convention, indicating the sizes of the factions.

A strong association exists between ethnic origin and membership in the different factions. Nearly two-thirds of the Westerners back
Shamir; fewer than 20 percent follow either Levy or Sharon. Those
whose origins are in Asia or Africa are almost evenly divided among
the four categories: slightly more than one-third for Shamir; 27 percent for Levy; 23 percent for Sharon, and 14 percent with no faction
loyalties at all. Native Israelis distribute themselves much like the party
as a whole. Few Westerners follow Levy (16 percent) or Sharon (13
percent). Asia-Africans predominate in both, 65 percent and 75 percent respectively. In addition, Westerners make up nearly half of
Shamir's faction. The data confirm the perception that the remnants
of Begin's "fighting family" and many of their Ashkenazi comrades
support Shamir and Arens.

Ethnicity, per se, however, has a weak effect on the choice faction. Sharon, born in Israel of Ashkenazi descent, and Levy, who was
himself born in Morocco, draw activists of very similar ethnic origins.
As challengers to the domination of Shamir and the remnants of the
"fighting family," Levy and Sharon draw the support of activists living
outside the oldest centers of Herut power, areas with relatively high
proportions of Orientals. In addition, veteran Herutniks, most of whom
are Ashkenazim, have banded behind Shamir to resist the rise of the

political professionals: "I support Shamir," a delegate, who first joined the Revisionist movement in Poland, told us.

> He served in Lechi. He sacrificed himself on behalf of the State, and he is the best. Arens too is a good man. Part of the Lavi [fighter plane] is his. Sharon too served in the army for many years and contributed to the State. Levy, who pronounced, 'You [Begin] have an inheritor,' is not acceptable to me. He didn't know Jabotinsky. he is not a party veteran. Let him wait. He took advantage of the fact that he is of Oriental origin, and pushed himself to the top. There are better men in the party, who didn't push themselves forward, and have had to stand aside. He jumped to the top, because he is Oriental. He will cause the party to split and fall from power. Katzav [another leader of Oriental origin] is a good man. He doesn't say that he must be the party leader."

This old-timer went on to condemn Benny Begin as well. "What did he do? A careerist, he studied abroad." Levy's methods of advancement rather than his ethnic origin are the object of disdain. The remnants of Begin's "fighting family," most of whom are Ashkenazim, have sought to defend their movement by rallying behind Shamir.

The factions vary in the extent to which they have been built around the control of patronage. Levy, the first to organize, has constructed a political machine around the control of government jobs and political offices. Nearly 60 percent of Levy's supporters work for the government, compared to 45 percent of the Shamir-Arens and Sharon factions, and about one-third of those in no faction. Two-thirds of Levy's backers also have held public office in the last three years compared to 62 percent of Shamir's faction, half of the Sharon supporters, and about one-third of those who claim no faction membership. Levy's faction, more than any of the others, is primarily composed of persons for whom politics is their career.

Conflict among the factions has increased the strategic and career reasons for joining the factions, at the expense of ideological and other loyalties. One of Levy's followers highlighted the tactical bases of his faction:

> I belong to Levy's faction because of my ties to Micha Reisser [his lieutenant]. I know what the factions are really about. Political life rests on alliances, such as the alliance between Levy and Reisser, themselves, and my association with them. This is the way to political survival. Obviously, I would prefer that the factions be abolished, but until then, you have to extract the maximum from them.

Another Herutnik echoed this point:

> I was treasurer of the branch four times, but now I have no position,
> because Levy's faction controls the leadership. Our branch was divid-
> ed into two groups. I wanted to remain active in the branch, but each
> side gathered followers. I opposed this, not because of David Levy,
> but because I wouldn't align with his local leader. I prefer the guy
> who was here before. It was because of him that I originally joined
> the branch. He was the only one I knew, and because of him, I got
> ahead, to become a member of Herut Center and the City Council.
> I wouldn't leave him.

A leader of the Shamir-Arens faction complained about these
developments. "In my youth, we discussed important issues, like the
settlement of the land and the meaning of the state. We cared deeply
and debated passionately. now, the activists seem to care only about
power, especially those who follow Levy and Sharon." An activist from
a city on the coast told us about Sharon's effort to break into the game:
"Didn't Arik send members of our branch to work in embassies and
consulates in Europe? Weren't they commercial, economic, and cultural
attaches?" The distribution of these trips abroad and jobs holds the
key to power in the local party. "This is called 'gathering power from
honors'. You can go to your friends here and.... You can help them
get jobs." The political return from the distribution of these jobs built
Sharon's faction in the city. Party conflict focuses on the control of
patronage not debate over policy differences or ideological principles.
    A circle of close followers composes the core of each faction. Key
members meet with Levy his office in the Ministry of Housing, forming his faction's "select forum." A larger group of about 70 composed
of leaders of party branches is the "extended forum." One of his
followers elaborated:

> I belong to Levy's group, which means that we discuss each decision
> in the group, sometimes with Levy, sometimes with Reisser, and
> sometimes with the other Knesset members in the faction. I emphasize
> the word 'group,' because when you compete in the party, the
> members of the group help each other. For example, I went to Ma'ale
> Adumim to assist our faction members there who were battling
> Shamir's supporters. Most of those who came to fight, did so because
> they belonged to factions.

A member of Sharon's faction told us: "Every month or so, Sharon
gathers 'the guys' together. He explains to them what's going on, not
that they should back him, which is understood, but where he stands

on various issues and what actions he will take." One Herutnik who works in Sharon's Ministry of Industry, described his links to the faction. "I have a direct connection to Sharon, and to Meir Shitrit, Miriam Glazer-Tasah, and to Kaugman (Sharon's closest associates). I turn to them, when I have problems, and they can solve them. I do not have a direct link to Levy or Arens. I can call Sharon at home, and I have done so." The Shamir-Arens faction remains the largest in the party and, consequently, asks the least of its members. Some denied the existence of a faction led by Shamir: "The one thing that unites us... is to stand behind Shamir and not to disrupt the government... I do not belong to any faction. I am for the Herut party and movement. That's all." Even so, Shamir's faction has organized in response to Levy's threat to their power. Most Saturdays, the leaders of Shamir's faction meet in the garden of one of their homes. "I make sure to go," remarked a former general and faction activist. "They called me before the meeting to confirm my attendance, because they are really interested in my being there. Tomorrow, we will meet there with Moshe Arens." They also use political connections to link some of the activists together: "I have many connections with MKs and Cabinet Ministers. If I need assistance, I can call anyone I want. I am a good friend of Ronnie Milo (Shamir's top aide). If I have a problem, I will first turn to the MKs and Ministers who are in Shamir's faction." In all three factions, the leaders' closest associates meet regularly, plan strategy, and maintain their links to faction activists.

Some of the delegates, even those who claim to support one of the leaders, do not take part in the activites of the factions. One of the delegates told us, "I don't follow anyone. For now, I'm not with anyone.... although, I am closest to Prime Minister Shamir." We asked him what he will do after Shamir steps down: "I will see the ideas presented at that time. I will see who speaks the most. Not like what happened at the last convention. I won't go with those people, who got up and carried on." Another echoed this theme: "Today, I don't belong to any faction. If I have to choose, I will.... I am closest to Arik Sharon. All the others are at the same level after him. There is no difference among Levy, Shamir, and Arens. Today, I see Sharon as the candidate to lead the party." A member of Levy's faction described the factions:

> I would never say that of the 2,000 at the convention, 1,500 were absolutely in factions and the others not, or the opposite. There is no way to know for sure. All the elections are conducted by secret ballot. You can't ever say that you know, unless the man himself says, 'I

belong to a particular faction.' And even then, three or four months can pass, and the man may change his mind. These things have happened.

Some activists are identified by their political connections and labeled as faction members. "How is it known that I identify with Shamir and Arens? Those in the faction count me as one of them, because of my ties to Milo, to Arens himself, and to Olmert. They list me as one of theirs, and that's how the other side knows." Faction identificaion is not always explicit. "I can tell very quickly, what faction someone belongs to. There is no recipe. It's my gut feeling. You've got to be around a while, in order to get these instincts. I can identify a man's faction as soon as he begins to speak." the cohesion of the factions varies with the opportunities for conflict within Herut and as the activists' careers require the assistance of faction leaders.

Herut conflict is faction conflict. David Levy and Ariel Sharon have organized their followers to challenge Shamir's control of the party. Their rise threatens the remnants of Begin's "fighting family," who have supported Shamir. Neither ideological divisions nor ethnic issues separate Herutniks into the competing factions. Rather, they jostle to extend their power by helping other members of their factions. Faction politics in Herut is the politics of personal favors and political connections.

Faction Conflict and Political Careers as the Bases of Activism

Herutniks vary in their devotion to political affairs. "Everyday, I am somewhere else," one told us. "Only on Friday night, do I belong to my wife. Ask her. She'll tell you that she never sees me during the rest of the week. There is an exception. I return home every afternoon for a nap. That is a fixed rule." Another reported:

> This is my daily calendar: Phone calls every day that are tied to politics; meetings everyday that are tied to politics; not necessarily meetings at the local party headquarters, but with all kinds of people. I am one of those who believes that in order to keep on top of things you have to make sure that your connections with your supporters are strong. I initiate meetings with them. I ask for their views. I am their address for requests for assistance.

Another described a less active political life:

> It's very difficult to describe how much time, I devote to politics, because it depends on the time of year. Most of the time, I put in four to eight hours each week at the local party branch, the national offices, and in phone conversations. I would estimate that I have a conversation every other day or so on political matters.

Others reported reducing their political work, when they had children, in order to spend more time with their families. Compared to other Israelis, the delegates spend an exceptional amount of time in political activities.

Some of their activities occur at meetings of party organizations. In small towns and out of the way neighborhoods of large cities, meetings vary with the political season. They are especially frequent before elections and party gatherings such as the congresses, but other times they may occur no more than once a month. There are also informal get-togethers at brances for "gossip and coffee," trips to national headquarters to "see and be seen" by party bigwigs, and even expeditions to the Knesset. Nearly 60 percent of the delegates reported attending party meetings at least two to three times per month, with one-third of the sample going once per week. Party meetings join formal and informal circumstances.

The exigencies of faction conflict help to account for the frequency with which Herutniks attend party meetings, during the period preceding the convention. The rise of Levy's faction generated a response from others with political careers, the vote brokers, and the controllers of patronage positions. Party meetings were their battleground. The drive to capture and defend political positions explain the frequency with which Herutniks attended party meetings.

Our analysis contrasts the effect of political variables with differences in ethnicity and educational level on the participation of Herutniks in the organizational life of their party. In order to sort the relative influences of these variables, we subjected our data to multiple classification analysis (MCA), which allows the analysis of interval level dependent variables with noninterval explanatory variables. MCA provides a useful way to display the results of analysis of variance and is analogous to multiple regression using dummy variables.[7] In Table 1, the F tests and their significance levels are taken from the analysis of variance for the main effects. The betas are equivalent to standardized regression coefficients, in the explanation of the dependent variable, when all other variables are held constant. The etas are correlation coefficients between each independent variable and the dependent variable, without taking into account the other variables. The table presents for each category of each explanatory factor the unadjusted mean for the dependent variable expressed as a deviation from the grand mean and the deviation from the grand mean of the category mean adjusted for the other factors.[8]

Table 1
Attendance at Herut Meetings

Variable + Category	N	Unadjusted Deviation Eta	Adjusted for Independents Deviation Eta	Mean Number of Meetings* per year, adjusted for Independents
Type of activist: level of statistical significance = .657				
Asia Africa	89	−0.20	0.57	30
Europe America	53	0.88	0.36	30
Natives	19	−1.13	−3.69	25
		0.03	0.07	
Level of Education: level of statistical significance = .002				
elementary or less	10	−14.22	−17.106	11
some and vocational	35	−7.78	−7.67	21
h.s. graduate	53	3.72	3.54	32
beyond h.s.	29	3.01	4.15	33
university	34	3.79	3.86	32
		0.32	0.35	
Branch: level of statistical significance = .306				
central cities	75	0.60	2.27	31
peripheral cities	63	2.03	−0.58	28
small towns	8	−5.92	−4.75	24
agricultural settlements	15	−8.39	−6.40	23
		0.17	0.15	
Friends in party: level of statistical significance = .204				
none or few	23	−3.35	−3.82	25
half	57	−1.02	−2.14	27
most or all	81	1.67	2.59	32
		0.10	0.14	
Politicized workplace: level of statistical significance = .171				
private and coop	77	−3.13	−2.90	26
Histadrut	8	−6.92	−9.09	20
private and government	76	3.90	2.42	31
		0.20	0.15	
Faction: level of statistical significance = .070				
No faction	44	−2.19	−2.90	26
Shamir or Sharon	83	−1.09	−1.16	28
Levy	34	5.49	6.57	35
		0.16	0.19	

Table 1 *(continued)*

Variable + Category	N	Unadjusted Deviation Eta	Adjusted for Independents Deviation Eta	Mean Number of Meetings* per year, adjusted for Independents
Year Joined Party: level of statistical significance = .074				
pre-1948	9	−9.36	−10.85	18
1948-66	63	2.41	2.95	32
1967-76	44	0.31	0.80	30
1977-83	35	0.28	−0.24	29
1984-86	10	−9.12	−11.48	17
		0.19	0.23	

Number of Meetings Attended Each Year, Grand Mean* = 29
Multiple R Squared = .249
Multiple R = .499
*Rounded to Nearest Whole Number

Table 1 presents the results of a multiple classification analysis, which assesses the relative effects of membership in Levy's faction, patronage (which distinguishes between those who work for the government and those who do not), occupying a political office, party branch, and the control vaiables, ethnicity and education, on the frequency with which Herut activists attend party meetings. Living close to the political center and taking part in the conflict to control the party lead to high levels of attendance. Members of Levy's factions attend most frequently. Not all the members of the other factions responded to Levy's challenge by battling his followers at party meetings. Those that did were the political professionals, persons who worked for the government and occupied political offices.

Political factors are the keys to high involvement in the party. Even though variation in the level of formal education has the highest beta and is statistically significant, it exhibits a curvilinear relationship with attendance at party meetings. Among Herutniks, having a university degree does not necessarily bring political success. Attending meetings and ''seeing and being seen'' do. One of the activists described how to make it in Herut:

> There are two ways of being successful in the local branch of the party. The first is personal. You introduce yourself as a lawyer, for example, and say that you would like to work on a particular task. Usually, people don't know you, and don't know much about you, but there is still a good chance that the lawyer will not be chosen for the task. Instead, many times, regular people, not especially smart, even the opposite, are chosen. When you check to see why this happened,

you find that 90 percent of those who voted are tied to the winner, whether through family or other connections. There is a general rule: whoever controls the most voters has the best chances of being selected.

A university education holds few political benefits for those in Herut. Most Israelis who have attended university do not usually vote for Herut; a university degree does not provide a Herutnik with many political resources. The ability to deliver votes counts. In addition, the MCA shows a weak tendency for Orientals to have the highest levels of attendance at party meetings. Political not ethnic factors are the keys to involvement. The differences in ethnicity are not statistically significant. When we substituted ethnic identification for ethnic origin, we found the nonidentifiers to be the most active and those identifying themselves as Sephardim to be the least active. The class and ethnic cleavages of the general society do not split the political world of Herut activists.

Political professionals in Herut are the most likely to attend party meetings. Sometimes, activists go to meet their friends, to gossip, and to pass the time of day. Sometimes, the meetings are formal occasions where committees attend to their assigned tasks. In the weeks and months preceding elections and party conventions, they are arenas in which conflict occurs. David Levy began his climb to the top of Herut by controlling local branches. His opponents have met his challenge by organizing their own factions. The political professionals who have created Herut's electoral successes compete at the local branches, the national offices, and the conventions for power over their party.

Conclusion

The changes in the Herutniks illustrate the transformation of Herut from a movement to a poltical party. Before coming to national power in 1977 and while Menahem Begin "commanded," Herutniks were political volunteers, who shared a nationalist vision of the land of Israel, opposition to the Labor movement, and a personal attachment to Begin. They sought each other's company as much as they worked to attract new suporters. As Begin maneuvered the party toward electoral victories, new activists, many of them of Oriental ethnicity, enlisted. The relative openness of Herut, not the dreams of the Revisionists attracted these activists. For many, joining Herut became a means to political and occupational mobility. Control of the national government brought access to jobs as much as it provided for influence over policy. Begin's retirement meant whoever could amass sufficent support in the party could rise to its top. The Herut movement emphasized ideology, symbol, and charisma. The Herut party is characterized by the conflict of factions.

Increasing numbers of Herut activists are political professionals. They meet with citizens, try to provide assistance in handling problems with government bureaucracies, in resolving issues of tax abatements, in obtaining government contracts, and in smoothing the other links between citizens and bureaucrats. They spend their days going from meeting to meeting, in restaurant and office, in a whirl of political activity. Not only do many Herutniks spend much of the professional lives engaged in political work, but much of their social and family time is filled with party activists as well. Activity in Herut is becoming a professional commitment.

Herut factions compete for positions in the party and government. Our respondents as well as other observers consistently maintain that ideological and policy differences do separate activists into warring camps. Rather, access to patronage, the ability to help political associates, to provide assistance for their friends and neighbors, are the terms of debate. The demands of political careers and conflict for control of the party induce high levels of activity. Party meetings are arenas to battle for new positions and defend old ones. They are places "to see and be seen," the places to build political careers. Conflict emerges in full force when the spoils of office are open for competition, as party leaders rank their candidates for elected office and as they make decisions at congresses over the party organization itself. Conflict disappears when the party is under attack, during election campaigns. At other times, conflict is the province of the professionals, those most involved in the activites of the party, jockeying to be in position for the next race. Herut politics is faction politics.

CHAPTER TWELVE

Better Late than Never:
Democratization in the Labor Party

Myron J. Aronoff

"The nature of the nominating procedure determines the nature of the party; he who can make
nominations is the owner of the party."
E.E. Schattsneider[1]

This essay focuses on the selection of the Labor party candidates
for the elections for the Twelfth Knesset. The analysis of the changes
in the nominations process is the key to evaluating the extent to which
Labor is undergoing internal democratization. From the rise of Labor
in the early 1920s and the establishment of its hegemony in the *yishuv*
(the Jewish community in pre-independence Palestine), through almost
three decades of its dominance of the political system of the sovereign
state, oligarchic control of the nominations process was a key
characteristic of Labor.[2] I have argued that the breakdown in responsiveness of the party, which derived in part from this process and which
led to a lack of genuine representation of important constituencies on
party institutions and the party's Knesset faction, was one of the

*This essay was written while I was resident director of the Rutgers Junior Year in Israel
program at Haifa University during the academic year 1987–88. I am grateful to Avraham
Brichta for his useful comments on an early draft of this essay. I wish to thank Knesset
Members Uzi Baram, Mordecai Gur, and Ora Namir, and former KM Yehuda Hashai
for granting me interviews.

major factors that contributed to Labor's loss of power in 1977. I have
also suggested that the failure to make the necessary reforms, which
such as analysis would have revealed, contributed to the defeat of the
party in the 1981 elections.[3]

Credit for the major impetus for democratization of the party must
be given to Uzi Baram, the party secretary-general. The election of the
former secretary of the Jerusalem district in a narrow margin (384–382)
over Micha Harish on October 30, 1984, paved the way for the reforms
in Labor. However, the ground had been laid by the election of Chaim
Bar-Lev in 1981 as party Secretary-General over his rival for the post,
Eliahu Spieser, secretary of the Tel Aviv district. Speiser follows the
tradition of his predecessors, the bosses of the Tel Aviv *gush*.[4] His election would have resulted in the continuation of oligarchic domination
of the traditional power centers.

Baram, son of the late former labor minister, Moshe Baram, had
actively pushed for greater internal party democracy since his days as
a student activist. He based his campaign for party secretary-general
on the platform of democratization. He wrote to each member of the
central committee arguing the case for the importance of changes in
the nominations process. Baram traveled extensively to the branches
campaigning for reform. Immediately after his election he met with
the ranking party leaders, Cabinet Members Shimon Peres, Yitzhak
Rabin, Yitzhak Navon, Moshe Shahal, and Gad Yacobi, and Secretary-
General of the Histadrut Yisrael Kesar to gain their support for his
plans. Although Baram met considerable resistance along the way, and
on at least one occasion actually resigned his post when it appeared
that some of his demands for reform would not be accepted, he
ultimately mobilized sufficient support to carry the day.

Major opposition to the reforms came from the settlement (*kibbutz*
and *moshav*) movements, which feared they would lose representation
through the proposed reforms. They ultimately agreed to accept
change, but insisted that they chose their own candidates (which they
were allowed to do as distinct units like the urban districts); they
demanded guaranteed positions on the list (which they did not receive).
A key supporter of reform was Professor David Liba'i, chairman of
the Preparation Committee, which is responsible for setting the agenda
of the national party conference.[5] However, the chairman of the subcommittee of the Standing Committee responsible for formulating the
changes in the nominations process was chaired by Yeheskiel Zakai,
a representative of a settlement movement and a member of the camp
of Yitzhak Rabin, who opposed the reforms.[6]

In a meeting attended by Shimon Peres, Yitzhak Rabin, Uzi Baram, Yeheskiel Zakai, and Yisrael Kesar, the latter argued that the party leader (Peres), the secretary-general of the Histadrut (Kesar), and the secretary-general of the party (Baram) should have their places at the top of the list guaranteed without having to stand for election. Zakai proposed that the head of the list either name the top ten on the list or that he appoint two or three on each panel to be elected. Baram argued for more far-reaching reform to give the members of the Central Committee the feeling that they had real influence and to overcome the stigma that the party had in the public mind of a closed, un-breathing, elderly, Ashkenzai, oligarchic party. Peres proposed that he be allowed to choose two people for guaranteed positions beside himself (Rabin and Navon). Zakai insisted that both the party and Histadrut secretaries-general (Baram and Kesar) also have secured positions on the list. The compromise was accepted.

The national party convention held in April 1986 — named by Baram the "Democracy Conference" — accepted the proposed reform agreed upon by the top leaders and formulated by the subcommittee of the Preparation Committee, which had passed it. The only change was the addition of the speaker of the Knesset (Shlomo Hillel) to the list of top leaders with guaranteed positions on the Knesset list, apparently as a concession to party members of Middle Eastern background. In addition Ezer Weizman had been promised a position toward the top of the list (along with two realistic positions for his sup-porters) when his Yahad list joined an alignment with Labor during the coalition negotiations after the 1984 election. The guarantee of the top seven places on the list to the top party leaders followed the Labor tradition of self-nomination by the elite, and was hardly a harbinger of significant democratic reform.

In 1981 half of the Labor candidates for the Knesset were chosen by a nominating committee of five members, which was appointed by the Political Bureau, and half were elected by the district branches. The all-important ordering of the names on the list (which determined who had a realistic chance to be elected) was done by an informal committee consisting of representatives from the kibbutz and moshav movements, and the three major urban districts (Jerusalem, Tel Aviv, and Haifa) with Baram and Speiser playing leading roles. This process ensured the renomination of the main national party leaders, and their major protégés, including representatives of the bodies that constituted the committee, who emerged with strengthened positions.[7] The decision to abandon the rule adopted by the party's second convention that members who had served two terms in the Knesset were required to receive a vote of at least 60 percent of the Central Committee (a rule that had already been seriously compromised during the selection of the candidates for the Tenth Knesset in 1981) also did not appear to be a good opening for democratic reform.

The 1986 party conference accepted the proposal of the party affairs committee that the candidates for Knesset be evenly divided between those to be elected by the districts and those by the Central Committee in the first round. The proposal was that twenty-three candidates be elected by each forum. However, the conference authorized the Central Committee to make changes in this ratio. Volatile debates were held in the Central Committee over how to implement the proposals passed by the convention and the party's constitutional requirement to guarantee places for five women, two young members, a Moslem, a Druze, and a representative of the "neighborhoods" (i.e., a Jew of Middle Eastern background from an inner city area). It was felt that these relatively politically weak categories lacked the power to gain representation on their own. Baram's interpretation that these guaranteed places should be applied to the candidates for the central list in the first round of voting only was accepted. Therefore, twenty-three Knesset candidates were elected by the councils of the district branches, and twenty-nine were elected by the Central Committee.[8]

The twenty-three candidates elected by their district councils conducted traditional campaigns among people with whom they were personally acquainted. Because the district secretaries have particularly strong influence in their districts, not surprisingly the secretaries of the largest districts were among those elected. However the eighty-five candidates for the twenty-nine places on the central list had to appeal for the votes of 1,267 Central Committee members most of whom they either barely knew or did not know at all. Many candidates spent between NIS 15,000 to NIS 20,000 (New Israeli shekels, equivalent to $10,000 to $15,000) from their personal funds for their internal party campaign.[9] Whereas previously they had to persuade the party bosses of their personal loyalty to gain access to the Knesset list, this time they had to convince their peers that their presence on the party list would contribute to the party's victory at the elections. For the first time in the history of the Labor party, there was American-style personal campaigning for the votes of the Central Committee members.

The members of the Central Committee were inundated with mail and telephone calls from the candidates. Many candidates prepared cassette tape recordings and videotapes (some of which were produced by professional public relations firms), which were sent to the Central Committee members. A seven- to eight-minute video cassette cost between NIS 3,000 and NIS 8,000 to produce. Public relations and communications consultant fees ranged between $2,000 to $3,000 a month.[10] Although many candidates hired professional advisers, most relied on friends and personal supporters who volunteered their services in helping their candidates canvass the Central Committee members. Most candidates logged thousands of kilometers traveling across the country to attend meetings with Central Committee members from the various branches, and endless other affairs while campaigning. This was a far cry from the old days when few ventured far from 110 Hayarkon Street in Tel Aviv (national party headquarters), and a visit to a local branch was termed "a descent" (*yorida*) to the periphery.[11]

Several "deals" (the English term was used with the Hebrew plural ending — *dealim*) were made by various candidates representing different groups and branches that promised mutual support. The largest support deal was made between Tel Aviv, Jerusalem, Haifa, the United Kibbutz movement, the Moshav movement, and the Shiluv, Kehila, and Mashov circles.[12] Among the eighteen candidates who were part of the deal, all but three were elected to the central list of twenty-nine, who were elected on May 25, 1988. The organization of such a deal was obviously to overcome the uncertainty resulting from free secret elections, and to guarantee the continued dominance of the traditional bastions of power in the party. Baram had campaigned actively against the deals and urged the members of the Central Committee to use their independent judgments.

The election was held in a carnival atmosphere. The entrance to the Tel Aviv exhibition and fairgrounds, where the elections were held, was lined for a mile with swarms of supporters of the candidates carrying banners and posters, many wearing T-shirts advertising their candidates, passing out brochures and leaflets, fruit, drinks, flowers, pens, badges, buttons, and various other gimmicks to boost their candidates. As I drove into the area on the bus carrying members from the Haifa district, one wag proclaimed "America! America!" as a clown on stilts passed advertising the candidacy of the secretary of the party's young guard. In addition to television camera crews who covered the colorful affair, several candidates had hired videotape cameramen to follow them around as they 'pressed the flesh' and requested last-minute support. The festive carnival atmosphere was not universally appreciated. One critic, former Secretary-General of the Histadrut Yitzhak Ben-Aharon, (who had always been one of the most effective spokesmen for democratic reforms in the party) considered the atmosphere "vulgar."[13]

A few candidates refrained from gimmickry. For example, Arieh 'Lyova' Eliav (former party secretary-general who had previously resigned from the party and served Knesset terms under different party banners) refused to allow his supporters to distribute the little sticker they had produced on his behalf because he felt it was undignified. Eliav, who was not part of any mutual support deal, received the second largest number of votes cast (nine less than Ora Namir, who was supported by the major mutual support deal). Ninety-eight percent of the Central Committee members voted. Namir received 962 of 1,247 votes cast. Each member was allowed to vote for up to twenty-nine candidates. The most striking result of the election was the large number of young, new candidates, many of whom represented Middle Eastern ethnic groups, who were elected on the central list. Some skepticism was expressed about how many of the fresh new faces would gain a realistic position when the Central Committee ranked the candidates.

The second phase of campaigning by the fifty-two candidates (twenty-three elected by the districts and twenty-nine by the Central Committee) for ranking of their positions on the list was intense. The positions of the top seven party leaders, the three representing Wiezman's Yahad, the Muslim Arab, and the Druze representatives were determined in advance. Because Labor received forty-four seats in the previous election, it could expect to receive approximately the same number in 1988.[14] A position beyond that was considered to be marginal to unrealistic depending how far down the position was on the list. The voting took place in four rounds in which ten candidates were elected in each round. Each candidate decided in which group of ten she or he wished to compete. Obviously the higher the group of tens, the greater the prestige and the greater the chance of entering the Knesset, but also the greater the competition. Candidates failing to gain election in earlier rounds were allowed to submit their candidacy in later rounds.

The first group of ten was contested by the younger generation of top party leaders who aspired to succeed those at the top whose positions had been guaranteed without election. Among the first ten elected were the six minsters who were serving in the government at the time who had not been granted guaranteed places (Moshe Shahal, Shoshana Arbeli-Almoslino, Gad Yacobi, Ta'acov Tsur, Mordecai 'Motta' Gur, and Haim Bar-Lev). Five of those elected had been part of a mutual support deal (Shahal, Namir, Arbeli-Almoslino, Tsur, Haim Ramon, and Avraham Katz-Oz), but not everyone who had been part of the deal was elected (e.g., Micha Harish). The other half of the top ten elected had not been party to any deals. Clearly the "deal" that had been relatively successful in the selection of the Central Committee's list of Knesset candidates was less so in the first round of the ordering of the candidates. The Central Committee members awarded the dedicated parliamentary work of Ora Namir (giving her the second highest vote and thereby moving her into contention for a ministerial post should Labor form the next government), Chaim Ramon (the youngest Labor member of the Eleventh Knesset at thirty-eight — giving him a wide lead over others of his generation), and Professor (of law) David Liba'i. Evidently this wider forum was more appreciative of dedicated and effective parliamentary performance than were the previous oligarchic nominations committees.[15]

If the "deal" was partially successful in the vote for the first ten, it completely broke down in the vote for the second. The second round was ironically termed by some the *"intifada* ten" (the Arabic term for the civil uprising that had rocked the Occupied Territoried since December 1987) to dramatize its radical nature. Five of the ten were entirely "new political faces" who had never previously served in the Knesset (except Avraham 'Beige' Shochat, who had just entered the Knesset to replace a Labor MK who had resigned). This did not count Lyova Eliav, an old new face, who was new to the Labor list after several years away from the party. This group also included five candidates of Moroccan origin, at least five who were under forty, three mayors of development towns in the Negev, and two who were religiously observant. This group also included several prominent political doves (including the two religious candidates).[16].

The members of the Central Committee showed an obvious preference for those on the central list whom they had chosen over the candidates elected by the districts. In the first round of ten not a single district candidate was elected. In the second round only two (Rafi Edri and Micha Harish) were elected—more for their personal parliamentary records and because of the strong support given to them by Peres (with whom they are closely associated) than because they represented districts. Of the six district representatives elected in the third round, only Professor Shevah Weiss (who competed unsuccessfully in the previous rounds) was elected on a basis of his parliamentary record and the support given to him by Rabin.

The independence of the Central Committee voters showed most clearly in their preference for fresh new faces over the dictates of the deals made by the district leaders. The moshav movement and the strongmen of two of the three major city districts, traditonal bastions of power in the party, did particularly poorly. This was in spite of the new deal they organized prior to the third round. No fewer than eight new faces were elected in this round. Responding to the pleas of Shimon Peres to support the moshav movement (which prior to the third round had failed to gain a single representative), they chose a newcomer, Gedalia Gal, over the veteran Ra'anan Naim, who had competed unsuccessfully in the first two rounds. They chose Haifa University Professor Shevah Weiss over Haifa district secretary Dov Garfunkel (who ultimately ended up fifty-fourth—a completely unrealistic position). Michael Bar-Zohar was elected as a representative of Tel Aviv over the secertary of the Tel Aviv branch, Eliahu Speiser, who in spite of being part of practically every deal going withdrew after unsuccessfully competing in the first three rounds. He had been a conspicuously inactive and unpopular parliamentarian.[17] Speiser's political ally Uri Amit (mayor of Ramat Gan) dropped out of the race also after not being elected in rounds two and three. Shriege Netzer, the boss of the national party machine during Ben-Gurion's premiership, never aspired to membership in the Knesset. His successors had higher aspirations and served in the Knesset and in the government.

The secretary of the Jerusalem branch, Emanuel Zisman (also spelt Sussman in some English sources), fared better and was elected fifth in the third round, which gave him a safe place of thirty-third on the list. However, a relative newcomer from his district, professor Shimon Shetreet (a young Moroccan academic) was ranked ten places higher. Another newcomer Efraim Gur, a 32-year-old deputy mayor of Ashkelon (the first person from Soviet Georgia to gain a realistic position on the Knesset list) gained the position after Zisman. The kibbutz movement barely got its representative, Edna Solodar, elected to the last place in the third round after the active lobbying of Yitzhak Rabin (although Tzur and Katz-Oz elected in the first round also represent the kibbutz movement.[18])

Approximately half of the candidates in realistic positions were new faces. Approximately 30 percent represented Middle Eastern ethnic communities (half of the fourteen Jews from Eastern communities are of Moroccan background), not including the Muslim Arab and Druze candidates. One-quarter of the candidates are forty years old or younger, two of whom are religious. Although only four women gained realistic positions (Nelly Karkabi, a Christian Arab has an outside chance in the 46th spot), Ora Namir's popularity may enable her to be the second woman minister if Labor forms the next government.[19]

In addition to producing the most representative Knesset list in its history in terms of age, ethnic, and geographical divisions, the

Knesset list is also equally balanced between doves and hawks. Avraham Tirush suggests that "approximately half of the first forty-one candidates are doves."[20] Orli Azuli-Katz counts "twelve doves and twelve hawks and six 'yon-tzim' "—a combination of the Hebrew terms *yonim* (doves) and *netzim* (hawks). She notes that the doves have received senior and visible placement.[21]

Across the political spectrum the Israeli press praised Labor's achievement. *Ma'ariv* led with a banner headline reading, "Revolution in Labor's list"; and the main editorial titled, "New Epoch," praised the process of "internal democratization."[22] Elan Schori, political correspondent of the Liberal *Ha'aretz*, spoke of a dramatic revolution in Labor. He noted that, "The members of the Labor Central Committee buried the system of arrangement committees."[23] The Histadrut-owned *Davar* highlighted the new faces claiming that Labor had changed its face by turning to the development towns and the neighborhoods, and by making a new covenant with the workers. In the main editorial it claimed that new system for electing the Knesset list had stood the test of democratization.[24] Aviezer Golan in the more conservative *Yediot Achronot* said, "You don't have to be a Labor supporter to feel satisfaction with the demonstration of democracy in Labor's internal elections."[25] In the same paper Ronit Vardi, in an article entitled "Suddenly in the middle of the night this was not the same party," wrote, "Amazing, simply amazing what the Labor Party did to itself last night. . .Finally Labor looks like an organization of live people with autonomous desires and ability to influence."[26] She observed that the members of Labor's Central Committee seem more independent and less dependent upon manipulations of the various camps that are their Likud counterparts.[27]

Michal Yudelman in the lead article in the traditionally pro-Labor English language *The Jerusalem Post*, wrote, "The Labour Party yesterday elected a younger, more representative and more Sephardi list to lead it in the elections for the 12th Knesset. Some called it 'a revolution' and 'an earthquake.' "[28] The main editorial observed,

> The party had just come out not only rejuvenated but intact from its first ordeal by internal democracy. That had not been preordained. . .
> For the first time ever it was not a handful of party oligarchs who chose Labour's electoral list in the solitude of their smoke-filled rooms. That decision was now made by the nearly 1,300-strong Central Committee. And yet the sky did not fall. . .The facelift undertaken by the Central Committee surgeons made Labour look younger, fresher, brighter, and more all-around Israeli than it had ever been before.[29]

Almost all editorials expressed regret that one of the victims of the democratization, which produced a more truly representative and "all-round Israeli" list, was the venerable Labor elder statesman, Abba Eban. Symbolically, while everyone dressed in extremely casual sports clothes in the sweltering summer heat, Eban was the only one wearing a suit and tie (although after failing to gain election in the first round he went home and changed into more casual clothing). In spite of a lifetime of service to his party and nation, Eban is viewed by most of his compatriots as an outsider—a foreigner.[30] Eban never had a popular base of support in the party. His rise to power was through the patronage of David Ben-Gurion, who recognized his unique talents, and he remained in power through the patronage of the finance minister and party boss, Pinchas Sapir. Just as the oligarchic nominations system allowed for the placement of colorless machine bosses in realistic positions on the Knesset list, it also enabled exceptionally talented, but unpopular figures like Eban to serve the party long and well.[31]

Yosi Werter seemed to express the consensus among Israeli political correspondents and pundits when he observed, "it is possible to officially declare the opening of the epoch of democracy in the Labor party."[32] Although there is little question that such a process has begun, it is not yet clear how far it will go and what the full ramifications of this process will be. I shall address myself to these questions in the remaining part of this essay, but first I shall summarize the nature of the changes that have taken place.

The most conspicuous change is the absence of a dominant national party machine that controls the nomination process. Shriege Netzer of the old "Gush" or Pinchas Sapir of the new "Gush" directly and through their surrogates could determine in many cases who would represent various internal party factions and interest groups, what the relative representation of many of the groups would be, and, most importantly, what would be the position of the candidates on the list.[33] Traditionally the Central Committee was a rubber stamp, which approved the list after it was completed. Even after reforms were introduced, which enabled the district branches to elect a proportion of the Knesset candidates, the vital stage of ordering the places of the candidates (both elected and appointed) was still done by an oligarchically controlled committee. For the first time in the history of the party, what was previously determined in the proverbial smoke-filled room was now determined in the polling booths of the central committee.

Whereas I have criticized the expansion of the size of party institutions, like the Central Committee, because it seriously detracted from their ability to act effectively as decision-making bodies, a distinct advantage is inherent in using such a large institution as the Central Committee for nominating and ordering the placement of Knesset candidates. In fact the next logical step would be either to utilize the even larger and more representative national party conference as the forum for the election of Knesset candidates, or to hold primaries of party members in their districts.[34]

The candidates elected through this process are more 'representative' of the various constituencies that make up the pluralistic Labor party in at least two different respects. First of all (as indicated earlier), the representation of various geographic areas, urban versus rural areas, age, and ethnic categories is proportionally closer to their distribution in the party and the nation than on any previous Knesset list. Categories and branches, which have been traditionally overly represented, e.g. veteran Eastern Europeans, Tel Aviv, Jerusalem, Haifa, and the kibbutz and moshav movements, have been somewhat weakened. Categories that have traditionally been underrepresented, such as younger generations, those from Middle Eastern background, and the development towns (particularly in the Negev), have been strengthened. Some categories, such as women, have not yet made gains through this more open process.

The second sense in which the new list is more representative than previous ones is that the personnel chosen to represent the various constituencies were chosen by a more widely representative body. In the past the bosses of the dominant national and district machines could easily assure their own nomination and that of their clients as the so-called representatives of various constituencies. This time the wider body frequently chose candidates to represent these constituencies who had qualifications other than being a party functionary or the client of a top party leader—although many, if not most, of those elected to realistic positions were functionaries and clients of Peres and Rabin.

In fact this was the most important element of continuity of traditional Labor practices. In their enthusiastic reaction to Labor's new list, most observers failed to note that even among the freshest of the new faces most were closely associated with the party's organization for many years. In fact of the so-called *intifada* ten elected in the second round only one, Eli Dayan, the young religious, dovish, Moroccan mayor of Ashkelon, has not had a long association with the party establishment. He was formerly associated at different times with the religious-ethnic Tami and the Democratic Movement for Change. His counterpart, Amir Peretz, the young (35-year-old), dovish Moroccan mayor of Sderot who came in first in the second round, worked for four years in the organization department of the central party head-quarters and was chosen by the municipalities department of party to lead the party's ticket in Sderot.

Among the other "new faces," there was a similar close associa-tion with the party organization and/or its top leaders. Avraham "Beige" Shochat served as mayor of Arad for twenty years and held many positions in the organization of heads of local councils before being appointed to head the organization of the 1988 national elections. He was the leading candidate of the Rabin camp in the second round of voting.[35] Avraham "Avrum" Burg (the young religious dovish son of the grand old man of the National Religious party) has served as the advisor to Shimon Peres on Diaspora affairs. The young dovish Dr. Yossi Beilin held many posts (including that of party spokesman) and is the right-hand man and protégé of Shimon Peres. Similarly, the "new faces" in the third round were not new to party insiders. For example, Eli Ben-Menachem, the young Moroccan representative of the "neighborhoods" was a party functionary for ten years, and Ra'anan Cohen has been a professional functionary of the party his entire adult life.[36]

What is most remarkable about the changes brought about through the vote of the members of the Central Committee is that to a large extent they themselves were the products of the old oligarchic system. I repeatedly heard elderly European members of major city districts in private conversations among themselves express the need to elect young and Middle Eastern candidates representing the disadvantaged neighborhoods and the development towns.[37] All of the members of the Central Committee with whom I spoke voted for can-didates for a variety of different reasons. Significantly, none of the various deals made attempted to determine an entire list of candidates for whom their followers were instructed to vote. Being realistic they left room for them to exercise their independent judgment.[38]

Not a single person with whom I spoke admitted to voting for all of the people on the list of a deal of which his group was a part. Many claimed to have voted for some people because of the deal, but to have exercised personal judgment in not voting for some who were part of the deal and for voting for others who were not part of the deal. The only personally based camp was that of Yitzhak Rabin. This camp, which is in a sense a mutual support alliance, made deals with the kib-butz movement (from which Rabin draws much of his support), the major city districts, and others. Shimon Peres, who did not have a formally organized camp that participated in deals, was successful in having a number of his close backers elected to realistic places (as mentioned previously), including his close adviser Dr. Yosi Beilin (who was part of a mutual support deal that included the Rabin camp). Only one person with whom I spoke admitted to having voted exclusively for doves. Most people indicated that they deliberately sought an ideological mix, if not balance, in the candidates for whom they voted. There were reports (which seem credible) that the kibbutz movement issued instructions to support the veteran leadership in addition to the members of their deals, and that after the first round Central Committee members from Middle Eastern background caucused to urge one another to vote for candidates from their ethnic background.

In sum the result of this more open and competitive process was a more attractive and representative list of Knesset candidates than Labor has even fielded. Many factors in addition to the list of candidates determine the outcome of national elections in Israel. In fact traditionally most voters are unfamiliar with any of the candidates beyond the top few party personalities. However, in the past the Likud has capitalized on having successfully projected the image of a young party that is more representative of and responsive to the Jews from Middle Eastern backgrounds. Given the positive publicity that accompanied the election of Labor's new list, and the acrimonious conflicts that produced Herut's list, which contained only a few fresh new faces, there is no question that Labor's list will be a major electoral asset in the coming campaign.[39]

The most crucial question is whether the spurt of democratization that was expressed in the nomination of Labor's Knesset candidates was an anachronism or whether it is a harbinger of wider reforms yet to come. Whereas it is to early to answer this question with certainty, a tentative prognosis is possible. First of all, it is important to recognize that there are many deeply entrenched vested interests perpetuating the status quo in Labor. These interests have produced the state of entropy that prevented the democratization of the party since the first waves of demands for reform arose in the aftermath of the Yom Kippur War through the fall from power in 1977 and thereafter. At every level of the party and the Histadrut (local through national), there are networks of functionaries whose livelihoods are dependent on the party and the Histadrut and who have traditionally been the base of power of local, district, and national bosses.

Reforming the Labor party and/or the Histadrut may be easier than reforming the Soviet Union, but the analogy is not as far-fetched as it may appear. The founding fathers and mothers of Labor (and the Israeli political system and culture) were products of revolutionary Eastern Europe. They left a legacy of an Israeli variation of Eastern

European democratic centralism wedded to a Western-style social democratic party. The melding of cultures in Israel is sometimes characterized as combining the *shtetl* and the *Casbah*, neither of which had particularly strong democratic traditions of the Western type.[40] A dynamic competitive democratic political system emerged in spite of the absence of these democratic traditions among important sectors of the population. However, democracy was conspicuously absent in the internal affairs of the parties. In addition to the aforementioned influence of political culture, this can largely be attributed to the country-wide proportional list system of elections, which encourages oligarchic control of nominations of parliamentary candidates.[41]

In spite of the aforementioned handicaps, the trend towards greater internal party democratization is definitely underway. The trend could be said to have begun with the reformist Democratic Movement for Change except that the disastrous results of the introduction of a direct and closed primary was used by the other parties as a negative example, and the DMC's experiment was never repeated even by the party (Shinui) that succeeded it.[42] Ironically, Herut, a party "commanded" by its leader Menachem Begin from its birth in 1948 until his resignation as prime minister in 1983, introduced in the election of its candidates for the Ninth Knesset the panel system of elections by members of the Central Committee. This model was adapted and adopted by Labor in 1988.

It will be hard to turn the clock back and revert to more oligarchic traditions of candidate nomination in Labor. Particularly if Labor fares well in the forthcoming election, part of the success is likely to be attributed to its attractive list, and the pressure will be to continue the more open selection process. On the other hand, if Labor fares poorly at the polls, there is the possibility of a backlash, which could result in regression to earlier oligarchic patterns. Particularly if Labor does well, the new spirit of freshness, invigoration, and change, which the reforms have produced, are likely to create pressures for even greater reforms in other areas. New candidates elected through more open processes may be less dependent upon party leaders and district bosses. While this may produce certain problems by weakening discipline in the parliamentary faction, it will undoubtedly be salutary for creating freer and more open debates and more democratic decision making in the party. The fact that even the "new faces" are closely identified with top party leaders and the party apparatus will be a strong check on "excessive" political independence on their parts. The new process can give the ministers who were elected a sense of greater independence from the prime minister, but has the danger of making them "slaves of the Central Committee."[43]

I do not predict a magical and instantaneous transformation of the party. Undoubtedly, active attempts will be made by individuals and groups detrimentally affected by the democratic innovations to either return to the old system of nominations, or to manipulate the new system more effectively to their advantage, e.g. by ensuring that the "deals" are more binding. Probably, many struggles will take place over the pace and nature of change in the party. However, I suspect that the direction of change has been established, and, while there may certainly be setbacks in the process, there is a good probability of its spreading into other areas of party (and national) life.

[Editor's Note: The Labor party reforms described by Professor Aronoff did not result in the hoped-for increase in Labor strength in the Twelfth Knesset; in fact, Labor's representation in the new Knesset (39 seats based upon 30 percent of the vote) is less than it was in the Eleventh Knesset (forty-four seats based upon 34.9 percent of the vote). Although the race between Labor and Likud became increasingly close as the election approached in 1988, Likud's position on national security was made especially salient by a terrorist bombing the morning of election day; many analysts suggested that the event itself was responsible for as much as a three- or four-seat swing in the election results.

Professor Aronoff adds that whereas on one hand the new faces of the Labor party were not conspicuously successful in terms of giving Labor an electoral victory, many of those faces have in fact already played an active role in putting pressure on the party leadership in a number of areas, including the conditions under which Labor would join the National Unity government. As well, the new members elected a new young parliamentary leader, Haim Doron, rather than the preferred candidate of Party Leader Shimon Peres, Micha Harish.

There is no evidence that the new, more democratic process of list construction described by Professor Aronoff was an electoral asset, but it must be noted that the democratic reforms were not clearly visible to the voting public: the top names on the list were not democratically chosen. Thus, the list did not give the average voter the impression of massive change in the makeup of the Labor party because the faces at the top of the list were, for the most part, the same faces that had been there in the past. Internally, however, democratization has produced a more dynamic Knesset delegation for the Labor party. The ultimate effect of this on the Israeli public remains to be seen.]

CHAPTER THIRTEEN

Recent Developments in
Israel's Religious Parties

Gary S. Schiff

Introduction

As they face elections to the Twelfth Knesset on November 1, 1988, Israel's religious parties appeared even more fractious than usual. Indeed, to some observers they may have seemed intent — in an almost masochistic way — upon further fragmenting themselves into assorted cliques and claques whose distinctions loom virtually Talmudic in origin to the uninitiated. The result of such further splinterization, it is argued (and in some cases hoped), might be the diminution of their overall impact on Israeli political life.

While the religious parties are beset with serious problems, both internally and externally vis-a-vis the larger political system, in fact many of the newly articulated divisions between and among them are deeply rooted in their pluralistic origins as umbrella parties covering a diverse spectrum of views that once was Orthodoxy. The recent spate of hyperfragmentation may well reflect the resurfacing of such internal tensions and factions, long inherent in these parties, triggered in large measure by the fundamental changes in the Israeli political system brought about by the rise of Begin and the Likud, rather than to any basic trend towards their dissolution.

As I have argued elsewhere[1], and continue to believe, the two core religious parties are very different from one another and should not be simplistically lumped together for purposes of analysis. Nevertheless, taken as a whole they do constitute what Elazar refers to as one of the three major "camps" in Israeli politics[2] (the other two being labor and civil). Viewed in this way the recent splits and mergers, recombinations, and permutations these parties have experienced may well constitute more of a realignment of forces within that "camp," rather than any fundamental breakdown thereof. Indeed, the pattern may more closely resemble the decline and disaffection of the old leftist Mapam, for example, from today's more centrist Labor party within the socialist camp rather than the disintegration of the short-lived Democratic Movement for Change.

Despite their fragmentation and relative decline, the religious parties continue to exhibit remarkable resilience and potency. Indeed, as I have suggested previously[3], given the crystallization of Israeli politics around two major poles — Likud and Labor — neither of which is capable of governing on its own; and given the relatively more durable staying power of religion over many other issues as a central concern in the Israeli polity, the religious parties' influence is likely to be enhanced, despite their ostensible divisiveness and decline. While voting for all the religious parties together declined from an all-time high of 15.4 percent and eighteen members of Knesset (MKs) in the Fifth Knesset elections of 1961 to an all time low of 11.3 percent and thirteen MKs in the Eleventh Knesset elections of 1984[4], the parties remain a potent political force.

[Editor's Note: The 1988 election resulted in 14.6 percent of the vote for religious parties, yielding eighteen seats in the Twelfth Knesset.]

Origins of the Religious Parties

What were the origins of these parties? And what were the diverse elements and forces that historically divided them into internal factions?[5]

First, it must be stressed that all Israeli parties aspiring to the label "religious," unlike those of Western Europe, claim to represent the same religion, indeed the same "denomination" thereof, Orthodoxy. As a result of this common professed allegiance to Orthodoxy, these parties are often indiscriminately lumped together and are alleged to have similar (usually "conservative, "extremist," "clericalist" or "right wing") political characteristics or behaviors.

(There is as yet no party claiming to represent the other two main denominations of Judaism in the world, Conservative and Reform, both relatively new to Israel — and, in the latter instance, to Zionism. However, recent developments, such as the formation of Reform and Conservative parties within the World Zionist Organization, suggest that these groups may be overcoming their previous American-derived inhibitions about mixing religion and politics. The eventual formation of two such parties, or one non-Orthodox religious party, cannot be ruled out. This scenario would be even more likely if the movements are frustrated in their present attempts at achieving their political ends via cooperation with one or the other major secular party[6] and/or if the prospect for electoral reform fades, both of which are likely.)

In fact, the two core religious parties are very different and have clearly distinguishable political and social characteristics, as well as often divergent roles in the Israeli political system. Initially, each of the two developed as different reactions to the modernization of Jewish life in Europe in the late nineteenth and early twentieth centuries, and particularly to the challenge of modern political, largely secular Jewish nationalism, or Zionism. At the same time, neither party was monolithic. From the very beginning each contained divergent internal strains and factions, divisions that have only become more manifest in recent years and in some cases have led to party splits.

Mafdal: the National Religious party

The oldest and largest of these parties — founded in 1902 as the first officially recognized faction within the World Zionist Organization — is the National Religious party (NRP), or in its Hebrew name, Mafdal. With an attitude that affirmed, or at least accommodated, religious tradition to modern life (including modern education and political activity), the party has a long history of active participation in the Zionist movement and later in the State of Israel, where it has traditionally played the role of essential but junior coalition partner to whichever of the two leading parties, Labor or Likud, was in power.

As a result of its loyal participation, Mafdal was able to achieve many gains within its overall objective of "nationalizing" or institutionalizing religion within the legal and political framework of the state[7]. Mafdal became the dominant force in the religious establishment of the state, which includes the chief rabbinate, the rabbinical court system that adjudicates all matters of personal status for Jews in Israel, and the religious state education system, as well as the principal proponent of religious legislation.

The party historically has had a broad socioeconomic, geographic, and ethnic base to draw upon, and was run by its lay (rather than clerical) leadership, derived in no small measure from its extensive labor organization, Ha-Po'el Ha-Mizrahi. (Mizrahi, short for Merkaz Ruhani

or Spiritual Center, was the original name of the party and remained
the name of the smaller, nonlabor sector until their reunification in 1956
under the umbrella of Mafdal).

Ostensibly a large (typically garnering nearly 10 percent of the
vote and twelve MKs as recently as 1977), unified party with a well-
articulated ideology, Mafdal has a long and at times bitter history of
factional conflict[8]. While some of these factions have been based on
personalistic cults of various leaders, the party has always had factions
that emphasized one of the three central pillars of its ideology over
the other: religion, nationalism, or socialism.

Bitter debates as early as that over the Uganda scheme (1903–05)
as to whether to accept an alternate, if temporary homeland (nationalists v. religionists); or later in the 1920s over whether to join the secular
socialist Histadrut labor organization, or whether to prefer an alliance
with other religious elements, including the non-Zionist Agudat Yisrael
(socialists versus religionists); or in the '30s whether to support the
Revisionists as against the established leadership of the World Zionist
Organization and the Yishuv on the partition of Palestine (nationalist
hawks versus religionist or socialist doves); or even whether to declare
independence in 1948, punctuated the history of the party. In different
periods one or the other view prevailed, but the tensions were never
fully resolved. These ideological divisions within the party were
crisscrossed and at times reinforced by interest groups that developed
within it, including those of the party's labor, agricultural, women's,
and rabbinic/educational sectors.

In fact, these three basic issues — the role of religion in the state;
the definition of nationalism vis-a-vis the territories and the Palestinian
Arabs; and the transformation of a once predominantly socialist,
egalitarian, communitarian economy and society into a postindustrial,
technological, individualistic and consumer-oriented one — constitute
three of the fundamental cleavages in post-Begin Israeli society. In
many ways the conflicts within Mafdal are a microcosm of those in
Israeli society at large.

Similarly, the party has not handled the knotty questions of
generational change of leadership or of ethnic (read Sephardi) politics
much better than most other Israeli parties, despite the fact that
Sephardim were involved in the party from very early on and that a
majority of its members has long been Sephardi. As a result of all these
internal tensions, when powerful forces of change in the overall Israeli
political system swept over Mafdal, beginning in the late '60s and early
'70s, and reaching epic proportions beginning in 1977, the stitches that
had long held party's patchwork quilt together began to give way.

Agudat Yisrael

The other core religious party, Agudat Yisrael (Society of Israel, founded in 1912), developed out of the opposite or negative reaction of traditional Orthodox European Jewry to the challenges of modernity, secularism, and nationalism embodied in the Zionist movement. Believing Divine intervention, rather than political self-help to be the only way to restore the Jewish people to its land, a land to be governed by the laws of the Torah not of man, Agudat Yisrael cultivated a separatist mentality vis-a-vis the rest of the Jewish community in general, and towards Zionism in particular. For the first few decades of its existence, then, it embraced a vigorously non- or anti-Zionist stance.

During and since the Holocaust, which led to the destruction of the wellsprings of its support in Eastern Europe, and the establishment of Israel, Agudat Yisrael adopted a more pragmatic view of the state, viewing it as a *de facto* legitimate secular political authority to be dealt with like other governments in the interests of its adherents. However, in Agudat Yisrael's view, that state (like the Zionist movement that gave it birth) has no religious significance per se.

While the party has always participated in the Knesset, it has tended not to join coalition governments except selectively when the interests of its constituents warranted it. Alternatively it has adopted the practice of supporting the coalition (in exchange for various concessions), but not actually participating in the cabinet. In this way Agudat Yisrael has been an effective advocate for the interests of its followers, especially in obtaining funding for its independent network of religious institutions, including a separate school system.

Agudat Yisrael was historically a clerically dominated party, with a limited socioeconomic, geographic, and ethnic constituency that was almost entirely confined to certain urban areas. Nevertheless, it, too, was far from monolithic. While its internal divisions were not ideological in the same sense that Mafdal's were — the party's principal platform was religion; as a non-Zionist group it had no use for nationalism, let alone socialism, which it viewed as yet another secular, alien ideology — they were no less profound.

Found under the umbrella of the early Agudat Yisrael, for example, were both German Jewish neo-Orthodox intellectuals of the Hirsch school of "Torah 'im Derekh Eretz" ("Torah and the Way of the World") who, while opposing Zionism, were advocates of modern education (many of them held doctorates from leading German universities), with all that implied; as well as Hungarian rabbis of the Hatam

Sofer school of thought, which believed that *"He-Hadash Asur min Ha-Torah"* ("Innovation is Forbidden by the Torah") and opposed modern education as the opening wedge that would destroy traditional Jewish life. Likewise found under its early banner were the followers of various major Hassidic rabbis, who very often were at odds with one another; as well as the disciples of the great *yeshivot* of Lithuania, whose Mitnagdic interpretation of Orthodoxy was poles apart from, and often in open conflict with that of the Hassidim.

Like Mizrachi, Agudat Yisrael also spawned a labor wing, Po'alei Agudat Yisrael (PAY). Unlike Mizrachi, the labor wing remained smaller than the parent party. Nevertheless, it did at times skirt perilously close enough to certain Zionist, even socialist ideas and practices (like the kibbutz) as to result in the eventual split of the two into separate parties.

Given its clericalist mentality, which tends to venerate age, the party has traditionally had a problem with what Pareto called the "circulation of elites." Over the course of the first thrity years of the state, for example, Agudat Yisrael had one of the oldest Knesset delegations[9]. Likewise, because of its heavily East European character and ambience — meetings were often conducted in Yiddish — the party missed the proverbial boat in securing the allegiance of the many Sephardim who were quietly becoming a significant segment of its voters by failing to advance any of Sephardi representatives into key leadership positions.

The Winds of Change: Mafdal

For Mafdal the winds of change can be identified as beginning at the 1967 Six-Day War, a process that was only intensified by the 1973 Yom Kippur War, and which culminated in major upheavals beginning with the accession of Begin and the Likud to power in 1977. Each of the aforementioned long-standing, if dormant conflicts came into play with great intensity during this period.

First, generational conflict erupted with the rapid rise of the Tze'irim or Young Guard faction, led by Zevulun Hammer and Yehudah Ben-Meir. Composed largely of Israeli-born and/or raised Sabras, products of Mafdal's own national religious education system and the army, the more militant Tze'irim were impatient to take over the reins of power and patronage long dominated by older European-born leaders like Yosef Burg and Yitzhak Refael. Under the latter the party, in its "historic partnership" with the then Mapai, largely confined itself to religious and educational issues, leaving broader matters of the economy and of foreign and defense policy to Mapai. As mostly upwardly mobile urban professionals — Hammer was an educator, American-born and educated Ben-Meir, a Ph.D. psychologist — this new leadership cadre had little interest in the socialist aspects of the party's ideology, especially with the opportunities opening up as a result of the rapid economic growth, foreign investment, and urbanization (particularly in Jerusalem) that followed the '67 victory.

More importantly the victory in the Six-Day War and the newly won control over territories that covered most of historic Eretz Yisrael (the Land of Israel) opened up whole new vistas for the party's long-standing, if largely dormant nationalist element. Suffused with a religious messianism long a part of religious Zionism, this new vision spawned a separate populist movement devoted to settling the land, Gush Emunim, which provided common ground and a convenient bridge between Mafdal and other nationalist parties, notably the Herut (later Gahal, later Likud) party of Menachem Begin.

Indeed, under the influence of the Tze'irim, the changing emphasis among the party's historic triad of ideologies toward the dominance of nationalism predisposed Mafdal to rethink its historic partnership with Labor and to seriously contemplate joining a Likud-based coalition if and when the time came, which it did in 1977[10].

Two additional factors militated in favor of that new connection. One was Begin's much vaunted personal traditionalism (viewed by some observers somewhat more cynically as the culmination of a process of manipulation of traditionalist symbols and myths in a largely successful attempt to remake Israel's "civic culture" that had begun earlier under the Labor party[11]). While not shared by his entire party, this attitude and behavior did mark a radical change from previous, Labor party prime ministers' avowed secularism.

A second and related factor was Mafdal's own somewhat belated attempt to give greater recognition and visibility to the Sephardi element in the party. The coming of political age of the Sephardim in 1977, and their rejection of previous allegiances to what they now viewed as a patronizing Labor party, precipitated the *mahapach* (revolution) of 1977. Insofar as Mafdal was able to ride on the coattails of this phenomenon of ethnic politics, it benefited from the Sephardi (and Likud's) rise to power.

Mafdal's joining of the Likud-led coalition in 1977 symbolized not only the ascension of the nationalist element of its ideology (and the concomittant decline of its socialist one), but also marked the coming to fruition of the long-sought ambition of the Tze'irim to break out of the confining mold the party had been placed in under Labor,

symbolized by its traditional control over the Ministries of Religion and
Interior and the Deputy Ministry of Education, which would oversee
the religious state education system.

Mafdal's aspirations to broader involvement in the general
political life of the country were now rewarded by its being awarded
the Deputy Ministry for Foreign Affairs, the entire Ministry of Education (not just its religious "ghetto"), and by having one of its senior
ministers chair negotiations with Egypt. As the third largest party, with
a restored twelve MKs to its credit, Mafdal began to view itself as a
broad-based, religiously affiliated party with wide national appeal à
la the Christian Democratic parties of Europe. Mafdal seemed to be
riding the crest.

These dreams came crashing down around Mafdal in the Tenth
Knesset elections of 1981, when the party's parliamentary delegation
was halved to six seats. About one quarter of Mafdal's votes (three
MKs) were siphoned off by a newly created, Sephardi (largely
Moroccan) ethnic party, Tami (The Tradition of Israel movement). Tami
was headed by a former Mafdal MK and minister of religious affairs
of Moroccan extraction, Aharon Abu-Hatzeira, who had been groomed
and touted as an example of how Mafdal was being solicitious of the
needs of its Sephardi constituents. Apparently it was too little too late.
Many of its long-time Sephardi adherents were turning away from
Mafdal, viewing it as a predominantly Ashkenazi-led and dominated
party, much as their confreres in the Labor party had done to it in the
previous elections. Again, developments in Mafdal often mirror those
in other, larger parties and in the Israeli political system as a whole.

Mafdal's turn to the nationalist right also provided the rationale
for significant numbers of its other voters to "go all the way" and vote
directly for Likud, the even more right wing Tehiya, or other extreme
nationalist parties like Meir Kahane's Kach. If, as Mafdal seemed to
be saying, the basic issues of religious life and law were well in hand
by now, thanks to its efforts and the central concern of Israeli politics
revolves around the territories and settlements, then why not vote for
right wing parties for whom those issues have always been paramount
and which, in any case, evince a generalized sympathy for religion?

The ascendancy of the nationalist right within Mafdal was in-
spired in no small measure by the mystical writings of the late Chief
Rabbi of Palestine Abraham Isaac Kook, and by the more explicitly
political teachings of his son, Rabbi Tzvi Yehudah Kook, head of the
prestigious Merkaz Ha-Rav *yeshiva* in Jerusalem. Inevitably, it
engendered a reaction from among the party's small, but vocal dovish
minority, based among the remnants of the party's old committed

socialist/labor/agricultural wing and among some younger academics and intellectuals, most of Ashkenazi extraction. Paralleling such movements as Shalom 'Ahkshav (Peace Now) in the general community, groups such as 'Oz ve-Shalom (Power and Peace) and Netivot Shalom (Path of Peace), emphasizing the elements of peace, accommodation, and the saving of human life in the Jewish tradition over those of territory, settlements and security, rose from within the ranks of the party. They found their own rabbinic patrons, several of American provenance (as are many of the leaders and members of the party's settlement movement as well).

The long and costly war in Lebanon gave further impetus to the peace movements generally, and to those in Mafdal orbit specifically. Whereas previous Israeli wars could be defined in traditional rabbinic terms as *milkhemet mitzvah*, defensive, obligatory wars of survival, the Lebanon war was increasingly viewed by some as *milkhemet r'shut*, an offensive, optional, political, unnecessary war, and the inevitable outcome of the unrestrained nationalism of the Begin era. Even one-time hawks like Hammer himself began to express reservations, both about the war and of Mafdal's ultranationalist stance.

At this time and out of similar concerns, Avraham Burg, son of Mafdal's long-reigning chieftain, Yosef Burg, abandoned the party and joined the Labor party, where he has since been given a secure spot on the list for the elections in 1988. (The Labor party has always had a small religious wing, Ha-'Oved Ha-Dati). Failing to make much headway within Mafdal, many other dovish members of the party have since moved over to the Labor camp as well.

With the party's leadership seeming to have second thoughts about its turn to the right, yet another break-away faction — this time to the right — appeared before the 1984 elections. Initially calling itself Matzad (The Religious Zionist party), the new party was led by former Mafdal MKs who were more unambiguously identified with the settlers in the territories. When they merged with the remnants of the old PAY, the party was renamed Morasha (Heritage). Under this banner it earned two seats in the Knesset, thereby almost directly reducing Mafdal's delegation to an all time low of four MKs. Subsequently one of these two returned to Mafdal after receiving assurances of Mafdal's continued devotion to the nationalist cause under its new leader, Avner Shaki. With only one MK, Morasha's political future as a separate political party is doubtful.

Shaki headed Mafdal's Knesset listing 1988. He was one of the few bright younger Sephardim (He is Israeli-born of Yemenite extraction.) who was belatedly fast-tracked by Mafdal for a leadership position in the very first Knesset election following the 1967 war (the

Seventh Knesset elections of 1969) in an attempt to pacify and secure the loyalty of its Sephardi adherents. A law professor at the party-affiliated Bar-Ilan University, which itself has since become the intellectual home of many of the party's right wing academics, Shaki was rapidly advanced from first-term MK to deputy minister of education, a post that traditionally presided over a key Mafdal fiefdom, the religious state education system.

However, when he displayed more interest in the overall educational advancement of Sephardi children, irrespective of educational track, than in the party's religious state education system, and when he broke party discipline to vote for an Agudat Yisrael-sponsored amendment to the Law of Return to limit conversions to those done according to Halacha (religious law), Shaki was deposed from his portfolio, declared himself an independent, and lost the confidence of the party leadership[12]. He clearly harbors no lost love for the old Mafdal elite that once ousted him and whom he is now replacing.

Known for his stridently nationalist views, Shaki's ascension to power in Mafdal marks the triumph of both its nationalist and remaining Sephardi elements. Symbolic of this transformation, the party announced the removal of its national headquarters from Tel Aviv to (East) Jerusalem in July of 1988[13].

The Arab uprising or *intifadah*, beginning in December of 1987, further polarized existing opinions within Israeli society as to what to do vis-a-vis the ("liberated," "administered," or "occupied") territories in general, and those of the West Bank of Judea and Samaria in particular, given their religious, strategic, demographic, and economic relationship to Israel. Again, the debate in Mafdal mirrored that in the larger society.

Now that what remained of Mafdal was once again firmly in the nationalist camp, and dominated by Sephardim to boot, some of its veteran members and others, mostly Ashkenazi in their ethnicity, liberal in their Orthodoxy, academic in their education and moderate in their nationalism, sought a new venue for political expression. Unlike those who had abandoned Mafdal for the Labor party for these reasons (or for Likud, for that matter, for the opposite ones), they sought the framework of a religious party.

Thus, a new religious party called Memad (the Religious Centrist party) was established in the summer of 1988 in anticipation of the elections. The party was headed by Rabbi Yehudah Amital, who heads the Har Etzion *yeshiva* (itself built beyond the "green line")[14]. Also placed on the new party's Knesset list was Dr. Naomi Cohen, a university lecturer in Jewish philosophy and wife of the Chief rabbi of Haifa[15].

This placement is indicative of an assertive new feminism found among the ranks of left wing Orthodoxy in recent years, which has seen Orthodox women successfully overcoming stiff legal, political, and social (although not really *Halakhic*) obstacles to serve in such once all-male preserves as local religious councils and even electoral bodies for city-wide chief rabbis[16]. This trend, too, has its roots in Mafdal and its women's organization. Mafdal had a woman MK as early as 1959. Yet, it is this very trend that underscores Memad's (and more broadly, modern Orthodoxy's) profound alienation from most other Orthodox religious groups and parties, be they in Mafdal or certainly in Agudat Yisrael, where the trend has been in the opposite direction.

Although some preliminary public opinion polls predicted as many as four seats, the party won less than one percent of the vote in the November 1988 election, winning no seats in the Twelfth Knesset. However, the very establishment of this new party itself harks back to antecedents in certain moderate factions of Mafdal extant in its very origins.

The triumph of the rightist, nationalist elements within Mafdal in recent years has not only alienated (and therefore led to the departures) of its veteran leftist, socialist, dovish wing, many of its once numerous Sephardi adherents, and even some of its ultranationalists who now prefer "the real thing," but it has also offended some of the party's "religionists," who have long evinced a deeper sympathy for other religious groups, like Agudat Yisrael, than for ties with either socialists or secular nationalists.

Indeed, Mafdal has long had to look over its religious shoulder not to be outflanked by Agudat Yisrael and even more extreme groups that have traditionally berated it for its compromises on religious issues, most notably on the question of "Who is a Jew?" for purposes of immigration and citizenship. The capturing of this issue by Agudat Yisrael — specifically the demand for an amendment to the Law of Return defining "Jew" in more strictly Halakhic terms — has only highlighted the vulnerability of Mafdal, historically a moderate, modernist religious party, at a time when Orthodox Judaism, in Israel and elsewhere — much like Christianity and Islam — is increasingly dominated by fundamentalists.

Nowhere is the difficulty in walking the tightrope between fundamentalism and modernism more palpable than in the state religious education system, once the pride and joy of Mafdal and the prime source of socialization and recruitment of new members and leaders. Rising from 24.5 percent in 1953–54 to a high of 29 percent in 1964–65, nationwide enrollment in the primary grades of religious

state education declined to a low of 20 percent in 1984–85. In inter-
mediate schools the decline was even more dramatic (from 37.5 percent
in 1969–70 to 16.3 percent in 1985–86); at the secondary school level
the decrease was more moderate (from 21.9 percent in 1969–70 to 19.6
percent in 1985–86)[17].

Most of these losses have been to the (secular) state school system,
which has increased markedly in all categories, indicating a movement
away from the party by younger generation parents (many Sephardim).
Some of the loss has been to the Independent Education schools
dominated by Agudat Yisrael, which have maintained fairly constant
enrollments, but which have shown remarkable growth at the key
secondary level. This pattern reflects a trend among even some of
Mafdal's own (mostly Ashkenazi) leaders to denegrate the religious
and/or educational attainments (and ethnic heterogeneity) of the party's
system and to opt for educating their children in the more traditionally
Orthodox (and supposedly largely Ashkenazi) schools of Agudat
Yisrael. However, the same trend towards the right in religious matters
has affected Sephardim as well, with increasing numbers of *yeshiva*
students (and their parents) being of Sephardi extraction. The growth
of the Sephardi sector in Agudat Yisrael is one of the key sources of
the upheavals that have wracked that venerable party in recent years.

The Winds of Change: Agudat Yisrael

While profound changes have taken place in the Agudat Yisrael
camp, too, given the very different nature of the party from Mafdal,
the changes are of a somewhat different character. As it never was a
nationalist, Zionist party per se, and as it (with the exception of PAY)
was never involved in land settlement or in military service, it was far
less troubled by the whole range of issues engendered by the territories.
Indeed, Agudat Yisrael, often portrayed as the "extremist" Orthodox
party, has been consistently dovish on these questions (while the supposedly "moderate" Mafdal has been counted among the leading
hawks).

Rather, Agudat Yisrael been far more concerned with social and
economic issues of direct import to its constituency (like the expansion
of child allowances for larger families, which its members tend to have),
as well as with the expansion and funding of its network of educational institutions. While not necessarily always a member of the
cabinet, the party exercised considerable influence in these areas via
its traditional chairmanship of the powerful Finance Committee of the

Knesset. The party's long-time incumbent in that position, Avraham Shapira, nicknamed "the country's director-general", was widely considered one of the most powerful politicians in the country.[18]

The party has always been concerned with religious issues, too, but there has been a significant change in its attitude in this area in recent years. Initially the party was most concerned with the creation of the basic conditions that would allow its adherents to maintain their religious life and institutions in an unencumbered fashion. In this spirit Agudat Yisrael, it is too often forgotten, served in the government from the establishment of the state until 1952, with its venerable leader, Rabbi Yitzhak Meir Levin, holding the Ministry of Social Welfare portfolio. Only when two issues that it viewed precisely as fundamentally inimical to such conditions, namely conscription of religious women for military service and the abolition of the separate Orthodox "trends" in education were raised, did the party reverted to an earlier pattern of separatist, isolationist behavior.[19]

Given its traditional separatism and nonaffiliation with either the Zionist movement or the official religious establishment long dominated by Mafdal, Agudat Yisrael was not initially overly concerned with religious legislation affecting the population at large, beyond the four basic tenets of the status quo agreed to between Ben-Gurion and both Agudat Yisrael and Mafdal immediately prior to the founding of the state. These arrangements provided for: kosher food in public facilities, personal status law for Jews adjudicated by rabbinical courts, separate religious education systems, and official observance of the Sabbath and Jewish holidays.

In more recent years, however, Agudat Yisrael has extended its purview in the religious sphere to embrace issues that not only affect its members directly, but also those which have an impact on the larger society (like the redefinition of the Law of Return to provide for recognition of converts to Judaism as being limited only to those converted according to Halakha). There are several reasons for this development.

First is the aforementioned rightist trend in Orthodoxy, both in Israel and among the growing and increasingly assertive Orthodox circles abroad, particularly in the United States, which exert important political and financial pressure on Agudat Yisrael. Many of the old accommodations and compromises under the status quo were simply no longer good enough; it was no long sufficient to be allowed to practice one's religion within one's own four walls. Rather, an aggressive outreach vis-a-vis the rest of society — whether it was welcomed or not — was now being sought. In American parlance, "equal opportunity" was now being replaced by demands for "affirmative action.'' Agudat Yisrael was under pressure from such elements within the party and to the right of it to produce results, whether in terms of legislation, funding, or other entitlements.

Second, as Mafdal turned its attentions increasingly to nonreligious issues such as defense, foreign policy, the territories, and the economy, as it was increasingly splintered by factional conflict, and later as it suffered withering electoral losses, making it a less key coalition partner, the field was now wide open for Agudat Yisrael to move in and stake its claim to be the upholder of "Torah-true" Judaism. From a senior coalition partner's point of view, Agudat Yisrael's assumption of Mafdal's old position of limiting itself mainly to religious issues made it a much more attractive junior partner than the new Mafdal that was seeking substantive involvement in other areas of national policy.

Furthermore, not only had the parliamentary and coalitional strength of Mafdal been reduced, but also many of the once-powerful institutions of the religious establishment it built and dominated were clearly in decline, including the chief rabbinate and the aforementioned religious state education system. By contrast, the number of (draft-exempt) students in mostly Agudat Yisrael-oriented *yeshivot* had increased from several hundred in the early 1950s to over 20,000 in the late 1980s. Enrollment in the Agudat Yisrael-affiliated Independent Education schools had essentially maintained its strength over the decades, declining from a high of 7 percent in 1953–54 to a low of 5.7 percent in 1979–80, recovering to 6.2 percent in 1985–86; enrollment in party-affiliated secondary schools jumped from 3.7 percent in 1969–70 to 5 percent in 1985–86.[20] Among the new students in the party's related schools were significant numbers of Sephardim.

If Agudat Yisrael was the principal beneficiary of the rightist trend in Orthodoxy and of high Orthodox birthrates and school enrollments, what accounts for its steep decline in electoral support from 3.7 percent and four MKs in 1981 (almost unchanged since the 1950s) to 1.7 percent and only two MKs in 1984?[21]

The sources of this decline lie deep in Agudat Yisrael's long history of its own unique brand of factionalism described earlier. Of the original component units, few of the always small, modernist-leaning German-Jewish intellectual and organizational leadership of the party survived the Holocaust. Of those that did, most were now attracted to the party's labor offshoot, PAY, whose intellectual leader, Yitzhak Breuer (himself a member of the Hirsch family), came closest to capturing the essence of their *weltanschauung*.

The principal groups that remained were the remnants of the large (mostly Polish, some Hungarian) Hassidic communities and their long-

time antagonists in Orthodoxy, the Mitnagdim of the (mainly Lithuanian) *yeshivot* that had been transplanted to Israel after the war. While
the Hassidim were well-represented in both major centers of party
strength, Jerusalem and B'nei B'rak, an almost all Orthodox satellite
city of Tel Aviv, the Mitnagdim were concentrated most heavily in the
latter, thus adding a geographic — and in some cases socioeconomic—
factor to the mix.

One additional group, which never existed in Europe, consisted
of the descendants of the Old Yishuv, the pre- and largely anti-Zionist,
largely pietistic Jewish community of Palestine which was concentrated
almost entirely in Jerusalem. As the original core group of Agudat
Yisrael in mandatory Palestine — which interestingly included some
Sephardim — the Old Yishuv element was particularly militant in its
anti-Zionism, spawning such even more radical antistate groups as the
Neturei Karta early on in its history.

For most of the history of Agudat Yisrael in Israel generally and
in the Knesset elections specifically, the party's traditional four seats
were allocated along these factional lines[22]: two seats for the numerically
superior Hassidim (one each to the Polish Gur sect, one to the
Hungarian Wischnitz), one to the Lithuanian *yeshiva* circles, and one
to the Old Yishuv Jerusalemites. Given the limited circulation of the
elites in clericalist Agudat Yisrael (one Agudat MK was "ousted" after
thirty-three years in office), the various factions became quite
entrenched. This alliance of factions, however uneasy, held solid for
the first twenty years of the state.

As in Mafdal, the ethnic complexion began to change — literally
and figuratively — following the 1967 war. In an unprecendented move,
one of the factional Agudat Yisrael MKs resigned his post during the
last year of the Seventh Knesset (1972–73) in favor of a Sephardi rabbi
of Yemenite extraction. (The Yemenites, while not strictly speaking
Sephardim, i.e., descendants of fifteenth century Spanish and Portu-
guese Jewish exiles, are one of the "Eastern communities" often loosely
referred to as Sephardim. They have tended to be more religiously
observant than some other such groups, and were among the earliest
Sephardi adherents of Agudat Yisrael). Even more than Mafdal's
belated attempts at mainlining Sephardim to retain and attract Sephardi
voters, however, this was a blatantly symbolic gesture; the individual
was afforded no real political power.

As demands for real representation by the party's growing (and
younger) Sephardi element grew stonger, and as the example of the
successful Sephardi break away party from Mafdal, Tami, appeared
on the scene in 1981, pressure grew within the old party elite in

determining whose seat was to be sacrificed for the newcomers. Growing personal and factional enmity, especially between leaders of the
Gur Hassidic and Lithuanian *yeshiva* factions, led to the latter giving
his blessing to a nascent Sephardi break away party that had earlier
run a successful list is the Jerusalem municipal elections to go national
for the 1984 Knesset elections. Its Hebrew name is Shas (Association
of Sephardi Torah Observers, not "Guardians" as often mistranslated).

Thus, drawing on the Sephardi element in Agudat Yisrael, plus
the (largely Ashkenazi) *yeshiva* faction, plus any other observant
Sephardim who may have been attracted from Mafdal, Tami (both of
which further declined that year) or elsewhere, the party achieved a
remarkable 3.1 percent or four MK showing, while halving Agudat
Yisrael's delegation to 1.7 percent or two MKs.[23] The remaining Agudat
Yisrael is essentially a Hassidic party, with some other, smaller
elements, such as the Old Yishuv, still in the fold.

The new Shas party emerged from the elections with the same
size parliamentary delegation as the veteran Mafdal, and quickly was
courted into the coalition with the lures of ministerial portfolios (including the Ministry of Religious Affairs, which must have made old
Mafdal-niks wince) and coalition promises. Subsequent disillusions
with some of the latter led to resignations from the former, while the
party itself of late is undergoing its own, largely personalistic internal
conflicts. Whether Shas will beat the historical odds and survive as
Israel's only ethnically based party is problematic at best.

More importantly, the development of Shas, like the rise and fall
of Tami before it, reflects the as yet incomplete political integration of
the Sephardim into the religious parties in particular, and into the Israeli
political system as a whole. Nevertheless, if the examples of the larger,
secular parties are instructive, the bridging of this ethnic gap appears
to be far more feasible over time than is overcoming the profound and
growing political and social chasms that continue to divide religious
(read Orthodox) from nonreligious Jews in Israel.

Summary

The religious political parties of Israel have experienced major
internal, structural—as well as external, behavioral—changes in recent
years. Many of these changes stemmed from long-standing internal
cleavages within the two core religious parties: Mafdal and Agudat
Yisrael.

These divisions in turn originated in various ideological, religio-ethnic and/or geographic factions that were inherent within these parties from their outset at the turn of the century, but which have been materially exacerbated in the wake of the rise of Begin and Likud to power. For it was precisely the same ideological issues relating to nationalism (the territories, the Palestinians, etc.); the nature of the society (socialist egalitarian v. free enterprise consumerist); and the relationship between religion and state, which the Begin *mahapach* thrust so forcefully onto center stage.

Likewise, it was the confluence of these issues with the rise of the Sephardim to political power that further compounded the problems of the once ethnically heterogeneous religious parties. As a result of these powerful ideological and ethnic cross-currents, the religious parties individually, and the religious "camp" as a whole, has experienced serious fragmentation, which in Israel has almost invariably meant decline in votes and Knesset seats.

In many ways the problems of the religious parties mirror those — albeit on a much smaller scale — of the highly divisive and fragmented political system as a whole. The religious camp, despite its seeming fragmentation and decline, remains a potent political force in Israeli politics. Their collective influence has, if anything, increased in recent years, as religion continues to play a pivotal role in political discourse in contemporary Israel.

[Editor's Note: The tension between and among the religious parties to which Gary Schiff alludes in his chapter continued through the 1988 elections for the Twelfth Knesset. In those elections, Shas captured six Knesset seats on the basis of almost five percent of the vote, and Agudat Yisrael captured five seats on the basis of just slightly fewer votes, more accurately reflecting Ashkenazic-Sephardic proportions in the population than had been the case in the past. Mafdal's representation in the Knesset went up from four to five Knesset seats on the basis of a very slight increase in voter support (from 3.5 percent to 3.9 percent). A new Orthodox party called *Degel HaTorah*, primarily made up of former Mafdal members supporting stronger government action promoting Orthodoxy, won two seats in the new Knesset.

Among the most interesting — and controversial for the general population — dimensions of religious party activity occurred immediately after the election, during which time the support of the Orthodox parties was sought by both the Likud (with forty Knesset seats) and Labor (with thirty-nine Knesset seats) leaders in quest of coalition support. The price demanded for their support by many of the leaders of the Orthodox parties was a promise of action on the "Who is a Jew?" question, seeking that the new government bring immigration and conversion standards closer to those positions advocated by Orthodox doctrine. In the end, the reaction of the Israeli public, and especially the reaction of the American Jewish community, was so strongly against these demands that another National Unity coalition was formed between Likud and Labor, without the government agreeing to the demands put by the Orthodox parties.]

CHAPTER FOURTEEN

Israel's Economy in the Post-Begin Era

Yakir Plessner

The Background: Israel's Economy Under Begin

The most remarkable attribute of Israel's economy during Menachem Begin's premiership concerns not what happened, but rather what did not happen: there were no changes in principle, as compared with the final years of Labor's tenure. In fact, one might say that the only changes that did take place involved the magnification of the worst aspects of Labor's policies.

The only nominal break with Labor's traditions came in October 1977, when the fresh Likud government implemented the economic *Mahapach* — the Foreign Exchange Reform. The reform concerned two aspects of Israel's foreign exchange policy. First, whereas the exchange rate had been under a crawling peg regime[1] since June 1975, it was now put under a regime of free float.[2] Secondly, whereas capital flows between Israel and the rest of the world had in the past been tightly controlled by the authorities, the new government abolished most of the restrictions. These acts were touted as a manifestation of the new government's orientation towards a more free economy.

In point of fact, the floating of the exchange rate was, under the circumstances, a bad mistake from the monetary standpoint, because it further destablilized the monetary system, thus setting the stage for the superinflation that was to follow. While the float in itself carried no message of economic freedom, the new government did not even contemplate reforming the one component of Israel's economy in which freedom could really be fostered: the capital market.

One might therefore conclude that if the Begin government did have an economic philosophy distinct from its predecessors, it managed to hide it quite well. Begin had no interest in economic affairs, nor did he understand economics. Therefore, even the attempts that were made to reform Israel's economic system, particularly during Aridor's tenure as minister of Finance, failed to enlist Begin's backing. Worse, Begin did back projects, such as the Lavi fighter and the Mediterranean-to-Dead Sea canal, which were unanimously opposed by his economic advisers, and rightly so.

The First Shamir Government: 1983-84

Shamir succeeded Begin as prime minister and stumbled right away into one of Israel's worst financial crises ever: the banking shares collapse. The affair had its origins in the mid-1970s, when Israel's major banks began to manipulate their own shares. The incentive to do so resulted from the fact that the banks had to invest most of the deposits in instruments designated by the government, and were seeking sources of finance for lending activites outside government control. The natural source was newly raised equity capital, and the banks were therefore very interested in making their shares as attractive as possible. The avenue chosen was share price manipulation.

By 1983, the market value of the banks' shares was out of any proportion to the banks' actual net worth based on their profits. As share values increased, their manipulation required larger and larger financial resources. The banks mobilized these resources by borrowing abroad, for which purpose they used their subsidiaries, mainly those in the United States. This practice was a dangerous one because it involved the banks in foreign exchange liabilities unmatched by foreign exchange assets. The banks were thus exposing themselves, for example, to devaluation risk. For example, suppose a bank borrowed $1 million to finance the purchase of its own stock, and suppose that this foreign exchange was converted to Israeli curency at a rate of NIS100 to the dollar. Suppose that a devaluation of 25 percent now takes place, so that the banks would now need NIS125 million to repurchase the foreign exchange upon debt repayment, instead of the NIS100 million that they received when they sold the foreign exchange upon borrowing it. Unless share values increased by 25 percent as well, so that the banks could mobilize the additional NIS25 million by reselling the purchased shares, the banks would be in trouble. It was only a question of time before such an event would occur, and it did occur in October 1983.

On the eve of October 7, 1983, the minister of finance announced that the Tel-Aviv Stock Exchange would be closed the following morning, and would remain closed until further notice. The new government thus found the banking shares problem in its lap. The logical and prudent way to deal with the problem was to assist the banks to the degree necessary to prevent the collapse of the banking system, and let the public take the losses in share values. This was particularly true in view of the fact that for most share owners, the "loss" would have meant nothing more than returns falling below what had been expected; most share owners could recover the sums invested in their shares, and often much more than that. Only those shares that had been purchased over the six to nine month period prior to the October collapse would have actually caused their buyers to incur a net loss.

With Shamir totally uninitiated in economic matters and, like his predecessor, largely disinterested, and with a great deal of pressure exerted on the new government, a decision was made to mitigate the loss incurred by the public to a considerable degree. The government adopted a plan according to which the shares were essentially turned into government bonds. The government promised that share owners who would agree to hold the shares for a period of five years could sell these shares at the end of the period to the government, and be paid the dollar value of the shares prior to the close of the stock exchange, plus an annual interest of 4 percent. What it all amounted to was the conversion of the banking shares to government bonds, indexed to the rate of exchange. The government assumed voluntarily an additional debt of several billions of dollars, a burden it could ill afford. The government now will have to discharge this obligation unless the net worth of the banks increases to such an extent that the market value of the bank shares will exceed the amount promised by the government. There is virtually no chance of that happening.

The collapse of the banking shares was associated, both as cause and effect, with mounting expectations of a substantial devaluation of the domestic currency. In fact, this is precisely what happened. On October 11, 1983, the dollar was worth 23 percent more in *shekel* terms than it had been on the day the stock exchange closed. In addition, the prices of various subsidized staples were raised. The inflationary results were not long in coming: while inflation during the first nine months of 1983 had proceeded at an annual rate of 130 percent, it jumped to an annual rate of 487 percent during the last three months of the year, as measured by the consumer price index.

Amid the negotiations, which ultimately led to the assumption of the banking shares liabilities by the government, Aridor resigned from the ministry of finance, after the plan known as "dollarization" became public. The plan was constructed by Aridor and his advisers

during the final six months of his tenure; had the nominal backing of
Begin, and upon taking over, Shamir agreed to go along with it. A
description of the considerations that led to the formulation of the plan,
and the plan's essentials will be helpful in understanding subsequent
developments.

The origins of the story are to be found around the turn of the
decade, when a few economists, most of them at the Bank of Israel,
voiced doubts about the validity of the conventional wisdom concerning the causes of Israel's inflation. The predominant view was that
Israel's inflation was brought about largely by persistent government
deficits, financed by printing money. According to this interpretation,
Israel's was a classic demand-pull inflation,[3] which would subside once
the government decided to balance its budget. The fact that this became
the predominant exegesis is itself a little strange, since during the first
inflationary years following the 1973 war, the Bank of Israel had
repeatedly pointed out that the inflationary process was of a cost-push[4]
variety. Statements to this effect are particularly clear in the bank's
annual reports until 1977. In 1978 the Bank still indicated that[5]

> "After an initial success in 1975, a deterioration took place, and the
> attempts to change relative prices resulted more and more in a cost-
> push inflation."

However, the Bank also stated:[6]

> "As pointed out, expectations played a significant role in powering
> the inflationary process."

by 1979, very little of the cost-push interpretation was left. the Bank
of Israel's version of what was going on suggested that[7]

> "Since the Yom Kippur War and the Oil Crisis, an inflationary pro-
> cess has been taking place in Israel's economy. The process is com-
> plex and is comprehensible only within its peculiar framework: large
> excess demand and profuse money-printing by the public sector; a
> monetary system in which most liquid financial assets are indexed,
> and a labor market in which no unemployment was revealed despite
> a decline in demand. As inflation wore on, expectations for further
> inflation developed, accelerated by the fact that institutional arrange-
> ments concerning wages, taxes and interest rates did not adjust to
> higher rates of inflation."

By 1980, the Bank of Israel was talking about cost-push inflation as
a thing of the past, attributing inflation to excess government demand
and inflationary expectations.

At that point a minority of economists promoted the view that nothing had changed in principle, and that the inflationary process was still the result of devaluations. The devaluations were intended to countervail excessive wage increases, which were seen as hurting Israel's exports and its ability to compete with imports. Such a policy, the economists pointed out, was counter-productive, because the government could not win the battle with high wages merely by devaluing the currency. Workers would desist from demanding excessive wages only under a credible threat. This was particularly true in view of the fact that, as the Bank of Israel pointed out, financial assets were mostly indexed, so the inflation generated by the devaluations could not erode the value of financial assets. Thus, workers did not need to fear inflation.

Why do devaluations create inflation in Israel? The answer lies with Israel's economic makeup. The country is poor in natural resources and energy, and so it depends entirely on imports for the supply of raw materials and fuel. The country also imports most of its capital goods. Consequently, the import component in Israel's economy hovers around 40 percent. A devaluation of, say 10 percent, therefore causes a price increase of 4 percent, even if wages do not adjust to increased price. Put differently, a 4-percent price increase would result even if the devaluation were fully effective.

In a normal free economy, labor would attempt, at this point, to restore the real value of wages to the predevaluation level, by demanding increased pay. Employers would resist, negotiations would ensue and, perhaps after some strikes, an agreement would be reached. Such an agreement would be characterized by labor achieving part of its objective. In Israel, workers typically succeeded in fully restoring the real value of their wages, since employers know that the government would rather compensate them than tolerate unemployment. Hence, a 10-percent devaluation would translate into a 10-percent price increase. This would be followed by more rapid devaluations, and this merry-go-round would gallop into the blue yonder, leaving in its wake ever more intense inflation.

As simple as this analysis was, it went unheeded, and the minister of finance who came into office at the end of 1979 pursued the old devaluation policy with renewed vigor. The results were loud and clear: inflation in 1979 amounted to 111 percent; in 1980, it reached 133 percent. Moreover, in the second half of 1980 it proceeded at an annual rate of 143 percent.

Against this background, Aridor, who by that time already shared the basic perceptions of the above-mentioned economists, took office in January 1981. After two failed attempts to slow down inflation, he came to the conclusion that the process could be halted only by a swift blow. This was to be accomplished by the dollarization plan, whose major components were: (1) A significant devaluation followed by a fixed exchange rate; (2) fixing of the wage rate in dollar terms (hence the name dollarization). This provision was designed to make it absolutely clear to employers that the government would no longer be able to correct for excessive wage concessions by devaluations. For wages, being linked to the exchange rate, would automatically adjust to changes in it; (3) Reduction in goverment expenditures to the extent necessary to forego inflationary taxation, estimated at the time to be about $700 million.

The media furor that followed the publication of the plan was caused primarily by the fact that one of the options that had been considered was the actual introduction of the dollar as legal tender. The basic logic of the plan was thus completely overlooked.

With Shamir uninterested in economics, the formation of economic policy was left to Orgad, who followed Aridor. The new minister of finance belonged firmly in the old school, and so reversed completely his predecessor's policies. He embarked on a rigorous devaluation policy. The result was that the rate of inflaiton in 1984 stayed at about the level it had reached in the last three months of 1983: 445 percent. When Orgad left office inflation was still accelerating: in the second half of 1984 it reached an annual rate of 500 percent.

One of the outcomes of the banking shares collapse was the perception that Israel was facing an imminent shortage of foreign exchange, as lenders abroad would refuse to extend credit. The professed objective of the new minister of finance was to head off such a crisis, by improving Israel's current account. I have serious doubts as to whether Israel actually did face a collapse of its credit rating. One very strong indication that there was no immediate danger is provided by the fact that there was no rush by foreign depositors to withdraw their deposits with Israeli banks. Another is that there was no decline in commercial credit extended to Israel by suppliers of import goods. This is particularly significant concerning suppliers of capital goods because credit associated with such goods is usually extended for longer terms.

Israel's current account deficit did decline in 1984. If direct defense imports are deducted[8], the 1984 deficit declined by about $500 million as compared with 1983. About one-quarter of the deficit reduction was contributed by a decline in imports, and the rest came from increased exports. This did not prevent Israel's net foreign debt from climbing by about $1.4 billion, to a level of about $19.7 billion at the end of 1984. This time, too, a price was paid for the temporary success in terms of future prospects, as real investment declined by 7.5 percent (after having grown by 12 percent in the previous year).

The policy had also a devastating effect on government finances. The immediate reason for this was a precipitous decline in real tax revenues. The decline came about because, on the one hand, Israel's tax brackets are fully indexed, so no fiscal drag emerges. That is, individuals are not pushed into higher income tax brackets by inflation. Hence, the government enjoys no inflationary gains on this score. On the other hand, corporate income taxes aren't indexed, but paid with a considerable lag. If inflation is severe, these corporate taxes are worth, by the time they are actually paid, a fraction of what they were worth when the tax liability was generated. So, on this score, the government loses.

The numbers are quite impressive: compared to 1983, real non-wage tax collection in 1984 declined by 29.4 percent. Corporate taxes declined by an astonishing 63.3 percent in real terms. Consequently, total real tax collections in 1984 declined by 13.9 percent.[9] Despite the fact that domestic public consumption grew only very slightly from 1983 to 1984, the public sector's domestic deficit doubled from 6 percent to 12 percent of GNP.[10]

Inflation in excess of 400 percent is damaging in many respects but the most aggravating aspect of it is that it ruins information. This happens primarily because nominal magnitudes don't mean anything anymore. Everything changes so quickly that people lose their orientation. This could be likened to somebody driving a car along a road, trying to keep constant velocity, while the length of the mile keeps changing all the time. The need for a fixed standard of measurement caused the increasing use of dollar terms in connection with prices, incomes, bookkeeping, and so on. Stores began to post prices in dollar terms, and cash registers were programmed to convert the dollar price into shekels, using the day's exchange rate. Other stores, tired of having to change price stickers so frequently, resorted to using codes instead. This was true especially of supermarkets. Consequently, consumers had to shop for food without knowing the prices of the goods they were pulling off the shelves. Only at the cash register could they find out how much they were paying for the various items.

Particularly prominent was the inability of cabinet ministers and lawmakers to control the government budget, as well as their inability to understand it. The situation became so bad that budget discussions were being conducted in dollar terms. However, since the budget was executed in shekels, there was no way to generate a common denominator for deliberations and actions. Among the budget items, the most irksome was the expenditure of subsidies for staples. Because these staples are manufactured from mostly imported materials (e.g. bread from wheat, milk, and eggs), production costs increased at roughly the rate of devaluation. The subsidies, the prices consumers paid could be changed only in discrete steps, involving each time an explicit decision. With the government trying to avoid both angering the public and aggravating the inflationary process, price increases for staples did not keep up with the rise in costs, thereby constituting a constant source of government deficit spending.

The reluctance to raise the prices of staples increased as the elections of 1984 approached. After the elections were held, however, the government again devalued the shekel, on September 17, by 8.7 percent, and reduced subsidies for staples. This, of course, caused inflation to surge even higher, and by the time the new Unity government took over in the fall of 1984, prices were rising at an annual rate of almost 1,000 percent (this describes inflation from September to November). In fact, October 1984, saw the highest one-month rate of inflation to date, when prices rose by 24.3 percent, or an annual rate of 1,265 percent.

The Unity Government: Phase I

The most important distinguishing characteristic concerning the new government, apart from its unusual composition, was that it assumed office with the economic problem at the top of its agenda. This had never happened before in Israel's short history, and it constituted a sharp departure for a country accustomed to considering war and peace to be the overriding issue. The election campaign that preceded the establishment of the new government had also been unusual in this sense. The new government brought with it the conviction that the inflationary problem, not the current account deficit, was the more urgent one. Only once before had a minister of finance assumed that position, but Aridor never found much support for it. Now the entire government was resolved to tackle the situation.

The first attempt at dealing with inflation came shortly after the establishment of the government. In early November 1984, a "package deal" was concluded between the government, the Federation of Trade Unions (*Histadrut*), and the Employers' Association. The main tenets of the deal were the institution of a price freeze and an agreement on the part of the *Histadrut* to forego one-third of the wage indexation payments due workers on account of past inflation.

The last provision merits an explanation. Cost of living allowances, or indexation payments, are made with a lag, in the sense that they compensate wage earners for past inflation. When rates of inflation subside, current indexation payments reflect rates of inflation in excess of current ones. Hence, real wages increase. The increase of real wages makes it difficult to keep price rises to the lower rates because increased real wages imply higher production costs and so reduce profits. The reduction in indexation rates was designed to avoid this development.

In general, the agreement was based on the perception that, while arresting inflation by tight monetary and fiscal policies might generate unemployment, an agreement to simply desist from price increases, while preventing real wages from rising, might accomplish the job without incurring unemployment. An interesting feature of the agreement, indicative of the conditions governing the economy at the time, was the form in which the price freeze was stated. The informational content of the price system had been completely blurred by that time and people were using dollar language; therefore, the agreement froze domestic prices at a rate of exchange of NIS527 to the dollar, which was the rate on November 2, 1984. From then on prices were to be figured as though the rate of exchange had remained at the November level.

The developments during the three-month period when the package deal was in force were very interesting.

Table 1
Inflation and Devaluation, Percent, Annual Rates

Period	XI/84-I/85	XII/84-I/85	I/85	II/85
Inflation	190	69	85	358
Devaluation[1]	207	144	113	310

1. Devaluation relative to the U.S. dollar.

The most remarkable feature revealed by Table 1 is the relative success of the plan, at least when looked at from the vantage point of the policy-makers, as they were watching the results unfold. After having witnessed inflation approaching 1,000 percent, 69 percent must have looked as a dream come true. Even the increase in January 1985, may have been perceived as a random fluctuation, rather than as a systematic return to higher rates of inflation.

Unfortunately, the policy followed by the government itself during the three-month period was bound to cause the plan to fail in the longer run. The government proceeded unwittingly to devalue the *shekel* at rates exceeding the rates of price increases. Thus, for the period as a whole, devaluation proceeded at 207 percent, as against 190 percent for inflation. More significant by far is the devaluation of 144 percent during the two months December 1984 and January 1985 while prices rose at a mere 69 percent. January 1985 also saw a substantial gap in this respect.

The implication was quite simple: with devaluation proceeding at a faster rate, costs were bound to increase faster than prices, making the slowdown untenable over the longer period. The evidence is provided by February, when inflation took off again, reaching 358 percent, a rate in excess of the 310 percent of devaluation. Prices were now catching up.

As the end of January 1985, approached, it became clear that the deal could not be sustained; it was thus replaced with a new one, to take effect at the beginning of February. The concept of the new agreement was different from the earlier one, and was based in essence on an idea that motivated the "five percent plan" in 1982-83. This time the objective was not to halt inflation, but slow it down to 3 to 5 percent per month. While the older plan had been based on a consistent approach, and failed because it had not been implemented as conceived, the new one was inconsistent to begin with. For it again failed to calibrate the rate of devaluation to the intended rate of inflation. The rate of devaluation relative to the dollar proceeded at 12.5 percent in February, 12.2 percent in March, and 10.9 percent in April of 1985. There was no way to achieve the plan's objectives under these circumstances.

Ironically, the government itself was the first to exceed the 3 to 5 percent target. With devaluations proceeding apace, subsidy expenditures for staples ballooned, causing a drain on the budget. So the government raised the prices of staples and other prices under its control (e.g. telephone rates, electricity, postal rates) at rates far in excess of the overall rate of inflation. For example, in the first quarter of 1985, government-controlled prices rose an average 15.4 percent per month, while all other prices included in the consumer price index rose only by 9.1 percent per month. The government was clearly defeating its own program.

In April it became clear that the plan, which was supposed to be in effect for eight months, was collapsing. So the partners to the deal agreed to a once-over price adjustment, which produced a price rise of 19.3 percent for April (737 percent at an annual rate). This became known as the "seam" between the second and the third agreement, which called for a price freeze for two months. However, like its two predecessors, it was an inconsistent plan; once again the rate of exchange was not synchronized with the inflationary target. While price increases slowed down a bit, inflation in May and June of 1985 proceeded at an annual rate of 242 percent, and that was mild when compared to the rate of devaluation over the same period, which reached an annual rate of 444 percent relative to the dollar. Again, there was no chance at all that inflation could be stopped in this fashion.

While all this was taking place, rates of interest on short-term commercial banking loans were beginning to rise, gathering real steam after the elections. For 1984 as a whole, interest on revolving accounts reached 60 percent in real terms. Then, in 1985, interest rates climbed to a peak of 94 percent in real terms — almost "loan-sharking' levels. The extent to which the credit market is distorted in the wake of decades of government mismanagement is manifested by the fact that through it all, banks were paying negative real interest rates on certificates of deposit: minus 7.1 percent and 8.2 percent in 1984 and 1985, respectively. Equally telling is the fact that while borrowing rates were skyrocketing, real bond prices actually increased, indicating a decline in yields. This implies that the credit market is so segmented, that wildly divergent interest rates can exist side by side.

The Unity Government: Phase II

The utter failure of the various attempts to combat inflation convinced the policy-makers that an altogether different approach was needed. Before going into the components and logic of the stabilization plan and assessing its outcome, it is worth pointing out that the very agony that accompanied the adoption of the plan revealed how hopeless the attempts of the preceding government at handling inflation had really been. If anybody needed proof, the Unity government, with its overwhelming parliamentary majority, provided it. For despite this awesome concentration of political power, the birth process of the stabilization plan was long and painful. There had not been a chance in a million that the previous Likud government, with its bare majority, could have done anything like it.

On July 1, 1985, the *shekel* was devalued by 18.8 percent, to NIS1500 per dollar, *and pegged at that rate*. The government adopted the following additional main resolutions: (1) The prices of subsidized goods were increased by from 38 percent for meal to 65 percent for milk and 100 percent for public transportation; also raised were the price of fuel, by 27 percent, and water, by 82 percent; (2) Prices of all goods and services were to be frozen for a period of three months; (3) All wages were to be frozen for the same period, after which the degree of compensation for the huge rise in prices would be negotiated with the employers and the unions; (4) The value added tax was reduced from 17 to 15 percent; (5) Israelis would no longer be permitted to own exchange rate linked bank deposits for a period of less than one year; (6) An array of cuts in government expenditures was to be implemented.[11]

In the negotiations that followed, a series of wage increments was decided upon, amounting to a total of 43 percent. These were to be paid over a period of six months, beginning with August 1. This was a crucial component of the plan, because the government's ability to maintain the pegged exchange rate was conditioned upon its ability to prevent real wages from increasing. Undoubtedly the Histadrut bore the brunt of the stabilization plan, something unimaginable under a Likud government. Two aspects of the plan must be considered in order to evaluate its results: inflation, the target of the plan; and government finances and wages, the instruments aside from the pegging of the exchange rate.

Starting with inflation, the plan definitely achieved its objective. After the initial price increase of 27.5 percent in July, inflation quickly subsided. In the last quarter of 1985 it declined to an annual rate of only 28.6 percent — almost negligible compared to the rates that Israelis had grown accustomed to. For 1986 as a whole, inflation was only 19.6 percent, and in 1987 it declined further to 16 percent.

While constituting a vast improvement, these rates were still unacceptable on a long-run basis. Why didn't inflation stop altogether? One explanation is to be found with the exchange rate, despite the pegging. The *shekel* was pegged to the dollar, but by 1985 the dollar was declining relative to some of the other major currencies. Consequently, between July 1985 and July 1986, the *shekel* declined by 52.6 percent relative to the yen, 35.9 percent relative to the mark and 28.6 percent relative to the French franc. Israel imports a lot of consumer goods from these countries. Therefore, such decline in the *shekel's* value shows up prominently in the consumer price index. Support for this explanation is provided by the fact that the industrial wholesale price index, increased in 1986 by 15.1 percent — considerably less than the consumer price index. There are probably other reasons for the continued inflation, however moderate, a point to which we shall return shortly.

Government finances provide a fascinating insight into the causes of the plan's success. Table 2 displays the necessary information, based on fiscal years, which begin on April 1 of each year.

Table 2
Government Finances, Percent of GNP[12]

Fiscal Year	1983/4	1984/5	1985/6	1986/7
Domestic expenditures	49.6	47.9	45.6	46.5
Domestic consumption	19.8	17.7	18.0	17.6
(Defense Consumption)	11.8	10.5	10.9	10.5
Investment	1.8	1.2	1.1	1.2
Other expenditures	28.0	29.0	26.6	27.7
Domestic revenues	43.4	35.3	42.2	43.9
Domestic deficit	6.2	12.6	3.4	2.6

The numbers reveal very clearly what it was that enabled the government to achieve an almost balanced budget in 1985 and 1986. The point is exceedingly important because most economists believe that stopping inflation requires absolutely a reduction of government expenditures, or an increase in taxes, in order to balance the budget. Otherwise, claim these economists, a stabilization plan could not be credible in the eyes of the public, and hence would be bound to fail Table 2 suggests that this line of argument is not valid.

The domestic deficit (domestic, since procurement of defense material paid for with United States aid is left out, because it plays no role in the balancing of the domestic economy) declined from 12.6 percent of GNP in 1984/85, to 3.4 percent in 1985/86 — a difference of 9.2 percent of GNP. An analysis of the sources of the reduction shows that while the decline in expenditures, from 47.9 to 45.6 percent of GNP, provided only 2.3 percent of the decline in deficit, the rise in revenues, from 35.3 to 42.2 percent of GNP, provided 5.8 percent of the deficit reduction. This resulted despite the fact that no tax rates had been increased. What happened?

The answer is, of course, that just as the acceleration of inflation had precipitated a tremendous erosion in the real value of tax receipts, its slowing down produced the opposite effect. A further look at some of the tax details reveals the depth of the phenomenon. Total real direct tax revenues increased by 13.6 percent in 1985 and by another 8.1 percent in 1986. Most impressively, revenues from corporate income taxes rose a staggering 159 percent in 1985 and another 35.5 percent in 1986. Tax revenues from self-employed persons also rose by 37.8 percent in 1985 and a further 18.6 percent in 1986.[13] The stopping of inflation brought order to government finances, rather than the other way around.

Still, the decline in government expenditures should not be belittled, not only because of its contribution to stability but also because it may have signalled, in some respects, the buds of changing attitudes. In particular, export subsidies declined from a peak of $767 million in 1984, to $428 million in 1985 and $356.5 million in 1986.[14] How significant this decline was can be comprehended upon observing that, while in 1984 export subsidies constituted 8 percent of the value of exports (excluding the subsidy), that ratio dropped to only 3.2 percent in 1986. If this were to signify a decline in the sway that the Manufacturers' Association had over the government, then a significant change for the better would have been accomplished. Subsidies for domestic output, mainly for staples, also declined significantly: 32.5 percent in 1985 and a further 41.4 percent in 1986. Again, if this should lead to the elimination of the staples sacred cow, something of a long-run benefit would have been achieved.

The weakest link in the stabilization program may be the complex of industrial relations. The immediate manifestation of these relations is the evolution of wages. For if real wages per unit of output resume their ascent, then Israel's ability to compete on international markets is likely to be imperilled. This would create pressure on the exchange rate, and hence threaten the foundation of stability. Wages are therefore very important, and deserve close scrutiny.

Table 3 provides this data. The first column for each year describes the purchasing power of domestic industrial wages in terms of export goods. In effect, the index here is calculated by dividing nominal wage rates by export prices, which consist of the foreign exchange price multiplied by the rate of exchange relative to the five currencies in the foreign trade "basket."[15] The higher the purchasing power of wages in terms of the export goods, the lower is export profitability.

Export profitability declined sharply in the second quarter of 1984, then increased gradually as the pace of devaluations quickened, but never quite returned to its first-quarter level. Then, in the first quarter of 1985, export profitability nose-dived again. The third quarter of 1985 marked the stabilization program. Indeed, real wage values in terms of export goods plunged, but from then on they rose continuously, implying gradual decline of export profitability, all through 1986. In fact, by the last quarter of that year wages were higher, in terms of

Table 3
Real Industrial Wage Index

Year	1984		1985		1986	
Quarter	Export returns	Consumer prices	Export returns	Consumer prices	Export returns	Consumer prices
I	100	100	109.2	109.8	104.3	102.7
II	111.5	107.2	103.7	102.4	109.2	102.2
III	110.5	110.2	85.9	86.9	108.3	103.7
IV	100.4	102.2	89.7	89.4	114.7	106.8

export goods, than they had been at any time during the three years covered by the data. So, it came as no surprise that the government devalued once again in January 1987, by 8 percent relative to the basket of currencies. This signified that the time to look back with pride had not yet come. The balance was a precarious one, and a lot would depend on what happened to wages and what the government's response to developments would be.

The second column for each year in Table 3 reports real wages in conventional terms; i.e., in terms of the cost of living. While both sets of indices move in the same direction, they are much more closely aligned before the stabilization than after it. The reason is that prior to stabilization, the consumer price index and the rate of devaluation were moving in tandem. After stabilization, devaluation proceeded at a slower pace than inflation, because most of it was caused by exchange rate changes among the currencies of the basket, rather than by deliberate devaluations. Hence, consumers were compensated for domestic inflation, without there being an offsetting increase in export prices. Consequently, wages rose relative to export prices by much more than they did relative to domestic ones.

Another aspect of the stabilization plan that merits mention is the situation in regard to private savings. For years, private saving rates have been very high. The preponderance of savings instruments consisted of obligations issued by the government. Israel's public is, therefore, unaccustomed to financing the private sector. When stabilization eliminated much of the government deficit, the government did not need to resort to the credit market. In the absence of new government issues, private savings rates plunged. Private savings out of net disposable income which amounted to 7.6 percent in 1983 and 18.8 percent in 1984, stood at a negative 1 percent in 1986. It is evident that a substantial change in attitudes towards the capital market is required, if the trend is to be reversed.

Conclusion

Decades of economic mismanagement by all of Israel's governments, including Begin's, produced the economic problems that the
Begin government was too weak and unwilling to uproot. The problems exploded in the face of the first post-Begin government, forcing
its successor to finally do something about Israel's economy. The jury
is not yet in: there is good reason to believe that if Israel cannot find
the economic growth path once again, the present delicate balance will
be unsustainable. Whereas the task of stopping inflation involved a
short, swift action, the task of resuming growth is long and hard, and
involves politically much more difficult changes. It remains to be seen
if any post-Begin government can bring these about.

Notes

Chapter One. Israel After Begin.

1. Gregory Mahler, *The Knesset: Parliament in the Israeli Political System*, Rutherford, N.J.: Fairleigh Dickinson University Press, 1981, p. 223.

Chapter Two. The Legacy of Begin.

1. Author's interview with Dr. Y. Bader, July 2, 1985.

2. People such as Eri Jabotinsky, H. Rosenbloom, R. Weinstein, H. Segal, Sh. Junichman, A. Grossman, A. Altman, B. Lubatzki, E. Shostak. Begin also forced out a few potential competitors from the IZL (H. Kook, Sh. Tamir, etc.).

3. Yitzhak Rabin, *Pinkas Sherut*, Sifriat Poalim, Tel-Aviv, 1979, Vol. 1, p. 227 [in English: *Rabin Memoirs*, Boston: Little, Brown, 1979].

4. "Coalition Under Strain," *Jewish Observer and Middle East Review* 17 (May 24, 1968), p. 5–6.

5. Armistice agreements between Israel and four of her neighbors were signed in 1949 on the Mediterranean island of Rhodes.

6. *Jewish Observer and Middle East Review*, January 1, 1969.

7. Benko Adar, "Majesty without Grandeur," *Al Hamishmar*, June 17, 1977 (weekly supplement), p. 3–4 (in Hebrew). Eban was the Foreign Minister in the governments of Eshkol and Meir. He was and has remained a leading Israeli dove.

8. A former IZL commander and a Herut member.

9. Gertrude Hirshler and Lester S. Eckman, *From Freedom Fighter to Statesman: Menachem Begin* (New York: Shengold Publishers, 1979), p. 267.

10. Uri Ra'anan, "Putting the Israeli Election under a Microscope," *New York Times*, June 4, 1977. Asher Arian, *Politics in Israel: The Second Generation*, Chatham House, 1985, p. 140.

11. Amitai Etzioni, "Alternative Ways to Democracy: The Experience of Israel," *Political Science Quarterly*, 74, 1959, p. 196–214.

12. Thus, in the early and mid-1950s there was a struggle between hawkish and dovish factions within Mapai.

13. Mark Segal, "After Begin," *Jerusalem Post*, Sept. 2, 1983; see also Yael Yishai, "Israel's Right-Wing Jewish Proletariant," *Jewish Journal of Sociology*, Vol. 24, Dec. 1982, p. 87–98.

14. Ibid.

15. See, for example, Hirshler and Eckman, p. 44–45, as well as Ahron Dola, "White Nights," in *Ma'ariv*, June 6, 1977.

16. For a full analysis of Neo-Revisionism as a concept, and its components, see Ilan Peleg, *Begin's Foreign Policy, 1977–1983: Israel's Move to the Right*, Greenwood, 1987, ch. 3.

17. Yitzhak Ben-Ami, "A Duty Done," *Jerusalem Post*, October 1, 1983.

18. This observation is based on a question regarding values posed to the author by Ian Lustick (personal communication, June 30, 1987).

19. *Jewish Week*, June 17, 1979, p. 2.

20. Myron A. Aronoff, "Establishing Authority: The Memorialization of Jabotinsky and the Burial of the Bar-Kochba Bones in Israel Under the Likud," in Myron J. Aronoff, ed., *Political Anthropology Vol. 5: The Frailty of Authority*, New Brunswick, Transaction Books, 1986, p. 105–130.

21. Jay Gonen, *A Psychohistory of Zionism*, N.Y., Mason/Charter, 1975, p. 3.

22. Bo'az Evron, "The Gimmick Does Not Work Anymore," *Yediot Ahronot*, June 20, 1980.

23. See Peleg, ch. 1–3.

24. The Gilad is a region east of the Jordan River. Begin published his declaration in *Herut*, the IZL paper, in May 1948 and later in an edited volume on the underground.

25. There is growing evidence suggesting that Ben-Gurion did not *want* to take over the area, fully understanding that such an action would forever make an Arab-Israeli peace impossible.

26. Uri Bialer, "David Ben-Gurion and Moshe Sharet: the crystallization of two political-military orientations in the Israeli society," *Medinah Umimshal* (State and Government), Vol. 1, No. 2, Fall 1977, p. 71–84.

27. Yehoshafat Harkabi, *Arab Strategies and Israel's Response*, New York, Free Press, 1977, p. 127–151.

28. Menachem Begin, "Concepts and Problems in Foreign Policy," *Ha'uma*, March 1966, p. 464.

29. Ibid., p. 465.

30. Howard M. Sachar, *A History of Israel: From the Rise of Zionism to Our Time*, New York: Knopf, 1979, p. 372.

31. Interview of the author with Mordechai Virshubsky, M.K. (July 1985).

32. Uzi Benziman, *Rosh Memshala Bematzor* (A Prime Minister Under Siege), Jerusalem, Adam Publishers, 1981 (Hebrew); William Quandt, *Camp David, Peacemaking and Politics*, (Washington, DC: Brookings Inst., 1986), p. 113.

33. Said Abba Eban in a personal interview with the author (August 8, 1985): "Begin managed the autonomy talks so that nothing could be possibly achieved. The first sign was the appointment of [Interior Minister] Burg to conduct the talks. Begin was afraid to allow Dayan or Weizman to be in charge, lest something will move."

34. Meron Benvenisti, *The West Bank Data Project: A Survey of Israeli Policies*, American Enterprise Institute, Washington, DC, 1984, p. 35. A dunam is one-fourth of an acre. According to some sources, 800,000 dunams were taken by the 1984 elections (see a series of articles in *Ha'aretz* under the title, "The Great Land Robbery," September-October 1985).

35. Thus, despite the urging of foreign minister Allon, Prime Minister Rabin refused to allow deep Israeli interference in Lebanon's internal affairs. See Ze'ev Schiff and Ehud Ya'ari, *Israel's Lebanon War*, New York: Simon and Shuster, 1984, ch. 3.

36. Amos Elon in *Ha'aretz*, Nov. 26, 1982.

37. *Ha'aretz*, July 9, 1982.

38. See Arei Avneri, *Hama'aluma* (The Blow), Tel-Aviv: Revivim, 1983 (Hebrew). Avneri's book deals with the air war in Lebanon.

39. See above.

40. Yoram Peri, "From Coexistence to Hegemony," *Davar*, October 1, 1982.

41. In fact, writers on the Right often complained that Israel never had clear territorial goals in launching wars. In the 1950-1960s Begin accused the Ben-Gurion government of purposely not taking the West Bank in 1948, an accusation that was, possibly, valid.

42. Thus, despite its complete control of the air in 1967, Israel refrained from massive attacks on Arab cities; compare this restraint with the bombardment of Lebanese cities in 1982 (and also the attack on Beirut in 1981).

43. These goals were often expressed by writers on the Right, but government officials, including Defense Minister Sharon and even Prime Minister Begin, did not conceal their expansionist goals either.

44. For the distinction between deterrence and compellence, see John Merrill and Ilan Peleg, "Nuclear Compellence: The Political Use of the Bomb," *Crossroads*, No. 11, 1984, p. 19–39.

45. See Zvi Lanir, "The Political and Military Objectives in Israel's Wars," in *War By Choice*, Kibutz Meuhad Publishers, 1985, Tel-Aviv, p. 117–156.

46. Such accusations were leveled, for example, at the late Prime Minister Golda Meir.

47. Zvi Shiloah, "The Mission of Greater Israel in the Ancient Land," in Ben-Ami, Aaron, ed. *The Greater Israel Book*, Tel-Aviv, Greater Israel Movement and Sh. Freedman, 1977, p. 213–226 (quote is on p. 225–226).

48. For the distinction between these types see Walter Jones, *The Logic of International Relations*, 5th edition, Boston: Little, Brown and Co., ch. 7.

49. Yoram Peri, "Coexistence or Hegemony? Shifts in the Israeli Security Concept," in Dan Caspi, Abraham Diskin and Emanuel Gutmann, ed., *The Roots of Begin's Success*, Croom Helm, London, and St. Martin's, New York, 1984, p. 191–215; Amos Perlmutter, "Begin's Rhetoric and Sharon's tactics," *Foreign Affairs*, Vol. 61, p. 67–83, Fall 1982.

50. Quoted in Peri (in Caspi), p. 203.

51. Following the attack on Osiraq, both Begin and Sharon made declarations to that effect.

52. *Yediot Ahronot*, January 5, 1983.

53. Dan Horowitz, "The Constant and Changing in Israel's Security Perception," p. 57–115 in *War by Choice*, p. 57–115 (quote on p. 60).

54. For the text see the Appendix to *A War of Choice*, p. 157–163. While the lecture was never delivered, because of passing obligations of the defense minister, the text is available.

55. Emphasis added.

56. Oded Yinon, "A Strategy for Israel in the 1980s," *Kivunim*, Vol. 14, February 1982, p. 49–59; *The Wall Street Journal* reported on Yinon's remarkable piece on December 8, 1982, p. 34.

57. *Ha'uma*, Vol. 27, January 1969, p. 329–339.

58. Aharon Davidi, "Israel's War Aims," in Ben-Ami, ibid., p. 199–203 (quote is from p. 199–200); see also, in the same volume: Eliyahu Amikam, "Palestine was born in Basle and buried in Lebanon," p. 335–339; Yedidyah Be'eri, "The Greatest Lie in History," p. 340–344.

59. The speech was published in *Ma'ariv* and *Yediot Ahronot* on August 20, 1982, and analyzed by Aharon Yariv, "A War by Choice or No Choice?," in *War By Choice*, p. 9–29.

60. Ian Lustick, "Israeli State-Building in the West Bank and Gaza Strip: theory and practice," *International Organization*, Vol. 41(1), Winter 1987, p. 151–1971.

61. On the possibility of violence in case of withdrawal, see Lea Inbal, in *Koteret Rashit*, No. 131, June 5, 1985, as well as Yoram Peri, *Between Battles and Ballots*, p. 284–287. One of the leaders of the West Bank settlers, Eliakim Haetzni published a booklet (*The Shock of Withdrawal in Eretz Israel*, Jerusalem, 1986) in which he explicitly declared any decision to withdraw as utterly illegal. See also Danny Rubinstein and Ilan Peleg, "Gush Emunim and Israeli Politics," *Reconstructionist*, Vol. 52(1), Sept. 1986.

62. Commentary on a first draft of this paper, meeting of the Association of Israel Studies, Burlington, VT, April 8, 1987.

63. Leon Wieseltier, "The Demons of the Jews," *New Republic*, November 11, 1985, p. 19.

Chapter Three. Illegalism in Israeli Political Culture.

1. Yithak Shamir quoted in *Ha'aretz*.

2. Ehud Sprinzak, *A Law Unto Itself: Illegalism in Israeli Society* (Hebrew), Sifriyat Poalim, Tel Aviv, 1986.

3. H. L. A. Hart, *The Concept of Law*, Oxford University Press, London, 1961, p. 197.

4. Cf. Amnon Rubinstein, *The Constitutional Law of the State of Israel* (Hebrew), Schocken, Tel Aviv, 1974, p. 155–165.

5. Cf. Gabriel A. Almond & Sidney Verba, *The Civic Culture*, Little Brown, Boston; 1965.

6. Cf. Theodor Weinshal, "How to Change the Public Administration in Israel," *Netivei Irgun Uminhal* (Hebrew), No. 131–132, June 1975.

7. Cf. Mark Zborovsky & Elizabeth Herzog, *Life is With People: The Culture of the Shtetle*, Schocken Books, New York, 1952.

8. For an elaboration on the notion of polinormativity in public administration see Fred W. Riggs, *Administration in Developing Countries: The Theory of Prismatic Society*, Houghton Miffin, Boston, 1964, p. 176–184, 277–285.

9. Cf. Yonathan Shapira, *Israeli Democracy* (Hebrew), Massada, Tel Aviv, 1977, p. 62–63.

10. Cf. E. Sprinzak, op. cit, p. 58–59.

11. Quoted in *The Palmach Book* (Hebrew), Hakibbutz, Hameuchad, Tel Aviv, 1955, Vol. 1, p. 678–680.

12. Yonathan Shapira, op. cit, p. 64–66.

13. Protektzia, a preferential treatment accorded by influential people to friends and friends of friends, has become a key feature of Israel's political culture. For a full analysis of the Protektzia phenomenon see Brenda Danet, *Roads to Redress: A Study of Israel's Hybrid Organizational Culture*, The State University of New York Press, New York (Forthcoming).

14. Cf. Shabtai Tevet, *David's Passion: David Ben Gurion, A Man of Authority*, Schocken, Tel Aviv, 1980, p. 349.

15. Yonathan Shapira, op. cit. p. 107.

16. Cf. Avraham Avichai, *Ben Gurion: The maker of the State* (Hebrew), Keter, Jerusalem, 1974, ch. 12; Michael Bar Zohar, *Ben Gurion* (Hebrew), Am Oved, Tel Aviv, 1977, Vol. III, p. 954–955.

17. Cf. Peter Medding, *Mapai in Israel: Political Organization and Government in a New Society*, Cambridge University Press, Cambridge, 1972, ch. 12.

18. Ibid.

19. Cf. S. N. Eizenstadt & Elihu Katz, "Some Sociological Observations on the Response of Israeli Organizations to New Immigrants," in Elihu Katz & Brenda Danet (eds.), *Bureaucracy and the Public*, Basic Books, New York. Also, Eliezer Don Yehiya, *Conflict and Cooperation: The Religious Camp and the Labor Movement and the Crisis of Education*. (Hebrew — A Doctoral Dissertation, The Hebrew University of Jerusalem, 1977), p. 735–740.

20. Cf. Ian Lustick, *Arabs in the Jewish State*, University of Texas Press, Austin, 1980, ch. 2.

21. On Ben Gurion's attitude towards the former members of Etzel and Lechi see Michael Bar Zohar op. cit, p. 926–929. Cf. Yohanan Bader, *The Knesset and I* (Hebrew), Edanim, Jerusalem, 1979, p. 24–26. This is also based on the author's long talks with Dr. Israel Eldad.

22. On the young Shimon Peres, his politics and conflicts, see Mati Golan, *Peres*, Widenfeld & Nicolson, London, 1982, chs 2, 3, 4; Also consult Moshe Sharett's terse remarks in *Moshe Sharett: Personal Diary*, Maariv Books, Tel Aviv, 1978, for example Vol. 8, p. 2325.

23. Cf. Shabtai Tevet, *Moshe Dayan* (Hebrew), Schocken, Tel Aviv, 1972, p. 556–559.

24. Cf. *United Nations Official Records of the Second Session of the General Assembly Resolutions, 16 September–29 November 1948*, Lake Success, New York, 1948, p. 132–148.

25. Cf. Sevach Weiss, *The Knesset* (Hebrew), Achiasaf press, Tel Aviv, 1978, p. 20–25.

26. Quoted by Weiss, op. cit. p. 20.

27. Cf. Natan Yania, *A Breach at the Top* (Hebrew), Levin Epstein, Tel Aviv, 1969, pts. 5–6.

28. Cf. Myron J. Aronoff, *Power and Ritual in the Israeli Labor Party*, Van Gorcum Assen, Amsterdam, 1977, p. 20–24; Medding, op. cit. p. 264–292; Eliahu Salpeter & Yuval Elitzur, *Who Runs Israel* (Hebrew), Levin Epstein, Tel Aviv, 1973, p. 81–90; Nathan Yanai, *Political Crises in Israel*, Keter, Jerusalem, 1982, p. 141–167.

29. *Maariv* (Hebrew), August 27, 1951.

30. Cf. Arye Avneri, *Sapir* (Hebrew), Peleg, Givataim, 1976, ch. 28; Eliahu Salpeter & Yuval Elitzur, *Who Runs Israel* (Hebrew), Levin Epstein, Tel Aviv, 1973, p. 53–58.

31. Cf. Shaul Evron, Razi Gutterman, Dov Genihovski et at. *The Break* (Hebrew), Special Edition, Tel Aviv, 1975.

32. Cf. Shmuel Tami "The Seeds of Evil," in Evron et Al. *The Break*, op. cit. p. 170–171.

33. Cf. Shevach Weiss, *The Switchover* (Hebrew), Am Oved, Tel Aviv, 1978, p. 59–60.

34. Cf. Asher Yadlin, *Testimony* (Hebrew), Edanim, Jerusalem, 1980, p. 213.

35. Cf. Ehud Sprinzak, "Extreme Politics in Israel," *The Jerusalem Quarterly*, No. 15, Fall, 1977, p. 40–41.

36. Cf. Yechiel Guttman, *The Attorney General Against the Government* (Hebrew), Edanim, Jerusalem, 1981, ch. 30.

37. Cf. Benjamin Akzin, "The Likud;" Ephraim Torgovnic, "A Movement for Change in a Stable System" in Allan Arian, *The Elections in Israel 1977*, Jerusalem Academic Press, Jerusalem, 1980. Nachman Urieli & Amnon Barzilai, *The Rise and the Fall of the Democratic Movement for Change* (Hebrew), Reshafim, Tel Aviv, 1982, p. 194–221; Amnon Rubinstein, *A certain Political Experience*, Edanim, Tel Aviv, 1982, chs. 3, 4, 5.

38. Cf. Asher Arian "Elections 1981: Competitiveness and Conflict," *The Jerusalem Quarterly*, No. 21, Fall, 1981.

39. Cf. Arye Avneri, *The Liberal Connection* (Hebrew), Zemora Bitan, Tel Aviv, 1984, chs. 18–36.

40. Akiva Eldar, "A National Nominations Government" (Hebrew), *Ha'aretz Magazine*, January 10, 1986.

41. Ibid.

42. Haim Shibi, "The Holy Land, The Holy Fund," *Yediot Achronot Magazine*, December 12, 1985.

Chapter Four. Tehiya as a Permanent Nationalist Phenomenon.

1. Yigal Allon, *A Curtain of Sand: Israel and the Arabs between War and Peace*, (Tel Aviv, Kibbutz HaMeuchad, 1959) p. 81–2, as quoted in Rael Jean Isaac, *Party and Politics in Israel*, (New York, Longman, 1981) p. 126–7.

2. Interview with Professor Amos Perlmutter, American University, January 1987.

3. Ibid.

4. Interview with Yisrael Medad, Tehiya's legislative assistant, July 1986.

5. *Jerusalem Post*, week ending 8/16/86, p. 4.

6. Interview with Yossi Goell, Jerusalem Post political correspondent, July 1986.

7. *Jerusalem Post*, week ending 3/30/85, p. 8.

8. Ibid.

9. Interview with Yuval Ne'eman, July 1986.

10. Interview with Ari Rath, editor of the *Jerusalem Post*, July 1986.

11. Yisrael Medad.

12. Gregory S. Mahler, *The Knesset* (Fairleigh Dickinson University Press, 1981) pp. 102–3.

13. Interview with Professor Ehud Sprinzak, June 1986.

14. Interview with Nahum Barnea, editor of *Koteret Rashit*, July 1986.

15. Yisrael Medad.

16. Interview with Rabbi Eliezer Waldman, July 1986.

17. Interview with Geula Cohen, July 1986.

18. Yisrael Medad.

19. Rabbi Eliezer Waldman.

20. Professor Amos Perlmutter.

21. Ibid.

22. Yisrael Medad.

23. Professor Ehud Sprinzak.

24. Interview with former MK Arie Lova Eliav, July 1986.

25. Interview with Gideon Altshuler, July 1986.

26. Jewish Telegraphic Agency in *Detroit Jewish News*, June 27, 1986.

27. Ma'ariv, April 28, 1987.

28. *Jerusalem Post*, week ending May 9, 1987, p. 5.

29. Nahum Barnea.

30. Rabbi Eliezer Waldman.

31. Rabbi Eliezer Waldman.

32. *Jerusalem Post*, week ending 8/31/85, p. 3.

33. *Jerusalem Post*, week ending 8/16/86, p. 10.

34. Interview with Professor Ian Lustick, Dartmouth College, June 1987.

35. Ibid.

36. Nahum Barnea.

37. *Jerusalem Post*, week ending November 28, 1987, p. 6.

38. Ibid.

Chapter Five. Israeli National Security in the 1980s.

1. This article draws primarily on two recently published works: Avner Yaniv. *Deterrence Without the Bomb: The Politics of Israeli Strategy.* (Lexington MA, D.C. Heath & Co., 1987) and Avner Yaniv. *Dilemmas of Security: Politics, Strategy and the Israeli Experience in Lebanon.* (New York, Oxford University Press, 1987).

2. The full text of the letter was reproduced in *Yediot Ahronot* on 13 April, 1984.

3. Cf. Steven J. Rosen, "A Stable System of Mutual Nuclear Deterrence in the Middle East," *The American Political Science Review* 71 (1977): 1367–1383; Shlomo Aronson, *Israel's Nuclear Options*, ACIS Working Paper No. 17 (Los Angeles, Center for Arms Control and International Security, University of California, November 1977); Shlomo Aronson, "Nuclearization of the Middle East: A Dovish View," *The Jerusalem Quarterly* 2 (1977): 27–44; Shai Feldman, *Israeli Nuclear Deterrence: A Strategy for the 1980s* (New York, Columbia University Press, 1982).

4. Aron S. Klieman, *Israel's Global Reach* (Washington D.C., Pergamon-Brassey, 1985).

5. Thomas Friedman, "Israelis Reassess Supplying Arms to South Africa," *New York Times*, 29 January, 1987.

6. Shabtai Teveth, *Kilelat HaBracha* (Jerusalem, Schocken, 1971).

7. See Moshe Maoz, *Palestinian Leadership on the West Bank* (London, Frank Cass, 1985) and Shlomo Gazit, *The Stick and the Carrot*, (Tel Aviv, Zmora-Bitan, 1985).

Chapter Six. Israeli-Soviet Relations.

1. For recent studies of Soviet policy in the Middle East, see Robert O. Freedman, *Soviet Policy Toward the Middle East Since 1970*, third edition (New York: Praeger, 1982); Jon D. Glassman, *Arms for the Arabs: The Soviet Union and War in the Middle East* (Baltimore: Johns Hopkins, 1975); Galia Golan, *Yom Kippur and After: The Soviet Union and the Middle East Crisis* (London: Cambridge University Press, 1977); Yaacov Ro'i, *From Encroachment to Involvement: A Documentary Study of Soviet Policy in the Middle East* (Jerusalem: Israel Universities Press, 1974); and Adeed Dawisha and Karen Dawisha (eds.), *The Soviet Union In the Middle East: Policies and Perspectives* (New York: Holmes and Meier, 1982). See also Yaacov Ro'i (ed.), *The Limits to Power* (London: Croom Helm, 1979).

For an Arab viewpoint, see Mohamed Heikal, *The Sphinx and the Commissar* (New York: Harper and Row, 1978). For a Soviet view, see E.M. Primakov, *Anatomiia Blizhnevostochnogo Konflikta* (Moscow: Mysi', 1978).

2. For studies of Soviet military aid, see Glassman, *op. cit.*, and George Lenczowski, *Soviet Advances in the Middle East* (Washington: American Enterprise Institute, 1972). See also Amnon Sella, *Soviet Political and Military Conduct in the Middle East* (New York: St. Martin's, 1981).

3. For a view of the role of Israel in Soviet Middle East strategy, see Freedman, *Soviet Policy Toward the Middle East, op. cit.* See Also Arthur Klinghoffer, *Israel and the Soviet Union* (Boulder, Colorado: Westview Press, 1985).

4. For studies of Soviet policy toward the Communist parties of the Arab world, see Robert O. Freedman, "The Soviet Union and the Communist Parties of the Arab World: An Uncertain Relationship," in Roger E. Kanet and Donna Bahry (eds.), *Soviet Economic and Political Relations with the Developing World* (New York: Praeger, 1975), p. 100–134; John K. Cooley, "The Shifting Sands of Arab Communism", *Problems of Communism*, vol. 24 no. 2, 1975, p. 22–42; and Arnold Huttinger, "Arab Communism at a Low Ebb", *Problems of Communism* vol. 30, July/August 1981, p. 17–32.

5. As a result of its April 1985 revolution, however, Sudan moved from the Egyptian camp to the centrist grouping of Arab states.

6. Cited in report in *The Washington Post*, 3 February, 1985.

7. Cited in report in *The Jerusalem Post*, 6 August, 1985.

8. Cited in report by Jonathan Randal, *The Washington Post*, 7 January, 1985. Jordan's difficulties in obtaining weapons from the United States, difficulties that escalated in 1985 due to the American Congress's opposition to arms sales to Jordan, were factors in Hussein's keeping open his options with the USSR.

9. On this point, see Robert O. Freedman, "Soviet Jewry and Soviet-American Relations: A Historical Analysis" in *Soviet Jewry in the Decisive Decade 1971–1980* (ed. Robert O. Freedman) (Durham, North Carolina: Duke University Press, 1984), p. 38–67.

10. Cited in report by Dusko Doder, *Washington Post*, 14 May, 1985.

11. Cf. *Pravda*, 14 April, 1985.

12. It turned out to be a signal to Israel, but there was to be no lasting change in the Soviet media's equating of Zionism and Naziism.

13. Cited in report by David Ottaway, *Washington Post*, 31 May, 1985.

14. Cited in report by Jim Hoagland, *Washington Post*, 8 June, 1985.

15. *Tass*, English, 20 July, 1985 (*Foreign Broadcast Information Service Daily Report: The Soviet Union* [hereafter *FBIS:USSR*], 22 July, 1985, p. H–2).

16. Jerusalem Domestic Service, in Hebrew, 19 July, 1985 (*FBIS:USSR*, 19 July, 1985, p. H–1, H–2).

17. Cf. comments by Soviet charge d'affairs in Kuwait, Vladimir Zentchner, as reported in KUNA on 23 July, 1985 (*FBIS:USSR*, 26 July, 1985, p. H–1) and comments by Leonid Zamyatin, head of the International Information Department of the Communist Party Central Committee, as reported in KUNA, 27 July, 1985 (*FBIS:USSR*, 29 July, 1985, p. H–1).

18. Cf. *Novosti* report, cited in *New York Times*, 7 August, 1985. See also Moscow Radio Peace and Progress, in Hebrew, 22 July, 1985. (*FBIS:USSR*, 23 July, 1985, p. H–3).

19. Cf. report of Peres's comments in the article by Michael Eilan, *Jerusalem Post*, 22 July, 1985.

20. For analyses of the diplomatic background of the summit, see the articles by Christopher Dickey, *Washington Post*, 6 August, 1985; Mary Curtis, *Christian Science Monitor*, 7 August, 1985; and Judith Miller, *New York Times*, 7 August, 1985. For a description of the issues concerning Moscow, see O. Fomin, "The Casablanca Summit," *New Times* no. 34, 1985, p. 10–11; *Pravda*,

7 August, 1985; and *Tass* report in English, August 8, 1985 (*FBIS:USSR*, 9 August, 1985, p. H–1).

21. Cited in article by Jean Gueyras, *LeMonde*, 11 August, 1985 (*Manchester Guardian Weekly*, 25 August, 1985).

22. *Manama Wakh*, in Arabic, 8 August, 1985 (*Foreign Broadcast Information Service Daily Report: Middle East and Africa* [hereafter *FBIS:ME*], 8 August, 1985, p. A–8).

23. Fomin, "The Casablanca Summit", *loc. cit.*

24. Cf. Moscow Radio, in Arabic, "Window on the Arab World" (Alexander Timoshkin), 10 August, 1985 (*FBIS:USSR*, 12 August, 1985, p. H–1).

25. For a background analysis of this development, see the report by Thomas Friedman, *New York Times*, 18 October, 1985. (A preliminary version of the agreement was broadcast over Israel radio on October 5, 1985). Of course, Poland, which also wished to influence United States Jewish opinion, had its own reasons for making this move, but it could not have done so without Moscow's approval.

26. Cited in *Jerusalem Post*, 6 October, 1985.

27. Cf. reports by Michael Eilan and Joshua Brilliant, *Jerusalem Post*, 31 October, 1985 and Judith Miller, *New York Times*, 26 October, 1985. The rumor was renewed after a December 1985 Bronfman visit to the Soviet capital (see the reports in the *Washington Post*, 23 and 24 December, 1985). Bronfman, it should be noted, was closer to Prime Minster Peres than to Foreign Minister Shamir, who often took a dim view of the World Jewish Congress President's quasi-diplomatic activities.

28. For a background analysis of the rise in terrorism, see the report by Thomas L. Friedman, *New York Times*, 3 October, 1985. A major seaborne attack on Israel in late April, authorized by Arafat's deputy Khalil Wazir (Abu Jihad) was prevented when the Israeli Navy sank the PLO ship carrying the terrorists. (See reports by G. Jefferson Price, *Baltimore Sun*, 23 April, 1985 and Reuters, *Jerusalem Post*, 10 May, 1985).

29. Cf. report by David Hirst, *Manchester Guardian Weekly*, 3 November, 1985.

30. To make matters worse for the PLO, Farouk Kaddoumi claimed, at the United Nations, that there was no evidence of Klinghoffer's murder.

31. Cf. Associated Press report, *Washington Post*, 21 September, 1985; *FBIS:ME*, 15 October, 1985, p. i and 16 October, 1985, p. i; and report by Jo Thomas, *New York Times*, 15 October, 1985.

32. It was rumored at the time that Hussein was seriously considering dropping Arafat (Cf. report by John Kifner, *New York Times*, 27 October, 1985).

33. Cited in report by Samara Kawar, *Washington Post,* 3 November, 1985. The Syrian and Jordanian Foreign Ministers had first met in mid-September under the auspices of the reconciliation committee set up by the Casablanca summit.

34. Cf. report by Bernard Gwertzman, *New York Times,* 31 October, 1985.

35. Cited in report by Walter Ruby, *Jerusalem Post,* 17 November, 1985. Vlasov was the deputy Soviet spokesman at the summit. Evgeny Primakov made the same point at another press conference in Geneva. (KUNA, 16 November, 1985 [*FBIS:USSR,* 18 November, 1985, p. H–7]).

36. Cited in report by Asher Wallfish, *Jerusalem Post,* 19 November, 1985.

37. Cf. report by Ihsan Hijazi, *New York Times,* 20 November, 1985. See also the report by David Ottaway, *Washington Post,* 8 November, 1985.

38. For the text of Reagan's speech on this subject, see *New York Times,* 25 October, 1985.

39. Arafat was particularly suspicious. See report by Ihsan Hijazi, *New York Times,* 20 November, 1985.

40. Moscow Radio International Service in Arabic, 17 November, 1985 (*FBIS:USSR,* 19 November, 1985, *Reportage on the Reagan-Gorbachev Summit,* p. 3).

41. *Jerusalem Post,* 4 December, 1985.

42. Cited in *Jerusalem Post,* 8 December, 1985.

43. For the text of Gorbachev's speech, see *Pravda,* 26 February, 1986. His foreign policy emphasis was on Soviet-American, Soviet-European, and Soviet-Asian relations, in that order.

44. For a background analysis on Soviet-Libyan relations at the time of the U.S.-Libyan clashes, see Robert O. Freedman, "U.S.-Libyan Crisis — Moscow Keeps its Distance", *Christian Science Monitor,* 24 April, 1987.

45. Cited in report by Celestine Bohlen, *Washington Post,* 26 March, 1986.

46. For an analysis of the events leading up to the Soviet-Israeli talks, see the article in the *Jerusalem Post,* 5 August, 1986. The Soviet warning to Libya and Syria came during Moscow visits by Syrian Vice President Abdel Khaddam, and Libya's No. 2 leader, Abdel Jalioud, in May.

47. Moscow was less happy, however, at King Hussein's crackdown on Jordan's Communist party and his arrest of leaders of the Jordan-Soviet Friendship Society, which the USSR may have feared might be the first step to a deal with Israel (Cf. *Pravda,* 29 May, 1986).

48. For the Soviet view of the talks, see the *Tass* report, in English, 19 August, 1986 (*FBIS:USSR,* 20 August, 1986, p. CC–1). For the Israeli view, see

Helsinki Domestic Service, in Finnish, 18 August, 1986 (*FBIS:ME*, 19 August, 1986, p. I–1) and Tel Aviv, IDF Radio in Hebrew, 18 August, 1986 (*FBIS:ME*, 19 August, 1986, p. I–1, I–2). One effect of Sharansky's coming to Israel had been to raise the political stature of the Soviet Jewry movement, which now had such important politicians as Moshe Arens on its side. Hitherto, the main Knesset activists were fringe politicians, such as Tehiya's Geula Cohen.

49. See the report by Bernard Gwertzman, *New York Times*, 23 September, 1986. In his United Nations speech, Shevardnadze noted that Israel owed its existence "to, among others, the Soviet Union," and also reiterated Moscow's call for a preparatory committee "set up within the framework of the Security Council to do the necessary work for convening an international conference on the Middle East."

50. For the State Department's view of the discussion of human rights in general and the issue of Soviet Jewish emigration in particular at the Reykjavik summit, see *Gist: The Reykjavik Meeting* (Bureau of Public Affairs: Department of State, December 1986).

51. Cited in report by Wolf Blitzer, *Jerusalem Post*, 20 February, 1987.

52. Cited in report by Benny Morris, Yossi Lempkowicz, and David Howowitz, *Jerusalem Post*, 24 February, 1987.

53. For the text of this document, see *FBIS:ME*, 23 March, 1987, p. 1–2, 3.

54. Cited in Reuters report, *New York Times*, 20 March, 1987. 871 Jews, the highest monthly total in six years, left in May 1987.

55. Cited in National Conference on Soviet Jewry Report, 1 April, 1987.

56. Cited in report by Walter Ruby and Andy Court, *Jerusalem Post*, 2 April, 1987.

57. Cf. Jerusalem Radio Domestic Service interview with Soviet Foreign Ministry spokesman Genady Gerasimov, 2 April, 1987. (*FBIS:ME*, 2 April, 1987, p. I–1). See also the article by Henry Kamm, *New York Times*, 3 April, 1987.

58. Cf. Jerusalem Radio Domestic Service interview with Yitzhak Shamir, 26 March, 1987 (*FBIS:ME*, 27 March, 1987, p. I–1). Shamir also downplayed the importance of the Bronfman-Abram visit (Cf. report by Thomas Friedman, *New York Times*, 1 April, 1987).

59. Cf. report by Joel Greenberg, *Jerusalem Post*, 27 March, 1987.

60. Reuters report, *New York Times*, 29 March, 1987. China's permanent United Nations representative, Li Luye, met with the Director General of the Israeli Foreign Minsitry, Abraham Tamir. See also the report by David Landau and Walter Ruby, *Jerusalem Post*, 29 March, 1987.

61. Cf. Jerusalem Radio Domestic Service interview with Soviet Foreign Ministry spokesman Genady Gerasimov, 2 April, 1987 (*FBIS:ME*, 2 April, 1987, p. I–1).

62. Jerusalem Radio Domestic Service interview with Peres, 2 April, 1987 (*FBIS:ME*, 3 April, 1987, p. I–1). In the interview Peres noted other changes in Soviet policy, including the release of nearly all the prisoners of Zion, the rise in exit permits from 100 to nearly 500 a month, and Soviet statements in diplomatic meetings that they wanted improved relations with Israel.

63. Jerusalem Radio Domestic Service, 5 April, 1987 (*FBIS:ME*, 6 April, 1987, p. I–1) and *Jerusalem Post*, 5 April, 1987).

64. Cited in report by John Tagliabue, *New York Times*, 8 April, 1987.

65. Jerusalem Radio Domestic Service, 8 April, 1987 (*FBIS:ME*, 9 April, 1987, p. I–1).

66. Jerusalem Radio Domestic Service, 9 April, 1987 (*FBIS:ME*, 10 April, 1987, p. I–3).

67. This information, reported by ''sources close to Peres'' was discussed in the *Jerusalem Post*, 10 April, 1987 in the report coauthored by Wolf Blitzer, David Horowitz, Jonathan Karp, and Robert Rosenberg.

68. Jerusalem Radio Domestic Service, 7 April, 1987 (*FBIS:ME*, 8 April, 1987, p. I–3).

69. Cited in report by Lea Levavi and Asher Wallfish, *Jerusalem Post*, 10 April, 1987.

70. Jerusalem Radio Domestic Service, 12 April, 1987 (*FBIS:ME*, 13 April, 1987, p. I–3).

71. Ibid.

72. Israeli Defense Forces Radio interview with Yitzhak Shamir, 13 April, 1987 (*FBIS:ME*, 13 April, 1987, p. I–4/I–5).

73. For the text of Gorbachev's comments, see *Pravda*, 25 April, 1987.

74. Cited in *Jerusalem Post*, 24 April, 1987. In early March, in another cultural exchange, Moscow had sent its Gypsy Theatre Troup to play in Israel.

75. Cited in report by Thomas Friedman, *New York Times*, 8 May, 1987.

76. Jordan's denial came in a statement by Jordanian Prime Minister Zaid Al-Rifal. The text of the denial was printed in the *Jerusalem Post*, 5 May, 1987. According to a report by David Shipler, *New York Times*, 12 May, 1987, Jordan had reportedly agreed to a limited role for the USSR in the conference which would be convened by the Secretary General of the United Nations based on United Nations Resolutions 242 and 338.

77. Cf. report by Glen Frankel, *Washington Post*, 15 May, 1987.

Chapter Seven. Israel in the Middle East.

1. While United States Secretary of State George Shultz made no trips to the region to negotiate in the period between the 1984 abrogation of the Lebanese accord and the Palestinian uprising, in 1988 he made four trips, but to no effect.

2. The distinction is not precise. Yet there is a key difference between Egypt's foreign policy under Nasser and Sadat, or Iran's policy under Khomeini and the shah. The former are self-described revolutionaries, the latter are not. Space does not allow for extensive discussion of the distinction here. For one effort, see Adeed Dawisha, *The Arab Radicals* (New York: Council on Foreign Relations, 1986) or generally, Henry Kissinger, "Domestic Structure and Foreign Policy," in *American Foreign Policy* (New York: W.W. Norton, 1974).

3. George Kennan, "The Sources of Soviet Conduct," *Foreign Affairs*, Spring 1947.

4. For a discussion of the periphery strategy and the erosion of its utility, see Shai Feldman, "Israel's Grand Strategy: David Ben Gurion and Israel's Next Great Debate," paper delivered at the Woodrow Wilson Center, Washington, 15 June, 1988.

5. Moshe Dayan, *Breakthrough: A Personal Account of the Egypt-Israel Peace Negotiations*, (New York: Knopf, 1981) p. 52.

6. Teshome Wagaw, "The Emigration and Settlement of Ethiopian Jews in Israel," *Middle East Review*, Winter 1987/8. Dayan's revelations also aborted a just-concluded agreement on emigration of Ethiopian Jews.

7. *New York Times*, 7 and 10 February 1978. This observation was made by Joseph Alpher, Deputy Director of Tel Aviv University's Jaffee Center for Strategic Studies *Ma'ariv*, 13 December 1987.

8. Thomas Friedman, *New York Times*, 7 September 1986.

9. As the arbitration decision neared, it seemed Israel's claim to Tabah was shaky. Then-Foreign Ministry Director General explained that Begin had been persuaded to allow a hotel to be built there on the basis of "a few documents." But the 1922 mandatory border, which became the basis for the Israeli-Egyptian border, put Tabah within Egyptian territory. David Kimche. *Jerusalem Post International*, 20 August 1988.

10. Negotiations described by Dayan, *op. cit.*, chap. 4, "Rendezvous in Morocco."

11. "Speech of His Majesty King Hassan II," July 23, 1986, Press Release, Embassy of the Kingdom of Morocco.

12. Paris Radio Monte Carlo and KUNA 22 July in *FBIS* 22 July 1986.

13. Islamic Republic News Agency, 24 July 1986 in *FBIS* 25 July.

14. George Joffee, *Middle East International*, 8 August 1986.

15. Ze'ev Schiff and Ehud Ya'ari, *Israel's Lebanon War* (New York: Simon and Schuster, 1984), p. 233–6.

16. Even before the war, Israeli military intelligence believed the Phalange were not dependable. Mossad pushed the relationship. Ibid., p. 53.

17. *Ma'ariv*, 1 January 1988, published a credible account of the accord in *FBIS* 4 January 1988, summarized here.

18. "Text of President Saddam Husayn's interview with Mr. Stephen Solarz, August 25, 1982" in al-*Jumhuriyah*, (Baghdad) 3 January 1983.

19. *Le Monde*, 8 January 1983.

20. Akiva Eldar, "Jerusalem: Baghdad Calling," *Ha'Aretz*, 1 July 1988, p. 82; *Mideast Report*, 1 August 1988.

21. Israel's Defense Minister reflected that sustained neutrality as he later explained to the author that he saw "Iran as an ideological threat, Iraq as a potential military threat," in Laurie Mylroie, "Iraq After the Ceasefire," *Jerusalem Post* 19 May 1989.

22. Damascus Television Service, 27 January 1987 in *FBIS* 29 January 1987.

23. *Keyhan*, 11 November 1987, *FBIS* 18 November 1987.

24. The Defense Minister explained, "Syria is striving for a strategic balance with Israel and as soon as this is established, Syria is ready to participate in an international Middle East conference." Weiner Zeitung, 25 April 1986, in *FBIS* 2 May. Five months later, he asserted Syria would reconquer the Golan Heights. When asked, "Will your liberation strike come soon?" he replied, "I will not tell you about our military plans." *Der Speigel*, 22 September in *FBIS* 23 September 1986.

25. This is even the estimate of some Israelis. See Avraham Tamir, Foreign Ministry Director General in *Haaretz*, 22 July 1988; and Aharon Levran, Chair, Military Balance Project, Jaffee Center for Strategic Studies in *Jerusalem Post*, 30 July 1988.

26. A similar point was also made by Aaron Miller, "Changing Arab Attitudes Toward Israel," *Orbis*, Winter 1988, and Moshe Maoz "Hafiz al-Asad of Syria," *Orbis*, Summer 1987.

27. I.e. Ariel Sharon, the defense minister warned, "support for Iraq may...lead to Soviet penetration into Iran" and sought to persuade the United States to support Israeli arms sales to Iran. *Ma'ariv*, 30 May 1982 in *FBIS* 1 June 1982; Jerusalem Domestic Television Service 1 February 1982 in *FBIS* 2 February 1982.

28. That was the last time the United States publicly protested suspicions of Israeli arms to Iran. The Defense Ministry then reissued orders then banning any sales. *Ha'aretz,* 16 November 1987.

29. As a *Ha'aretz* editorial complained, "The impression is that Israel had a policy of aiding Iran for the last five years and just changed its arguments every now and then." 26 November 1986.

30. *Washington Post,* 30 October 1987.

31. David Menashri, "Khomeini's Policy Toward Minorities," in M. Esman and I. Rabinovich (eds.) *Ethnicity, Pluralism, and the State in the Middle East,* (Ithaca, NY: Cornell, 1988), p. 226.

32. Youssef Ibrahim, "Key Official Stresses Iran's Backing of Palestinians," *New York Times,* 3 May 1979.

33. *Jerusalem Post* 23 September 1987; 18 and 25 November.

34. *Jerusalem Post,* 22 November 1987.

35. See Alain Gresch's *The PLO: the Struggle Within* (London: Zed Books, 1983) for a sympathetic account of divisions within the PLO and their consequence.

36. Zafir al-Masri, appointed mayor of Nablus with PLO, Jordanian and Israeli approval, was killed by Syrian-backed Palestinians in early 1986. Fahd al-Qawasima was assassinated after the 1984 PNC by pro-Syrian elements as a warning to the PLO not to go too far in the peace process, also the reason for Sartawi's murder. Asher Susser, "The Palestine Liberation Organizaiton," in *Middle East Contemporary Survey 1984–85,* p. 194.

37. Cairo Domestic Service, 10 February 1988, in *FBIS* 11 February 1988.

Chapter Eight. Israel and Morocco.

1. For an extended discussion of this point, see the introduction and several of the contributions in Rene Lemarchand (ed.), *The Green and the Black: Libyan Policies in North and Sub-Saharan Africa.* Bloomington, Indiana: Indiana University Press, 1988.

2. Yitzhak Rabin, *The Rabin Memoirs* (Boston: Little, Brown and Co., 1979), p. 320–321.

3. Quoted in *The Jerusalem Post,* 23 July 1986.

4. See Matti Golan, *Shimon Peres: A Biography* (London: Weidenfeld and Nicolson, 1982), p. 217, 222–224, 250–253.

5. Quoted in *The Jerusalem Post,* 25 July 1986.

6. Hirsh Goodman, "Limited Mission Accomplished," *The Jerusalem Post*, 25 July 1986.

7. The communique is reprinted in *The New York Times*, 25 July 1986.

8. Hassan's speech is reprinted in full in *The Jerusalem Post*, 30 July 1987.

9. Quoted in *The New York Times*, 24 July 1986.

10. Amir Taheri, "Hassan II — Peres: un dialogue impossible," *Jeune Afrique*, 6 August 1986.

11. For fuller discussions, see Richard B. Parker, *North Africa: Regional Tensions and Strategic Concerns* (New York: Praeger, 1984), especially p. 162–164; and John Damis, *U.S.-Arab Relations: The Moroccan Dimension* (Washington: National Council on U.S.-Arab Relations, 1986), p. 10–17. See also Claudia Wright, "Journey to Marrakesh: U.S.-Moroccan Security Relations," *International Security* 7 (Spring 1983): 163–179; and John Damis, "United States Relations with North Africa," *Current History*, May 1985, p. 193–195.

12. An illustration of Congressional reservations about United States support of Morocco is provided by Stephen J. Solarz, "Arms for Morocco?" *Foreign Affairs* 58 (Winter 1979/1980): 278–299. See also Parker, *op. cit.*, p. 116.

13. For details, see Mark Tessler, "Continuity and Change in Moroccan Politics, Part II: New Troubles and Deepening Doubts," *Universities Field Staff International Reports*, May 1984. See also Mark Tessler, "Explaining the 'Surprises' of King Hassan II, Part I: Tensions in North Africa in the Mid-1980s," *UFSI Reports*, December 1986.

14. Differences and similarities between King Hassan's regime and that of the Shah of Iran are discussed in Mark Tessler, "Image and Reality in Moroccan Politics," in I. W. Zartman (ed.), *The Political Economy of Morocco* (New York: Greenwood Press, 1987).

15. The administration did state, however, that it would permit the sale of "defensive" weapons to Morocco, and in February 1979 it accordingly approved the sale of six heavy-lift helicopters. For details, see Damis, *op. cit.*, 1986, p. 14.

16. *New York Times*, 25 January 1980.

17. Quoted in Damis, *op. cit.*, 1986, p. 15.

18. A detailed account of the formation of the Arab-African Union, including a chronology of events associated with its implementation through the end of 1984, is provided in *Panorama Economique & Social* (Casablanca: Maroc Soir, 1985). See also Francois Soudan, "UAA: Maroc et Libye un an apres," *Jeune Afrique*, August 14/21, 1985. The further evolution of the union is traced in Mark Tessler, "Explaining the 'Surprises' of King Hassan II, Part II: The Arab-African Union between Morocco and Libya," *UFSI Reports*, January 1987.

19. Other accounts of the Arab-African Union, which also assess the motivation behind it and its significance for United States-Moroccan relations, are provided by John Damis, "Morocco, Libya and the Treaty of Union," *American-Arab Afairs* 13 (Summer 1984): 44–55; Mark Tessler, "The Uses and Limits of Populism: The Political Strategy of King Hassan II of Morocco," *The Middle East Review* (Spring 1985): 44–51; and Richard B. Parker, "Appointment in Oujda," *Foreign Affairs* 65 (Summer 1985): 1095–1110. See also the epilogue in the revised (1987) edition of Parker. *op. cit.*, 1984.

20. Quoted in *The New York Times*, 23 and 24 October 1982.

21. Quoted in *The Jeruslaem Post*, 24 July 1986.

22. Quoted in *The Christian Science Monitor*, 25 July 1986.

23. Asher Wallfish, "Visit Could Ease Hassan's Position," *The Jerusalem Post*, 22 July 1986.

24. The circumstances of Morocco's Jewish community are discussed in Mark Tessler, "The Protection of Minorities in the Middle East," in Robert Wirsing (ed.), *The Protection of Minorities* (New York: Pergamon, 1981); and Mark Tessler, "Minorities in Retreat: The Jews of the Maghreb," in R. D. McLaurin (ed.), *The Political Role of Minority Groups in the Middle East* (New York: Praeger, 1979).

25. Quoted in *The Christian Science Monitor*, 25 July 1986.

26. Quoted in *The Jerusalem Post*, 27 July 1986.

27. For an extended discussion, see Mark Tessler, "The Impact of the Intifada on Israeli Political Thinking," *Journal of Palestine Studies*, forthcoming.

Chapter Nine. The Guarded Relationship Between Israel and Egypt.

1. The following paragraphs are based on the author's "Egyptian-Israeli Relations: Normalization or Special Ties?," Universities Field Staff International (UFSI) *Report*, No. 35, 1986, p. 2; reprinted in *Israel, Egypt, and the Palestinians: From Camp David to Intifada*, Ann M. Lesch and Mark Tessler, Bloomington: Indiana University Press, 1989. Detailed footnotes on Arabic sources are available in the original.

2. Discussion of the summit meeting is based on the author's "The Egyptian-Israeli Summit: Protracted Negotiations and Reduced Expectations," UFSI *Report*, No. 33, 1986, p. 1–2; reprinted in *Israel, Egypt . . .*

3. The section on normalization is based on the author's "Egyptian-Israeli Relations."

4. Joel Beinin, "The Cold Peace," *MERIP Reports*, No. 129, January 1985, p. 5.

5. Figures were obtained from Isaac Bar Moshe, press attaché, Israeli Embassy, Cairo, 2 September 1986.

6. *Middle East Times (MET)*, 3 September 1988.

7. Ibid.

8. *Wall Street Journal*, 8 March 1984.

9. *MET*, 17 January 1988.

10. *MET*, 10 January 1988.

11. *Al-Wafd*, Cairo, 25 February 1988.

12. On early trade contacts see Beinin, p. 6; *Financial Times*, London, 6 October 1981; *Washington Post*, 28 April 1980; Marie Christine Aulas, "The Normalization of Egyptian-Israeli Relations," *Arab Studies Quarterly*, 5:3, Summer 1983, p. 230–232. Trade figures were provided by Bar Moshe, 2 September 1986; also *Jerusalem Post*, international edition *(JPI)*, 20 September 1986.

13. Figures from Bar Moshe; Beinin, p. 7; *International Herald Tribune (IHT)*, 12 September 1982.

14. *Ha'aretz*, Tel Aviv, 15 June 1986.

15. MET, 3 September 1988.

16. *MET*, 20 September 1987.

17. Aulas, pp. 234–235; see letters by Dr. Muhammad Sha'alan in *JPI*, 23 January 1981 and 1 August 1981.

18. *October*, Cairo, 9 November 1980.

19. *October*, 6 June 1982; interview with Dr. Sha'alan, 21 August 1986.

20. Comment by a senior Egyptian diplomat, summer 1986.

21. Information drawn from IAC *Bulletin*, No. 1 (Fall 1982) to 7 (Summer 1986); interview with Dr. Gabriel Warburg, the second director, 8 September 1986.

22. Dr. Avivi Yavin, director of Research Project on Peace, Tel Aviv University, who visited Egypt in September 1979 and February 1980; personal discussions and correspondence, 1979–80.

23. *JPI*, 4 January 1986; *al-Ahali*, Cairo, 19 February 1986.

24. Patterns of Agricultural Technological Exchange and Cooperation (PATEC) received $3.49 million funding over four years from USAID, September 1984. Information based on research proposal, January 1984, and additional grant documents.

25. Cooperative Arid Lands Agricultural Research (CALAR), funded in 1982 with a $5 million USAID grant, received supplementary support in 1985. See *Arid Lands Newsletter,* Office of Arid Lands Study, University of Arizona, No. 22, September 1985, pp. 2–13.

26. Agricultural Ministry Under Secretary Muhammad Dasouqi, quoted in *JPI,* 30 March 1985.

27. Quoted from mid-term evaluation by RONCO Consulting Company, Washington, D.C., September 1984, p. 2; appendix 6, p. A–45; and draft proposal, 28 January 1985, p. 141.

28. *AID Congressional Presentation FY 1987,* Annex II: Asia Program, p. 399.

29. *New York Times (NYT),* 5 May 1985; see also *JPI,* 4 and 11 May 1985.

30. *MET,* 29 November 1987.

31. Dr. Sherif al-Sayid, "Epidemiology and Control of Arthropod-Borne Diseases in Egypt," presentation to USAID, 23 April 1986, p. 12, 15.

32. *JPI,* 24 November 1984.

33. Based on the author's "Irritants in the Egyptian-Israeli Relationship," UFSI *Report,* No. 34, 1986, p. 1–2. The section on Egypt's Revolution is based on *ibid.,* p. 2–3.

34. Associated Press, quoting the first communiqué, 5 June 1984. Mahmud Nuriddin's views are also quoted in *al-Sha'ab,* Cairo, 23 February 1988.

35. *MET,* 22 October 1988.

36. Details come from *al-Sha'ab,* 23 February 1988 and 8 March 1988, and *al-Ahali,* 2 March 1988.

37. Based on the author's "Irritants," p. 3.

38. Ibid., pp. 3–4.

39. The events surrounding Tabah up to September 1986 are detailed in the author's "The Egyptian-Israeli Summit." Research was based on documentation from the Israeli, Egyptian, and international press and interviews in summer 1986 with diplomats in the American and Israeli embassies in Cairo and key Egyptian negotiators.

40. *IHT,* 15 January 1986; Egyptian foreign minister's testimony to the Peoples Assembly, *al-Ahram,* 20 January 1986.

41. The question stated: "The Tribunal is requested to decide the location of the boundary pillars of the recognized international boundary between Egypt and the former mandated territory of Palestine, in accordance with the Peace Treaty, the Agreement of 25 April 1982, and the Annex." The Annex noted that "each party has indicated on the ground its position concerning the location of each boundary pillar."

42. *MET*, 13 September 1987, 17 January and 21 February 1988.

43. *NYT*, 30 September 1988; *MET*, 1 October 1988.

44. *MET*, 29 November 1987, 25 June, 2 July, 6 August 1988.

45. *NYT*, 30 September 1988.

46. *MET*, 1 and 8 October 1988; *NYT*, 18 October 1988.

47. There are two unresolved issues involving Coptic properties. The Jordanian government had allocated land for a Coptic college in Jerusalem, but Israel rejected the plan on security grounds because the college was located next to the military central command. Egyptian negotiators raised the issue in bilateral talks in 1984–85, and Peres agreed that the construction could proceed. Nevertheless, ultrorthodox religious politicians delayed action, as part of their opposition to any increase in the Christian presence in Jerusalem. The second problem concerned Deir al-Sultan, property of the Egyptian Coptic Orthodox Church until Ethiopian Coptic monks seized it in April 1970. The Israeli high court ruled on 16 March 1971 that the Deir should be returned to the Egyptian church, but the Israeli government failed to implement the ruling. After the peace treaty, Pope Shenuda II decreed that no Copt could visit Jerusalem until Deir al-Sultan was returned to the church's control. Israel, however, did not want to jeopardize its relations with Ethiopia, with which it negotiates over the status of Ethiopian Jews and which grants overflight rights to Israeli planes. The problem has therefore not yet been resolved.

Canada Camp is a Palestinian residential area on the Egyptian side of the border with the Gaza Strip, which was established by Israel in the early 1970s for Palestinians whom it had expelled from refugee camps within the Strip. After the return of Sinai in April 1982 to Egypt, the 560 families who resided in Canada Camp were supposed to be transferred back to the Strip within six months. They have remained in limbo for more than six years, isolated from their relatives, jobs, and schools within the Strip. In March 1986 Egypt agreed to provide $8,000 per family and Israel agreed to provide $9,000 worth of land and support for construction for each family in a housing zone northwest of Rafah. Nevertheless, the families are still stuck in Canada Camp. The Israeli government and public procrastinate on implementing the accord, not wanting to add 5,000 persons to the volatile population of the Gaza Strip.

The issues of Coptic properties and Canada Camp are detailed in the author's, "Irritants", p. 4–6.

48. *Yediot Ahronot*, Tel Aviv, 2 November 1984.

49. *MET*, 27 December 1987.

50. *MET*, 26 November 1988.

51. Dr. Boutros Boutros-Ghali, minister of state for foreign affairs, *MET*, 27 December 1987. The police crackdown on attempted demonstrations and marches is described in *MET*, 10 January 1988, and *Middle East Report*, May-June 1988, p. 45.

52. *MET*, 29 October 1988.

Chapter Ten. The Not-so-Silent Partnership.

1. For the text of Ben-Gurion's statement, see *In Vigilant Brotherhood* (New York: American Jewish Committee, 1964); p. 64–66; Blaustein's response is on pp. 66–69.

2. Interview with Abraham Rabinowitz, *Jerusalem Post*, 13 March 1987.

3. *In Vigilant Brotherhood*, p. 65.

4. Ibid., p. 68.

5. Response to a question by the author.

6. Joel Brinkley, "Israel Feels Growing Anguish As Immigration Flow Falters," dispatch from Mevaseret Zion, *New York Times*, 18 June 1988.

7. AP dispatch from Jerusalem, *New York Times*, 20 June 1988.

8. The joint statement was adopted by the American Jewish Committee, American Jewish Congress, Anti-Defamation League of B'nai B'rith, Coalition to Free Soviet Jews, Council of Jewish Federations, Hebrew Immigrant Aid Society (HIAS), National Conference on Soviet Jewry, National Jewish Community Relations Advisory Council, Union of Councils for Soviet Jews, United Israel Appeal, and World Zionist Organization/American Section.

9. *In Vigilant Brotherhood*, p. 65–66. Professor David Sidorsky of Columbia University, who had served as a volunteer in the Israeli army during the War of Independence, questions whether free choice was really accepted as a universal principle or only as a necessary concession to Jews in democratic societies. He notes that in 1948 the term *Mahal* (Mitnadvei Hutz La'aretz), Volunteers from Outside Israel, was applied only to those from the United States, Canada and other Western democracies. Those who were recruited from the displaced persons camps of postwar Europe were referred to as *Gahal* (Giyus Hutz La'aretz) Draft from Outside Israel. In other words, Israeli leaders felt that Jews being aided by Israel to flee from persecution had an obligation to the Jewish state and were therefore "draftable." Conversation with the author, Jerusalem, July 1988.

10. As quoted in the *Baltimore Jewish Times*, dispatch by Helen Davis in Jerusalem, 13 May 1988, p. 35.

11. Ibid., p. 34.

12. New Israel Fund, *Annual Report*, November 1987, p. 23.

13. See Jewish Telegraphic Agency *Daily News Bulletin*, 2 August 1987.

14. Dispatch by Glenn Frankel in Jerusalem, *Washington Post*, 9 July 1987.

15. AP dispatch from Jerusalem, *Newsday*, 15 June 1988. The votes were 60 to 53 against amending the Law of Return and 60 to 51 against giving the Israeli rabbinical authorities power over immigration and conversion certificates. See also *Ha'aretz*, 15 June 1988.

16. An outspoken advocate of reform has been Cleveland-born Eliezer Jaffe, professor of social work at the Hebrew University in Jerusalem. See his article, "The Crisis in Jewish Philanthropy," *Tikkun*, Sept./Oct. 1987, p. 27–31, and the responses by Jerold C. Hoffberger, former chairman of the Jewish Agency's Board of Governors, and Gottlieb Hammer, for 35 years vice chairman of the Jewish Agency and United Israel Appeal in New York, ibid., March/April, p. 76–80, and Jaffe's response, p. 80–82.

17. Dispatch by Glenn Frankel, Jerusalem, *Washington Post*, 13 December 1987. The Reform and Conservative movements were each allocated $1.8 million. A Reform representative was named to head the WZO's education department and a Conservative to head the organization department.

18. See Toby Axelrod and J. J. Goldberg, "Veteran Jewish Activists Here Stunned by Sharansky's Criticism," *Jewish Week* (New York), 20 May 1988, p. 21.

19. Daniel J. Elazar, "Enough of all the Zionist-bashing," *Jerusalem Post*, January 5, 1988. See also Elazar, *Some Concrete Steps for the Improvement of Jewish Agency Programs*, *Jerusalem Letter/Viewpoints*, Jerusalem Center for Public Affairs VP:66, 19 October 1977.

20. See J. J. Goldberg, "Zionists See 'Takeover' Threat in Jewish Agency Reform Plan," *Jewish Week* (New York), 17 June 1988, p. 11.

21. These arguments, and the opposing ones summarized below, are excerpted from George E. Gruen, "Solidarity and Dissent in Israel-Diaspora Relations," *Forum* (Jerusalem), Spring/Summer 1978, Nos. 30–31, p. 33–53.

22. As quoted in "Soul-Searching," by Albert Vorspan, *New York Times Magazine*, 8 May 1988, p. 54.

23. Ibid., p. 56.

24. For the complete text, see *New York Times*, 21 February 1988, p. E22.

25. From Gruen, "Solidarity and Dissent," p. 47–48.

26. Conversation by the author with Israel Ellman, a visiting Israeli scholar who is researching relations between American Jews and non-Jews.

27. From "Partners," in *Present Tense,* January/February 1988, p. 11.

28. Quoted in George E. Gruen, "The United States and Israel: Impact of the Lebanon War, *American Jewish Year Book: 1984,* p. 85.

29. Ibid., p. 86–87.

30. Ibid., p. 88.

31. See *Christian Science Monitor,* 6 July 1982, story by Daniel Southerland.

32. Jonas was quoted in a full-page article in the *New York Times* headlined, "Discord Among U.S. Jews over Israel Seems to Grow," 15 July 1982.

33. See Geraldine Rosenfield, "U.S. Public Opinion Polls and the Lebanon War," *American Jewish Year Book: 1984,* p. 105–16.

34. Herbert Scheer, "U.S. Jews for Peace Talks on Mideast," *Los Angeles Times,* 12 April 1988.

35. Mark J. Penn and Douglas E. Schoen, "American Attitudes Toward the Middle East," *Public Opinion,* May/June 1988, p. 45.

36. *Los Angeles Times* Poll, Number 149, question 25, from full text of poll, courtesy of the *Los Angeles Times.* Slight differences among the subgroups may not be statistically significant. In its introduction on methodology the poll notes that "for the 90 Orthodox Jews, the sampling error is plus or minus 10 percentage points; for the 336 Conservative Jews, it is plus or minus 5; for the 304 Reform Jews, it is plus or minus 6; and for the 240 non-affiliated Jews, the sampling error is plus or minus 6 percentage points."

37. Similar divergent trends were noted in the period 1983–1986 by Steven Cohen, who attributed the difference in part to reaction over the increasing militancy of the Orthodox in Israel. See Steven M. Cohen, *Ties and Tensions: The 1986 Survey of American Jewish Attitudes Toward Israel and Israelis* (New York Institute on American Jewish-Israeli Relations, American Jewish Committee, 1987), p. 19–21.

38. Campaign Update to the Semi-Annual Meeting of the American Jewish Joint Distribution Committee Board of Directors, New York, May 19, 1988. The Israel Radio reported on July 27 that $620 million in Israel Bonds had been sold in the past year.

39. A *Los Angeles Times — CMN* poll of 4,203 delegates to the National Democratic Convention in Atlanta in July found that 36 percent of the delegates favored cutting military aid to Israel, as against 5 percent who wanted to increase it. The other 59 percent were for keeping aid at current levels. Nearly 75 percent favored cutting foreign aid in general. (Walter Ruby dispatch from Atlanta, *Jerusalem Post,* 18 July 1988).

Chapter Eleven. The Party's Just Begun.

1. Yonathan Shapiro, "Politics of the Plaza," *Politika* 11:2 (October–November, 1986), 30–32.

2. See Roland Cayrol and Karlheinz Reif, "Conscience Individuelle et Discipline Partisane," *International Political Science Review* 4:1 (1983), 36–47; H. McCloskey, P. J. Hoffman, and R. O'Hara, "Issue Conflict and Consensus Among Party Leaders and Followers," *American Political Science Review* 54:3 (1960), 406–27; Warrren Miller and M. Kent Jennings, *Parties in Transition: A Longitudinal Study of Party Elites and Party Supporters* (New York: Russell Sage Foundation, 1986); Oscar Niedermayer, "Methodological and Practical Problems of Comparative Party Elites Research: The EPPMLE Project," *European Journal of Political Research* 14 (1986), 253–59; Walter Stone and Alan Abramovitz, "Winning May Not Be Everything, But It's More than We Thought: Presidential Party Activists in 1980," *American Political Science Review* 77:4 (1983), 945–56; P. Whiteley, "Who are the Labour Activists?" *Political Quarterly* 52 (1981), 159–68.

3. Jon Pierre, "Attitudes and Behaviour of Party Activists: A Critical Examination of Recent Research on Party Activists and 'Middle-Level Elites'," *European Journal of Political Research* 14 (1986): 468.

4. Many studies point to the power of ethnicity over various characteristics of the Israeli society and mass politics. Israeli Jews of the same ethnic and class positions usually share policy preferences and vote choices. Since the mid-1970s, election results have shown a strong association between Asian-African origin and vote for the Herut party and Europe-America ethnicity and support for the Labor party (see, for example, Arian, 1986; Ayalon, et al. 1985; Ben-Rafael, 1982; Eisenstadt, 1985; Goldscheider and Zuckerman, 1984; Gonen, 1984; Klaff, 1973, 1977; Matras and Weintraub, 1976; Nachmias and Rosenbloom, 1978; Shamir, 1986; Shamir and Arian, 1982; Smooha, 1978; Weingrod, 1974; Weimann, 1983). There is reason, however, to argue that power of ethnicity is a political and social construction (Herzog, 1984, 1985a, 1985b).

5. These results match those obtained by the Herut's section on organization.

6. We defined ethnic identification by the response of Jewish party activists to the question, "Do you think of yourself as a Ashkenazi, a Sephardi, both Sephardi and Ashkenazi, or neither one?" Everyone answered the question, dividing the sample into three equal groupings: 31 percent claimed an Ashkenazi identity; 33 percent defined themselves as Sephardi, and the remainder, 36 percent, claimed both ethnic identities (2 percent) or neither (34 percent).

7. Frank Andrews et al., *Multiple Classification Analysis* (Ann Arbor: The Institute for Social Research, 1973), chapters 5 and 6.

8. We should add one further note on the statistical technique. It is generally accepted that MCA may be used when the interaction terms in the Analysis of variance are not significant and may be ignored. Unfortunately, given the number of variables and categories in our model as well as the number of cases, we could not test for interaction effects. We resolved the problem by the theoretical route, testing for specific interactions that we considered likely to be meaningful, so as to incorporate them with the main effects.

References for Chapter Eleven

Abramowitz, Alan, John McGlennon, and Ronald Rapoport. 1983. "Party Activists in the United States: A Comparative State Analysis." *International Political Science Review*. 4, 1, p. 13–19.

Andrews, Frank J. et al., 1973. *Multiple Classification Analysis*. Ann Arbor: The Institute for Social Research.

Arian, Asher. 1986. *Politics in Israel*. Chatham House.

Ayalon, Hannah, Eliezer Ben-Rafael and Stephen Sharot. 1985. "Variations in Ethnic Identification Among Israeli Jews." *Ethnic and Racial Studies*. 8, 3 (July) p. 389–407.

Ben-Rafael, Eliezer. 1982. *The Emergence of Ethnicity: Cultural Groups and Social Conflict in Israel*. Westport, Conn.: Greenwood Press.

Cayrol, Roland and Karlheinz Reif. 1983. "Conscience Individuelle et Discipline Partisane," *International Political Science Review*, 4,1 p. 36–47.

Eisenstadt, S.N. 1985. *The Transformation of Israeli Society*. Weidenfeld and Nicolson.

Goldscheider, Calvin and Alan S. Zuckerman. 1984. *The Transformation of the Jews*. Chicago: University of Chicago Press.

Gonen, Amiram. 1984. "A Geographical Analysis of the Elections in Jewish Urban Communities." D. Caspi, A. Diskin, and E. Gutmann, eds., *The Roots of Begin's Success: The 1981 Israeli Elections*. London: Croom, Helm, p. 59–87.

Herzog, Hanna. 1984. "Ethnicity as a Product of Political Negotiation: the Case of Israel." *Ethnic and Racial Studies*. 7, 4 (October) p. 517–33.

Herzog, Hanna. 1985a. "Political Factionalism: the Case of Ethnic Lists in Israel." *Western Political Quarterly*. (June)

Herzog, Hanna. 1985b. "Social Construction of Reality in Ethnic Terms: The Case of Political Ethnicity in Israel." *International Review of Modern Sociology*. 15, 1.

Klaff, Vivian. 1977. "Residence and Integration in Israel." *Ethnicity.* 4.

Matras, Judah and Dov Weintraub. 1976. "Ethnic and Other Primordial Differentials in Intergenerational Mobility in Israel." Paper presented to International Sociological Association Seminar on Stratification and Mobility, Jerusalem.

McCloskey H., Hoffman, P.J. and R. O'Hara. 1960. "Issue Conflict and Consensus Among Party Leaders and Followers." *American Political Science Review.* p. 406–27. 54. 3.

Miller, Warren E. and M. Kent Jennings. 1986. *Parties in Transition: A Longitudinal Study of Party Elites and Party Supporters.* New York: Russell Sage Foundation.

Nachmias, David and D. H. Rosenbloom. 1978. "Bureaucracy and Ethnicity." *American Journal of Sociology.* 83, 4, p. 963–75.

Niedermayer, Oscar. 1986. "Methodological and Practical Problems of Comparative Party Elites Research: The EPPMLE Project." *European Journal of Political Research.* 14. p. 253.59.

Pierre, Jon. 1986. "Attitudes and Behaviour of Party Activists: A Critical Examination of Recent Research on Party Activists and 'Middle-Level Elites'." *European Journal of Political Research.* 14. p. 465–79.

Shamir, Michal. 1986. "Realignment in the Israeli Party System." in A. Arian and M. Shamir, eds., *The 1984 Israeli Elections.*

Shamir, Michal and Asher Arian. 1982. "The Ethnic Vote in Israel's 1981 Election." *Electoral Studies.* 1. p. 315–31.

Shapiro, Yonathan. 1986. "Politics of the Plaza," *Politika.* October–November no. 10–11, p. 30–32.

Smooha, Sammy. 1978. *Israel: Pluralism and Conflict.* Los Angeles: University of California Press.

Stone, Walter J. and Alan I. Abramowitz. 1983. "Winning May Not Be Everything, but It's More than We Thought: Presidential Party Activists in 1980," *American Political Science Review.* p. 945–56, 77. 4. (December)

Weimann, Gabriel. 1983. "The Not-So-Small World: Ethnicity and Acquaintance Networks in Israel." *Social Networks.* 5, p. 289–302.

Weingrod, Alex. 1974. "Recent Trends in Israeli Ethnicity." *Ethnic and Racial Studies.* 2 p. 55–65.

Whiteley, P. 1981. "Who are the Labour Activists?" *Political Quarterly.* p. 159–68. 52.

Chapter Twelve. Better Late Than Never.

1. *Party Government* (1942:64).

2. See Gorni (1973), Shapiro (1976), Medding (1972), and Aronoff (1977), especially chapter 3 *The Power of Nominations*. The key nominating committee has gone under various names, e.g. arrangement committee, selection committee, and ordering committee. I use the term nominations committee, which is the English translation of the Hebrew term most frequently used.

3. Aronoff (1977, 1979, and 1982). For example, "Since the top leaders of the Labor party failed to comprehend the full causes and significance of their party's defeat in 1977, they failed to press for the more fundamental structural reforms that would have been required to democratize the party and make it more responsive to the party membership and wider public." (1982:85).

4. The name of the old Tel Aviv based national party machine. See Medding (1972). Spieser is the author of a book, which is like Machiavelli's *The Prince* applied to Israeli politics. It is called *Politica Shimushi* (Applied Politics).

5. See Aronoff (1977) for an analysis of the exceptional importance of this committee.

6. According to Mordecai "Motta" Gur (in an interview on July 27, 1988) Rabin called the proposed reform "idiocy and a disaster" (*timtume v'asone*). Gur claims that initially Peres was not much more enthusiastic about Baram's push for democratization, but that he is more careful with his words than is Rabin.

7. For a description of the nomination of Labor's Knesset list for the 1977 election see Goldberg (1980: 109–10), and for the 1981 election see Brichta (1986: 22–24), and Goldberg and Hoffmann (1983: 64–67). At the time of writing no published scholarly analysis of nominations in Labor for the 1984 Knesset list was available.

8. The Likud attacked this "undemocratic" aspect of Labor's nominations process. Whereas the dominant Herut component of the Likud virtually unanimously elected its leader Shamir to the top spot on the list (He was challenged by an little known and uninfluential person.), there was a bitter struggle between David Levy, Ariel Sharon, and Moshe Arens for the next three positions. It was suggested by a number of observers that Herut would have been better off emulating Labor than engaging in the public airing of internal party antagonisms. The Liberal party, Herut's partner in the Likud, guaranteed the positions of its top three leaders. There was also considerable contention in Herut over the number and position of places on the Knesset list reserved for the Liberals as well as over the places that Shamir had promised to Aharon Abuhatzira (Tami), and Yigal Hurwitz (Ometz) in return for their votes against the international peace conference proposed by Peres.

9. Whereas this may seem a relatively modest sum to the American reader, it is approximately a year's salary for most of the candidates. These expenses did not come from party coffers, but from the pockets of the candidates (with the help of family, friends, and perhaps a few close supporters).

10. Michal Yudelman, "Political Diary," *The Jerusalem Post* 29 April 1988, p. 5.

11. See Aronoff (1977), particularly chapter 7 "Party Center and Local Branch Relationships."

12. See Yael Atzmon, "The Labor Party and Its Factions," *The Jerusalem Quarterly* (31, Spring 1984, p. 118–29) for a discussion of the different types of internal groups and factions in Labor.

13. Yosi Wertner, "Namir first, Lyova Eliav Second," *Hadashot* 27 May 1988, p. 3.

14. Mapam was granted six realistic places on the joint Alignment list with Labor based on the number it had prior to the electoral alignment with Labor, which took place in 1969. However, over the years Mapam had lost much of its electoral support, so it actually received more Knesset seats than its electoral strength warranted. During the negotiations over the formation of the National Unity government, Mapam split from the Alignment with Labor and joined the opposition. Ezer Weizman's Yahad list (with three Knesset members) joined the Alignment with Labor thereby receiving the promise of three realistic places on the Labor list for the 1988 election. Weizman is likely to bring Labor approximately the same amount of electoral support as did Mapam. Reports of scientific public opinion polls commissioned by Labor indicated that if the election were to take place in July it would increase its representation in the Knessset. However, the results of the vote for the Alignment in the previous election were used as a guide for estimating realistic expectations for the 1988 election by most participants and observers of the internal party elections.

15. According to Abraham Brichta (in a personal conversation), Shriege Netzer, boss of the dominant party machine, the "gush," justified the oligarchic nominations process because (among other reasons) places could be assured for various interest groups and for excellent parliamentarians who might lack a power base in the party.

16. Because the National Religious party (NRP) became increasingly hawkish over the past few years, a group of former activists in the NRP joined Labor. The appearance of two dovish observant candidates on the Labor list (including the son of the former leader of the NRP — who some Orthodox Jews consider to be insufficiently observant to quality for the Hebrew term *dati* which is generally translated as religious or Orthodox in English), is likely to attract votes from moderate supporters of the NRP who are dissatisfied with

the extremism of their party. Also, as a reaction to the rightward swing of the NRP, a new religious party was established. The moderate Rabbi Amital heads the Knesset list of this new Religious Center party (Mamad). If it gains representation in the forthcoming election, it will be a likely coalition partner in a Labor-led government.

17. On the bus carrying members of the Central Committee from the Haifa district to the elections one of the members announced over the public address system that the rumor that the deal with Tel Aviv excluded Eliahu Spieser was not true, that he was part of the deal. He claimed that this announcement was made in the name of the Haifa district secretary. The announcement appeared to be greeted by knowing smiles and laughter. Later on while a video promoting the candidacy of Professor Shimon Shitreet (Jerusalem) was playing on the overhead television screen, someone again spoke over the public address system saying ironically, "Who is Spieser? Oh, he is part of the deal?" This provoked a certain amount of laughter. It appears likely that the exclusion of Speiser was deliberate and organized.

18. For a descripition of the behind-the-scenes activities see Shlomo Nakdimone, "Its all Politics," *Yediot Achronot* 7 July 1989, p. 36.

19. Herut failed to elect a single woman (or Druze or Arab) to a realistic place on their Knesset list. Their Liberal partners on the Likud have only one woman on the lowest position that could be considered realistic. Although 65 percent of the 2,092 Herut Central Committee members are of Middle Eastern background, less than 20 percent of their Knesset candidates elected in July 1988 are from this background. See Michal Yudelman, "Male, Jewish and mostly Ashkenazi," *The Jerusalem Post*, 8 July 1988, p.4.

20. Avraham Tirush, "Behind the News," *Ma'ariv*, 16 June 1988, p. 1.

21. Orli Azuli-Katz, "Surprise," *Yediot Achronot*, 16 June 1988, p. 2.

22. *Ma'ariv*, 16 June 1988, p. 14.

23. Elan Schori, "Carnival in Efal," *Ha'aretz*, 16 June 1988, p. 3.

24. "Democracy Tested," *Davar*, 16 June 1988, p. 7.

25. Aviezer Golan, "Today's Reactions," *Yediot Achronot* 16 June 1988, p. 2.

26. Ronit Vardi, "Suddenly in the middle of the night this is not the same party," *Yediot Achronot* 16 June 1988, p. 2.

27. This observation was conclusively borne out by the sharp infighting of the disciplined personal-based camps in the Herut elections.

28. Michal Yudelman, "'Revolution' as party chooses slate, Labour goes for youth," *The Jerusalem Post* 16 June 1988, p. 1.

29. "Face lift for Labour," *The Jerusalem Post* 16 June 1988, p. 24.

30. In an interview after Labor's defeat in 1977 Yoram London asked Eban if he felt that he had been 'absorbed' in Israeli society. When I asked my students at Tel Aviv University what they thought of the question, they unanimously replied that they applauded the interviewer, because they, too, felt that Eban was somewhere not truly Israeli. When I asked them if Eban were to wear his shirt unbuttoned to his navel and spit the shells of sunflower seeds as he chewed them (rather than smoking a Havana cigar) would they consider him more Israeli, they replied in the affirmative.

31. Eban claims to regret not having challenged Rabin and Peres for the leadership of the party. (see Yehoshua Ben-Porat, "Conversation with Abba Eban," *Yediot Achronot*, 1 July, 1988, p. 9.) He fails to understand how futile such a challenge would have been without the dedicated and full support of Pinchas Sapir, which was not forthcoming. For an explanation of why this support was not given to Eban, see Aronoff (1977).

32. Yosi Wertner, "We made a deal," *Hadashot* 27 May, 1988, p. 16.

33. See Medding (1972) and Aronoff (1977).

34. Both Baram and Mordecai 'Motta' Gur (in personal interviews on July 27, 1988) suggested that they would prefer primary elections in the districts as the system for nominations to the Thirteenth Knesset. On the other hand Ora Namir (in an interview the same day) suggested that Labor would not go further with reforms, but would repeat the same system in the future. She said the wisdom of guaranteeing the top leader's positions was proven by the divisive contest in the Likud.

35. He is also the son-in-law of a former Labor prime minister, the late Levi Eshkol.

36. I am grateful to Yehuda Hashai (former Knesset member and former head of municipalities department of the party) for calling this to my attention. Baram (in an interview on July 27, 1988) readily agreed that to be elected by the Central Committee a candidate had to have been actively involved in the party. However, he pointed out that few of the candidates were in a position to award patronage. Hashai disputes this suggesting that many were indeed in such a position.

37. Since I traveled with the Haifa delegation (I was living in Haifa during this period of field work), I have heard more expressions of this kind from them. However, given the results of the voting this attitude was obviously more widespread.

38. This is in sharp contrast with the published reports of the Herut party internal elections, where the three major camps bases around the personal leadership of Yitzhak Shamir and Moshe Arens, David Levy, and Arik Sharon handed down instructions for voting for all candidates in every round of voting.

According to reports, camp discipline was much stronger in Herut than in Labor. Also tensions between the camps was much greater in Herut.

39. Although it has fewer fresh faces than Labor, the Likud gained a media star and serious claimant to future leadership in the form of the former Israeli Ambassador to the United Nations Benjamin ''Bibi'' Nathanyahu (brother of Yonathan — a national hero who was killed leading the successful rescue of the kidnap victims in Entebbe airport in Uganda). He will undoubtedly be a major electoral asset to the Likud in the campaign. None of the new Labor recruits to the Knesset list (or the veterans) has as yet revealed the television charisma of Nathanyahu.

40. The *shtetl* symbolizes the stereotyped way of life of the Eastern European Jews at the turn of the century, and the *Casbah* symbolizes the stereotyped traditions of North African Jews, who constituted the bulk of new immigrants in the early years of the state.

41. Brichta (1986: 20) cites Max Weber's observation (from *Politics as a Profession*) that such systems tend to produce either charismatic leaders backed by party machines or nominations systems based on manipulation and bargaining by party politicians and functionaries.

42. See Avraham Brichta (1986: 29–30).

43. This point was made by Motta Gur in an interview on July 27, 1988.

References for Chapter Twelve

Aronoff, Myron J. 1977. *Power and Ritual in the Israeli Labor Party*. Amsterdam/ Assen: Van Gorcum.

———. 1979. The Decline of the Israel Labor Party: Causes and Significance. In *Israel at the Polls: The Knesset Elections — 1977*. Ed. Howard R. Penniman, p. 115–45. Washington, D.C.: The American Enterprise Institute.

———. 1982. The Labor Party in Opposition. In *Israel in the Begin Era*. Ed. Robert O. Freedman, p. 76–101. New York: Praeger.

Atzmon, Yael. 1984. ''The Labor Party and Its Factions,'' *The Jerusalem Quarterly* (31, Spring, p. 118–29).

Azuli-Katz, Orli. 1988. ''Surprises,'' *Yediot Achronot*, 16 June 1988, p. 2 (Hebrew).

Ben-Porat, Yehoshua. 1988. ''Conversation with Abba Eban,'' *Yediot Achronot*, 1 July 1988, p. 9 (Hebrew).

Brichta, Avraham. 1986. Selection of Candidates to the Tenth Knesset: The Impact of Centralization. In *Israel at the Polls, 1981: A Study of the Knesset Elections.* Eds. Howard R. Penniman and Daniel J. Elazar, p. 18–35. Bloomington: Indiana University press.

Davar. 1988. "Democracy Tested," *Davar* (editorial), 16 June 1988, p. 7. (Hebrew).

Golan, Aviezer. 1988. "Today's Reactions," *Yediot Achronot,* 16 June 1988, p. 2 (Hebrew).

Goldberg, Giora. 1980. Democracy and Representation in Israeli Political Parties. In *The Elections in Israel — 1977.* New Brunswick: Transaction.

Gorni, Joseph. 1973. *Achdut Haavoda 1919–1930. The Ideological Principles and the Political System.* Ramat Gan: Hakibbutz Hameuchad Publishing House (Hebrew).

Jerusalem Post, The. 1988. "Face Lift for Labour," *The Jerusalem Post* (editorial), 16 June 1988, p. 24.

Ma'ariv. 1988. "New Epoch," *Ma'ariv* (editorial), 16 June 1988, p. 7 (Hebrew).

Medding, Peter. 1972. *Mapai in Israel.* Cambridge: Cambridge University press.

Nakdimone, Shlomo. 1988. "Its All Politics," *Yediot Achronot,* 17 July 1988, p. 36 (Hebrew).

Schattsneider, E.E. 1942. *Party Government.* New York: Farrer and Rinehart.

Schori, Elan. 1988. "Carnival in Efal," *Ha'aretz,* 16 June 1988, p. 3. (Hebrew).

Shapiro, Yonathan. 1976. *The Formative Years of the Israeli Labor Party.* London and Beverly Hills: Sage Publications.

Tirush, Avraham. 1988. "Behind the news," *Ma'ariv,* 16 June 1988, p. 1 (Hebrew).

Vardi, Ronit. 1988. "Suddenly in the middle of the night this is not the same party," *Yediot Achronot,* 16 June 1988, p. 2 (Hebrew).

Wertner, Yosi. 1988a. "Namir first, Lyova Eliav Second," *Hadashot,* 27 May 1988, p. 3 (Hebrew).

———. 1988b. "We made a deal," *Hadashot,* 27 May 1988, p. 16 (Hebrew).

Yudelman, Michal. 1988a. "Political Diary," *The Jerusalem Post,* 29 April 1988, p. 5.

———. 1988b. " 'Revolution' as party chooses slate, Labour goes for youth," *The Jerusalem Post,* 16 June 1988, p. 24.

———. 1988c. "Male, Jewish, and mostly Ashkenazi," *The Jerusalem Post,* 8 July 1988, p. 4.

Chapter Thirteen. Recent Developments in Israel's Religious Parties.

1. Gary S. Schiff, "Israel After Begin: The View From the Religious Parties," in Steven Heydemann (ed.), *The Begin Era: Issues in Contemporary Israel* (Boulder and London: Westview Press, 1984), p. 41–43.

2. Daniel J. Elazar, *Israel: Building a New Society* (Bloomington: Indiana University Press, 1986), p. 71–72.

3. Gary S. Schiff, "Israeli Politics: The Renewed Centrality of Religion," in Bernard Reich and Gershon R. Kieval (eds.), *Israel Faces the Future* (New York: Praeger Publishers, 1986), p. 43–48.

4. State of Israel, Ministry of the Interior, *Results of Elections to the Eleventh Knesset, 23 July 1984* (Jerusalem: Central Bureau of Statistics, 1985), p. 9, 11.

5. For a comprehensive history of the religious parties of Israel see Gary S. Schiff, *Tradition and Politics: The Religious Parties of Israel* (Detroit: Wayne State University Press, 1977), especially chapter 2, "The Parties of Participation," and chapter 3, "The Parties of Separatism."

6. Peter Steinfels, "Conservative Judaism Tilts Toward Israeli Left," *The New York Times*, 11 September 1988, p. 21.

7. Schiff, *Tradition and Politics*, chapter 6, "Mafdal and the Nationalization of Religion."

8. Ibid., p. 54–62.

9. Ibid., p. 113–117.

10. Moshe Krone, "Political Zionism in the Political Arena," in Yitzchak Pessin (ed.), *Year Book, Religious Zionism, 1987* (Jerusalem: Mesilot, 1987), p. 32.

11. Charles S. Liebman and Eliezer Don-Yehiya, *Civil Religion in Israel: Traditional Judaism and Political Culture in the Jewish State* (Berkeley: University of California Press, 1983), p. 181–182; and Charles S. Liebman and Eliezer Don-Yehiya, *Religion and Politics in Israel* (Bloomington: Indiana University Press, 1984), p. 53.

12. Schiff, *Tradition and Politics*, p. 118–119, 204.

13. Micheal Yudelman, "NRP Plans Move to East Jerusalem," *The Jerusalem Post*, 21 July 1988, p. 1.

14. Yakir Tzur, "Rabbi Amital Will Run at the Head of Memad," *Davar*, 15 July 1988, p. 1 (Hebrew).

15. Haim Shapiro, "Rabbi's Wife Says Woman's Place Is in House," *The Jerusalem Post*, 15 July 1988, p. 2.

16. Thomas L. Friedman, "In Israel, A Confluence of State, Temple and Gender Issues," *The New York Times*, 12 October 1986, p. 7E; Hugh Orgel

(Jewish Telegraphic Agency), "For the First Time in the History of Israel, Panel Electing Chief Rabbi Includes Women," in *The Jewish Exponent,* 9 September 1988, p. 93.

17. Schiff, *Tradition and Politics,* p. 180, Table 7.3; State of Israel, Central Bureau of Statistics, *Statistical Abstract of Israel, 1986* (Jerusalem: Central Bureau of Statistics, 1986), p. 581, Table XXII/16.

18. Avi Temkin, "The Country's Director-General," *The Jerusalem Post,* 22 July 1988, p. 7.

19. Schiff, *Tradition and Politics,* p. 83.

20. Ibid., p. 180, Table 7.3; *Statistical Abstract of Israel, 1986,* p. 581, Table XXII/16.

21. *Results of Elections to Eleventh Knesset, 23 July 1984,* p. 9, 11.

22. Schiff, *Tradition and Politics,* p. 97–101.

23. *Results of Elections to Eleventh Knesset, 23 July, 1984,* p. 9–11.

Chapter Fourteen. Israel's Economy in the Post-Begin Era.

1. Editor's note: A "crawling peg" exchange rate is one in which a currency is set to increase (or decrease) in value at given intervals (e.g. every so many days, weeks, or months) as a function of government policy. That is, changes in the value of the currency are a function of previously determined government policy, not fluctuations in the free market.

2. Editor's note: A "free float" exchange rate is one in which a currency increases or decreases in value simply as a function of market forces, without prior planning from the government.

3. Editor's note: "Demand-pull" inflation is a function of how much purchasing power there is in the economy. If there is a lot of economic growth and income, people will demand more things (e.g. cars, television sets, refrigerators). When people demand more items relative to their availability, prices rise, leading to inflation.

4. Editor's note: "Cost-push" inflation is a function of the producer's side of the relationship. If the inputs used by producers (suppliers, labor, oil, etc.) become more expensive, their prices go up, leading to inflation.

5. Bank of Israel, *Annual Report 1978,* p. 43 (Hebrew).

6. Bank of Israel, *ibid.,* p. 10.

7. Bank of Israel, *Annual Report 1979,* p. 5.

8. Israel imports from the United States defense materiel financed by United States aid funds. These imports are thus financed in a way that doesn't create future obligations, and they therefore do not compete with other import requirements. Also, the rate at which these imports proceed is dictated by noneconomic considerations.

9. Bank of Israel, *Annual Report* 1984, p. 116.

10. Bank of Israel, *Annual Report* 1986, p. 243.

11. Government of Israel, "Emergency Plan for the Stabilization of the Economy", *Jerusalem*, 2 July 1985, mimeo. (Hebrew).

12. Bank of Israel, *Annual Report* 1986, p. 116.

13. Bank of Israel, ibid., p. 117.

14. The dollar figures were calculated from the national accounts figures, using the average annual exchange rate.

15. The basket representing Israel's foreign trade, as constructed by the Bank of Israel, consists of 60 United States cents, 41.77 German pfennigs, 6.7p sterling, 33.94 French centime, and 7.7 yen. The exchange rate data relative to this basket are published monthly by the Bank of Israel; the price index of exported goods and wage rates are published quarterly and monthly, respectively, by the Central Bureau of Statistics.

Contributors

Myron J. Aronoff is professor and chair of the Department of Political Science at Rutgers University. He is the author of *Frontiertown: The Politics of Community Building in Israel* (Manchester University Press, 1974), *Power and Ritual in the Israeli Labor Party* (Van Gorcum, 1977), and most recently *Israeli Visions and Divisions* (Transaction, 1989). He has edited six books and is editor of the Transaction series on Political Anthropology.

Robert O. Freedman is Peggy Meyerhoff Pearlstone Professor of Political Science and Dean of the Graduate School at Baltimore Hebrew University. He is the author of *Soviet Policy Toward the Middle East Since 1970* (Praeger, 1982), now in its third edition, and is the editor of *Israel in the Begin Era* (Praeger, 1982), *The Middle East Since the Israeli Invasion of Lebanon* (Syracuse University Press, 1986), and *The Middle East Since the Iran-Contra Affair* (Syracuse University Press, 1990).

George E. Gruen is director of the Israeli and Middle East Affairs Division of the American Jewish Committee and is also an associate of the Columbia University Seminar on the Middle East. He is the editor and a coauthor of *The Palestinians in Perspective: Implications for Mideast Peace and U.S. Policy*, as well as a collection of essays on *The Resurgence of Islam and the Jewish Communities of the Middle East and North Africa*. His major monographs include *Water and Politics in the Middle East*, *Refugees of Arab-Israel Conflict*, and *Turkey Between East and West*.

Hanna Herzog is senior lecturer in Sociology at Tel-Aviv University. She is the author of *Political Ethnicity: The Image and Reality and Content of Symbols: The Sociology of Election Campaigns Through Israeli Ephemera*, as well as other monographs and articles on ethnicity and gender in Israeli politics. During 1989-1990 she was a visiting associate at the Center for Jewish Studies, Harvard University.

Ann M. Lesch is associate professor of Political Science at Villanova University and has published widely in the field of Middle Eastern politics. Her recent books include *Political Perceptions of the Palestinians on the West Bank and Gaza Strip* (Middle East Institute, 1980), and most recently, *Israel, Egypt, and the Palestinians: From Camp David to Intifadah,* coauthored with Mark Tessler, (Indiana University Press, 1989).

Gregory S. Mahler is professor and chair of the Department of Political Science at the University of Mississippi. Among his many books and journal articles are several dealing with Israeli politics, including *The Knesset: Parliament in the Israeli Political System* (Fairleigh Dickinson University Press, 1981), *Readings on the Israeli Political System* (University Press of America, 1982), *Bibliography of Israeli Politics* (Westview, 1985) and most recently *Israel: Government and Politics in a Maturing State* (Harcourt Brace Jovanovich, 1989).

Laurie Mylroie is a Bradley Fellow at Harvard University's Center for Middle Eastern Studies. She received her B.A. from Cornell and her Ph.D. from Harvard. She has a book forthcoming on regional security in the Persian Gulf.

Ilan Peleg is head of the Department of Government and Law of Lafayette College in Easton, Pennsylvania. He has published several books and articles on Israeli foreign policy and weapons policies in the Middle East. His most recent books include *Begin's Foreign Policy, 1977 – 1983: Israel's Move to the Right* (Greenwood Press, 1987), and *The Emergence of Binational New Israel: The Second Republic in the Making,* coedited with Ofira Seliktar (Westview Press, 1988).

Yakir Plessner is senior lecturer at the Hebrew University of Jerusalem and prepared this paper while he was a Visiting Professor at Dartmouth College. He has worked as deputy governor of the Bank of Israel, as an economic advisor to the Minister of Finance of Israel, and as a research consultant at the Development Research Center of the World Bank, as well as consulting for numerous government agencies in Israel. His recent publications have dealt with inflation, debt, and economic stabilization in Israel.

Aaron D. Rosenbaum is president of Aaron Rosenbaum and Associates, a Washington, D.C. consulting firm specializing in international politics and defense.

Gary S. Schiff is president and professor of Middle East studies at Gratz College in Philadelphia. He is the author of *Tradition and Politics: The Religious Parties of Israel* (Wayne State University Press, 1977), and numerous articles, monographs, and book chapters on Israeli politics and society. He has previously taught at the City University of New York and Yeshiva University.

Michal Shamir is associate professor of Political Science at Tel Aviv University. Her major areas of research are comparative and Israeli politics. She has co-authored the book *Political Tolerance in Context: Support for Unpopular Minorities in Israel, New Zealand, and the U.S.*, and co-edited *The Elections in Israel – 1988* (with Asher Arian, Transaction Books, 1986).

Ehud Sprinzak is a member of the Political Science Department at Hebrew University of Jerusalem. His recent research interests have focused upon the concepts of terrorism and illegalism in Israel. His most recent book is *The Emergence of the Israeli Radical Right* (Oxford University press, 1988).

Mark Tessler is professor of Political Science and coordinator of the International Relations Major at the University of Wisconsin, Milwaukee. He has published many books and articles in subjects dealing with the Arab world and Israel and is currently president of the Association for Israel Studies. His most recent books include *The Evaluation and Application of Survey Research in the Arab World* (Westview, 1987), *Political Elites in Arab North Africa* (Longman, 1982), and most recently *Israel, Egypt, and the Palestinians: From Camp David to Intifadah*, coauthored with Ann Lesch (Indiana University Press, 1989).

Avner Yaniv is professor at the Department of Political Science at the University of Haifa. He has published numerous papers dealing with Israeli national security; his most recent books include *Dilemmas of Security: Politics, Strategy and the Israeli Experience in Lebanon* (Oxford University Press, 1987), and *Deterrence Without the Bomb: The Politics of Israeli Strategy (D.C. Heath, 1987)*.

Alan S. Zuckerman teaches at the Department of Political Science at Brown University. He has published widely in fields related to Jewish philosophy, European politics, and voting behavior. His most recent books include *The Transformation of the Jews* (with Calvin Goldscheider, University of Chicago Press, 1984) and *Societies of Jews in Modernity* (with Calvin Goldscheider, Beacon Press, 1988).

Index